D'Annunzio in typical pose at the Capponcina

GABRIELE D'ANNUNZIO,

DEFIANT ARCHANGEL

JOHN WOODHOUSE

OXFORD
UNIVERSITY PRESS

OXFORD
UNIVERSITY PRESS

Great Clarendon Street, Oxford OX2 6DP

Oxford University Press is a department of the University of Oxford.
It furthers the University's objective of excellence in research, scholarship,
and education by publishing worldwide in

Oxford New York

Athens Auckland Bangkok Bogotá Buenos Aires Calcutta
Cape Town Chennai Dar es Salaam Delhi Florence Hong Kong Istanbul
Karachi Kuala Lumpur Madrid Melbourne Mexico City Mumbai
Nairobi Paris São Paulo Shanghai Singapore Taipei Tokyo Toronto Warsaw
and associated companies in Berlin Ibadan

Oxford is a registered trade mark of Oxford University Press
in the UK and in certain other countries

Published in the United States by
Oxford University Press Inc., New York

British Library Cataloguing in Publication Data
Data available

Library of Congress Cataloging in Publication Data
Data available

ISBN 0–19–818763–7

1 3 5 7 9 10 8 6 4 2

Typeset by Graphicraft Ltd., Hong Kong
Printed in Great Britain
on acid-free paper
by Biddles Ltd.,
Guildford and King's Lynn

FOR
COUNT PIETRO ANTONELLI

Preface

This is the first fully documented biography of Gabriele D'Annunzio in any language, and, within the limits of reason, given the bizarre nature of D'Annunzio's career, the first objective appraisal of the man. An English reassessment of D'Annunzio implicitly cuts across the great partisan approaches visible in Italy where the history of Dannunzian biography falls into two broad categories: pre-1938 and post-1945. The earlier studies, written during the poet's life, or just after his death in 1938, are uniformly laudatory, and even the best of them, Mario Giannantoni's sumptuous volumes of 1933 and 1939, are eulogies, though it is true that objectivity is more visible in the sometimes curious collections of *realia* put together by bibliographical scholars such as Camillo Antona-Traversi in 1934, Roberto Forcella in 1937, and, more recently, Filippo Masci in 1950, each of whom did a great service to Dannunzian scholarship by assembling documentary evidence often contemporaneously with events in the poet's life.

After the defeat of fascism and the rise of heavily biased left-wing criticism in Italy, D'Annunzio's fame and fortune reached their nadir. Post-1945 biographies in Italy have varied in quality and approach: serious scholars such as Eurialo De Michelis, doyen of them all, urged objectivity, and stressed D'Annunzio's writings; others were more concerned with cashing in on the pornographic and sensationalist elements in the poet's life. Guglielmo Gatti had a foot in both camps with his excellent book of 1957, the most scientifically based study to date, and his collection of essays of 1951 which studied D'Annunzio's most significant relationships with women. Of Gatti it must also be said that, unlike any other biographer of the adventurer-poet, he was willing to revise his opinions, and certain later 'corrections' to his biography are a testimony to his integrity. Giuseppe Sozzi's combination of biography and literary criticism, published in 1964, was well researched and contained many sensitive judgements. Like Gatti, Sozzi was keenly aware of the intensely subjective nature of D'Annunzio's creative work and regarded it as essential to have an accurate biography in order fully to appreciate the allusions of D'Annunzio the artist. Piero Chiara's influential biography of 1978 was a journalist's essay—stylishly written and very readable—but, as De Michelis's fifteen-page review demonstrated, Chiara was not always careful about checking his facts, and pandered to a populist view of D'Annunzio as a little man preoccupied all his life with sex, money, and travel. Chiara's account was also over-reliant at times on anecdotal evidence often culled without acknowledgement from earlier scholars. That method of studying D'Annunzio's life, as a series of anecdotes, was another danger which De Michelis highlighted in his review of Paolo Alatri's volume (1983); in De Michelis's opinion the anecdotal approach risked trivializing the whole. To a degree this is self-evident, but D'Annunzio's own auto-biographical reminiscences were mainly cast in the form of anec-dotes and lend themselves to being used in similar ways in a less personalized study. Alatri himself has acknowledged that his other work concerning particular aspects of the poet was scientifically more rigorous than his biography, which, despite its great merits, shared with earlier biographies a lack of authenticating references (not compensated for by the selective reading-lists for each chapter), and a Marxist bias which seems strangely old-fashioned in our post-Gorbachev epoch. In fact, however, Alatri's biography proper remains fuller and more informative than any previous life of the poet, and the present volume owes many debts to its author.

There are other biographical studies in Italian which are duly acknowledged in the footnotes and bibliography that follow, but the foregoing are the best. No biographer can pass on, however, without mentioning the influence of D'Annunzio's private secretary, Tom Antongini, even though most critics have regarded his three volumes as full of trifling detail; 'trivial' (*futile*) was one of De Michelis's adjectives for Antongini's work. The truth is that much material, including unpublished documents (D'Annunzio wrote Antongini over 700 letters), was for many years available only in Tom Antongini's work, and critics (and biographers) have drawn generously on that particular source. At certain times Antongini's irony, his method of reading into D'Annunzio's actions questionable interpretations of his own, have no doubt irritated the aficionados. He was, on the other hand, one of D'Annunzio's most constant companions over a period of thirty years and no one can ignore his opinions or the facts, trivial or not, which his books reveal.

Of Anglophone studies, the Nardelli–Livingstone biography of 1931 derived from the original well-informed if nonchalantly written study published in Italy by Federico Nardelli the same year; the original was translated with the occasional footnoted aside by Arthur Livingstone. In 1935 Gerald Griffin's sometimes whimsical but always readable volume concentrated largely on D'Annunzio's military exploits, but cannot now be taken seriously as academically reliable, and a large section of his book depended derivatively, though without acknowledgement, on J. N. Macdonald's account of D'Annunzio's seizure of Fiume. Frances Winwar's *Wingless Victory*, first issued in 1956, was in effect a dual biography of D'Annunzio and Eleonora Duse, and concentrated somewhat on the romantic side of their lives, an aspect also reflected in its style, but the book still convinces by the excellent documentation of its sources. Winwar did considerable work on unpublished archives, which Italian biographers, even Gatti and Sozzi, were quick to utilize for their own volumes. Anthony Rhodes's ironical portrait of 1959 has much to commend it even nowadays; written with verve and humour, most of its statements are substantiated with reference to ascertainable documents. Last, but by no means least, in 1988, Charles Klopp produced a brief but workmanlike account of D'Annunzio's life and work, stimulating for certain intuitive comments, and noteworthy for its welcome value judgements concerning the merits of some of the poet's writings.

In his fine preface of 1957, Guglielmo Gatti modestly suggested that his work could not seriously be considered definitive because D'Annunzio's correspondence had not been fully available to him. During the decade that followed, Emilio Mariano co-ordinated the cataloguing of 30,000 major manuscript items (some over 1,000 folios in length) conserved in the Vittoriale archive. The compilation of that huge inventory in 1968 opened up Dannunzian studies at a time when Italy was once again ready to appreciate the work of one of its most famous sons; publication of significant collections of *inedita*, including hundreds of important letters, followed almost automatically. More recently Annamaria Andreoli's editions of further miscellanea from the archive have shown that even now many documents remain to be published. On the one hand, her books have confirmed for the biographer many obscure facts about D'Annunzio which were previously no more than hearsay; on the other, her latest work (1996) may have uncovered subtle difficulties for textual critics of D'Annunzio's writings, by revealing the possible presence in D'Annunzio of an attitude previously unsuspected and not unlike the legendary determination of James Joyce to bequeath to generations of future academics a heritage of unfindably abstruse references: deliberately or not the poet may have sown throughout his papers, perhaps during his final eighteen years, hundreds of loose leaves, containing undated allusions and implications connected with his published work. Suddenly, for the textual critic at least, the old certainties of the vast *Inventario* of 1968 would now appear to have less solid foundations.

Despite the archival work of a generation of conscientious editors, Gatti's question still remains: D'Annunzio's immense, and still in large part unpublished, correspondence raises particular problems for the biographer. Several ample collections are now available in volume form; other letters have to be searched for not only in archives, but also in the body of personal reminiscences of correspondents (Vincenzo Morello, Giuseppe Fatini, Tomaso Fracassini, Enrico Nencioni, Ugo Ojetti, and others) who happen to have been recipients of D'Annunzio's letters and telegrams and who made the most of them to add novelty and originality to their own studies. Every effort has been made in the present volume to trace and consult unpublished documents, including letters, which might better provide a more complete account. In certain circumscribed areas, such as D'Annunzio's individual love affairs, his political campaigns, or his seizure of Fiume, almost all the documents necessary have been available and there have been some brilliant essays by fine scholars who have succeeded in investigating almost all the important evidence; their first-class monographs have been indispensable for my own study.

In the text itself no assumptions have been made about the reader's knowledge of Italian, and all quotations have been translated. This may be to the chagrin of scholars who regard such translations as academic betrayals, or as patronizing gestures; nevertheless it is true that outside the Peninsula a first-hand knowledge of Italy's cultural heritage, albeit the richest in Europe, has traditionally been restricted to a small band of Italianists or modern-day Grand Tourists. In those instances where the Italian text is essential, this has been included alongside the translation, a practice particularly adhered to in the quotations from D'Annunzio's poetry, which has always been cited in the original language. For Italianist critics, it should be stated from the outset that, although inevitably 'a literary life', the book is not meant to participate in fashionable trends in literary theory; if for no other reason, its inclusion of the occasional value judgement rigorously eliminates it from the contemporary canon of literary criticism.

Any author suggesting that his volume is the first fully documented biography of D'Annunzio in any language, and insisting upon the need to check sources where at all possible, lays himself open to a twin charge of arrogance and pedantry. But if D'Annunzio is not to remain the folkloristic, almost fairy-tale figure discernible in biographies such as those of Phillipe Jullian, and often indivisible from his fictional heroes, then some attempt has to be made to confirm the truth of his adventures and proclivities. De Michelis has shown that some biographical studies of D'Annunzio are so full of fanciful errors 'that incredulity vies with hilarity at the sight of some of the mistakes'. In the present volume every effort has been made to certify the truth of an occurrence through reliable documents, published and unpublished; it is hoped that the pedantry of footnotes will show that truth, even in the case of D'Annunzio, was often stranger than fiction.

Acknowledgements

I have debts of gratitude to many friends: to the trio who first set me on this route, Eurialo De Michelis, Ettore Paratore, and Edoardo Tiboni; to Pietro Antonelli, whose encouragement helped bring the volume to completion; to Philip Horne for his constant advice, support, and his practical and tasteful suggestions during the first draft; to Denis Mack Smith for his wise counsel concerning the Public Record Office documents; to Raimondo and Germana Luraghi, both for their spontaneous friendship and for Raimondo's reading of the final version of the text; to Francesco Perfetti and the personnel of the Vittoriale, Elena Ledda, Mariangela Calubini, and Michela Rizzieri, who (often thanklessly) do so much work for others in the library and archive there; I also wish to thank the Vittoriale for permission to reproduce photographs from their Fototeca. Three other libraries have proved unfailingly helpful and courteous: the Taylor Institution Library, the Public Record Office, and the Bodleian Library; to the personnel of those wonderful institutions, in particular to David Thomas, I extend warmest thanks. To Jason Freeman and his associates at Oxford University Press I am, as ever, grateful. In my efforts to trace other unpublished letters and documents of the period, I have incurred particular debts: to the Ceccherini heirs for the rich store of *inedita* regarding D'Annunzio's administration of Fiume, in particular for the correspondence with his commander-in-chief, General Sante Ceccherini; to the D'Alessandro family and particularly to Dr Talbot D'Alessandro, whose Dannunzian autograph manuscripts and other material have now been bequeathed to Oxford's Taylor Institution; to the family of Gabriele Sovera Latuada, whose documents continue to keep alive the memory of their 'Fiuman' grandfather Colonel Giuseppe Sovera. Most importantly I am grateful to Gaynor Woodhouse, not only for her critical reading of the English of this book but also for her tolerance of the substitution of my recent *fissazione dannunziana* for certain earlier *manie borghiniane*. Needless to say I am wholly responsible for any shortcomings the work may have.

J.W.

Contents

List of Plates

All photographs reproduced by kind permission of the Sovrintendenza of the Vittoriale.

Frontispiece: D'Annunzio in typical pose at the Capponcina

[between pp. 210 and 211]

Introduction

ITALY is a country more accustomed than any to the problems of living with genius, but Gabriele D'Annunzio presented symbiotic difficulties which his fellow countrymen found particularly trying. In their time-honoured fashion the Italians resolved the problem by creating a dilemma: they divided into opposing camps, and for over a century, since indeed the publication of his precocious *Primo vere* of 1879, D'Annunzio's name has, with a few rare moments of objective scrutiny, aroused either passionate support or vitriolic opposition in that country. On the wider European stage, as well as in Italy, D'Annunzio's flamboyant life-style, his unashamed dedication to personal glory, and his unapologetic pursuit of pleasures, pure and perverse, meant that for over fifty years, his figure was surrounded by permanent controversy. In particular his apparent support for Nietzschean values, his disdain for the proletariat, his enthusiasm for military accomplishments and accoutrements, and the élan with which he threw himself into World War One, lent his personality, rightly or wrongly, a pre-fascist aura which caused some writers and critics to regard him as the John the Baptist of fascism. Yet all the evidence shows that he despised the fascists, considered Mussolini his social and political inferior, wrote a liberal charter for his new State of Fiume as early as August 1920, and tried to stop the alliance between Berlin and Rome in September 1937. It was, rather, his anarchic life-style and the complete disregard for authority, fashionably imitated by his followers and admirers, which prepared the political climate after World War One for a fascist revolution. Ironically, however, it must be said that *Me ne frego*, his obscene slogan at that time ('I don't give a toss'), also contained the seeds of Mussolini's downfall. *Me ne frego* was taken over by Mussolini and his crew and became the watchword of an influential majority of the population; it was the sentiment behind the Italian presence at the League of Nations in the early 1930s and particularly during the Abyssinian crisis of 1935. But when things began to go wrong for the regime the Italians were able to turn the famous slogan against their fascist hierarchs, and there was little these last could then do to recover popular loyalty or favour.

In Britain, at least during the early part of the twentieth century, and amongst the literate and upper-middle classes, D'Annunzio was read and more or less appreciated by such as Arthur Symons, Ouida, Henry James, James Joyce, Osbert Sitwell, W. B. Yeats, Harold Nicolson, D. H. Lawrence, and Marguerite Radclyffe Hall. He enjoyed a reputation and notoriety not dissimilar to those of Swinburne or Wilde. British attitudes fluctuated capriciously: from awe at his brilliance to middle-class acclaim for bowdlerized versions of his sensual novels; from puritanical disgust at his decadent life to envy at the arrogant elegance with which he carried it off; from lionization following his heroic exploits in World War One to the most virulent denigration when he refused to accept the Allied line and what he called Italy's 'mutilated victory' at the Versailles peace negotiations of 1919. In particular his piratical capture of the Yugoslav port of Fiume (Rijecka) (where he first hoisted his *Me ne frego* standard) turned the British Establishment's superficial adulation, evidenced, for instance, in the *Times*'s famous leader of 24 August 1918, into vituperative attacks which at their mildest questioned his sanity. Even the sympathetic, if gently ironic, Osbert Sitwell was of no avail against the ire of the Establishment. Indeed, after the enforced retreat from the Yugoslav port in January 1921, D'Annunzio was given no serious mention in the British press until the obituaries of 1938, which were almost unanimous in their positive appraisal of his life and work.

By the time of the celebrations to honour his centenary in 1963 he was, for the British, a distant recollection, lurking perhaps in the folkloristic memory of a disappearing upper-middle class. That anniversary passed unheralded in Britain. In 1963 Roberto Weiss, then holder of the Panizzi Chair of Italian in London, was asked to contribute to the centenary conference at the Vittoriale, D'Annunzio's residence overlooking Lake Garda; he had to confess that his researches had failed to find interest in or knowledge of the poet amongst British contemporaries. 'The British once talked a lot about D'Annunzio, but read little of him. Now in Britain no one talks of him or reads him.'[1] Weiss exaggerated the situation for effect, but even now, in British universities, only Oxford, home

---

[1] The remarks are made in R. Weiss, 'D'Annunzio e l'Inghilterra', in E. Mariano (ed.), *L'Arte di Gabriele D'Annunzio* (Milan, 1968), 463; this and other observations made in the present Introduction will be explained, expanded, and annotated in the chapters which follow, and in the bibliography.

of lost causes, has regular courses on D'Annunzio's literary work. Yet, leaving aside the political and military impact of D'Annunzio's influence during fifty tumultuous years of European history, his prolific exploitation of every literary genre has meant that no Italian writer since 1900 has been able to remain free of his influence. Since 1963 and those centenary celebrations, his critical fortune in Italy has been boosted considerably by the acknowledgement of his authority, and D'Annunzio's works are now selling in even greater numbers than at any time in the past. His reputation has been promoted further by frank statements such as that of Nobel laureate Eugenio Montale, who, as long ago as 1956, and courageously in that critical climate, wrote a preface to Lucio Piccolo's *Canti barocchi* of 1956, which likened D'Annunzio's significance in Italy to that in France of Victor Hugo, and declared that for any Italian writer not to have learned from D'Annunzio would be a bad sign.

D'Annunzio was, and continues to be, one of those outstanding writers (D. H. Lawrence and Ezra Pound are others), whose critical fame has oscillated wildly according to variations in society's political or moral attitudes. His entire works were placed on the Catholic Index of proscribed books in 1928 (the very year, incidentally, that *Lady Chatterley's Lover*, prohibited in Britain, was being published in Florence—in English), and throughout Italy during the anti-fascist reaction after World War Two D'Annunzio's name was particularly identified with a right-wing brand of politics. In Britain, after an eccentric allusion to him in 1924 by Sisley Huddleston, who was the first to describe him in print as Mussolini's John the Baptist, ten years passed before the short-lived Union of British Fascists began to regard the poet as one of their own. In 1936 one slightly unbalanced correspondent of their magazine, *The Blackshirt*, wrote to him, enclosing a copy of the cyclostyled *Overseas Bulletin* of the party, which D'Annunzio ignored; note and newsletter are both now tucked away in the general archive of the Vittoriale. The ephemeral journal of the British fascists, *Action*, carried a strange obituary on 2 March 1938, with an inappropriate historical parallel, praising this D'Annunzio–Machiavelli who had died happy having seen his Prince–Mussolini safely installed.

D'Annunzio was sublimely indifferent to public criticism. From his earliest years he deliberately set out to create a unique personality for himself—one which was by definition inevitably controversial. 'Inimitable' was the adjective he often used to describe his character and his writings. In the early years friends helped by inventing myths about his life and early work, and, as time passed, other stories, not always fostered by D'Annunzio, accumulated and attached themselves to his public persona, until truth and fiction became indistinguishable. Had he been born during a storm at sea, on the deck of the sailing-ship *Irene*? Had he experimented with cannibalism during a journey through Libya? Did he compose an ode to his appendix as it was being extracted under local anaesthetic? Had he colluded in the disappearance of the *Mona Lisa* in 1911? Did he, Doolittle-like, compile a canine lexicon? Was he, in the end, assassinated by a Nazi spy for his opposition in 1937 to a treaty between Mussolini and Hitler? These were just a few of the more bizarre legends which pursued him literally from cradle to grave, and D'Annunzio, never one to shun publicity, welcomed the myth-making.

The authenticity of such events was further complicated by D'Annunzio's own preference for incorporating into his fictional writing any episode which he considered worthy of his creative pen, from the squalor of an abortive and noisome visit to a Phrygian prostitute in Patràs, to the exuberant joy of cocking a snook at superior Austrian forces in World War One. Every experience was grist to D'Annunzio's artistic mill, and there is no doubt that all his creative work casts more or less direct light on his life, and that psychologically speaking it often has autobiographical characteristics, not least in its pursuit of unrealizable ideals. D'Annunzio's biographer has to learn to differentiate between fact and fiction, and above all not to be deceived by self-glorifying reminiscences. Even with more normally reliable sources, such as diaries and letters, the same problem presents itself. His letters to his mistresses, for instance, were often deceptive attempts to persuade victims of his fidelity while simultaneously betraying them with their rivals or successors. In his *taccuini*, or notebooks, he was sometimes capable of erasing or rewriting episodes in order to avoid an incriminating reference, or to exaggerate an erotic experience. And from letters and diaries he derived the stuff of his later biographical reminiscences.

For most of his life D'Annunzio's sole concern was self-gratification and glory: to make his existence as interesting and preferably as joyful as possible for himself, whatever the consequences for others; to create a work of art from his life and to immortalize it in words. There were, it is true, moments when nationalism or patriotism seemed important, particularly during his youthful discovery of the beauty and power of ships and naval power after his first journey on the Adriatic in 1887, but more often than not the greater glory of his native land served only to throw into greater relief the lustre of his personal brand of glory. And when inspiration for creative writing ran out, after his expulsion from Fiume in 1921, he spent the next sixteen years in the creation of a vast physical arte-fact which might reflect his life and achievements: the Vittoriale. That was the untranslatable name he gave to the palatial residence and museum which overlooked Lake Garda. 'Vittoriale' implies the reward of victory as well as the symbol of victory itself, and the estate constituted a theatre of memory guaranteeing D'Annunzio immortality, not only in the eyes of his readers, but also in the minds and hearts of those too young or too illiterate to understand his writings, who still continue to flock there in their thousands and gaze with awe.

One of D'Annunzio's most affectionate, and most brilliant, crit-ics was the late-lamented Eurialo De Michelis. In 1979 De Michelis gave an important paper at the Vittoriale, later published, with the title 'Towards an Ideal Biography of D'Annunzio'. The article was in effect an attack on most recent biographical studies of the poet; and to it De Michelis was later to add strictures on the latest bio-graphy he could have known, that of Paolo Alatri. His main con-tention was that critics should not pass moral judgement on writers such as D'Annunzio, indeed should take no account of his life in assessing his work, and least of all celebrate his philandering while ignoring his literary merits. As if to demonstrate the truth of what he had been saying, Ferruccio Ulivi's biographical volume, the next to come out of Italy after Alatri's, was, despite its academic preten-sions, no more than a novel in biographical form, and a novel which concentrated largely on D'Annunzio's love affairs. De Michelis's views are understandable. But D'Annunzio himself made it clear on many occasions that he considered life and art a seamless unity. He incorporated his life and activities into his creative work as perhaps no other writer before or since, and, when his vein of literary ori-ginality dried up, he went on to immortalize his life's experiences, as a model and inspiration for others, in the physical surroundings of his redesigned home.

Some biographers have, as De Michelis implied, stressed D'Annunzio's sexual gymnastics, often to the exclusion of his literary work, but it must be said that to discuss D'Annunzio without mentioning his priapic tendencies is to omit a most important aspect of his life. D'Annunzio counted his sexual liaisons with women as an essential inspiration for his art, and he made use of his women in every possible way. Here, again, lay controversy: the affection and admiration felt by the public for some of the women he misused, particularly the universally respected Eleonora Duse, created strange enmities for him. He insisted, 'Today, tomorrow, until death, the work of the flesh is in me the work of the spirit, and both harmonize to achieve one sole, unique, beauty. The most fertile creatrix of beauty in the world is sensuality enlightened by apotheosis.' In this area, too, critics are divided in their attentions: some have exploited D'Annunzio's erotic conquests in order to sell what is nothing less than soft pornography, some have passed over his libertinism with a patronizing smile, and throughout Europe there has been widespread, prudish reaction against the lurid and voyeuristic reportage of his many love affairs. Such controversy, understandable as it may be, should not obscure the rapport between sexual activity and literary creativity, which in D'Annunzio's life and work were indivisible. Towards the end of his life he noted that it was an astonishing thing that he had not been devoured by what was most voracious in the world: *Femmine e Muse* (Women and the Muses), and he often expressed regret, hardly credible to those who knew him well, that his devotion to sexual pleasures weakened or diminished his artistic prowess. *Femmine e Muse* was the all-embracing title he wanted to give to his *Opera omnia* when the first tome of the substantial national edition of his writings appeared in 1927. The present volume will not make the mistake of ignoring his love affairs, though for the reader who wishes to dwell more fully on the sexual aspects of his relationships it may prove disappointing.

There is another strand of Dannunzian criticism which needs mentioning and which De Michelis also took to task, and that is the ironic approach, especially discernible in early Italian critics of his work, as well as in later non-Italian biographers. D'Annunzio certainly took himself and his art very seriously, and at times wrote about them with theatrical pretentiousness. Apart from the humour inherent in such pomposity, D'Annunzio was a gift to the caricaturist: at under five feet six inches tall, he was short enough to have to obtain a height-exemption certificate in order to re-enrol in the cavalry in 1915; prematurely balding at the age of 22, he came to regard his egg-like cranium as one of the beauties of creation and as a mark of higher evolution, hair being unnecessary in a modern civilized society; blinded in one eye during the war, he used that disability as the inspiration for one of his best pieces of literary prose, and, though unscarred, seemed thereafter to try to ensure that he was photographed only in right profile; blessed with what his secretary–factotum called unfortunate teeth, he never smiled into the camera. He was an obvious target for irony, and, since the beginning of this century, has not only provided much material to caricaturists, but also supplied critics and biographers with amusing anecdotes and comic punch-lines, leading some Anglo-Saxon critics to treat him with something approaching the humour of P. G. Wodehouse. It would be wrong to ignore the risibility of some of his actions, indeed it might be politically dangerous to take them seriously. The present volume will attempt to steer a middle course, but if irony should break through it should be ignored.

I

Early Life and Experience

EVEN surrounded by the tasteless speculative building of present-day Pescara it is not difficult to imagine the environment into which D'Annunzio was born on 12 March 1863.[1] The family house, glamorized by redesign in 1927, still stands 300 yards from a golden seashore on which the port encroaches annually, the Pescara river still pours its stone-grey waters into the blue Adriatic, local fishing-boats still tie up in the estuary. Most of the dense pine forest which used to cover much of the area above the foreshore has been scraped away, to be replaced by reinforced concrete, but there are still enough Mediterranean pines to provide a dark-green nuance to the foothills running up to the dominant peaks of the Gran Sasso range. D'Annunzio's Abruzzi homeland constituted his province in many senses. The customs and character of its people, its art and architecture, the landscape and sea vistas of this rugged area were ever-present in the poet's consciousness. The Abruzzi supplied enthralling themes to inspire much of his creative writing, pro-vided a backdrop for his love affairs, a haven for his elopement and marriage, and, in a literal sense, periodically offered a retreat (albeit in a deconsecrated convent) from the anxieties and pressure of urban life in Rome.[2] The fact of his birth in the Abruzzi, as well as the importance of the region in his life and work, are discernible in the epithets 'the Abruzzese' and 'the Pescarese' which are instantly re-cognized in Italy as synonymous with 'D'Annunzio' (while other Abruzzesi, from Ovid to Benedetto Croce, have achieved great fame but would not be so honoured).

[1] The myth of D'Annunzio's birth on board the brigantine *Irene* sailing between Pescara and Trieste was first publicized by Edoardo Scarfoglio in the newspaper *Capitan Fracassa*, 8 May 1882; for D'Annunzio's embellishment of the myth see his correspondence with Georges Hérelle, below, p. 123.

[2] Interesting recent studies by Ermanno Circeo and other members of Edoardo Tiboni's Centro Studi Dannunziani concerning the many reminiscences of the Abruzzi throughout D'Annunzio's work have been published in E. Circeo, *L'Abruzzo in D'Annunzio* (Pescara, 1995).

As late as 1935, three years before his death, D'Annunzio noted with feeling:

On the soles of my shoes, the heels of my boots I carry the earth of the Abruzzi, the mud of my estuary. When I find myself amongst strangers, isolated, different, wildly hostile, I sit down, cross my legs and gently shake my foot, which to me seems weighty with that ground, that bit of earth, that moist sand, and it is like the weight of a piece of armour—an iron defence.

Suo se pondere firmat, (Its very weight adds firmness).[3]

And D'Annunzio's earliest informal jottings recall adolescent experiences of his native town, and particularly of the River Pescara flowing into the sea:

Lying on the soft grassy carpet, beneath a cool dome of poplars, the sun playing marvellously amongst the leaves. The sky obscured with white vapour. The leaves of the willows in the sunshine seem silver. The emerald water flows past; flows from between the willows. Green folly, joy, inebriation. Tall plants ripple and murmur. Green solitude, where the wind sings in your Muse, Theocritus, and where I hear, floating on the evening your soft, soft Greek hexameter.

The harbour, the sand, the washerwomen's linen on the shore, sailing-boats and gulls, the surrounding mountains, an ancient fortress, the heat and aridity of the rocks, the colours and scents of summer, all are details observed in the first of his so-called *taccuini* (notebooks).[4] These particular notes date from 1881 and D'Annunzio's eighteenth birthday, and reflect the natural environment in which he grew up. Jottings of this kind, when worked up in literary vein, provided him with inspiration for later prose and verse.

---

[3] GD'A, *Cento e cento e cento e cento pagine del libro segreto* (A Hundred and a Hundred and a Hundred and a Hundred Pages of the Secret Book), in GD'A, *Prose di ricerca di lotta e di comando* (Prose Works Concerned with Research, Struggle, and Command), ed. E. Bianchetti (Milan, vol. i 1947, vol. ii 1950, vol. iii 1947), here ii. 883.

[4] The notebooks provide one of the least unreliable sources for D'Annunzio's biography; two large volumes of these jottings have been published: *Taccuini*, ed. E. Bianchetti and R. Forcella (Milan, 1965), here 6–7, and *Altri taccuini*, ed. E. Bianchetti (Milan, 1976). The notebooks, unless more are discovered in the unpublished Vittoriale archives, end with the fall of Fiume in 1919; in his interesting, if at times ingenuous, account of D'Annunzio's schooldays, T. Fracassini, *GD'A convittore* (Rome, 1935), 54, reproduces a drawing by the 15-year-old of 'A sailor on a winter shore'; the environment could easily be Pescara.

It must have been a cause of satisfaction to the mature poet when, in 1927, the provincial and municipal boundaries of his native region were redefined, giving Pescara the status of provincial capital. Undoubtedly the fame of D'Annunzio's achievements had brought about the transformation in status of his small fishing village, wresting it from the adjacent province of Chieti, and allowing it to supplant its larger neighbour Castellammare as the centre of a new conurbation. The elevation of Pescara was also an indication of the threat that D'Annunzio was then thought to represent to Mussolini's new fascist government, which was anxious to appease a figure more popular and charismatic than its own leader. Like so many concessions to the poet (the redesigning of the family house being a similar favour), the fascist hierarchy believed it helped keep his mind off rival political ambitions, and left the road clearer for Mussolini, at a time when the Dictator was being given plenipotentiary powers.[5]

Some of the earliest personal reminiscences we have of D'Annunzio's life in Pescara concern his experiences as a child in what were excitingly adventurous surroundings for a young boy. The village was still full of the memories of the Bourbon regime, which, until Garibaldi's victorious campaigns, had imposed its decadent, if sleepy, rule upon that part of the Kingdom of Naples. A rickety Customs barrier, the Porta Sale, still stood close to the D'Annunzio house. Ancient cannon were upended as improvised mooring bollards at the water's edge, and crumbling fortifications, some dating back to the sixteenth century, were scattered along the shoreline. One particular incident from D'Annunzio's memories of childhood in Pescara was, in his view, prophetic of his later spiritual development. It concerned a friendly local fisherman from Ortona who would sometimes give the solitary boy a mussel or shrimp from his catch. On this occasion one of the mussels had an especially stubborn shell which the young D'Annunzio battered in vain against the cast-iron stock of an old cannon. Only when he took his knife to the mollusc did it yield, and then only after one of the boy's frustrated jabs had driven the blade deep into his left thumb. He had matched his obstinacy against that of the mollusc, and had won. He celebrated his triumph by gulping down, with a blend of pain and defiance,

---

[5] For a good account of D'Annunzio's birthplace and its subsequent development until the present day, see L. Renzetti, *La casa natale di GD'A: Ieri e oggi* (Chieti, 1989).

the cartilaginous contents, whose salt mingled with the blood from his wound.[6]

That early incident contained in germ one aspect which would characterize D'Annunzio's adult life: an indifference to pain and injury, though it must be said that hostile critics challenge the myth of his courage. But the story of the obstinate bivalve contains other elements which foreshadowed later events: the boy, bleeding profusely, did not immediately run home. Instead he wrapped the hand in a bandage improvised from his shirt-sleeve, and, calling to mind his recollections of local women who used cobwebs to heal such cuts and wounds, he made his way down to an abandoned ammunition store infested with spiders, and in the growing darkness used their webs to bind his wound before fainting away for hours. Finally, in pain but uncomplaining, he staggered home to startle his mother with the gory result of his adventures. Whenever, in future years, he returned from his wanderings to his native home, his mother would hold his hand and run her finger over the scar, which remained a living reminder of the episode for the rest of his life. His conclusion to the paragraphs in the reminiscences of *Il secondo amante di Lucrezia Buti* (The Second Lover of Lucrezia Buti) is that for him 'the great spiritual value of that memory lies in the sign which fate impressed upon my soul, the first secret token of my future destiny'. A disregard for personal danger, an ostentatious self-sufficiency, a vital interest in the lore of his region, and the sensual implications of the salty tang of blood and shellfish were characteristics which recurred in later years in sometimes bizarre creative forms.

The sentiments are anyway typical of D'Annunzio, who wrote up the episode thirty-five years later, in 1907. More significantly, however, for his literary biography, his re-evocation demonstrates how the smallest incident could be incorporated into his writing. He was soon to formalize this method in the notebooks. These *taccuini* comprised drawings or jottings of the kind noted above, usually on a single sheet of notepaper, often folded to fit easily into a breast pocket; on them he captured any incident, such as the idyll of Pescara in the springtime, which could potentially be useful to him

---

[6] The episode is narrated and elaborated in GD'A, *Il secondo amante di Lucrezia Buti*, *Prose di ricerca*, ii. 181–5; a wonderful account of river and seascape in Pescara is given in A. Grossi's *La poesia del fiume e del mare in GD'A* (Chieti, 1963).

in his creative work. When his attention turned from surrounding nature to the observation of individuals he could be merciless in his portraits, since those sketches invariably ignored the personal feelings of people who might later find their characteristics permanently enshrined in his pages.

The authenticity of the family name D'Annunzio has often been questioned; it enabled Gabriele to make high-sounding play of his own name, Gabriel of the Annunciation. Could this have been another of the poet's fictions? At the time that Roberto Weiss took up the Panizzi Chair, D'Annunzio's works were catalogued in the library of University College London under the surname Rapagnetta. That surname recalls an incident narrated by Harold Nicolson, invited to hear D'Annunzio recite two of his poems during a soirée at the Florentine home of the Countess d'Orsay; in self-confessedly snobbish vein, Nicolson meditated with his fellow noblemen, the Marquis de Chaumont and Enrico Visconti, on the question of the poet's ancestry. All three agreed that he was not 'a man of family', and found considerable amusement in discussing what Visconti alleged was his true surname, not D'Annunzio (or, more nobly, d'Annunzio), he said, but Rapagnetta. '"Mais dans tous les cas", commented de Chaumont, decisively, "c'est un garçon qu'on ne peut pas voir". Visconti, who was older than either of us, was very much amused at this, and laughed a great deal.'[7] In fact D'Annunzio's father, Francesco Paolo Rapagnetta, had been adopted at the age of 13 by a childless uncle, Antonio D'Annunzio, and had been brought up with the surname Rapagnetta-D'Annunzio. In 1858 Francesco Paolo married Luisa De Benedictis, by whom he had three daughters and two sons. Gabriele, the middle child of the five, had three sisters, Anna, Elvira, and Ernestina, and a younger brother, Antonio. At the time that Gabriele came to be baptized, the Rapagnetta element had been allowed to drop from the family name, and he was registered as Gabriele D'Annunzio. The question of the spelling of the name, d'Annunzio or D'Annunzio, is still debated. D'Annunzio always signed himself 'Gabriele d'Annunzio', the form which implied

---

[7] H. Nicolson, *Some People* (London, 1927), 91–2; their view contrasts with that of the duke of Leeds, who at the Waterloo Cup coursing in February 1914 told D'Annunzio that 'An Italian of class such as yourself could easily pass as an Englishman [. . .] as long as no one saw him eating spaghetti. No offence meant— especially since I've never seen you personally eat spaghetti'; reported by T. Antongini, *Un D'Annunzio ignorato* (Milan, 1963), 154.

a noble origin. More down-to-earth compilers of library indexes incline to 'D'Annunzio' in all circumstances.[8]

The family was initially reasonably well off. Francesco Paolo had inherited half of the D'Annunzio fortune, and had control of the half inherited by his two sons. He was a dealer in wine and agricultural products, and in 1873 became mayor of Pescara. But he had a deserved reputation as a womanizer and hard drinker, and at his death in 1893 Gabriele discovered that there were heavy family debts to pay; he was forced to sell the family's country house, the Villa del Fuoco, where his father had kept his mistresses, but which had in earlier times provided rural excursions for the young family, and had served Gabriele for his honeymoon in 1887. Although initially the young man would write with pride to his father concerning his achievements at school and immediately afterwards, and although in his turn Francesco Paolo was proud to help publish his son's first poems, D'Annunzio came to despise him. The break between the two seems to have begun in the summer of 1882, when Francesco Paolo opposed irascibly the intention of both Gabriele and his sister Ernestina to marry their youthful lovers.[9] There were undoubtedly other, psychological, reasons for D'Annunzio's rancour as he came to recognize in his father the germ of sensuality which he believed had contaminated his own genes, and which, he unconvincingly alleged, impeded his artistic creativity. D'Annunzio's novel *Il trionfo della morte* (The Triumph of Death) includes a pitiless portrait of a debauched sensualist, generally acknowledged to be that of his father; and it was significant that he received news of Francesco Paolo's death without emotion, refusing to make a small journey to be with him at the end.[10] But it must also be added that throughout his lifetime Gabriele never seems to have demonstrated disinterested affection for anyone, with the possible exceptions of his mother and his baby daughter, Renata. On his mother's death,

[8] This last practice will be followed in the present volume. The problem is discussed by D'Annunzio's distant relative Amedeo Rapagnetta, *La vera origine familiare e il vero cognome di GD'A* (Lanciano, 1938).

[9] For a year Francesco Paolo had tried to obstruct the affair between Gabriele and his first love, Giselda Zucconi (for whom see below, p. 25). The development of the relationship between son and father is particularly well illustrated in D'Annunzio's correspondence with Giselda Zucconi; see GD'A, *Lettere a Giselda Zucconi*, ed. I. Ciani (Pescara, 1985), 425.

[10] For these events, see below, p. 106; F. Monicelli, *Il tempo dei buoni amici* (Milan, 1975), discusses D'Annunzio's family relationships, including his apparently heartless reaction to his dying father.

in 1917, the poet was far away in the north, having seen her only rarely in the previous twenty years; he declared himself sad that the public thought him incapable of tears, and was devoted to her memory.

D'Annunzio had private tutors in Pescara; at first he attended the lessons of two sisters, Adele and Ermengilda Del Gado, who taught him to read and write, and then Giovanni Sisti, who prepared him for secondary school. Both of these early educational experiences were to have literary outcomes. The Del Gado sisters were to be immortalized in the *Contessa d'Amalfi*, one of the short stories of *Le novelle della Pescara* (Tales of Pescara), and again, or so the sisters believed, in the semi-biographical portraits of frustrated spinsters in the opening of the scurrilous novella of *Il libro delle vergini* (The Book of the Virgins) later restyled as *La vergine Orsola*. To Giovanni Sisti, who went on teaching in Pescara until 1910, D'Annunzio was to write affectionate, if often boastful, letters, useful now for revealing his early psychological development.[11] At 11 years of age he was old enough to be sent by his father to a private, and prestigious, boarding-school in Prato, the Collegio Cicognini. This was a grammar school, founded originally by the Jesuits in 1699, but, after many changes in management, it had developed into a secular institution, and one which D'Annunzio afterwards described as 'a great lay seminary, created to sterilize and shrivel the seeds of greatest fervour, a plantation made in the images of the second Circle [of Dante's *Inferno*], reducing the most vivacious of human saplings to "dried twigs with poison" '.[12] He was later to send both of his own sons there as soon as they were old enough. D'Annunzio remained at the Cicognini for the next seven years, four of them permanently spent in Tuscany, without so much as a school holiday at home, though he was allowed to come back to the Abruzzi in 1878 in order to take a state examination which

[11] Details of their relationship are available in F. Masci, *La vita e le opere di GD'A in un indice cronologico e analitico* (Rome, 1950), 9–10. This was not the Filippo Masci from whom D'Annunzio was to inherit the constituency of Ortona a Mare in 1897/8 (for whom, see below, p. 163). Indeed in an unpublished letter in the Vittoriale archive (Archivio Generale, VI. 1) the biographer Masci, almost as if to emphasize the distance from his earlier namesake, makes it clear to D'Annunzio that he was born on 26 May 1896 at Chieti and that his father's name was Alessandro, a point needing to be made in view of his attempted objectivity.

[12] GD'A, *Il compagno dagli occhi senza cigli* (The Companion with Browless Eyes), *Prose di ricerca*, ii. 503; similar sentiments are expressed in *Il secondo amante*, ibid. 328.

might exempt him from a year's school fees. That early period of his life, including those unflattering portraits of the old maids, finds expression in his first writings and in the reminiscent musing typified in the three memoirs of *Il venturiero senza ventura*, *Il secondo amante di Lucrezia Buti*, and *Il compagno dagli occhi senza cigli*.[13] Those recollections blend certain stream-of-consciousness techniques with an admixture of Proustian memory-triggers in an entirely new kind of poetic prose, and while they certainly reinforce D'Annunzio's egotism, as autobiographical reminiscences they are more romantically than factually reliable.

Yet his father was really quite clever to get his son to the Cicognini, having fortunately followed the advice of an old Florentine friend, Francesco Coccolini, with whom D'Annunzio was to lodge during some of his school holidays. One particularly interesting memory of the Collegio Cicognini is D'Annunzio's reflection on the constant need to practise voice control and elocution in order to rid himself of his Abruzzese accent, mocked by fellow students when he first arrived at school. That was probably one of his father's preoccupations in sending him to Tuscany. Many years later, in *Il secondo amante di Lucrezia Buti*, Gabriele was to note his harrowing experience: 'Back into my memory flows the ferocious derision of my fellow pupils in the Prato school when, called upon for the first time, I got up from my desk to decline the noun *rosa* and pronounced it as though it were the past participle of *rodere* [to gnaw].'[14] And in the memories of his *Il compagno dagli occhi senza cigli* he reflected in retrospect upon the providential vision of his father: 'He forbade me the barbarous territory of the Abruzzi until I had Tuscanized myself incorruptibly.'[15]

[13] Collectively known as *Le faville del maglio* (Sparks from the Hammer), most of which were serialized in the *Corriere della sera* before being published as three separate volumes in 1924; the memoirs now comprise certain of the so-called *Prose di ricerca*; the first title, *Il venturiero senza ventura*, literally 'Adventurer without Adventure', also implies 'Soldier of Fortune without Fortune'.

[14] *Il secondo amante*, *Prose di ricerca*, ii. 152–3; the equivalent of his provincial pronunciation might be the northern English dialect pronunciation of *rose*, compared with its equivalent in received pronunciation; Fracassini, *GD'A convittore*, and G. Fatini, *Il cigno e la cicogna: GD'A collegiale* (Pescara, 1919), describe well the young boy's triumphs and tribulations at school in Prato; Fracassini's volume includes entries from an interesting and prophetic notebook of D'Annunzio's (indicating his attraction to such heroic figures), which contained extracts from a series of authors ranging from Cicero to Benjamin Franklin, 16 bis–53 bis (the volume consists of two undifferentiated parts).

[15] *Il compagno dagli occhi senza cigli*, *Prose di ricerca*, ii. 450.

Even nowadays, amongst certain middle-class Italians, there is a prejudice against the sound of a thick southern accent, akin to English snobbery, or as far as it is possible for Italians to approach English snobbery. So, in view of D'Annunzio's later triumphs as a public orator and, more intimately, as a reciter of his own poetry, the acquisition of a pure Tuscan accent may be seen as one of the more important benefits of his schooling in Prato. One could go further: the intense concentration at such an early age on voice modulation and the cultivation of the essential musicality of poly-syllabic Tuscan pronunciation (compared with his native apocopated Abruzzese), were major factors in giving him such facility both for improvising and for technical composition in his later career. Those attributes were added to his academic study and absorption of the classical tradition from Virgil to Carducci; they created a formid-able basis for D'Annunzio's prolific output in every literary genre, and gave him the self-confidence to deliver sometimes formal, but often improvised, public speeches on a great variety of topics. D'Annunzio's secretary and confidant, Antongini, reflecting upon the poet's accent and voice, stressed the lack of any regionalism in his voice, and emphasized his ability to change its pitch from the caressing tone he employed when reciting his poetry to the metallic timbre and urgent delivery he used when haranguing crowds.[16] Harold Nicolson testified to the spellbinding quality of D'Annunzio's voice in the episode already noted in part:

I leaned back in the large red sofa revelling in the languors of that lovely voice, in the amazing finale of that lovely sonnet [. . .] I was enthralled. I crouched back among the cushions, conscious of an emotional pressure such as I had not as yet experienced [. . .]. We left eventually and walked along the quay. I was still fervent with excitement.[17]

It is an appropriate, if ironic, reflection on the episode that while Nicolson praised the sublimity of D'Annunzio's vocal performance, he also took the opportunity to criticize adversely the English pro-nunciation of his own noble friend the marquis de Chaumont, on the grounds that the marquis spoke the language with a Cockney accent, having learnt it from a serving-girl in the London house where he had stayed.

---

[16] Antongini, *Un D'Annunzio ignorato*, 107–8.
[17] Nicolson, *Some People*, 90–1; for other instances of D'Annunzio's ability to sway an audience, and of his quality of voice, see below, p. 318.

By the time the young Gabriele was 15 years old a vein of rhetorical self-glorification had become visible in his letters home to his parents and to his former tutor, Sisti. The boy consistently (though with the exception of mathematics) obtained very high marks in his lessons and examinations, and he reports those successes in his early letters. One such missive, written on 27 March 1877, thanks Sisti for encouraging him to work so hard in order to honour family, tutor, and country, and concludes:

My first mission on this earth is to teach people to love their country and to be honourable citizens, the second is to hate to the death all the enemies of Italy and constantly to combat them. Ah! if all Italians were like me, they would pay dearly for all the blood they have sucked from us with their cowardly betrayals.[18]

That originally naïve patriotism was to develop and strengthen in the years to come. There were other symptoms of his own self-esteem, for instance in the well-known dedication of a juvenile photographic portrait in 1878, 'To Glory, this figure of my most distant melancholy', the forerunner of countless signed photographs for which his fans were in later years to clamour.[19]

Similar aspects of his personal psychological state at the time are further revealed by other letters home and to friends. Thus, several years before the pompous dedication beneath his portrait, he also sent an affectionate letter to his father, written on the back of an essay dated 27 November 1874, marking the end of his first term at the Cicognini:

Dearest Papa,

The jubilation which my heart is experiencing makes me take up the pen to let you know the good news that I am top of my class. Oh, how sweetly those words spring to my lips; what joy I feel at having come up to what you and Mama and my good teacher wanted for me (I shall honour him more than ever since he put me on the path to study).[20]

[18] Fatini publishes the letter: *Il cigno e la cicogna*, 38.

[19] D'Annunzio took unusual advantage of this vogue when, as late as 1916, possibly to forward his ambitions in the armed forces, he sent a similar photograph of himself aged 16 to the Italian commander-in-chief General Cadorna, with the 'prophetic' dedication: 'To Captain Luigi Cadorna, future Generalissimo of a victorious Italy, Gabriele D'Annunzio, July 1869'; reported by his friend Ugo Ojetti, *Cose viste*, 7 vols. (Milan 1937), i. 42.

[20] R. De Felice, G. Pampaloni, and M. Praz, *D'Annunzio* (Florence, 1978) contains appendices of rare or unpublished letters; here the letter is available in E. Bodrero's transcription, pp. 106–8; Fatini, *Il cigno e la cicogna*, 239 n. 7, suggests a later date that same year for the missive, preferably after D'Annunzio's first term of schooling.

His affection for his father is expressed in other letters during that first year, one of which pleads with Francesco Paolo to write to him more often:

You see, father, this is the only real pleasure, the one real comfort which I have from my labours: I love praise, because I know that you will enjoy praise offered to me; I love glory because I know that you will exult to hear glory attached to my name; I love life because I know that my life must be a support and a consolation for yours.[21]

The 'praise' he described in that letter of 25 April 1878, as elsewhere, is that which was accorded to him by his school masters, particularly by Father Angelo Tonini. This may repay further investigation here, though the questions raised also need to be discussed at a later stage in this study. One occasion for such an academic compliment was when Tonini set D'Annunzio an essay: the description of a visit to an art gallery. D'Annunzio was fond of art and was a frequent visitor to the nearby Uffizi galleries. But the essay he wrote for his teacher was simply a re-elaborated copy of the art gallery described by Edmondo De Amicis in his *Spagna*. D'Annunzio was rewarded by the naïve Tonini with full marks, 10/10. On a later occasion, he was asked to write a description of a hill. This he copied in large part from Raffaello Giovagnoli's *Spartaco*; for that second effort he was rewarded with 9/10.[22] Detractors were later to characterize these two incidents as the first of many instances of D'Annunzio's plagiarism; his supporters consider them examples of his *furbizia* (cunning), a derogatory way perhaps of saying 'intelligence'. The schoolboy scribblings of a 14-year-old, even of such a precocious 14-year-old, may seem trivial nowadays, but that youthful success at being able to pull the wool over his teacher's eyes may well have lent, in later adult life, conviction and determination to some of his legitimate imitative ambitions.[23]

Brilliance at his studies was one of the reasons why, according to Fatini, most of the masters at the school turned a blind eye to some

---

[21] Published in Fatini, *Il cigno e la cicogna*, 48.

[22] See ibid. 30–2 for transcriptions of the essays, and cf. p. 240 for the long and important notes (nn. 11–14) on the essays and their effect on later criticism; other such juvenile essays, available only in rarely seen private copies, are published in Masci, *La vita e le opere*, 11–12.

[23] This has been discussed more fully in J. R. Woodhouse, 'Creative Plagiarism: D'Annunzio's Varied Sources', in G. Bedani, R. Catani, and M. Slowikowska (eds.), *The Italian Lyric Tradition* (Cardiff, 1993), 91–107; see below Ch. 2 n. 31.

of D'Annunzio's scapegrace activities, clambering over the roof, insubordination, fighting in the dormitory, and the rest. 'Exuberant, resolute, quick to anger, jealous of his prestige, and above all dominated by a limitless pride which led him to rebel against any reproach which he considered unjustified and to impose his will on his companions and laugh at those in authority whose intellectual inferiority he knew.'[24] When teachers less favourable to the boy were in charge of his activities, Fatini notes that his name appeared in the punishment book. Thus the censor Bireni stops his allowance of fruit and wine with meals 'for indiscipline in the dormitory', and Fatini's study continues with quotations from the form punishment book for 1877–88, showing, for instance, that between April and July 1878 D'Annunzio had eight punishments, usually loss of food privileges, for such offences as 'insubordination', 'interrupting studies', 'creating indiscipline in the dormitory', 'talking back to the teacher', 'breaking a carafe', 'indiscipline', and, on 10 July 1878, for 'insulting the prefects with offensive words', for which he was given four days of solitary confinement.[25]

During the Easter vacation of 1877, D'Annunzio, as usual not allowed home for the school holidays, was a guest in the house of Francesco Coccolini, where, as the autobiographical *Secondo amante di Lucrezia Buti* describes, in an account rather too epic for its subject-matter, he kissed Coccolini's daughter Clemenza, during a visit to the Etruscan Museum in Florence, in front of the bronze statue of a Chimera; he later, with typical pretension, called the experience 'The hour of the Chimera'.[26] In August of the following year, 1878, he pawned his grandfather's gold watch to get money to visit a brothel, an episode which seems so to have saddened him that it was many years before he ever again paid for sex. The motherly prostitute, Lucrezia, 'a great Gorgon whose serpent locks had been reduced to a wig of reddish tow', gave him more comfort than passion, and the session ended when she sold him a battered old violin. That experience he entitled 'The hour of the Hetaira'.[27] By that time, at the age of 16, the precocious young student's character

[24] Fatini, *Il cigno e la cicogna*, 55.   [25] Ibid. 54.
[26] The episode is described at some length in *Il secondo amante*, *Prose di ricerca*, ii. 225–9. Some doubt is cast upon D'Annunzio's account, not least because Clemenza was ten years his senior; see G. Gatti, *Le donne nella vita e nell'arte di GD'A* (Modena, 1951), 20; Fracassini, *GD'A convittore*, 32–5, mentions even earlier 'love affairs'.
[27] *Il secondo amante*, *Prose di ricerca*, ii. 363–6.

was more or less formed and would alter little for the rest of his life. A year after the brothel episode, on 20 May 1879, he wrote to Cesare Fontana, a Milanese acquaintance, offering him a self-portrait:

First of all I will draw a psychological portrait of myself, just so that you may know, anyway, with what kind of animal you are about to become friends. I shall be brief and truthful. I am sixteen years of age and already I feel thrilling in my soul and brain the approach of the first fires of youth. Fixed in my heart is an unlimited desire for knowledge and glory, which often produces dark, tormenting melancholy in me, driving me to tears. I cannot suffer any yoke upon my freedom; I am as quick to anger and to take offence as to forgiveness; loyal and fiercely contemptuous of cowards; opposed for the most part to everything the world does; an ardent lover of new art and beautiful women; most individual in my tastes; most tenacious in my opinions; frank to the point of harshness; generous to the point of prodigality; enthusiastic to the point of madness.[28]

Adulthood merely gave him the physical and financial possibility of publicly showing those attributes to the world.

In November 1878, on his journey back to Prato from the examination at Chieti, and about to begin the new school term, D'Annunzio paused at Bologna to acquire the newly published *Odi barbare* (Barbarian Odes) of the future Nobel laureate, Giosuè Carducci. By definition these were cult models of nonconformity; their title reflected the fact that their metre depended on the *quantity* of Greek and Latin vocabulary and was hence alien or barbaric in the context of the romance quality of Italian. Carducci's shaggy appearance and his iconoclastic views on politics and literature also gave the impression that the 'barbarous' quality of his poetry contained within it the vigour of an untamed mind. It is difficult to exaggerate the influence which Carducci had upon budding intellectuals in post-unification Italy. His famous 'Inno a Satana' (Hymn to Satan) exalted symptomatically a life of action and enjoyment, set against asceticism and stagnation. For Carducci's younger contemporaries it was not difficult to view current political and economic conditions as a sluggish, bureaucratic, and often corrupt contrast with the optimistic heroism of the earlier Risorgimento. Young Italian patriots easily identified with Carducci's views; for

[28] The letter is published in R. Forcella, *GD'A (1863–1883)* (Rome, 1926), i. 90; and is available in fascsimile in *Varietas* (Dec. 1905); such facsimiles of D'Annunzio's handwriting were a popular feature of many pro-D'Annunzio journals from this point onwards.

them he was the personification of Mazzinian republicanism, and at the same time he undeniably had a powerful physical presence, anti-clerical, anti-Christian, and austerely incorruptible. Almost every poem of Carducci's exudes the atmosphere of ancient Greece and Rome; his values were pagan values.

D'Annunzio devoured the *Odi barbare*, and in January 1879 he sent Carducci his visiting-card from Prato, and was delighted to receive the great man's card in return. The exchange gave the 16-year-old the courage to write to the idol at some length on 6 March 1879, expressing his reverence, love, and admiration, and his ambition to follow his example:

I wish to follow in your footsteps. I, too, wish to fight courageously for this school of letters which they call new, destined as it is to see triumphs very different from those of the Church and the School of Manzoni. I, too, feel in my brain the spark of combative genius, which makes every fibre tingle, and sets in my soul a tormenting mania for glory and for battle. I, too, wish to consecrate to the true art the most brilliant flashes of my intellect, the strongest forces in my life, the most sacred beatings of my heart, my golden dreams, my youthful aspirations, the most tremendous bitternesses and the most supreme joys.
And I wish to fight at your side, O Poet![29]

It is doubtful whether Carducci replied to the young man's rhetorical exuberance. If he had done so, D'Annunzio would certainly have made sure that people heard of such a reply; there is no trace of it among his papers.

The end of D'Annunzio's long exile was at hand. On 8 June 1879 he wrote his most affectionate letter to his father in response to two notes (*letterine*) from Francesco Paolo, in which the latter had evidently said 'My son, I am waiting for you', words which the boy repeated to himself over and over, wondering how to compensate his parent for his affection and for the joy the words had given him. All the world's applause, every poetic laurel, all the cries of admiration and emotion would, he wrote, be nothing beside his father's greeting, 'Father, smile on me and kiss my forehead; a kiss from you is worth more than the whole world.'[30] The poignancy of his

---

[29] Published in G. Gatti, *Vita di GD'A* (Florence, 1956), 25.
[30] Fatini, *Il cigno e la cicogna*, 104–5; also published with other letters of the time by R. Tiboni, 'I giorni della "chiusa adolescenza": Lettere al padre alla madre e alle sorelle', *Nuova antologia*, 74/1620 (16 Sept. 1939), 126.

sentiments would contrast starkly with the bitter relationship which later developed between the two.

By the summer of 1879 D'Annunzio had written thirty poems in Carduccian vein, and by December they were published, following a subvention from his father. *Primo vere*, the title of the small collection, maintained, in Carducci's neo-Latin style, the masculine form of the noun for spring, and the first ode, in neo-Sapphic metre, was dedicated to Carducci himself.[31] What is clear, however, is that Carducci's almost puritanical austerity was not for D'Annunzio. A good example of the contrast is in the way Satan also supplied the younger poet with his inspiration in the 'Ora satanica' (Satanic Hour) where D'Annunzio's Satan lacks any of Carducci's pagan virtue:

> Voglio l'ebbrezze che prostrano l'anima e i sensi,
>   gl'inni ribelli che fan tremare i preti:
> voglio ridde infernali con strepiti e grida insensate,
>   seni d'etére su cui passar le notti:
> voglio orgie lunghe con canti d'amori bizzarri;
>   tra baci e bicchieri voglio insanire.

> [I desire the inebriation which prostrates soul and senses,
>   rebellious hymns which make priests tremble:
>   dances from hell, with noise and senseless cries,
>   breasts of courtesans on which to spend my nights
>   long orgies serenaded with bizarre love-songs;
>   I want to lose my mind among cups and kisses.]

It fell to Giuseppe Chiarini, increasingly important as one of Italy's leading critics, to review the collection in the influential newspaper, *Il fanfulla della domenica*. On 31 December 1879 D'Annunzio had taken the precaution of writing to Chiarini a subtle and well-composed letter which he enclosed with a complimentary copy of the poems:

I have been sitting at my desk for half an hour tormenting pen and inkpot, and I have been unable to find an appropriate opening. You know? I feel like one of those country fellows who, when they find themselves in the

---

[31] A second and enlarged version of *Primo vere* was published a year later, containing seventy-six lyrics (of which only fourteen had appeared in the earlier volume), and twenty-three translations from Latin and Greek. The Carduccian influence in the volume is only too obvious, though most critics agree that D'Annunzio also drew on several other poetic sources, and there are indeed hints of Ugo Foscolo, Giacomo Leopardi, Aleardo Aleardi, the bohemian Scapigliatura, Lorenzo Stecchetti, and Giuseppe Chiarini.

presence of a grand personage blush as red as prawns in a saucepan and stammer goodness knows what, passing their hat from one hand to the other. I really feel like one of them.[32]

D'Annunzio need have had no such preoccupations. Chiarini's piece, which was published on 2 May 1880, was headed 'A proposito d'un nuovo poeta' (Concerning a New Poet), no doubt in itself a wonderful boost to D'Annunzio's already swollen ego. Chiarini's over-all judgement was positive, despite some reservations concerning D'Annunzio's over-exuberance and his imitation of others; here was a new poet with genuine inspiration and great technical abilities: 'To me this verse clearly attests to an uncommon aptitude for poetry.' Not so favourable was the judgement of the college authorities in Prato, where a copy was sent to the library, and where a debate was initiated among that provincial and rather prudish hierarchy on whether to expel the young man for his scepticism and sensuality. In the end the director, Flaminio Del Seppia, relented and simply issued an official warning to Gabriele, meanwhile attempting to confiscate the copies of the volume bought by the young man's fel-low pupils. The minutes of the relevant college meeting in January 1879 make fascinating reading, mainly for the tension between Del Seppia's need to avoid a scandal in such a provincial centre as Prato, and his ambition to promote his leading pupil's obvious literary talent. Under college rules members were (theoretically at least) for-bidden to submit items for publication, even in local newspapers, and Del Seppia had reason to remember his recalcitrant pupil when in a later report to his school governors, he drew their attention to the negative aspects of having a 16-year-old publish a book of poetry, decrying what he called the current mania for publishing.[33] D'Annunzio, however, continued to work on the second edition of *Primo vere*, passed his examinations, and, at the end of the 1878/9 academic session, returned to Pescara. In June of that same year, 1879, D'Annunzio had published *In memoriam*, eighteen sonnets, two four-strophe lyrics, and an envoy, dedicated to the memory of his grandmother, Rita Lolli. The collection elicited only poor

[32] Fatini, *Il cigno e la cicogna*, 129.
[33] Ibid. 115–16, where Fatini reproduces the minutes of the college meeting, and, in a long note at p. 245, gives the warning by Del Seppia to his governing body; for the episode generally see G. Sozzi, *GD'A nella vita e nell'arte* (Florence, 1964), 60–1; for a discussion of the relationship between Chiarini and D'Annunzio, see L. Pescetti, 'D'Annunzio, Marradi e Chiarini', *L'Italia letteraria* (25 Mar. 1934).

reviews, and, perhaps as a reaction, in another letter to Fontana, dated 12 August 1879, D'Annunzio tells how that summer he had turned to more physical activities in Pescara: swimming, riding, sailing by moonlight, dancing, drawing, fencing, singing, courting beautiful women.[34] There, to judge from other letters to friends, he was lionized by the local bourgeoisie. It was while he was at home, celebrating the publication of the second edition of *Primo vere*, that on 14 November the Florentine newspaper, the *Gazzetta della domenica*, published the following announcement:

GABRIELE D'ANNUNZIO, the young poet, already well known in the republic of letters and often mentioned on our pages, some days ago (5 November) on the Francavilla road, fell from his horse and died on the spot.

The new edition of his *Primo vere* is expected daily!

Following the news of his death numerous other newspapers took up the story, regretting the passing of such a promising young genius, and sending condolences to his astonished parents. Almost all the newspapers published complimentary obituaries, even praising the poor compositions of *In memoriam*, copies of which D'Annunzio did his best to destroy. And all mentioned the imminent publication of the revised edition of his *Primo vere*. Rumour had it that at the Cicognini a mass was said for his soul. D'Annunzio, over the signature of a bogus G. Rutini, had himself supplied the news of his accidental death. The incident is typical of the way he was to manipulate public opinion, and the press, in order to get maximum attention for himself and his work. The second edition of *Primo vere* sold well and was reviewed in newspapers from Palermo to Florence.[35]

Almost without exception, D'Annunzio's Italian biographers mention, even at this adolescent stage in his life, his brief love affairs involving some of the women with whom he came in contact. Two such incidents in Florence have already been mentioned. The attention paid to such trivial affairs has an importance which goes beyond the prurience with which some Italian critics treat the subject. The power of sex and his attraction to women were, throughout his life, to be D'Annunzio's main spur and inspiration for creative writing.

[34] The letter is published in Fatini, *Il cigno e la cicogna*, 156.
[35] Fatini (ibid. 161–6) reproduces some of the obituaries, including the one above, and describes the consequences for D'Annunzio's fortunes thereafter. There are many accounts of these events: see P. Chiara, *Vita di GD'A* (Milan, 1981), 26 and Sozzi, *GD'A* 63.

D'Annunzio's Anglophone critics have not taken that fact seriously and have reacted puritanically or ironically to his philandering. (The exception which proves the rule was poor, supportive, appreciative Arthur Symons, so proud to be able familiarly to refer to the poet by his first name.[36]) Simultaneously with his two amorous experiences in Florence D'Annunzio occupied his time, during visits to Pescara, with a provincial flame, Teodolinda Pomarici; he was to correspond with her for the next three years. Those brief encounters were to surface later in his literary work, as did most other events from his life, disguised with exotic names and surroundings; thus Clemenza, for instance, became Clematide and Malinconia in the memoirs of *Il secondo amante di Lucrezia Buti*. But the only name of any importance, and then because she was his first real inspiration for a personal kind of sensual poetry, was Giselda Zucconi, called affectionately Elda, later transformed into Lalla in the poems of *Canto novo*, the collection which celebrates in large part their youthful love.

Elda was the daughter of D'Annunzio's language tutor at the Cicognini and this time the affair was more serious. In view of the passionate language with which D'Annunzio celebrates her beauty in his letters, and given the sensuality of the poetry which he composed under her inspiration, unprepossessing photographs of the young woman present a much more plain and demure appearance than readers might have expected. In her most famous portrait, perhaps owing to the formality of the *fin de siècle* pose, perhaps because of her disillusionment after D'Annunzio had played with her emotions for nearly four years, Elda's rather heavy features, distinguished only by a fine forehead and brows, carry a desolate expression; the mouth is sad, the eyes look with an almost defiant unhappiness into the distance right of camera. The vast correspondence between the two continued until 1883,[37] and in June 1882,

[36] For forty years in reviews, articles, and translations, Symons consistently supported D'Annunzio's work; see, for instance, his introduction to GD'A, *Child of Pleasure*, trans. G. Harding (London, 1898), his *Studies in Prose and Verse* (London 1904), his 'A Reading at Count Primoli's', in his *Eleonora Duse* (London, 1926), 111–29, and, more recently, his *Selected Letters 1880–1935*, ed. K. Beckson and J. M. Munro (London 1989), where in letters to his wife he mentions nonchalantly his meetings in Rome with 'Gabriel': see pp. 115, 253, 258–9.

[37] There are some 470 letters from D'Annunzio alone, published in Ivanos Ciani's edition of the *Lettere a Giselda Zucconi*; the appendix to Ciani's edition contains eleven letters from Elda, pathetically appealing for D'Annunzio's aid during the 1920s (see Ch. 2 n. 17); for her appearance see Plate 9.

during his only visit to Florence since leaving the Cicognini in May 1881, the affair was renewed sufficiently for Gabriele to return to Pescara and ask his mother's permission to marry the girl. So much is implied in the letters he wrote during that summer, at times assisted by his sister Anna, or Nannina as he called her, whom he persuaded to enclose the occasional letter of her own which would emphasize to Elda both the loving feelings of her brother and the affection that she and her mother felt for this unseen love of D'Annunzio's life. But by January 1883 D'Annunzio had written his final letter to Elda, three months later he had seduced and impregnated Maria Hardouin, and by August of that year he and his new flame were married.

The title of his second volume of verse, *Canto novo*, was meant to assert the young poet's new freedom from Carduccian influence: 'That wizard Carducci was crushing me, and one day I'd have ended up like so many young hopefuls', he wrote to Guido Biagi during the period of composition:

I've had the strength to rebel, and with a slow and most laborious process of *selections*, I've managed to come out as myself, just me. All that remains is for me to break the final weak chains and then plunge into my own sea. What would do me the world of good now is a slice of freedom, a submersion in pure air, to be drunk with sunshine, greenery and wild scents.[38]

Certainly the sixty-three poems of *Canto novo* had a sensuality of their own which marked them out as what was later universally recognizable as Dannunzian. Love for Elda and an exultation in nature, and especially the sea, formed his main subject-matter, while his extravagant expressions of joy and sensuality were made in a language which was characteristically exotic and far from the language of everyday speech. The poems were also a hymn to youth, and to the necessary irresponsibility of the young, an attitude, one might add, which spiritually did not leave D'Annunzio until he had reached his mid-sixties. His particular song of joy, for instance, 'Canta la gioia', might be regarded as his own programme of action for the next forty years (some biographers might say until the end of his days):

[38] The correspondence with Biagi is kept in the Biblioteca Nazionale in Florence; the letter of 24 May 1881 is published in part by Ivanos Ciani in his fine article on the original inspiration for *Canto novo*, 'La nascita dell'idea di *Canto novo*', in *Canto novo nel centenario della pubblicazione*, ed. E. Tiboni and L. Abrugiati (Pescara, 1982), here p. 24.

Canta l'immensa gioia di vivere,
d'essere forte, d'essere giovine,
di mordere i frutti terrestri
con saldi e bianchi denti voraci,

di por le mani audaci e cupide
su ogni dolce cosa tangibile,
di tendere l'arco su ogni
preda novella che il desio miri [. . .].

[Sing the immense joy of living
  of being strong, of being young,
  of biting the fruits of the earth
  with firm, white, voracious teeth,

of putting audacious and covetous hands
on every sweet tangible thing,
of bending the bow against every
new prey that desire has in its sights [. . .].]

The generic allusions to love and excitement which were present in *Primo vere* now became particularized, made more realistic, and so proved more shocking to his readers. There were further changes from the earlier collection: D'Annunzio's relationship with the external world becomes more intense, at times he seems one with nature in a way which foreshadows the greater lyrics of *Alcyone*, where humanity assumes mythical qualities in the poet's imagination. In *Canto novo*, Elda takes on the characteristics of surrounding nature, her blood becomes lymph, her limbs and features become sensual plants, while the trees and wild creatures in turn take on human characteristics, reminding the poet of the scents and sights of love. Many of the poems are vitiated by D'Annunzio's obsessive use of recherché vocabulary and by his delight in employing obscure classical allusions, both of which tendencies forced his principal editor, Enzo Palmieri, to include more footnotes than text, simply to explain the poems' erudite references.[39] But elsewhere in the collection there are sublime moments of poetic beauty, such as his three verses on the waning moon, 'O falce di luna calante' (O Sickle

---

[39] Typical are Palmieri's notes on the third 'Offerta votiva' (Votive Offering), an over-complicated vehicle for such personal sentiments, which begins with a convoluted description of the cithara-playing Eunomus of Locris in Delphi, consecrating to the god a cicada worked in bronze (*una di lavorato bronzo cicala al dio*); see *Crestomazia della lirica di GD'A: Interpretazione e commento* ed. E. Palmieri (Bologna, 1944), 18–21.

Moon), which provided inspiration for Tosti and Respighi, who were among several composers to set the song to music.[40] Some of the mood of 'O falce di luna calante' is rendered by George Arthur Greene:

> O falce di luna calante
> che brilli su l'acque deserte.
> O falce d'argento, qual mèsse di sogni
> ondeggia al tuo mite chiarore qua giù!
>
> Aneliti brevi di foglie,
> sospiri di fiori dal bosco
> esalano al mare:
> non canto non grido
> non suono pe 'l vasto silenzio va.
>
> Oppresso d'amor, di piacere,
> il popolo de' vivi s'addorme . . .
> O falce calante, qual mèsse di sogni
> ondeggia al tuo mite chiarore qua giù!
>
> [O sickle of moonlight declining
> That shinest o'er waters deserted,
> O sickle of silver, what harvest of visions
> Is waving down here, thy mild lustre beneath!
>
> Ephemeral breathing of foliage,
> Of flowers, of waves from the forest,
> Goes forth to the ocean, no cry and no singing,
> No sound through the infinite silences goes.
>
> Oppressed with its loves and its pleasures
> The life of the world lies in slumber;
> O sickle declining, what harvest of visions
> Is waving down here, thy mild lustre beneath!][41]

Canto novo was inspired, then, by Elda Zucconi, and the first edition of 1882 included allusions to his 'great, beautiful, most adored inspiration', as well as an initial poem dedicated to her. If Elda was in effect no great beauty, D'Annunzio had the imagination to make her so. What really counted on this and future occasions was the stimulation of his hormones. The book sold well, and provided

[40] *Canto novo* was also one of the earliest collections to be known to his English audiences; thirteen of its poems were translated by G. A. Greene in his admirable anthology, *Italian Lyrists of Today* (London, 1893).

[41] Ibid. 8–9.

young people with an expression of passionate sexual love, normally repressed in their bourgeois society. It had elements of realism, and even of Socialism, if we are to believe a note which D'Annunzio wrote to Paolo De Cecco concerning 'the blasts of fierce Socialism' which he had inserted in the poems.[42] But an interesting reflection on D'Annunzio's character, and his attitude to the women who inspired him, was that in the definitive edition of 1896 Elda's name and the dedication disappear, along with two-thirds of the original poems which particularly revealed D'Annunzio's more human (and by definition more fallible) side. In the 1896 edition, the figure of the woman becomes, instead, more idealized, while in the new poems D'Annunzio is made out to be less obviously involved on a personal level in a sensual love affair. The intervening period had, as may be seen, added sophistication and cynicism to the egotism already present in the young poet. To these harder characteristics D'Annunzio added a further incidental stratum of fashionable Nietzschean philosophy. The German thinker's ideas simply gave an impersonal, abstract, or theoretical justification to the self-centred behaviour patterns and attitudes which D'Annunzio had adopted spontaneously since the age of 15. But above all the reworked *Canto novo* showed D'Annunzio self-consciously constructing for himself a public image; he was beginning, it might almost be said, to write his own obituary, from which personal feelings of a trivial or domestic nature had to be expunged in order to highlight a more heroic figure, his own version of a Nietzschean superman.

At the same time that he was publishing *Canto novo*, and demonstrating his new-found freedom from Carduccian 'chains', he also published the naturalistic collection of short stories, *Terra vergine* (Virgin Land). Naturalism was in vogue on the Continent, partly because of powerful French influences, but it had also been taken over by several leading Italian littérateurs, notably Luigi Capuana and Giovanni Verga, the latter one of D. H. Lawrence's favourite authors and one whom he openly preferred to D'Annunzio. It was Verga who, after achieving a national reputation for novels of a Romantic, bourgeois nature, had begun to write harrowing tales of the poverty-stricken Sicilian peasantry, in a new realistic style

---

[42] The note to De Cecco and a long and interesting letter to Elda's father Tito Zucconi concerning the aim and content of *Canto novo* are published in Ciani, 'La nascita dell'idea del *Canto novo*', 32.

heavily influenced by Zola. In 1881, just a year, that is, before the publication of D'Annunzio's *Terra vergine*, Verga had published the masterpiece *I Malavoglia* (Lawrence translated Verga's second novel, *Mastro-don Gesualdo*). *Verismo*, the Italian variant on *naturalisme*, was becoming fashionable: Salvatore Di Giacomo and Matilde Serao were also among verist writers achieving a national fame. With the confidence of youth D'Annunzio undoubtedly thought that he could do as well as, if not better than, they had done, and the short stories, already prepared for publication in April 1881, a good two months, that is, before he left school, were intended to break into this fashionable market. Some of those stories, added to other small collections, *Il libro delle vergini* of 1884, and *San Pantaleone* of 1886, were published in 1902 under the comprehensive title of *Le Novelle della Pescara*.

Several critics have seen parallels between D'Annunzio and other naturalist contemporaries; some have accused him of copying Verga's ideas and plots,[43] while certain of his characters had evident psychological affinities with Verga's peasantry. Such criticisms are quibbles when seen in the light of the many differences between Verga and his younger contemporary. D'Annunzio's sketches of Abruzzese life have in common with Verga only the degradation of grinding rural poverty, and from the differences between the two may be gained an important insight into D'Annunzio's character at the time. A fundamental contrast lay in the attitudes of the two writers. Aware of the grimness of peasant life in his native Sicily Verga was, at least fictionally, dominated by a concept of a melancholy Fate, a Mediterranean *moira*, which dogged the footsteps of all his veristic characters. That awareness caused him to depict scenes of pathos with most of which his readers, even without his authorial intervention, could spontaneously sympathize. D'Annunzio, on the other hand, was concerned with observing human derelicts whom he then depicted through the imagination of an adolescent with a penchant for the grotesque and shocking; significantly, the earliest versions of the short stories were more harrowing than their revised later editions. On the rare occasions in the short stories when

---

[43] Many of the arguments are sensitively and succinctly set out in E. Paratore's *Studi dannunziani* (Naples, 1966), especially in the essay 'D'Annunzio e Verga', 119–47; Verga's *La Lupa*, for instance, seemed to provide the source for D'Annunzio's *Bestiame*, but Paratore shows how D'Annunzio developed the ideas of his older contemporary, if not always for the better.

his protagonists triumph over their degradation it is a triumph of raw, often bestial, unthinking courage or hardiness. Paratore suggests a musical comparison between the two writers: Verga, he suggests, obtains his effect through the submissive tone of a trio, while D'Annunzio uses the sound of the full orchestra, complete with brass.[44] Let two examples suffice to illustrate what other biographers tend to leave unsaid.

In *Gli idolatri* (The Idolaters), originally the title story of the small collection *San Pantaleone*, the fight between the fanatical rival villages of Radusa and Mascalico leaves nothing to the reader's imagination. The murder of Radusa's village champion, Pallura, in the atmosphere of a religious festival to celebrate San Pantaleone, inflames the wrath of his fellow peasants, urged on by the fanatical Giacobbe, who leads the Radusani in a cruel raid against Pallura's assassins in neighbouring Mascalico. The story has much in common with Verga's *Guerra dei santi* (War of the Saints), but in D'Annunzio's tale we are spared nothing of the crudity of the conflict. The villagers, bizarrely carrying their statue of San Pantaleone, succeed, after much slaughter and wounding, in advancing their burden into the Mascalicesi's church (consecrated to the rival saint, Consalvo); there a growing, instinctive sense of purpose drives them to attempt to set the statue upon the main altar of their rivals. The villagers' murderous progress, wielding scythes and reaping-hooks, leaves a trail of dead and dying as far as the steps of the altar, where Giacobbe, his bones whitely visible from the depth of his wounds, is finally disembowelled by five of the enemy, his entrails spilling out as he dies. The statue falls to the ground and is lost to the foe.

The choral horror of *Gli idolatri* becomes, if anything, more harrowing in the sequel to the story, *L'eroe* (The Hero), which, like the horrific contemporary story, *Il cerusico di mare* (Sea Surgeon), relies heavily on tactile images. D'Annunzio's scenes and characters continue to be surrounded by an unmistakable Abruzzi atmosphere; here the Mascalicesi, buoyed up by their victory, celebrate the festival of San Consalvo, spending the hard-earned profits of the harvest on decking out their village in the saint's honour. Amid the atmosphere of joy and self-congratulation, eight of the strongest

---

[44] Ibid. 128; often Verga's more thoughtfully created characters are artistically superior: his Jeli is better delineated than D'Annunzio's Dalfino; whether the spontaneity of D'Annunzio's peasants outweighs this technical superiority is a matter of opinion and dispute.

men are chosen to carry in procession the enormous bronze effigy of San Consalvo, its silver head and hands lending it further massy weight. But someone is clumsy, the statue falls, crushing the hand and wrist of Ummalido, one of the Herculean bearers. He cries out. The statue is raised. Women shudder at the now formless limb which was his hand. Ummalido insists on continuing with his sacred duty, putting his shoulder beneath the heavy statue. He collapses before the church is reached, but recovers his senses in a neighbour's house while Vespers are being celebrated. Making his way through the heat and sweat of the congregation, and with a brief, 'I offer it to you, San Consalvo', he runs his knife around his wrist, slowly detaching it from the rest of his arm. Further shudders from the congregation, a mention of the final dangling cartilaginous filaments as the hand falls into the offertory basin, and the story closes with a repetition of Ummalido's dedicatory words.

There is about nearly all D'Annunzio's stories an unfeeling quality which reinforces the brutally poor life of the peasants and underlines their three main preoccupations: religion (or their primitive interpretation of Christianity), reproduction (there is no love here, only sex of a bestial kind), and economic survival, exemplified by the horror of another tale, *La madia* (The Bread Chest). No one can deny, however, that there is a novel power about D'Annunzio's descriptions which grips the reader's imagination and which certainly touched a chord in the minds of his contemporaries, well aware of the primitive conditions current in southern Italy. It is worth recalling that at the same time that D'Annunzio was describing his seemingly grotesque creations, his friend, the artist and pioneering photographer Francesco Paolo Michetti, was actually recording similar events. Michetti's camera immortalized, for instance, certain primitive pilgrimages to local sanctuaries, one of which, the pilgrimage to Casalbordino, was, in 1894, to become the focus of an important episode in D'Annunzio's fourth major novel, *Il trionfo della morte*. It is also undeniable that D'Annunzio is unique in creating the Abruzzese atmosphere, with the sights, sounds, and smells of local villages, adding the primary colours of an unrelentingly harsh landscape, or the white horses of a storm at sea, using, where necessary, enough dialect speech to complete the authenticity of the whole. At the same time it must be said that D'Annunzio's descriptive pieces are full of that rich, at times precious, vocabulary which he uses to characterize less plebeian environments. It formed part of his obsession with the power of words, and with his later well-publicized stand for restoring dignity and brilliance to the nation's language. But its appropriateness in such peasant environments is at times questionable. Unquestioning, however, were the appreciative words of the only competent English critic consistently to approve of D'Annunzio. In 1919, at a time when D'Annunzio was proving particularly irritating to the British Establishment, C. H. Herford delivered a eulogy of the poet, concentrating his attention on D'Annunzio's verbal qualities. His appreciation of the *Idolatri* is particularly relevant here:

D'Annunzio's sensuality asserts itself still, as always; but it appears here as a Rubens-like joy in intense impressions; now a copper-coloured storm sky, now a splash of blood, betrays his passion for the crude effect of flame and scarlet, most often where they signify death or ruin. He imagines voluptuously as always, but his voluptuousness here feeds not in the lust of the flesh, but in the lust of wounds and death.[45]

The reaction of the more influential Italian critics to D'Annunzio's veristic work was favourable, but from the point of view of D'Annunzio's critical fortunes abroad, judgements in English journals and biographies were important since they helped to crystallize his reputation in Britain and America. Thus Ouida (sobriquet of Marie Louise de la Ramée), despite her outward admiration for D'Annunzio, was to condemn his realism and sensuality. Writing in 1897, she noted the popularizing effect which the French translations of D'Annunzio's work had had through Europe, though she seems to regret the French censorship, for instance of the Lourdes-like pilgrimage to Casalbordino, which she translates from the original in D'Annunzio's *Trionfo della morte*, remarking: 'What strength is here? What admirable choice of descriptive phrase and truth of design, as in a Callot or Hogarth! What sense conveyed of press, of haste, of noise, of confusion, of stench, of uproar! We live in this crowd as we read.'[46] On the other hand, when D'Annunzio dwells on the naked charms of his heroine, Ippolita Sanzio, Ouida coyly sends her readers to the original Italian with the comment: 'What is, I think more offensive to taste and more injurious to art than any

[45] C. H. Herford, 'GD'A', *Bulletin of the John Rylands Library* (1919), 5, 424.
[46] Marie Louise De la Ramée (Ouida) had spent a considerable time in Florence and was one of the few Anglophone critics capable of judging the original text of D'Annunzio's work. Her essay 'The Genius of D'Annunzio' was published in the *Fortnightly Review*, 67 (Mar. 1897), here 305.

sensual excess in description, is mere nastiness, mere filth; and of this D'Annunzio is as guilty as Zola is, and as Zola has been, always.'[47] Eugene Benson, meanwhile, is more concerned with the stench of the crowd, and in an unconsciously amusing essay in the *Yellow Book*, judging from D'Annunzio's willingness to include the agreeable and the disagreeable with the indifference of a surgeon, he surmises: 'I confess Italian hardihood is always a surprise, and one is induced to think that the race lacks *delicacy* in things moral and physical.'[48] Benson goes on to wonder whether the 'nasal nerve' is more robust in the Italian. 'That organ does not sniff the offence in the way, nor nose the rat on the stairs, nor the corpse behind the arras. The Italian ignores villainous odours.' Benson is in fact trying to find an excuse for D'Annunzio's indifference to what Gerald Griffin was later to describe as 'the sadistic gloating which makes one shudder on reading the *Novelle della Pescara*'.[49] The views of Ouida, on the other hand, not least because she was able to read D'Annunzio in the original Italian, were most influential in her own day. And, although she may be unfashionable nowadays on account of her insipid fiction and lack of intellectual weight, her opinions continued to resurface, indeed to be plagiarized in English articles and reviews, until the death of D'Annunzio. One effect of such repetition was to strengthen the anti-Dannunzian (and, it must be said, anti-Italian) bias of the British Establishment, creating prejudices which had repercussions for D'Annunzio's reputation in later years.

It is interesting to note that, twenty years after their first definitive edition, and forty years from the first composition of some stories, a selection from the *Novelle della Pescara* was translated into English in 1922. The anthology is prefaced by a bizarre if authoritative-looking introduction by Joseph Hergesheimer, full of praise for the style and content of the book, and implying that D'Annunzio was writing 'for any who are moved by the heroic spectacle of humanity pinned by fatality to earth, but for ever struggling for release'. D'Annunzio's depiction of brutality and evil reflected, according to Hergesheimer, a universal need for hope and sympathy, his creations

---

[47] *Fortnightly Review*, 350–1. She is specifically criticizing *Il trionfo della morte*, for which see below, pp. 117 ff.

[48] E. Benson, 'GD'A: The New Poet and his Work', *The Yellow Book*, 11 (Oct. 1896), 286.

[49] G. Griffin, *GD'A: The Warrior Bard* (London, 1935), 275.

were 'troubled by modern apprehensions, a social conscience unavoidable now to any fineness of perception'.[50] This anachronistic judgement seems to be the only serious allusion to D'Annunzio's having a social conscience. Hergesheimer was moved to make his comparisons by the post-war poverty and destitution visible in Britain's inner cities and in areas of unemployment in Wales and Scotland. But if the opinion had any influence with the British Establishment in the period after 1919 (immediately following D'Annunzio's piratical capture of Yugoslav Fiume) it would probably have been to strengthen the *Times*'s view that in D'Annunzio Britain was dealing with a lunatic.

[50] GD'A, *Tales of my Native Town*, introd. J. Hergesheimer (London, 1920), here 14–15.

2

The Conquest of Rome

ALTHOUGH the publication of *Canto novo* and *Terra vergine* was of paramount importance in encouraging D'Annunzio independently to develop his literary talents, the immediate next steps in his career were traditional enough. Following his final year at the Cicognini he enrolled for the first term of the new academic session in the Humanities Faculty of Rome University. He seems scarcely to have attended a lecture in the Faculty, much less to have taken any examinations, though he did frequent the lessons of Jacob Moleschott, the Flemish physiologist, in great vogue and well known for his positivist philosophical views.[1] But the simple fact of being enrolled as a student postponed D'Annunzio's legal requirement to do military service, a ploy he was also to use later to avoid a potentially awkward meeting with Elda Zucconi. More immediately, D'Annunzio's main interest was in Rome's burgeoning social life, its new and exciting newspaper offices, outrageous intellectuals, its race-tracks, beautiful women, and fashionable personalities. It went without saying that although Elda suspected that her lover's energies were being devoted to an enjoyment of Rome's many diversions, D'Annunzio did his best, after his first month there, to give her the impression that the city meant hard work and loneliness.

Rome had become Italy's capital city only ten years before D'Annunzio's arrival there on 20 November 1881. Until the French could be persuaded to relinquish their military support for papal sovereignty in Rome, Turin and latterly Florence (1865–71) had

---

[1] Moleschott is given pride of place in D'Annunzio's 'Per una festa della scienza' in the *Tribuna* of 4 Nov. 1887; articles from *Tribuna*, which D'Annunzio was always reluctant to publish as a collection, were anthologized, with an interesting introduction, by A. Baldini and P. P. Trompeo: *Roma senza lupa: Cronache mondane (1884–88)* (Milan, 1948), a collection now superseded by the comprehensive twin volumes of *Le cronache de La Tribuna*, with a preface by R. Puletti, 2 vols. (Bologna, 1992); hereafter, where possible, reference will be in the text to the date of individual articles, thus facilitating reference to the original journals as well as to the two collections, while at the same time not overloading the footnotes.

served as Italy's capital. Rome under papal rule had been reduced to a quiet backwater, where goats still grazed in the Forum. Francis Wey, in an amusing if squalid aside during his first visit there, describes the muddy streets, the unpaved squares, the danger of fever, the poor quality of food, the lack of public transport, and above all the stench of the place, which he characterized as 'more poetically speaking, the perfume of Rome': 'It is a local exhalation of cabbage or broccoli broth, mixed with the raw smell of roots, sulphurous emanations to which one has to become accustomed, for the pavement and the black mud of the streets are impregnated with that essence, which has not become pure in becoming ever-lasting.'[2] In 1870 the population of Rome was around 220,000, a figure which, by the time D'Annunzio arrived, had risen to some 300,000 inhabitants—not a considerable increase when account is taken of the descent upon the city after 1871 of king and court, statutory military garrisons, unpaid politicians by the score, the Piedmontese civil service structured upon centuries of French-style bureaucracy, and a full array of foreign diplomatic corps—each of which brought in its train hosts of support personnel.

By 1881, then, the city had all the potential for the kind of expansion and exploitation associated with a frontier town, developing a bustling economy which attracted immigrant workers from the impoverished south, along with businessmen, entrepreneurs, and speculators ready to take advantage of them. All these elements, as Piero Chiara has remarked, 'conferred upon the Capital its character as an inexhaustible source of corruption, which it has not lost in the course of over a century'.[3] But Rome was certainly less provincial and more stimulating than Pescara, and, after first succumbing to a feverish illness, D'Annunzio reacted favourably, even excitedly, to his new surroundings: wonderful sunshine, springlike weather, monuments, churches, fountains, ruins—all sparkling, gold, silver, diamond; splendid walks surrounded by a crowd of friends, 'a brilliant red gaiety glows all around me'.[4] Such unconcealed enthusiasm in his correspondence with Elda was short-lived. Over the next few months his letters to her disguised or toned down the exhilaration in response to her natural jealousy that he should be away from her enjoying himself and possibly considering pastures

---

[2] F. Wey, *Rome* (London, 1872), 4–5.   [3] Chiara, *GD'A* 33.
[4] *Lettere a Giselda Zucconi*, 291.

new; what for the biographer might have been valuable indications of his experiences of the capital are dissimulated.

On this first visit to Rome D'Annunzio fell in with Edoardo Scarfoglio, an older fellow pupil from the Cicognini, who had also come up to the Eternal City from the Abruzzi the year before. Scarfoglio had in 1881 become editor of the weekly newspaper *Il Capitan Fracassa*, founded in 1880 by Luigi Vassallo; D'Annunzio accepted at once an invitation to write for the newspaper, and through his influential contact made the acquaintance of some of the leading artists and writers of the capital. The new editor and his friends had created in their newspaper a definite cultural and political bias which would have chimed with D'Annunzio's personal ambitions at the opening of the 1880s. Scarfoglio recalled that its incidental object was to support a kind of Carduccian literary stand-point (as well as popularizing and eulogizing Carducci himself), to steer the Italian literary tradition back towards its more austere clas-sical roots, and culturally to exalt and beautify the newly born Italy.[5] Scarfoglio also showed that journalism could provide a promising outlet for penniless intellectuals such as D'Annunzio. Like other pio-neering fields in the new capital, journalism and newspapers seemed to offer golden opportunities for the entrepreneur, not least because, prior to 1870, thanks in no little part to the high rate of illiteracy in the city, Rome had only three journals, all of them clerical and all organs of the Vatican (whose *Osservatore romano* is today left as the remarkable modern survivor of that trio). Within two years of D'Annunzio's arrival a dozen fledgling newspapers were circulating in the capital, and D'Annunzio was busily writing for at least six of them, *Capitano Fracassa* and the *Domenica del Fracassa*, the *Cronaca bizantina*, *Tribuna*, *Il fanfulla*, and *Il fanfulla della domenica*.[6] His

---

[5] E. Scarfoglio, *Il libro di Don Chisciotte* [Rome, 1885], now repr. in a fine new volume ed. and annotated by C. A. Madrignani and A. Resta (Naples, 1990), chron-icled the period in lively prose; Scarfoglio's allegiance to Carducci is particularly vis-ible in the essay 'La critica del Carducci' (see pp. 324–5), though Scarfoglio always had an independent and often pugnacious attitude of his own.

[6] For a good account of newspapers and journalists, including D'Annunzio at this period, see E. Sormani, *Bizantini e decadenti nell'Italia umbertina* (Bari, 1975); V. Castronovo has a broader account in his *La stampa italiana dall'unità al fascismo* (Bari, 1970). An account of D'Annunzio's personal situation, as well as a lively description of the journalistic ambience of the time, are given by V. Morello, *GD'A* (Rome, 1910); the poet's work as a journalist has been analysed by several critics in the essays in E. Tiboni (ed.), *D'Annunzio giornalista* (Pescara, 1983); see also nn. 8, 25, and 26 below.

activity as a journalist was to be his principal profession (outside his more artistically creative writing), continuing for the next forty years and reaching its peak, both within and beyond the frontiers of Italy, during the period of his co-operation with the *Corriere della sera*, shortly before, during, and immediately after World War One. Yet, not unexpectedly, he could write to Elda on 28 January 1882, 'What craven humiliations, Elda, what brutality, what cynicism in this journalistic world. A few days have sufficed to nauseate me. Here men are sold like cattle – no more, no less.'[7]

One entrepreneur to whom D'Annunzio was introduced was Angelo Sommaruga, the ambitious 24-year-old son of a Milanese businessman. Having just abandoned his previous employment in mine management on Sardinia, Sommaruga was anxious to use his undoubted entrepreneurial skills to make a quick fortune through the new world of Italian publishing. Like D'Annunzio, Sommaruga had only recently arrived in the capital, where in 1880 he had immediately seized his opportunity to publish the best-selling Carducci's *Confessioni e battaglie* (Confessions and Battles). This was of great mutual benefit for both publisher and author; Carducci was one of the first writers to be launched from the new national platform provided by a publisher in the heart of Italy's new capital, and Sommaruga, for his part, gained financially. Significantly, when Sommaruga's publishing empire collapsed a few years later, Carducci was the one famous personage to give him moral support. Sommaruga's next two major publications were to be D'Annunzio's *Canto novo* and *Terra vergine* (1882), a dual enterprise which again made a considerable profit for him, as well as helping to increase D'Annunzio's reputation in Rome's cultural circles. Sommaruga's weekly newspaper, *Cronaca bizantina* (Byzantine Chronicle), founded in June 1881, was also made available to D'Annunzio both as a vehicle for his opinionated views, and as another proving ground for poems and short stories which might later be worked up and collected into independent volumes. Sommaruga's immediate and major concern was to increase circulation and make the largest profits he could, and he intended his journalism to appeal to a wider audience than had been possible earlier; the conversion of Rome to capital city had brought an artificial infusion of new literacy. He also saw the popularity of radical political ideas at a time when the country was

[7] *Lettere a Giselda Zucconi*, 319.

being torn by what really amounted to Socialist riots, and he was not averse to publishing reports and articles which society at that time considered outrageous, or dangerous to public order. His first title, implying Byzantine degeneracy, could itself be seen as a permanent criticism of the corrupt state of government of the city, as well as of the decadent society it contained. As Sommaruga's empire spread, that combination of anti-Establishment views along with certain scandalous allegations made by his uncontrollable journalists were to lead, in 1885, to his catastrophic downfall, hounded by a determined prime minister, Agostino Depretis, at a time of political crisis.[8]

Rome must have been an exotic and enchanting experience for the young barbarian from Pescara. Scarfoglio describes with affection his first meeting with D'Annunzio at the offices of *Capitan Fracassa*, in November 1881, 'a little fellow with curly hair and gently feminine eyes'.[9] A combination of protectiveness towards his fellow Abruzzese–Cicogniniano, and boredom at the empty chatter in the office increased the warmth of Scarfoglio's welcome; D'Annunzio was soon introduced to assembled journalists and authors as the new prodigy whose work had already received the approval of such a critic as Giuseppe Chiarini. Scarfoglio was to remember his first year of friendship with D'Annunzio as 'the most delightful of all the wearisome and turbulent years I had to spend boring my literary neighbours'. Two years after the first meeting Scarfoglio could still report:

Gabriele was for all of us the object of an almost incredible cult and fond delight. He was so gentle, so affable and so modest, and he bore the weight of his rising glory with such grace that all ran to him out of a spontaneous attraction and friendship, as to a kind miracle that in the vulgarity of the literary life very rarely occurs.[10]

That particular naïve charm was soon to be, literally, dissipated.

Scarfoglio also proved to be of great assistance in gaining entry to the higher circles of Roman society which were to enchant D'Annunzio in the coming years. Indeed, despite his unofficial

---

[8] See below, pp. 57–8; Angelo Sommaruga chronicled his personal rise and fall in the autobiographical *Cronaca bizantina (1881–1885)* (Milan, 1941); an important description of Sommaruga's career is included in G. Lega, *Cinquant'anni di giornalismo* (Rome, 1930), and in the very readable account of R. Drake, *Byzantium for Rome* (Chapel Hill, 1980), esp. 30–92.

[9] Scarfoglio, *Il libro di Don Chisciotte*, 154.   [10] Ibid. 155.

engagement to Elda Zucconi, D'Annunzio made all excuses possible to avoid leaving the capital and his new-found pleasures. He was already a popular figure, and with the publication of the two most recent books, capable, he thought, of reaching the heights of art and glory. If further proof were required, he had met his old idol Carducci in Sommaruga's office, and had been presented to the great man while Carducci was actually reading through the page-proofs of *Canto novo*, exclaiming with pleasure, 'Thalatta! Thalatta!', as he turned the last page.[11] Thoughts of Elda must have been of secondary importance to D'Annunzio by now, though he continued to busy himself composing his usual extravagant love-letters to her.

It seems fairly clear that D'Annunzio was holding back from a return to Florence and a renewal of the affair with Elda. He next used a well-tried if complicated justification for staying away from her: the military draft, the postponement of which required his presence in Rome, there to be exempted from army service because of his enrolment as a student for a further year at the university. Unfortunately, soon after a typical series of letters containing excuses or passionate apologies for his absence, a complimentary copy of *Canto novo*, in which Elda could recognize herself on every page, was, on D'Annunzio's instructions, sent to her by the printer. The poet may have been trying to be kind, but she must have been angered or at least saddened that D'Annunzio had not brought the volume himself. It did nothing to ease her disappointment that his next letter informed her that on 1 May 1882, at precisely the same time that the complimentary copy arrived in Florence, he had left Rome to spend a fortnight in Sardinia. In fact the decision to make the trip had been made on the spur of the moment; without even taking a spare shirt, he chose to accompany Scarfoglio and Cesare Pascarella on a fact-finding trip to research an item for *Capitan Fracassa* concerning the 'mysteries' of the island. D'Annunzio had simply accompanied them to the ferry; as they stood on the dock waiting to go aboard, he became enchanted by the sight of the sun on the sea and exhilarated by the salt breeze in his lungs, and, with an impulsiveness which was to characterize him in future years,

[11] D'Annunzio recalls the episode in his *Di un maestro avverso*, see *Prose di ricerca*, ii. 548–9. Xenophon's famous words, 'The sea; the sea', implied the relief of his Greek troops at their sight of the Mediterranean after the hardships of a Persian campaign. D'Annunzio takes Carducci's words to imply some glorious revelation in his new poetry.

decided to join them.[12] During the crossing he was violently sea-sick, a physiological weakness which thereafter afflicted him on every sea journey he would undertake. After some nineteen days observing the beauties of Cagliari and environs, and after expressing their particular admiration for the charm of the women they saw, the three young men ended their stay abruptly when they were chased back to the ferry by a hostile crowd of offended Sardinians, unused to the less inhibited mores of their Roman visitors.[13]

D'Annunzio had continued to write to Elda from Sardinia, stressing what he described as the melancholy aspects of the island, as well as his own weariness and discomfort at having no change of clothing. Elda did not reply until his return to Rome on 21 May 1882, when she appears to have written him a bitter letter. Her sorrow at what she considered a personal snub was not lightened by a letter from D'Annunzio on 24 May in which he refused to apologize, saying that he should have killed himself at the thought that, despite his constant protestations of love, written in blood, she should feel displeasure. The sad but accusatory tone of his letter distinguished it from any previous missive:

I have a terrifying abyss all around me; I am alone upon a point of rock. Abyss, abyss around me. I see no light; I have no hope. You have taken everything from me. You have even taken from me the relief of telling you what I have in my heart. But do you really love me?[14]

Nevertheless the letter ended affectionately, even passionately, 'Yours, yours, yours, all yours, Gabriele', and during the following weeks the exaggerated declarations of love and passion continued as the correspondence again took on its usual quasi-daily rhythm. In mid-June D'Annunzio travelled to Florence to pick up the threads of their relationship, returning at the beginning of July to Pescara, where, surprisingly, and despite initial opposition from his parents, he obtained his mother's consent (though never his father's) to

---

[12] D'Annunzio writes to this effect on 2 May 1882: see *Lettere a Giselda Zucconi*, 386; the impression of exhilaration, played down in what follows of the letter, is confirmed independently by Scarfoglio in *Il libro di Don Chisciotte*, 157.

[13] This according to Frances Winwar, *Wingless Victory* (New York, 1956), 45, a version followed by Sozzi, *GD'A* 73; Morello, *GD'A*, limits the undignified incident to an unnamed town on the island (pp. 38–9); in Scarfoglio's accounts, during May 1882 in *Capitan Fracassa*, no reference is made. Full documentation of the journey has now been assembled by I. Ciani, 'Alla scoperta della Sardegna', *Rassegna dannunziana*, 14 (Dec. 1988), 18–37.

[14] *Lettere a Giselda Zucconi*, 392.

marry Elda. However, he then remained alone in Pescara for the whole of the summer, and when finally he left the Abruzzi, in November, it was not for Florence, but for Rome. There Scarfoglio found him much changed in character. The young Romantic who, Scarfoglio reported, previously could hardly be persuaded to wear a collar and tie, now, even at a comradely get-together of fellow Abruzzesi, perfumed himself and dressed up as if for some festival, watching his cuffs lovingly, and becoming annoyed when Scarfoglio accidentally spilled crumbs on his black suit. But, worse than these superficial affectations, Scarfoglio was disgusted by D'Annunzio's indiscriminate choice of companion during the six months which followed, and regretted that the young genius was squandering his great gifts. He feared that D'Annunzio, 'like a lap dog with a silk collar around his neck', was frittering away his life at aristocratic dinner-tables, society dances, riding parties, and suchlike. He was willing to surround himself with adulatory sycophants or fashion-able, empty-headed women who had never understood (if they had indeed read) a line of his poetry, but who asked him to write verses in their albums or on their fans, in return for a few moments of trivial admiration. That, thought Scarfoglio, was symptomatic of the waste of D'Annunzio's talent. Art, which had earlier been a driving factor in his life had become a child's game to amuse soci-ety idlers.[15]

In January 1883 D'Annunzio wrote the final five letters to Elda Zucconi, 'Farewell, farewell, farewell, my saintly, my beautiful, pale and suffering child. Farewell, farewell, farewell. [. . .] I am worn out, convulsed.'[16] The passionate effusions of 472 love-letters had come to this; there followed a final brief letter and five one-line telegrams, concluding with the final staccato message of farewell written on 22 March 1883: 'Received your letter. I write. I am half-ill, very sad. Goodbye. Gabriele.' On 5 February 1883 he had met Maria Hardouin; on 28 July they were married.

The breakdown of an adolescent love affair may seem a trivial matter, though Elda seems to have been grief-stricken at the end, but it was also symptomatic, at this early age, of D'Annunzio's utter failure to show any consideration for others' feelings. Since early 1881 he had effectively trifled with Elda's affections, writing letters which at times could be regarded as nothing more than sadistic

[15] Scarfoglio, *Il libro di Don Chisciotte*, 159.   [16] *Lettere a Giselda Zucconi*, 500.

teasing aimed to keep alive her emotions, from which he might derive the sensual images which fill *Canto novo* and other contemporary writings. For the next forty years no further word passed between the two. Elda married and had three children. Then, on 20 October 1921, she wrote appealing to Gabriele for financial aid to help her second son, Gianni (her first, Lamberto, had committed suicide at the age of 25, and Gianni seemed afflicted with the same nervous illness); in exchange Elda seemed to be willing to return his love-letters to him. There is no record of D'Annunzio acceding to her request, though he did write one more letter on 24 January 1922, enclosing a copy of his recently published book, *Il notturno* (Nocturne), and inviting Elda to hand the letters to his lawyer Eugenio Coselschi, son of the Francesco Coselschi who had worked for him in earlier times in Florence. When she next wrote, four and a half years later, on 25 November 1926, he had still not responded to her appeal. In 1936 the letters were sold to the well-known collector Mario Guabello and variously dispersed among his descendants until traced and properly edited by Ivanos Ciani. Committed to a mental asylum in 1937, Elda finally died there in 1942. She was the first in a line of women who, all in their own particular ways, suffered from D'Annunzio's general indifference to the feelings of others.[17]

D'Annunzio's addios to Elda in the spring of 1883 were also symptomatic of the end of any innocent love affairs. The lascivious nature of his life in Rome found expression in the largely pornographic poems of *Intermezzo di rime* (Poetic Intermezzo) which D'Annunzio began to publish sporadically in *Cronaca bizantina* before collecting together twenty-six of them in a single volume in 1883. Most of these poems are inspired by the languorous voluptuousness of his life in Rome, though Enzo Palmieri, when compiling his popular anthology of this early verse, was successful in finding eight poems innocuous enough to edit for Italian sixth-formers. More typically, *Animal triste* (Sad Animal) is one series of sonnets which express the bored satiety of the poet after copulation. 'L'imagine'[18] (The Image),

---

[17] For Elda's plight, see the appendix to Ivanos Ciani's edition of the *Lettere a Giselda Zucconi*, 505–14.

[18] It may be worth mentioning here D'Annunzio's unconventional spelling of Italian words, such as *imagine*, instead of the standard and orthodox *immagine*; the archaic spelling added a Latinate flavour as well as giving the vocabulary an inimitable Dannunzian quality.

the first of the sonnets, contrasts a pure, almost pre-Raphaelite vision of the woman in the poet's imagination, 'golden hair upon slender stem, like an asphodel', with his post-coital revulsion:

> Tristezza atroce de la carne immonda
> quando la fiamma del desio nel gelo
> del disgusto si spegne e nessun velo
> d'amor l'inerte nudità circonda!
>
> E tu sorgi ne l'anima profonda
> pura Imagine. Come su lo stelo
> èsile piega un fùnebre asfodelo,
> su 'l collo inclini la tua testa bionda.
>
> [Sad atrocity of the unclean flesh
>   when the flame of desire is doused
>   in the ice of disgust, and no veil
>   of love surrounds the inert nakedness!
>
> And in the depths of the soul you arise,
>   pure Image. As on its stem
>   a funereal asphodel droops slender,
>   so on your neck you incline your blonde head.]

Other poems develop sado-masochistic themes, including in particular the two lengthy concluding poems added in the 1884 edition, 'La tredicesima fatica' (The Thirteenth Labour), and 'Il sangue delle vergini' (The Blood of Virgins), which plumb the depths of tasteless grotesquerie, but contain important notions concerning the 'superman' and the inevitability of violence which may point towards D'Annunzio's future actions as a soldier and politician. Their subject-matter, which is given an almost Swinburnian atmosphere, also contains in germ the thematic motifs which animated some of his productions for the stage a few years later. The first poem sketches the tale of a demi-god, a handsome hero, discovered by an old peasant in the shade of an almond tree, a Hercules redivivus, who soon attracts an entourage of adoring concubines, the more virginal 'offering the red flower of their youth, while wives left their marriage-beds for the robust embrace of the hero'. The athletic, horse-riding genius 'spreads his love serene and abundant; seeing to that carnal work with inexhaustible vigour [. . .] casting the good seed of the future species'. The gnarled locals take a dim view of this activity and plan to get rid of him and his Bacchae-like followers as they sleep exhausted in a particularly drought-affected forest. There 'the new Hercules' dies on the pyre of his 3,000 concubines, 'his head unbowed'. The second poem concerns the revenge of an unknown god for the death of his daughter at the hand of a mortal archer, for which crime the territory around is punished with decades of war. Despite the kindly words of another creative deity urging the inhabitants to dedicate their days instead to an enjoyment of their paradise-like surroundings, instinct and violence come to the fore. 'Before the celebratory sacred fires of friendship die down in the night' and 'before the circling dancers break up, hearts longed for the rape and plunder', the enemy archers ravish their virginal hosts, and the land runs again with the blood of the slaughtered.

D'Annunzio was immediately attacked for the immorality of the new collection. His critics included two who had formerly praised his work, Chiarini and Carducci, as well as many others who were beginning to be revolted by his life-style, or who had been made envious because of his growing popularity in uncritical high-society circles. Strangely enough, D'Annunzio seemed to agree with his adversaries and wrote to Sommaruga on 24 June 1884: 'You tacitly reprove me for the *Intermezzo*, but the *Intermezzo* is the product of an infirmity, a weakness of the mind, a momentary decadence. The motives for the *Intermezzo* are to be found in the tenor of my life during that period of falsity.'[19] Some of the poems themselves confirm a paradoxical regret at the sameness of the sexual experience, ('Quousque eadem'; Everywhere the Same), and even an awareness of the waste of his energies, as in 'Sed non satiatus' (But not Satiated). 'The strength of my barbarous youth lies slain in the arms of women' he notes in two lines of that sonnet, 'a slow poison creeps up every artery, a long languor comes upon my sinews and I have no further power to struggle'. And that decadent torpor continues in 'L'inconsapevole' (The Unconscious One): the poet's awareness of a new motive for his composition is made clear, no longer exuberant joy, but the nullity of physically sated sex; the rottenness of a new dying fleshliness involves nature and poet in a

---

[19] Quoted in P. Alatri, *GD'A* (Turin, 1983), 44; the theme of immorality in literature was one hotly debated by the 'Bizantini'; A. Sommaruga's *Alla ricerca della verecondia* (Rome, 1884), was a response to the G. Chiarini's attacks in 'Alla ricerca dell'inverecondia', *Domenica letteraria* (19 Aug. 1883); the contributions of E. Panzacchi, E. Nencioni, and Chiarini himself were edited by L. Lodi, in an identically entitled *Alla ricerca della verecondia* (Rome, 1927).

grotesque union. The mood is partly captured in G. A. Greene's translation of that particular sonnet:[20]

> Come da la putredine le vite
> nuove crescono in denso brulicame
> e truci piante balzano nudrite
> dai liquidi fermenti d'un carname;
>
> s'apron corolle simili a ferite
> fresche di sangue, con un giallo stame;
> si schiudono crisalidi sopite
> ne le rughe del carneo fogliame:
>
> cosí dentro il mio cuore una maligna
> specie di versi germina. Le foglie
> vanno esalando un triste odore umano.
>
> Attratta dal fulgor de la sanguigna
> tinta la inconsapevole ne coglie;
> e il tossico le morde acre la mano.
>
> [As from corrupted flesh the over-bold
>   Young vines in dense luxuriance rankly grow,
>   And strange weird plants their horrid buds unfold
> O'er the foul rotting of a corpse below,
>
> As spreading crimson flowers with centred gold
> Like the fresh blood of recent wounds o'erflow,
> Where vile enormous chrysalids are rolled
> In the young leaves, and cruel blossoms blow,
>
> E'en so within my heart malignant flowers
> Of verse swell forth; the leaves in fearful gloom
> Exhale a sinister scent of human breath.
>
> Lured by the radiancy of the blood-red bowers,
> The unconscious hand is stretched to pluck the bloom,
> And the sharp poison fills the veins with death.]

[20] See Greene, *Italian Lyrists*; Greene uses a certain freedom in the last tercet of the sonnet. Greene was an early acquaintance of W. B. Yeats, his fellow Irishman, and Yeats's subsequent hostility to Greene's 'Italian' initiatives in the Rhymers Club, and to his translations, may well have impeded any chance D'Annunzio had of fame as a lyric poet in Anglophone countries. It is true that Yeats, thirty years later (and following D'Annunzio's support for Sinn Fein), invited D'Annunzio to Dublin 'to be Ireland's guest', and had some of his work reviewed, but after 1893 Greene's tiny anthology remained the largest body of D'Annunzio's poetry in English until the translation of *Alcyone* in 1990; some of the controversy is discussed in J. R. Woodhouse, '*Il Canto novo* e i nuovi rimatori inglesi: Un'occasione perduta?', in E. Tiboni and L. Abrugiati (eds.), *Canto novo nel centenario della pubblicazione* (Pescara, 1983), 149–66; for Yeats' invitation see below, p. 313.

D'Annunzio obviously thought that the poems of *Intermezzo*, like so much of his literary output, also reflected part of his biography, and he was reluctant to abandon them. Indeed in the definitive edition of 1894 he added two further sonnets in a new *Invocazione*, celebrating the joys of oral sex, a topic which obsessed him throughout his life and to which he was to return in literary terms a few years later, notably in the major novel, *Il trionfo della morte*. Of more immediate significance, the definitive edition of the *Intermezzo* included 'Il peccato di maggio' (Sin of the Month of May), itself hardly a paean to chastity: during the course of this particular poem, for example, the protagonist fears at one point that Yella, the virgin he has ravished, has died from her orgasm. Readers familiar with D'Annunzio's style might have considered Yella an unlikely pet name, particularly in view of D'Annunzio's preference for listing rather more exotic names of classical heroines. Indeed one major fault in some of his work was his willingness, in certain circumstances, to use too many such evocative names (and in the *Intermezzo* itself the names evoked in 'Le adultere' (The Adultresses) are typical examples).[21] But Yella was an abbreviation for Maria, Mariella. His 'sin of May' was Maria Hardouin, and the poem, which first appeared in the *Cronaca bizantina* of 16 May 1883, was as autobiographical as anything in the rest of the collection.

Maria Hardouin seemed to offer D'Annunzio an entrance into the high life of Rome which he had been enjoying for the previous three months. 'She was a year his junior, a flower of grace and beauty; fair-haired, delicate, with a fine bone-structure, blue-eyed, petite.' Guglielmo Gatti's description chimes with Maria Hardouin's appearance in the famous photographs by Gégé Primoli, and in her portrait by Antoine de la Gandara.[22] In *Il fanfulla* on 13 April 1883, D'Annunzio's column contained an account of a society gathering, presided over by Maria's mother, Donna Natalia, concluding with a description of 'two lovely turquoise eyes, full of flecks of gold which sparkle beneath wonderful long lashes, dispensing enchantment against which no talisman has any power'. The eyes with flecks of gold recur in 'Il peccato di maggio'.

---

[21] He is sometimes capable of using such an exotic name as a substitute for a whole descriptive passage; thus Lucrezia might evoke heroic chastity, Niobe, motherly grief, Daedalus, fatherly pride, and so on.

[22] Gatti, *Le donne*, 45; Gatti reproduces the portrait by Antoine de la Gandara at p. 48. See also Plate 3.

Maria Hardouin was the daughter of a former French lieutenant who had come to Italy with the troops sent by Louis Bonaparte in 1849, ostensibly to protect Pope Pius IX. Her lineage was not as venerable as it might have been and, in view of the controversy surrounding her noble origins (not unlike that surrounding D'Annunzio's name), perhaps calls for a brief explanation here. It was while Jules Hardouin was billeted in the Palazzo Altemps, hereditary home of the dukes of Gallese, that he found favour with the widowed duchess, Lucrezia Alessandrina. She married him and petitioned the Pope to allow the now defunct title to pass to her new husband. On the death of Duchess Lucrezia, Jules, or Duke Giulio as he preferred to be known, remarried; his new wife, Natalia Lezzani, was a noblewoman of well-proven standing, an intimate member of Queen Margherita's court. Natalia bore him two children: Luigi, who inherited the title, and Maria, born in 1864.

Maria was among the young society women of Rome who were fashionably infatuated with D'Annunzio; he, in turn, no doubt felt flattered to be admired by such a beautiful girl, who was at the same time scion of a noble house, and, at first glance, a potentially rich heiress. Whatever his ulterior motives may have been, D'Annunzio also declared his love and seems to have been equally infatuated. 'I am finally in love', he wrote to Enrico Nencioni on 6 April 1883, 'love with complete abandon, forgetful of myself and of everything else.'[23] The poet's courtship was a whirlwind thing, but the path of true love was by no means easy for the young couple. The social distance between them was great: on the one hand a fledgling poet and journalist who specialized in gossip columns, on the other the daughter of a noblewoman high enough in the social scale to be lady-in-waiting to the queen herself. Maria's parents certainly disapproved of D'Annunzio, and on 28 June the two lovers were forced to elope. Their escapade lasted only a couple of days. Caught at Florence by influential friends of the Gallese family, including the local prefect of police, they were taken back to Rome, where the scandal hit the headlines in all the newspapers. But the sin of May had left Maria pregnant, and marriage was inevitable. The duke never approved of their wedding, did not attend the ceremony (in the private chapel of the family palace), and never acknowledged

[23] De Felice *et al.*, *D'Annunzio*, 57.

D'Annunzio. The marriage, indeed, dealt the final blow to Duke Giulio's own tottering union, and it is doubtful that he was ever reconciled with his daughter. The newly-weds, after a month in Rome, left for Pescara, where they set up house temporarily in the family Villa del Fuoco, and where Maria gave birth to their first-born, Mario, on 13 January 1884.

Contemporaneously with his new domesticity, and with the uncommitted self-indulgence of the *Intermezzo*, D'Annunzio was also promoting views which left-wing critics in particular have seen as foreshadowing violent years ahead. One interesting letter to the composer Vittorio Pepe blends domesticity and thrusting ambition in bizarre ways:

Dear Vittorio,

[. . .] So. I have a child, a son, a beautiful son, with two unfathomable blue eyes and five blondish hairs. He's a soft, pink, warm, palpitating thing, moves sporadically, gropingly like a spider, he possesses the pretty graces of a young monkey, a voice which is sometimes bestial sometimes super-human. Oh paternity! I have named him Mario because it would seem pretentious to give him a more recherché name. Would you have liked Bellerophon or Draghignazzo or Zorobabele?

But the letter continues with a note of disdain and regret at the lack of culture, particularly musical culture, in his native region. In Pescara the only music is played by 'bands in the town squares, bands rather more akin to the *robber-band* sense of the word'. The cultural desert reminds him of the musical soirées and concerts of Rome and persuades him to spur on Pepe and his colleagues to work hard at their creative tasks. And here he introduces a fashion-able note, blending Darwin and Nietzsche:

Work, work, you young people, full of joy and power. There still remain many peaks to conquer [. . .] Cast from you all timid fears and hesitations; be bold, always bold; never tire of the search, the quest, the endeavour. The path of Art is long, rough and precipitous and to climb it you need good loins, armed with valour [*valore*] [. . .] Have no fear of the battle. It is a battle for life, Darwin's *struggle for life*, the inevitable and inexorable struggle. Woe to the disheartened, to the humble! Do not be scandalized by these un-Christian maxims. Pay attention to me; I'm your true friend and I have much experience of having lived among people, fighting, furiously elbowing my way forward. By now the realm of nullity is at an end. Let the valiant and worthy [*valenti*] arise.[24]

One effect of their marriage was, for the time being at least, to resolve the sexual problems which D'Annunzio himself declared were contributing to his artistic sterility. He had finished a manuscript of four novellas at about the same time that *Intermezzo* was published. In June 1884 Sommaruga, still with an eye to a quick profit, agreed to publish these, and sought to exploit the recent lurid turns in D'Annunzio's reputation by cashing in on the new title *Il libro delle vergini*. Without consulting the author, Sommaruga published the volume with what D'Annunzio, not normally so squeamish, considered an obscene cover: three naked women elegantly framed within a festoon of roses. D'Annunzio immediately wrote to several newspapers protesting at the vulgar titillation and inviting the public not to buy the volume. Later, for reasons best known to himself, he attempted to withdraw his letter from the newspapers, but was too late to prevent its publication in *Il fanfulla* on 25 June 1885. The situation was further complicated by accusations that the cover design had anyway been copied from an earlier semi-pornographic volume published in Naples.[25] In self-justification Sommaruga protested that D'Annunzio had earlier written to him, explaining that the background to the book ranged from brothel to church, from the perfume of incense to the stench of putrefaction.[26] Paolo Alatri hypothesizes, probably correctly, that D'Annunzio's protests and the subsequent publicity were typical ploys of his in order to obtain wider coverage in the press and elsewhere. But D'Annunzio may also have been hedging his bets on another account:

[24] The text of the letter, lost during the war, but earlier transcribed with accuracy by the trustworthy Raffaele Tiboni, was published by him in *Lettere inedite di GD'A alla famiglia di origine* (Pescara, 1984), p. xxiii; other critics have replaced, mistakenly in my view, D'Annunzio's concept of 'valour', 'worth' (*valore, valenti*) with other terms which serve a biased purpose, cf. the 'Marxist' judgement of Alatri, *GD'A*, 46, based on the reading *violenti*.

[25] These details are discussed by G. Squarciapino, *Roma bizantina* (Turin, 1950), 295–6.

[26] Sommaruga's letter reproducing D'Annunzio's earlier description was published in the *Domenica letteraria* of 13 July 1885. Both were again reproduced in Sommaruga's *Cronaca bizantina*, along with other information published (with much pathos of tone) 'to correct the inexactitudes earlier published', pp. 119–42. For further discussion of this and other details, see GD'A, *Il libro delle vergini*, ed. R. Scrivano (2nd edn., Milan, 1990), 8–9.

self-preservation. Piero Chiara's view of the quarrel goes further: he suggests that D'Annunzio could see the imminent moral and financial ruin of Sommaruga, and so used the 'obscene' cover illustration as an excuse to distance himself from the inevitable collapse of the Sommaruga publishing house.[27]

Sommaruga had begun to support the journalistic enterprises of Pietro Sbarbaro, an unsavoury character even by the standards of Rome's more unscrupulous newspapers. It may be that the group to which D'Annunzio belonged saw risks to their own reputation in being seen to be associated with Sommaruga's new venture, but Chiara's view perhaps attributes too much foresight to the poet, when, in fact, Scarfoglio was the more likely initiator of the letter which appeared in Rome newspapers on 1 October 1884; its import was that the signatories had nothing to do with Angelo Sommaruga. The protest was in large part motivated by the way Sommaruga, eager as ever to increase his revenues (and possibly weakened by recent losses), had financed what was generally considered to be the frankly yellow journalism of his new protégé, Pietro Sbarbaro. The open letter of 1 October contained the signatures of the major 'Byzantines': Scarfoglio, Matilde Serao, Giulio Salvadori, Luigi Capuana, Gerolamo Rovetta, Carlo Dossi, and D'Annunzio—a formidable group.[28]

Whatever the reason for their protest, or indeed for D'Annunzio's quarrel over the cover design of the latest volume, his new collection needed all the publicity it could get. The universal opinion of critics was (and is) that only one of the long short stories, *Le vergini* itself, was of any artistic value. Even D'Annunzio seemed to recognize this: the harrowing title story (renamed *La vergine Orsola*) was the only one to survive into *Le novelle della Pescara*, the later anthology of short stories already noted. In view of D'Annunzio's habit of reproducing in fictional form almost every event from his life's experiences, it is interesting to see that the Del Gado sisters feared that they could see themselves, portrayed as part of D'Annunzio's earliest childhood memories, immortalized in the original version of *Le vergini*. Their protests to D'Annunzio's mother were said eventually to have brought about the changes in the definitive edition, though this is unlikely. The final version of the tale was revised mainly for style and language in order to produce a more artistically

---

[27] For a summary of these events see Alatri, *GD'A*, 50, and cf. Chiara, *GD'A* 51.
[28] Sommaruga reproduced the letter in a generous if defensive section of his *Cronaca bizantina*, 47–8.

successful work; many of the more bizarre and immature descriptions were also omitted. Nevertheless the renamed *La vergine Orsola* is still a harrowing story, taking the atmosphere of D'Annunzio's earlier verist stories into a petit bourgeois environment. Orsola, after an already traumatic illness which is described in vivid detail, is raped by the drunken water-carrier Lindoro, has recourse to a back-street abortionist, and dies in a pool of blood at a friend's house on the outskirts of Pescara. As she falls to the ground, Mua, her friend's blind and deformed father, probes around him uncomprehendingly with his walking-stick. The finale of the tale in its original version was more harrowing: the blind and incapacitated Mua, thinking that the gravedigger's dog had come into the room and flopped on the floor, lashed out with his stick at Orsola's now dead body, crying 'Get away! Get out of it!'

For the time being D'Annunzio had been working from Pescara and Francavilla, held back from an earlier return to Rome partly because, following his marriage to Maria Hardouin, he had left so many creditors in the capital; these included (as some commentators always report with a chortle) Francesco Gentiletti, a waiter at the Caffè di Roma, who was to pursue him for years to come.[29] In November 1884 he was able to return to the capital, after securing appointment to the editorship of the *Tribuna* thanks to the approbation and support of its new owner, the wealthy Prince Maffeo Sciarra Colonna. Between December 1884 and August 1888, partly for want of articles from those friendly journalists he hoped would support him as editor, D'Annunzio was himself forced to compose some 260 pieces.[30] His output ranged over the most diverse subjects, in the most diverse styles, and using the most diverse and sometimes bizarre sobriquets: Il Duca Minimo, Sir Charles Vere de Vere, Bull Calf, Happemouche, Shiun-Sui-Katsu-Kava, and several others. Some of these names might consistently be attached to specific topics, and his readers soon came to associate him with certain sobriquets which covered familiar ground. Thus as Happemouche he discussed such topics as fashion or perfumes, periodically using French terms; Vere de Vere was his racing (and society) 'correspondent', not averse to dropping the occasional Anglicism into his articles; Il Duca Minimo discussed the most varied of topics; Shiun-Sui opened with

[29] Amusing accounts are given by Alatri, *GD'A*, 49 and 122, and by Chiara, *GD'A* 46, 72, 86, and 88.
[30] See above, n. 1.

the new Japanese ambassador's reception at the royal palace but went on to advertise a fashionable Japanese shop (Maria Beretta's) in the Via Condotti. At the same time that D'Annunzio was engaged in the daily chore of the *Tribuna* he was also busy composing the short stories of *San Pantaleone*, as well as the poems which make up the collection *Isaotta Guttadauro*. And he had continued to collaborate on his other newspapers, including the *Capitan Fracassa*, the *Fanfulla* (the daily and Sunday versions), and the *Domenica letteraria*.

In later years, notably after 1914, D'Annunzio became Italy's most renowned newspaper correspondent, but this early journalistic work in Rome was one of the most important formative influences, both in his literary career and in his spiritual and psychological development. The experience taught him to write even more quickly than before (by concentrating on the need for an elegant prose which needed little retouching); it focused his mind, though not necessarily with any great profundity, on various areas of the arts and literature about which he had previously had less time or inclination to take thought: music, painting, sculpture, philosophy, fashion, society, and new literary trends. Journalistic necessity forced him to pursue and propose exciting or novel ideas which would ensure that his column was always fashionably in the lead over rivals and competitors. All these aspects were to be most useful in the novels which began to flow from his pen. In particular, his first novel, *Il piacere* ([The Child of] Pleasure), published in 1889, encapsulates the *vie mondaine* of the years between. He began the work in earnest when temporarily forced to retire exhausted from his journalistic labours in 1888. But there were other less obviously literary benefits from his journalism.

Apart from helping to fill the pages of the *Tribuna* with multi-sobriqueted articles one of D'Annunzio's main tasks was to continue with his society column, the *Cronaca mondana*. It must soon have become obvious to him that this gave him enormous power over certain empty-headed devotees in fashionable Roman society. He noted the anxiety, particularly of his female readers, to obtain a mention by name or an obvious allusion in his column, preferably to be seen in a positively complimentary light, but, above all, not to be ridiculed. That manipulative authority allowed him to control people, showed him the power of the press, and permitted him to glimpse the particular effects which he and his words could have upon an audience. The Roman newspapers for which he wrote had a relatively small print-run compared, for example, with an English national daily (though Pietro Sbarbaro's scandalous *Forche caudine* (Caudine Forks) sold 150,000 copies twice a week in the Rome of 1885). Nevertheless D'Annunzio's articles were widely read by the society at which they were aimed, the kind of society with which D'Annunzio was associating daily and from whose reactions he could gauge the immediate results of his journalistic skill. Through his columns he was able to promote the careers of new artists and writers (and a eulogy of his great friend Francesco Paolo Michetti was one of the first, and most elegant, efforts in this regard), or even of the owner of a modish furnishing boutique. That ability to manipulate the public was to reach a point in 1887 when, as will be seen, he was capable of forging poems (allegedly written by a 'new' English aesthetic poet), so as to be able to 'review' them favourably in his column. Thereafter he was able to 'imitate' the new school by composing poems 'of his own' in the same vein. It is arguable that he thus created an interesting if spurious new school of pseudo-pre-Raphaelite poets and artists, founded on his own spoof. His contemporaries, convinced by his apparently authoritative statements, were thus willing to admire and imitate, and consider him again to be a continuing leader in literary fashion.[31]

A good example of how D'Annunzio's gossip column could promote a favourite, remarkable in this case for several reasons, was his description of an ash-blonde beauty, who appeared thinly disguised under the name of Donna Claribel in the column of Sir Charles Vere de Vere (in other articles she also became Lady Claribel). The lady in question was in reality a Neapolitan journalist, Olga Ossani, a colleague on *Capitan Fracassa*, who wrote under the pseudonym Febea. D'Annunzio and she were to have a love affair which lasted from his return from Pescara in November 1884 until March 1885, when Olga left him (without rancour on either side) in order to marry one of his great admirers and supporters, Luigi Lodi.[32]

---

[31] Other of D'Annunzio's spoofs are discussed in Woodhouse, 'Creative Plagiarism'; cf. below Ch. 5 n. 38.

[32] In view of subsequent developments, it is interesting to note that in *Tribuna* on 14 Feb. 1885 D'Annunzio wrote a piece on a society gathering in Palazzo Tittoni in which the names of Olga Ossani and Eleonora Duse appear in the same sentence as guests at the same soirée; for Lodi's name as an editor, see n. 19 above.

Olga Ossani was later to be used as the model for the character Elena Muti in *Il piacere*, the novel with a Roman setting; in particular D'Annunzio created from his final actual farewell scene with Olga the short story, *Il commiato* (The Farewell), later to be incorporated into *Il piacere* as the parting scene between Andrea Sperelli and Elena Muti on Rome's Nomentano bridge. Olga seems also to have inspired in D'Annunzio another literary obsession which was never to leave him, the martyrdom of St Sebastian. Since that particular fetish casts light on his life-style at the time as well as in future years, one mysterious and involved episode in their brief relationship deserves a special mention at this point.

D'Annunzio's fixation on the saint, martyred for his Christianity by being used as the target for his company of archers, was significantly different from the attraction which St Sebastian had for one of the poet's contemporaries: on Oscar Wilde's rough penitential uniform, the prison department arrows were seen by Wilde as symbols of his personal martyrdom, and may have inspired part of his pseudonym Sebastian Melmoth.[33] But D'Annunzio's obsession, typically, had a more sensual, sado-masochistic origin, which only became clear half a century later. In February 1932 D'Annunzio wrote to Olga concerning his personal St Sebastian experience, recalling the night he had stripped naked in the moonlight in the woods of the Villa Medici, and became for her 'the speckled archer'. This particular letter followed a visit by Olga, who had come to see the poet at the Vittoriale to ask him to intervene with Mussolini in order to promote her husband Lodi's election to the Accademia d'Italia. To N. F. Cimmino belongs the honour of solving the mystery of the speckled archer. In the archive at the Vittoriale he seems to have been the first to find D'Annunzio's description of a night of sensuality, which left him covered in love-bites, 'My body speckled with violent kisses', followed by the continuation of the episode the next evening when the poet stripped off:

I call her, leaning against an oleander, arranging my limbs as though bound to the tree. The moon bathes my naked body and all the livid marks appear. 'St Sebastian!' she cries. When she comes to me I first visualize, with a

---

[33] Melmoth was a Wilde family surname; Oscar was also inspired to write of Keats as a Sebastian-like figure. For these and other parallels with D'Annunzio, see J. R. Woodhouse, 'GD'A e la cultura anglosassone: La testimonianza del silenzio', in E. Tiboni (ed.), *GD'A a cinquant'anni dalla morte* (Pescara, 1988), ii. 629–30.

lyrical thrill, the sensation and illusion that the arrows disappear into my wounds and pierce the oleander.[34]

The sight of the love-bites which Olga Ossani had left all over his pale body may have reawakened or created the obsession with St Sebastian, which continued for much of the rest of his life, leading on notably to his composition of *Le Martyre de Saint Sébastien*, the drama, written during the poet's exile in France after 1910, and produced in Paris in 1911 with one of Diaghilev's celebrated ballerinas, Ida Rubinstein (another of D'Annunzio's mistresses, of a much later vintage), scandalously chosen for the saintly title role.[35] But the episode in the Villa Medici gardens with Olga Ossani as witness to his 'martyrdom' illustrates well how every experience was grist to D'Annunzio's literary mill, and an invitation (or a warning) to his acquaintances that they might well find themselves immortalized in his flamboyant prose. Olga was no doubt proud to find literary immortality as the elegant society beauty, Elena Muti, and as the archer to D'Annunzio's Sebastian, though until Cimmino's discoveries she would remain anonymous in this last role. Other women were not so flattered.

In the meantime, back in the newspaper offices in Rome, D'Annunzio's quarrel with Sommaruga, apparent or genuine, proved to be diplomatically useful during the opening months of 1885, since it meant that he could avoid involvement in the ensuing criminal proceedings against his former friend and associate. Sommaruga had always relied upon a provocative style of journalism to sell his newspapers, and in June 1884 he had published the immensely popular *Forche caudine*, edited by Pietro Sbarbaro, a noted opponent of the Establishment, not averse to scandalously provocative pieces, including personalized attacks on the monarchy, and on leading figures in the Depretis government. Sommaruga was arrested in August 1885 on a variety of charges, including extortion, bribery,

---

[34] N. F. Cimmino, 'Appunti inediti sul *San Sebastiano*', *Dialoghi* (July–Aug. 1953), 67; Olga is the 'Signorina X' of Winwar, *Wingless Victory*, 62; the excerpt from the archives has now been published in GD'A, *Di me a me stesso*, ed. A. Andreoli (Milan, 1990), 218–19. As late as 1933 D'Annunzio recalled, on 20 Jan. (St Sebastian's Day), 'Am I not transfixed like a St Sebastian even today?' (ibid. 143). These and other self-identifications with the saint are further discussed by A. Andreoli in *D'Annunzio archivista: Le filologie di uno scrittore* (Florence, 1996), 192–3.

[35] See below, p. 256. In this 'Mystery', G. Nicastro, *Il poeta e la scena* (Catania 1988), 143, sees other parallels with Wilde, in particular comparing *Le Martyre de San Sébastien* with Wilde's *Salome*.

and corruption. D'Annunzio, who by then had taken to addressing Sommaruga with the polite *voi*, instead of the familiar *tu* previously used by both men, refused to interrupt his holidays in the Abruzzi to return for the trial in Rome. Officially he declared himself too ill to attend, but his presence could have had only a harmful effect, to judge from the evidence he gave to the judicially appointed investigator from Chieti; his affidavit concluded that 'Sommaruga was a man of few scruples, rarely observed the rules of decorum or even those of honour [*onestà*]'.[36] Carducci, Sommaruga's first author, in poor health because of a stroke, came from Bologna to testify that the good that Sommaruga had done outweighed any criminal act of which he might be accused. That was a view which seemed to find strong support throughout the capital, though it was not endorsed by the court; the Establishment won. Sommaruga was condemned to six years' imprisonment, and a fine of 506 lire.[37] He escaped gaol by leaving the country while waiting for an appeal to be heard, and he subsequently hoped that a change of government would produce the usual amnesties and enable him to return; this was not to be. A not dissimilar case in London three years later, in 1888, undoubtedly had an inhibiting effect on Heinemann's bowdlerized translations of D'Annunzio's novels; there another Italian, Henry Vizetelly, was punished by the British Establishment, when he was prosecuted for publishing an already heavily censored edition of Zola's *La Terre* (The Soil: A Realist Novel). Convicted, fined (£300 in all), and gaoled for three months, Vizetelly died shortly afterwards, and with him his publishing house. When Heinemann subsequently came to publish D'Annunzio's novels, caution affected his attitude to their style and content until after World War One.[38] For the moment, anyway, editorial standards were laid down throughout Europe by institutionalized puritanism.[39] Sommaruga was later

---

[36] Masci, *La vita e le opere*, 50, where there is also an account of the proceedings. It might be added that in Masci's account the word *onestà*, with undertones of 'honesty' as well as 'honour', concludes the statement as here.

[37] A good account of the events is given in Squarciapino, *Roma bizantina*, 234, which confirms the six-year gaol sentence and the fine of 506 lire; it is difficult for me to feel sympathy with Squarciapino's disgust at the sentence; Masci, *La vita e le opere*, 50, suggests a sentence of five years; Alatri's 'six months' *GD'A*, 64 must be a typographical error, possibly generated by an unconscious refusal to believe the harsh judgement.

[38] See below, pp. 85, 121.

[39] Other examples of this puritanism are visible in S. L. Hynes, *The Edwardian Turn of Mind* (Princeton, 1968).

to set up a publishing house in Argentina; in 1911, according to Filippo Masci, in badly reduced circumstances, he tried again to see D'Annunzio at Arcachon, but he was refused admission. More recently discovered letters published by Ivanos Ciani show that after 1910, despite many frustrations, he gradually won back some of D'Annunzio's favour, until, as late as 1936, the poet sent him *Aux Bons Chevaliers Latins de France et d'Italie*, with the dedication: 'Ad Angelo Sommaruga, il poeta del *Canto novo* semper idem'.[40]

With Sommaruga *hors de combat*, D'Annunzio's new employer, Maffeo Sciarra, not slow to seize an opportunity, founded a new weekly journal to coincide with Sommaruga's departure and with the simultaneous demise of his popular *Cronaca bizantina*. The new organ bore the title the *Domenica letteraria–Cronaca bizantina*, nominally edited by Attilio Luzzato, but with D'Annunzio's influence paramount. And by the time Sommaruga had left Europe another journal altogether, a revived *Cronaca bizantina* under D'Annunzio's sole direction (a new Sciarra enterprise) began to appear, on 15 November 1885. His anxiety to recruit a team of glittering talents to write for the new journal is visible in letters written during this period, notably to Enrico Nencioni.[41] But D'Annunzio's hopes of persuading a fresh group of gifted littérateurs to write for him ultimately failed, and by 28 March 1886 that third series of the *Cronaca bizantina* had ceased publication.

The period of Sommaruga's trial had coincided with the 1885 summer holidays, during which D'Annunzio had withdrawn his family from Rome to the seaside at Pescara. On 27 September 1885 a local part-time journalist, Carlo Magnico, who felt that D'Annunzio had offended him at an official reception the night before, wrote a frivolous account of the evening in the provincial newspaper, *Gli Abruzzi*, including ironical references to D'Annunzio as the spurious son of Carducci, the godson of Sommaruga, and 'the small Gargantua of Italian poetry'. D'Annunzio challenged Magnico to a duel, and on 30 September 1885, with Michetti and Scarfoglio as

---

[40] Masci, *La vita e le opere*, 50; cf. *Lettere a GD'A*, ed. I. Ciani, *Rassegna dannunziana*, 20 (5 May 1992), 1–16, here 16 n. 36.

[41] A striking unpublished letter in the Conservatorio library at Parma, Carteggio di Arrigo Boito [100831], pleads with the composer to send him an article; I am grateful to Dr Rosa Wroth for drawing this letter to my attention. Twelve other such letters to Nencioni are published by R. Forcella as an appendix to De Felice *et al.*, *D'Annunzio*, 82–94. For an account of the resurgent newspaper see R. Forcella, *D'Annunzio: Guida bibliografica*, vol. ii (Rome, 1928), 279–86.

his seconds, met his opponent, with sabre at the ready, outside the railway station at Chieti. Despite his reputation as a fencer, thanks to lessons at the Cicognini and practice in Rome's gymnasia, the poet was struck on the head by one of Magnico's clumsy lunges. The surgeon rushed forward to stanch the flow of blood and, according to Matilde Serao's account, poured the entire contents of a bottle of iron perchlorate over the poet's scalp. The effect of this was certainly to stanch the flow of blood from the three-inch wound, but, reported Serao, 'on either side of the wound, his hair began to fall out; there was a hope that, given the poet's youth and vigour, the hair would grow back'. However, the chemical had reputedly destroyed the roots of most of the hair and already, at the age of 22, D'Annunzio had to resign himself to what in effect was the gradual, though relatively rapid, loss of his crowning glory.[42] Not slow to turn any situation to his advantage, D'Annunzio later claimed that baldness was a sign of a higher evolutionary stage in the development of mankind, since hair no longer fulfilled any useful function in modern civilized life. 'Unlike Julius Caesar and Domitian', noted Tom Antongini, 'he never complained about this premature baldness; in fact when a French woman impertinently asked his opinion about baldness, he replied, "Madame, la beauté future sera chauve!"'[43] His view failed to find many converts, though as late as the 1980s certain fanatical Dannunzians were known to appear at conferences with shaven heads, in imitation of the Master. The duel itself provided an important part of the plot for *Il piacere*, the novel set in this period, though published some four years later.

D'Annunzio undertook all the work that came his way in order to try to support a growingly affluent life-style: every day he had

---

[42] For the duel see also Sozzi, *GD'A* 101, and Gatti, *Le donne*, 66–8; for Matilde Serao's account, see C. Antona-Traversi, *GD'A: Curriculum vitae*, 2 vols. (Rome, 1932–4), i. 178. Masci, *La vita e le opere*, 50, casts doubt on whether D'Annunzio's baldness was caused by this heroic stroke. Tom Antongini says that his patron used the 'far-off incident' as a reason to explain his complete baldness a few years later (*Un D'Annunzio ignorato*, 228). Certainly photographs of D'Annunzio even before the duel show a self-consciousness about the combing of his hair to hide possible thinning patches.

[43] T. Antongini, *D'Annunzio* (London, 1938), 4 (this is a translation of his *Vita segreta di GD'A* (Milan, 1938); D'Annunzio is also quoted there as declaring his cranium as among 'the four most expressive beauties of the world'. It is a view that contrasts with a letter to Fontana of 12 Aug. 1880, which attributes part of his success with women to his 'forest of curly hair' (*ho una selva di capelli ricciuti*); for the letter see R. Forcella, *Guida bibliografica dannunziana*, vol. i (Rome, 1926), 89.

to work assiduously, very often unaided, to find something new to write. That problem reinforced his habit of making every experience a literary event, and added to his ability creatively to develop in an artistic manner and with linguistic brilliance the most apparently banal happening. But it was hard work to complete his daily stint. Some of his distress became visible after the definitive failure of the *Cronaca bizantina* in March 1886, in a long letter he wrote to Prince Sciarra on 6 April, explaining his life-style and regretting that Rome had defeated him:

Rome has vanquished me. By temperament as well as by instinct I have a need for the superfluous. My spiritual education draws me irresistibly to the desire for and the acquisition of beautiful things. I could quite easily have lived in a modest house, sat on Vienna chairs, eaten from ordinary plates, walked on carpets made in Italy, drunk tea from a threepenny cup, blown my nose in a Schostal or Longoni handkerchief. Instead, and fatally, I have wanted divans, precious fabrics, Persian carpets, Japanese china, bronzes, ivories, knicknacks, all those useless and beautiful things which I love deeply and passionately. And further I did not want Maria, brought up in a noble household as she was, to live in an environment different from that to which she had become accustomed. I have done what I could not do. Rome has beaten me. I shall go back home.[44]

His missive might have been a subtle begging letter. It is difficult to see how a departure for his home village could have provided any solution for his woes. Such a luxurious life could simply not have been continued at Pescara, where anyway his father was running up debts which D'Annunzio had periodically to pay off, or for which he signed promissory notes. His own financial needs became greater on 10 April 1886 when Maria presented him with another son, Gabriellino. Whatever the purpose of the famous letter to Sciarra, he was to remain with *Tribuna* for a further two years.

As a postscript to his career on the *Tribuna*, it is interesting to see that by 1887 the blasé D'Annunzio often made no effort to conceal his boredom with his work on the gossip column. On 27 January 1887 he wrote a piece entitled 'Il sogno del cronista' (The Dream of the Gossip Columnist). The article anticipated a *vade mecum* of the perfect columnist, where the budding writer might

[44] Published in A. Alberti, 'Ho una gran voglia di mettermi a lavorare', *Nuova antologia*, 77/1694 (16 Oct. 1942), 219–21. The letter is also printed with apposite comments as part of the introduction to the anthology of *Tribuna* articles, *Roma senza lupa* ed. Baldini and Trompeo, pp. x–xi.

look, on a given page, for the epithet best suited to his subject. Adjectives and entire phrases would be grouped around each and every subject (invariably women) and, once familiar, could be regurgitated on other occasions. D'Annunzio gave an example of what he meant by citing the case of Miss Multon, a character who recurred in his columns:

Miss Multon will be 'a great beauty'; she will have a head that Alma Tadema might depict 'on a background of oleanders'; she will have on that head 'flaming red hair'; her 'perfect' shoulders will be 'of pure ivory'. She will have a 'pre-Raphaelite dress of yellow and sea-green voile'. At times she will have 'sprung out of a sonnet of Dante Gabriel Rossetti', at other times 'from a Scandinavian saga'.

In the period following the publication of *Intermezzo di rime* up to the end of 1886, D'Annunzio worked on the short stories which made up the collection *San Pantaleone*, published in mid-1886, and on the poems of *Isaotta Guttadauro* (Isolde Drop of Gold) which saw the light in December of the same year. The delay in publication of the poems was due to D'Annunzio's desire to recruit the best artists of the day, in order, allegedly, to illustrate the volume in a way worthy of a possible dedication to his wife, Donna Maria. Diego Angeli's entertaining history of the Roman artists' haunt, the Caffè Greco, tells the story of D'Annunzio's energetic organization of the project,[45] and the inspirational effect he had on artists of the calibre of Marius de Maria, Alessandro Morandi, Aristide Sartorio, Vincenzo Cabianca, Alfredo Ricci, Giuseppe Cellini, and the others who, under the leadership of Giovanni (Nino) Costa in 1886, formed the group In Arte Libertas, which would put on its first public show the following year, 1887, in the gallery of Scipione Vannutelli; it later came to London in 1890.[46]

The pompous title of D'Annunzio's new collection, *Isaotta Guttadauro*, probably derived from a recherché anthology, the *Liber*

[45] D. Angeli, *Cronache del Caffè Greco* (Milan, 1930), 107–9 and *passim*; in fact only the second edition bore the dedication to the duchess. The best account of the artistic production of the *Isaotta* is given by C. De Leidi, 'Gli illustratori di *Isaotta Guttadauro*', *Rassegna dannunziana*, 28 (Nov. 1995), 25–40.

[46] G. Brema's review of their 1892 exhibition parallels the movement with the English pre-Raphaelites: published in *Fanfulla della Domenica* (14 Feb. 1892); also informative is G. Piantoni, *La Cronaca bizantina, Il Convito e la fortuna dei pre-Raffaelliti a Roma* (Rome 1972), esp. pp. xxxvii–xxxviii. R. D'Anna brings these surveys up to date in his masterly *Roma preraffaellita* (Rome, 1996), a whole volume forming a fascicule of the proceedings of the Lincei, *Memorie*, ser. IX/7, fasc. 3.

Isottaeus, put together by Basinio Basini in 1439 to honour Isotta, the lover of Sigismondo Malatesta. It was typical of the kind of exotic titles which D'Annunzio mentally collected in order to startle or surprise his readers, though it is true that much later he would study the history of the Malatesta in great detail in order to provide himself with subject-matter for his dramas. Edoardo Scarfoglio thought that the title was pretentious, and the delay in publication gave him the opportunity to play a joke on his friend by publishing a parody (condoned if not actually written by Scarfoglio) over three editions of the *Corriere di Roma*, in October 1886. The satirical piece was entitled, not *Isaotta Guttadauro*, but *Risaotto al pomidauro* (a garbled version of 'risotto with tomato sauce'). D'Annunzio challenged him to a duel (which took place outside Porta Pia on 20 November 1886), and was lightly wounded in the arm.[47] Perhaps it was another publicity stunt; certainly D'Annunzio had an urgent need to sell a few volumes that year. The two men were anyway firm friends again soon afterwards, and in less than a year were indulging in another escapade at sea.

The strangely titled volume came out in December 1886, with a run of 1,500 numbered copies on hand-made paper, illustrated with twenty-two plates executed by D'Annunzio's 'pre-Raphaelitic' friends from the Caffè Greco. Its publication had been guaranteed by the munificent Prince Sciarra. Yet, despite the luxurious production, and the announcement in the *Tribuna* that by January 1887 it had been sold out, all the evidence points to its having had very little commercial success. When on 22 August 1889 D'Annunzio suggested a second edition of the poems to his new editor, Emilio Treves, he began with a frank admission that the collection was almost unknown. Whatever D'Annunzio really felt about the offence given to him and his poems by Scarfoglio's parody, he took care, for that second edition, to change the title of the collection, and renamed it *L'Isotteo*.

The original 1886 volume of *Isaotta Guttadauro* had included certain compositions, more personally amorous in tone, concerned indeed with mythological or imaginative love affairs which derived

---

[47] For accounts of the duel with Scarfoglio see Masci, *La vita e le opere* 59–60; E. De Michelis, *Roma senza lupa* (Rome, 1976), 10 (and a useful note at p. 32); and D'Annunzio's not unboastful account in *Libro segreto*, *Prose di ricerca*, ii. 826–7, where he alleges that he deliberately offered Scarfoglio his arm in order, by accepting a slight wound, not to overwhelm his old friend with his superior fencing skills.

from D'Annunzio's own experience. These, and other poems, seventy-five lyrics in all, less obviously reminiscent of the Tuscan fifteenth century, though certainly having in some cases a pre-Raphaelite air, were not included in *L'Isotteo*. D'Annunzio had envisaged a separate collection for them, but Treves wisely decided that the idea of two separate volumes was uneconomical. The poems were eventually published in the definitive edition of 1890 under the dual title *Isotteo–La Chimera*.[48]

The *Isaotta* collection had once again taken D'Annunzio into unknown poetic waters in the sense that here he deliberately wrote in forms which would recall Tuscan poetry of the fourteenth and fifteenth centuries. In the now famous letter to his French translator, Georges Hérelle on 14 November 1892, he made a useful distinction between the poems of the now separated collections: 'In the book of verse entitled *Isottèo*, I wanted to renew the traditional metrical forms of ancient Italian poetry and reproduce Italian fifteenth-century life in a vast tableau, singing ballads in the manner of Lorenzo il Magnifico.'[49] D'Annunzio made himself a master of the fourteenth- and fifteenth-century style and metre, and the poems in these collections bubble with sonnets, ballads (*ballate*), madrigals (*madrigali*), sestine, octaves, and *nona rima*. Not untypical is the 'Thirteenth Ballad':

> [. . .] Scendemmo il piano margine; e commise
> in sí dolce atto Isotta
> il fior de la sua bocca ad una vena
> e sí fresco e vermiglio e vivo rise
> quel fiore in tra la rotta
> onda e s'aperse, ch'io ritenni a pena
> un grido e in su la piena
> bocca più baci e più, cupido, impressi [. . .]

> [[. . .] We descended the smooth bank and Isolde
> with such sweet act pressed
> the flower of her mouth to the fountain's
> rivulet, and so fresh and crimson and vital
> did that flower open to catch the divided flow
> that with a scarce contained cry,

[48] Sozzi, *GD'A* III, describes well the complex negotiations and the reworking of the volume.

[49] GD'A, *Lettere a Georges Hérelle*, ed. M. G. Sanjust (Bari, 1994), 61.

> on that full mouth I pressed kiss on kiss,
> cupidinously [. . .]].

In the same letter to Hérelle, D'Annunzio characterized the *Chimera* as being evocative of the frescoes in Florentine chapels and Lombard palaces, life, he said, as seen through fifteenth-century eyes, half-Christian, half-pagan, as seen by a disciple of Fra Filippino Lippi. Here and there a clearer pre-Raphaelite tone is sometimes visible, as in his 'Due Beatrici' (Two Beatrices):

> O Viviana May de Penuele,
> gelida virgo prerafaelita,
> O voi che compariste un dí, vestita
> di fino argento, a Dante Gabriele,
> tenendo un giglio ne le ceree dita,
>
> Viviana, non più forse a la mente
> il ricordo di me vi torna mai.
>
> [Oh Viviana May de Penuele,
> cool pre-Raphaelite virgin,
> who one day appeared to Dante Gabriele,
> dressed in fine silver,
> a lily held in waxen fingers
>
> Viviana, perhaps no longer to your mind
> returns at all remembrance of me.]

In the original 1886 edition, this poem was illustrated by D'Annunzio's artist friend Sartorio, in a painting which showed Dante in the act of drawing a figure, while Beatrice appeared giving her blessing. The composition echoed two paintings of Dante Gabriel Rossetti, his *Beata Beatrix*, now in the Tate Gallery, and *Dante Drawing an Angel* in Oxford's Ashmolean Museum. Both artists may have been inspired by a single source, Dante's *Vita nuova*. But the coincidence here seems too great to be absolutely fortuitous. D'Annunzio's poetic direction was in this case clearly not far removed from that taken by Dante Gabriel twenty years before, and Sartorio deliberately reflected the relationship. Indeed, in view of the fact that Dante Gabriel's family was hardly a generation removed from its origins in the town of Vasto, just a few miles down the coast from Pescara, it may well have been that D'Annunzio felt a special affinity with the Rossettis. That view gains strength when one considers that Dante Gabriel's father (another Gabriele), was regarded in Italy as one of the exiled heroes of the Italian war of independence, and had been celebrated as such by none other than Giosuè Carducci. The pre-Raphaelite nuances increased D'Annunzio's growing reputation as the supreme equivalent of the English pre-Raphaelite poet, an impression reinforced during the next few years by the content of *Il piacere* as it was by other essays, poems, and critical reviews.

3

Life into Art

D'ANNUNZIO'S creative efforts seemed to be running into the sand with *Isaotta Guttadauro*, essentially an experiment in beautiful form. But this artistic sterility was soon to change: inspiration was close at hand. In the spring of the following year, on 2 April 1887, D'Annunzio met Elvira Natalia Fraternali. As was his invariable practice when he met a new lover, he rebaptized Elvira with a name of his own coining which he believed harmonized better with the personality of his new conquest; in Elvira's case it was Barbara. Just three months older than he, she was alienated, though not actually separated, from her husband, Ercole Leoni, whom she had left two years earlier in 1885, after only a few weeks of married life. Much to D'Annunzio's chagrin, her husband continued to make appearances at regular intervals in order to demand his marital rights, thus interfering seriously at times with this, the poet's latest adulterous idyll. Elvira's marriage had left her with a uterine illness, which some chroniclers ascribe to a disease which she had contracted from her husband, others to an abortion, which had left her sterile. That piece of medical gossip was to prove of literary value to D'Annunzio in his physical depiction of Ippolita Sanzio, the heroine of *Il trionfo della morte*. He later wrote in *Il libro segreto* (The Secret Book) concerning Barbara's identification with Ippolita Sanzio;[1] in particular her illness aroused a morbid kind of interest in him, which was to resurface in his depictions of the illnesses of other women in his life, notably Alessandra di Rudiní and Giuseppina Mancini. Two years into the relationship with Barbara, on 18 April 1889, he wrote her a strange letter as she lay ill in bed: 'Sick and listless thus you please me. I think that when you are dead you will reach the supreme light of beauty: spiritless and

---

[1] *Il libro segreto, Prose di ricerca*, ii. 676; cf. below n. 28.

bloodless.'[2] The sentiments are typical of one particular bedside manner of D'Annunzio's which would recur again and again in his novels. 'She is very beautiful today', the hero of *Il trionfo della morte* reflects on his lover Ippolita, 'She is pale. She would gratify me if she were always afflicted and always ailing.'[3]

In Rome, between April and late June of that year, 1887, D'Annunzio and his new mistress met almost daily, first in the studio of Guido Boggiani, another of D'Annunzio's artist friends, and then in a *pied-à-terre* which the poet acquired in Via Borgogna. Their affair was to continue for the next five years, and was to provide a wealth of material for several of D'Annunzio's most inspired creative works, notably, but not only, that first 'Nietzschean' novel, *Il trionfo della morte*. More immediately, in the *Elegie romane* (Roman Elegies), composed at intervals during their love affair, Elvira reappeared under the pseudonym Vittoria Doni. Indeed, although D'Annunzio's immediate pet name for her had been Barbara (and Barbarella), Ippolita, Miranda, Jessica, and, significantly, Gorgona were other names he used over the course of the next five years. In the main she was known to him and to his biographers as Barbara Leoni, and to minimize confusion she will here be referred to as Barbara. Most contemporary commentators refer to Barbara's beauty, *Barbara the Beautiful* is the title of Mario Guabello's slight bibliography of the relationship, and Luigi Trompeo combines both her association with the *Trionfo della morte* and her beauty in the title of his essay 'The Most Beautiful Eyes in Rome: D'Annunzio's Ippolita'.[4]

The beauty of Barbara Leoni was surely in the eyes of the beholder, and she was not without flaws. It may be risky to take at

---

[2] GD'A, *Lettere a Barbara Leoni*, ed. with a preface by B. Borletti and a note by P. P. Trompeo (Florence 1955), 116; this edition has a rich appendix which points out the close parallels between particular letters and certain parallel episodes in *Il trionfo della morte*, *Il piacere*, and *Elegie romane*, works which were composed or planned during the years of their love affair.

[3] *Trionfo della morte*, I. 1. henceforth, to economize on footnotes, references to the novels will, where feasible, be inserted in the text in the form of book and chapter. There are many editions of the novels; quotations here will be taken from GD'A, *Prose di romanzi*, ed. E. Bianchetti (Milan, 1940). Barbara Leoni as the model for Ippolita Sanzio is particularly studied in *Il trionfo della morte*, ed. G. Ferrata, (5th edn., Milan, 1980), here the relevant pages are 62 and 245–6.

[4] M. Guabello, *Barbara la bella Romana* (Biella, 1935) (in effect a brief bibliographical essay); L. Trompeo, 'I più begli occhi di Roma: l'Ippolita dannunziana', in his *Ricordi romani di GD'A* (Rome, 1938); Gatti gives a good account both of her and of the affair in *Le donne*, 75–110.

face value D'Annunzio's fictional representation of her, but the passage in the *Trionfo* where he comments upon Ippolita's illness also makes it clear that 'Materially she is not beautiful. Sometimes, looking at her I have experienced the painful shock of disappointment [. . .]. She does have, however, three divine elements of beauty: her forehead, her eyes, and her mouth: divine.'[5] And D'Annunzio's concentration in the novel on eyes, brows, and mouth underlines the fascination of those features for him. In fact in the pastel of Barbara by Emil Fuchs those features mitigate a heavy jaw, and add a certain interest to an otherwise solemn portrait, while a drawing by G. N. Vitelleschi, entitled *Ippolita*, published by one of Barbara's greatest admirers, Adolfo De Bosis,[6] also depicts her fine eyes and beautiful mouth in a determinedly set jaw, and gives her an air of challenging sensuality. Considering these and other representations of Barbara alongside earlier photographs of Elda Zucconi, an image begins to appear of a certain type of face which D'Annunzio found particularly attractive.[7] The image becomes clearer over the years as D'Annunzio continued his rake's progress. There is a notable resemblance between D'Annunzio's preferences in lovers (his wife being an exception) and youthful pictures of his mother, Luisa De Benedictis, no beauty herself, who had similar physical characteristics.[8]

Barbara had studied at the Milan Conservatoire and was an accomplished pianist; probably the most literate and cultivated of D'Annunzio's lovers, she also proved a correspondent more worthy of D'Annunzio's own literary talents than his other lovers had been or would be, and, in the period 1887–92, over a thousand letters were exchanged between the two. Many of these, particularly those written by D'Annunzio, figured large in the form of transcriptions in the *Trionfo della morte*, adding to the autobiographical quality of that novel. Since Barbara later refused to return D'Annunzio's original letters, their appearance in the book suggests that D'Annunzio

[5] *Trionfo della morte*, I. 1.

[6] In his extravagantly expensive journal *Il convito*, dated 12 Feb. 1896; De Bosis and D'Annunzio were already firm friends.

[7] In a similar way Dante Gabriel Rossetti's 'stunners' were said to have defects, including goitres, which Dante Gabriele made into fetishes.

[8] The most striking similarity between Donna Luisetta and Elda Zucconi, for instance, is visible in photographs (see Plates 1 and 9); the broad brow and the firm line of the jaw are also visible in other photographs of D'Annunzio's women, notably Eleonora Duse, who during most of their relationship referred to him as her 'son' (see Plate 12 and cf. Plate 10).

had kept notes or copies of his correspondence with her. Barbara–Ippolita was cast aside in 1892, and might with reason have complained at the way her experiences during the previous five years, often including some personal sexual revelations, were utilized to lend zest and flavour to the novel; but perhaps like Olga Ossani she felt privileged to have provided a genius with inspiration. Nevertheless, even more than the experiences of Elda Zucconi and Olga Ossani, Barbara's particular treatment by D'Annunzio should have been seen by other women as a presage of the more cruel literary portraits that were to be drawn by D'Annunzio in later years.

Apart from their almost daily assignations in Via Borgogna, the couple used to meet in Rome's deserted art galleries, or they would follow wooded walks in the gardens of the great houses, partly to find privacy, but no doubt also avoiding the fierce heat of summer in the capital. Since staying in Rome was the only possibility D'Annunzio had of being alone with Barbara, he made a virtue out of necessity, and during the summer of 1887 his columns in the *Tribuna* were filled with the newly discovered experiences of Rome in summer. Under the rubric *L'estate a Roma* (Summer in Rome), he wrote four pieces on how to find amusement in the capital, as though he were compiling hints on potential activities for the amusement of tourists during the summer holidays. The first piece, 'Preludio', had about it something of the sour-grape assertiveness which critics have observed in his views on the evolutionary superiority of baldness: D'Annunzio declared that he had always felt pity for those people who, out of habit or because of fashionable dignity, had forced themselves to stay away from Rome in the summer. They were, he wrote, 'Unfortunates, who do not know, and perhaps never will know the infinite delights which Rome, even in the summer months, can give to its faithful'.[9] In fact the column, dated 20 July 1887, over the signature of Duca Minimo, along with the three following articles, is simply a description of his own strolls with Barbara around the Villa Medici and the Galleria Borghese. Others were concerned with local painting exhibitions, or depicted the pretty window displays in fashionable shops. One described what he termed the refreshing quality of Catholicism during the summer in Rome.

[9] For these and other references see above, Ch. 2 n. 1 on *Tribuna*.

Summer Catholicism in Rome especially is a fount of inexhaustible freshness. Wise people, instead of going to splash around laboriously in the pol-
luted waters of some bathing establishment, or leaving to contemplate the
cows in the over-green artificiality of the Swiss countryside, remain in Rome,
or come to Rome from the provinces to profess their Catholicism.

Pleasurable as his daily associations with Barbara might have been,
there can be little doubt that the great sun-worshipper D'Annunzio
would have preferred to be disporting himself on the golden sands
of the Adriatic. From the artistic point of view what was important
about those desperate but undoubtedly amusing attempts to divert
his readers was that his descriptions, and his words and expressions,
would crop up again in his major novels. In particular the experience of Rome, both before and after that summer of 1887, became
the substance of his first novel *Il piacere*, while more specific aspects
of his relationship with Barbara are directly incorporated into the
Trionfo della morte.

The happiness of the lovers' meetings was offset from time to
time by their enforced separations. When Barbara eventually left
Rome that summer of 1887 to stay briefly with parents and relatives
in Rimini, D'Annunzio's letters to her declared that he was beside
himself with sorrow and boredom. But there was a genuine possibility of legal scandal if the two had, for instance, decided to live
under the same roof, even though Donna Maria was by now becoming inured to her husband's infidelities and would not herself have
initiated proceedings. That there was a genuine danger for the two
lovers was demonstrated ten years later when D'Annunzio, caught
in his next extramarital affair, was sentenced by a Neapolitan court
to five months in gaol for adultery. One of D'Annunzio's letters,
dated 31 July 1887, laments: 'My grief is so great that since yesterday I have been living almost unconscious of life, closed in on
myself, with the thought, with the desire, acute and unceasing of
your love.' And the poet's misery is increased even more when no
letters arrive from his Barbara:

I shall remain here these two long hours fantasizing and torturing my soul.
[. . .] I have no news of you! I have just come home. It is almost midnight.
I came slowly down the stairs of the Trinità dei Monti where we used to
walk up and down exchanging loving words and glances. Remember? [. . .]
I went alone to the English Cemetery [. . .] what a melancholy, serene spot.[10]

---

[10] *Lettere a Barbara*, 16–17.

In the previous June D'Annunzio had also been forced to return to Pescara briefly, in order to deal with some of the worst of the financial chaos being generated by his father. It was during this period of the lovers' two-month separation, a separation much favoured by Barbara's family, that Donna Maria had accidentally intercepted certain letters and discovered the real intensity of the affair between the two.

The letters to Barbara also mention the *Lady Clara*, the yacht of his friend Adolfo De Bosis, who proposed a trip in the Adriatic during that August of 1887. It seemed a godsend for the bored, if not distraught, D'Annunzio, who prepared to free himself for the voyage by taking his wife back to Pescara on 13 August, where a month later she would give birth to their third son. The two men embarked at Ancona on the first of September, with a crew of two, Ippolito Santilozzo and Valente Valori, the former unused to sailing-boats, the latter, in the words of Vincenzo Morello, 'half-cretinous' (*un semicretino*); D'Annunzio approved of them because they bore heroic-sounding names.[11] For as long as they were able to steer by following the line of the coast the voyage went reasonably well, if a little tediously. Much to the amusement of local inhabitants and holiday-makers, the two friends would pause occasionally to go ashore, fling down their Persian carpets, and brew tea or coffee in a silver service. But when they arrived at the level of Rimini De Bosis, looking for more exciting sailing, headed out towards the open sea. Once out of sight of land, D'Annunzio succumbed to his habitual seasickness, as the yacht, steered by De Bosis himself, began to roll helplessly in the rougher water, rapidly becoming a hazard to shipping. At that point the Italian royal naval cruiser *Agostino Barbarigo* came to their rescue, winched the yacht humiliatingly on board and took the quartet to Venice, where they were set down.[12]

That apparently trivial, even semi-comic, episode was to have enormous consequences for D'Annunzio's later artistic, spiritual, and political development. Already familiar as he was with the

[11] Morello, *GD'A* 49, repeated word for word by Chiara, *GD'A* 57; years later in Paris D'Annunzio selected a cook sight unseen from a short-list of three because of her name: '*Victoire*? Engage her immediately', Antongini, *D'Annunzio*, 260–1.

[12] The voyage figures large in *Trionfo della morte*, but more factual accounts are given in Morello, *GD'A,* and in Gatti, *GD'A*, esp. pp. 79–82, where novel and journey are shown to coincide, and by D. Angeli, in a commemorative piece after the poet's death published on 6 Mar. 1938 in *L'illustrazione italiana*.

domestic charm of the Adriatic, its wider reaches now began to captivate him with their beauty and historical associations. That new delight was temporarily eclipsed by the enchantment of Venice, which, thanks to the *Barbarigo*, he was visiting for the first time. Thereafter the power and beauty of Venice were to be indissolubly bound up in his mind with the history and political destiny of the Adriatic. But, to begin with, it was the effect of being at sea on the cruiser, and his sense of the steely, throbbing power of the ship, which brought home to him the realization of his country's need for such naval strength if she were to maintain a hold over the fate of Italy's inheritance, both in Venice and on the Adriatic. All these influences worked simultaneously on him and, indeed, from that point on never left him. Their immediate and most important effect was political; he began writing a series of ten major articles in *Tribuna*, which ran between 27 May and 6 July 1888 under the title *L'armata navale* (The Sea Force); unlike his normal gossip-column items, all the articles were signed with his real name, a mark of the serious attitude which dictated them. The pieces were almost immediately collected in a single volume and published later the same year with a new title, *L'armata d'Italia*.[13] Paolo Alatri sees in the alacrity of their publication the hand of wealthy ship-builders, anxious to whip up an armament trade for themselves, and willing to subsidize and forward D'Annunzio's ambitions in this as in other profit-making spheres when the opportunity arose.[14]

In 'Le navi d'Italia', the prefatory article to *L'armata d'Italia*, D'Annunzio made clear his almost delirious excitement at being on board the *Barbarigo*, surrounded by other ships of the line with evocative names such as *Castelfidardo*, *Affondatore*, *Dandolo*, *Palestro*. He recalled in that first piece the image of the fleet standing off Ancona in review, acclaimed by hundreds of spectators on shore visible against the ancient outlines of historic churches and palaces, the sea blue-green and splashed with violet where the clouds rushed over the surface, Mount Conero in the background, pink with the rising sun, the breakwaters stretching out like white arms. All Italians, his prologue declared, should tremble with pride at the sight and thought of such a vision:

---

[13] The combined essays, *L'armata d'Italia*, are available in GD'A, *Prose di ricerca*, iii. 3–54; other notes and additions continue at pp. 55–67; quotations are taken from these pages.

[14] For further comments see Alatri, *GD'A* 68–9.

There lives in Italy, profound and immutable, the love of the sea and of naval glory, just as at the time of the Roman Republic. It is a fine and noble heritage, perpetuated from century to century in the spirit of the Italian people. No other aspiration is more vast, more universally recognized, more deeply national. And the three colours never appear so brilliant, so free or so victorious to the eyes of the people as when they are seen wafting above a powerful ship, as *magnetic*, in the words of the poet, *as the eyes of a woman*.[15]

The only impression the reader gains from his words is that D'Annunzio was an honoured guest on the most imposing of the ships in review. Very understandable to critics, who now recognized D'Annunzio's style, and very typical of the poet's creative imagination, even in these apparently factual descriptions, is the omission of any reference to the initial disaster which had occasioned his being winched aboard the *Barbarigo*.

Other articles in the series attacked the apparent penny-pinching methods of the naval minister Benedetto Brin and his acolytes. D'Annunzio's diatribe here became vitriolic, leaving pen-portraits in his readers' minds in the way he was to do in more serious moments during World War One, when attacking prime ministers Nitti and Giolitti. 'What forces', he asked, 'will provide Italy's future greatness?' and he scornfully rejected the glory of Bernardino Grimaldi's agriculture or Senator Saracco's railways. 'Italy will either be a great naval power or it will be nothing.' In a jingoistic 'epilogue' to the articles (which concludes with the not unexpected prayer: 'God protect Italy'), he declared that he did not wish to be a mere poet, a mere prosodist like Théodore de Banville, 'able only to say "Je ne m'entends qu'à la métrique!" ': 'All manifestations of life and all manifestations of intelligence attract me in equal measure'. He was preparing to enter the political arena: 'I have complete freedom to carry my research and study into all fields.' In a statement of his political ambitions on 14 August 1897, he was later to inform his new publisher Treves, 'The world must see that I am capable of everything'.[16]

---

[15] *L'armata d'Italia, Prose di ricerca*, iii. 6 and 3 respectively.

[16] For the letter to Emilio Treves see A. Sodini, *Ariel armato* (Milan, 1931), 368; the important correspondence with the Treves house has now been edited by Gianni Oliva, *G.D'A: Lettere ai Treves* (Milan, 1999), rendering obsolete the typescript of Treves letters long held in the library at the Vittoriale; see Oliva, p. 205.

The experience of the voyage on the *Barbarigo* remained with D'Annunzio for a long period; poetically his feelings found expression five years later in the *Odi navali*, published in 1893. In the meantime the city of Venice entranced him with its beauty, its history, and its cosmopolitan atmosphere. Barbara managed to get away from Rimini for a day in mid-September, and for twenty-four hours the two were together at the Hotel Beau Rivage, an episode which gets a more up-market treatment in *Trionfo della morte*, where Giorgio Aurispa and Ippolita Sanzio stay at the Danieli. Just after Barbara's departure from Venice, news came that Donna Maria had given birth to her third son. D'Annunzio, still excited about Venice, was in no hurry to get back to his wife's bedside, but he did send a telegram asking for the boy to be named Veniero, in celebration of Venice's most famous naval commander. Although Donna Maria personally favoured the name Ugo, she humoured D'Annunzio in his new-found enthusiasm for Venice and the city's traditional sea power by having the name Veniero added to the child's first name. Business commitments called Adolfo De Bosis away from Venice at the end of September, and since D'Annunzio was entirely dependent on his friend for financial support he, too, was forced to leave the city immediately afterwards, and so returned to Rome.

Since June 1887 D'Annunzio had been publishing in the *Fanfulla della domenica* the series of poems, later to be edited in four books, with an envoy, under the title *Elegie romane*. In these complex lyrics the summer visits to museums, palaces, and cemeteries described in the *Tribuna* combine with the passionate feelings expressed in letters exchanged between the two lovers. Thanks to Bianca Borletti's edition of the previously unpublished correspondence between D'Annunzio and Barbara, it is now possible for the biographer accurately to document the events which inspired the poems.[17] The finished volume of *Elegie* was ultimately dedicated to the poet and critic Enrico Nencioni, one of his most favourable reviewers, and was calculated to echo the title of Goethe's *Römische Elegien*, intended, that is, to celebrate both the Eternal City and a love story acted out against that magnificent backdrop. It is interesting to see the dissimilarity between the artistic temperaments of the two poets, separated as they were by a century during which the techniques of

---

[17] See n. 3 above; typical of such events is the poem *Sul lago di Nemi* which corresponds to references in a letter of 17 June 1890 concerning their visit to the lake.

expressing literary emotion had developed so intricately. D'Annunzio probably saw, in the contrast between the two resulting collections, evidence of his own inimitability; at the same time the experience also strengthened his growing belief in the power he possessed to set up and target a literary model of his own choosing, in order, he believed, to surpass it in artistry. Goethe's mood was one of classical imperturbability; Rome gave him a luminous vision which provided a consoling background to the love of Faustina. D'Annunzio's mood was constantly fluctuating and his reactions to the beauty of Barbara–Elvira's *alter ego* (now confusingly in certain poems given the other pet names of either Ippolita or Vittoria) at times varied with the pallor of her cheeks.[18] Eurialo De Michelis suggested that this fluctuation between voluptuousness and sad elegy was typical of D'Annunzio's mood at the time, brought about by forced separation from Barbara and by uncertainty concerning their future. Thus, for De Michelis, the changing moods visible in the *Elegie* simply formed part of a coherent and authentic chronicle of the love story.[19] Paolo Alatri, more sceptical in his approach, agrees with De Michelis's view of the mood of the poems, but adds his own opinion that some of the fluctuations were the result of D'Annunzio's own fickleness and inconstancy *vis-à-vis* Barbara.[20] The second stanza of one of the later lyrics, 'Villa Chigi', reflects well some of the tone: part satiety at the continuing permanence of their association, part fear of losing the woman's love, part melancholy that she was saddened by their last embraces:

> [. . .] Vano ogni sforzo. Un freddo suggel mi chiudeva la bocca;
> torbido, invincibile, contro di lei, dall'ime
> viscere mi sorgeva non so quale odio; moriva
> ogni pietà di lei nel saziato cuore.
> Muti, cosí, vagammo: cosí, l'uno a fianco dell'altra [. . .]
> Ella non più bevea l'anima mia ne' baci
> Ella bevea soltanto le lacrime sue ne' miei baci.
> Lacrime di quelli occhi, pur vi sentii su 'l cuore
> ardermi fra 'l disgusto che a flutti salía dal profondo,
> lacrime di que' dolci occhi ove il cielo io vidi!

[18] For further interesting comments on the relationship, see GD'A, *Di me a me stesso*, 37, where it seems clear that the poet had Goethe in mind when writing his elegies (it is also interesting to see there the mention of *Elegie* associated with the statement 'My life is my art'); see also R. Bertazzoli, 'Le *Elegie romane* tra Goethe e D'Annunzio', in P. Gibellini (ed.), *D'Annunzio Europeo* (Rome, 1991), 195–204.

[19] E. De Michelis, *Tutto D'Annunzio* (Milan, 1960), 101–7.

[20] Alatri, *GD'A*, 73.

[[. . .] Every effort is vain. A cold seal closed my mouth;
      a tumult, unsuppressible, rose from deep within me—
      of hatred, could it be? All compassion for her died
      in my sated heart. Silently thus we wandered, side by
        side [. . .]
      She no longer drank in my soul with our embrace,
      only her own tears in my kisses. Tears from those
      eyes I felt burning in my heart, amid the disgust,
      which rose wavering from the depths of my being,
      Tears from those sweet eyes where I had seen heaven.]

That particular poem was written towards the end of their relationship, and begs certain questions which will be answered as further lacunae in this account are filled in. The documentary nature
of the collection, as well as its adulterous shadow, prejudiced many
Italian critics against *Elegie romane*. As if to confirm its quality as
a chronicle of events, D'Annunzio, for the 1892 edition, did not
change words or text, a unique departure from his normal practice.

The early months of 1888 were occupied with D'Annunzio's usual
journalistic activities; in particular he worked hard to investigate
naval history: the engineering, architecture, and technical specifica-
tions of men-of-war; researches of this kind enabled him to acquire
the knowledge to write such authoritative articles in *Tribuna* on
Italy's need for naval reform. He was also turning out a prodigious
amount of other, more obviously creative artistic work, notably the
lyrics which made up the *Elegie romane*. The burden of having daily
to concoct new articles had become no less irksome. The same
difficulties which he had mentioned in his letter to Sciarra two years
earlier still persisted,[21] and in July 1888 D'Annunzio did resign
from the newspaper and left Rome for Pescara. After some days in
his native town, he moved down to the neighbouring village of
Francavilla. There he was given sanctuary by his friend, the artist
Francesco Paolo Michetti, who took him into his exotic, if crumbling, home, the deconsecrated convent of Santa Maria Maggiore,
which he had bought as dwelling-cum-studio in 1883. Michetti there
gave him the use of a simple upper room. In those surroundings,
and with D'Annunzio's vivid imagination, it was not difficult for
him to regard his study-bedroom as a monk's cell and his work as
a sacred literary mission. He was obviously determined to seize the
opportunity to carry out the plan at which, over two years earlier, he had hinted in his letter to Sciarra. In that apparent attempt

---

[21] For the letter to Prince Sciarra, see above, Ch. 2 n. 44.

at resignation, on 6 April 1886, D'Annunzio had noted his new ambition:

I have many things to attend to, many pieces to bring to a conclusion. I have a great desire to get down to the serious task of writing a long work of capital importance for me. My character and my commitment mean that daily collaboration on a newspaper distracts me too much; it dissipates and weakens my powers.

In giving up his regular salary (500 lire per month)[22] and leaving behind his Roman connections, he was staking everything on his ability to become an independent writer. For years, consciously or otherwise, he had been preparing himself to write *Il piacere*, the novel which would shock Rome and bring him international fame.

The departure for the Abruzzi put a temporary halt to the affair with Barbara, though their correspondence continued unabated. It gave them both a breathing-space and allowed her temporarily to allay the anger and suspicion of her husband, who, to D'Annunzio's continuing disgust, seems to have persisted in regular marital visits. The seriousness of the poet's commitment to more grandiose literary ambitions was not in dispute: he wrote for hours at a time, pausing only for meals and sleep; he also refused two opportunities to meet Barbara, in Turin in mid-October, and later in Rome when she returned to the family home. His letters to her were full of protestations that his workload was so heavy that an absence from Francavilla would have been unthinkable. D'Annunzio's view that as a poet he required a special kind of heroic strength and endurance in order to hammer out literary works of art is a recurrent theme in letters, notebooks, and diaries written both at the time and later at similar periods of high-speed composition. He was undeniably a swift and assiduous worker, and has consistently won the plaudits of critics for his ability to close out everything else in his drive to finish a work for publication. With all that concentrated effort in his monk's cell at Francavilla, D'Annunzio succeeded in completing the text of *Il piacere*, some 120,000 words, during the six months between 26 July and Christmas 1888; the manuscript was ready for dispatch to Emilio Treves in January 1889.

Il piacere, dedicated to Francesco Michetti, was the opening volume in the so-called trilogy of the *Romanzi della rosa* (The Novels

---

[22] This was the equivalent of 3 million lire at today's values, around £1,250 sterling; in 1890 a top civil servant in Rome earned a maximum of 850 lire per month.

of the Rose), whose title was meant to imply that the volumes were intended as a love sequence, a notion probably only later excogitated once it became clear to D'Annunzio that a trilogy might be completed with his next two novels, *L'innocente* and the *Trionfo della morte*. As will be seen, he later became fond of inventing such comprehensive titles, often for literary projects which never took off. It is evident from his letters to Barbara at the time that, following a long and venerable literary tradition, the rose of the title was D'Annunzio's pet name for the female genitalia, an impression confirmed by a lifetime of references in his less formal writings and, more immediately, by the sadistic language of the contemporary sonnet to Godoleva in the 'Adultere' of the *Intermezzo*. The more prudish critics have limited their references to the rose as though it were a generic allusion to voluptuousness.

Il piacere was certainly important for D'Annunzio's subsequent literary career; it also captured well the decadent atmosphere of Rome's high society in the 1880s, and, although not necessarily autobiographical, most critics see it as an important reflection of D'Annunzio's existence in the 'Byzantine' capital. The protagonist of the novel is the highly refined and sensitive Count Andrea Sperelli-Fieschi d'Ugenta, egotist, poet, painter, general aesthete, and immoralist. Enamoured of the society beauty Elena Muti, he is forced to dissipate his energies in other frivolous and amorous adventures at the point in the story when Elena, already three years a widow, leaves Rome suddenly to remarry. Her second husband is the grotesque Lord Humphrey Heathfield, marquis of Mount Edgcumbe and count of Bradford, renowned collector of pornographic prints and editions, whom, it transpires, she has married in order to write off her family debts. Another aspirant to Elena's favours is man-about-town Giannetto Rutolo; one of Andrea Sperelli's adventures involves him in a duel with Giannetto from which Andrea emerges severely wounded. During his convalescence, which gives him time to contemplate with some disgust his libidinous past, aesthetic inclinations return to him, bringing in their wake profound reflections on artistic composition.

A casual meeting with the uncorrupted Maria Ferres, Sienese wife of a wealthy Guatemalan politician, encourages Sperelli's renewed artistic feelings; but he and Maria fall in love. His subsequent recovery from the duelling injury, and his return to the metropolis, bring Sperelli once more into contact with Elena, which inevitably reawakens the old libido. At that point, he uses Maria as a substitute for Elena, his imagination helped by a certain physical resemblance between the two women, and on poor, sweet Maria he unleashes the voluptuous desires he felt and still feels for Elena. The deceit is, to Maria's distress, discovered when, after one session of love-making with her, in an excess of passion (and absent-mindedness) he calls out the name 'Elena'. Maria's husband, meanwhile, has been ruined financially and, in their once magnificent apartment, the family effects have to be sold at auction. The novel ends on a note of sterile emptiness, dominated by Maria's desolate sadness and Andrea Sperelli's feelings of loneliness and futility.

The first reaction to the manuscript novel from Treves himself was one of alarm; he was particularly anxious about the propriety of some of the episodes in the story. The story itself quite evidently had autobiographical elements to it, as well as being full of recognizable figures from Rome's society, blended in with authentic historical events from the capital's most recent past. At the same time there were scenes which reflected an upper-middle-class desire for titillation which could not but affect the sensitive Treves. Thus during a charity sale some of the upper-class 'saleswomen' offer cigarettes to their noble public, heavily moistened from their own lips, at exorbitant prices, while one noblewoman offers for auction a cigar, held for a time beneath her armpit, for another high fee, and in one ineffable scene (I. 4), D'Annunzio indulges in one of his favourite fetishes, forcing Maria to give Sperelli a cup of tea by taking it into her mouth and allowing him to drink, not from the cup but from her lips. The scene reaches an unconscious level of absurdity when Maria insists upon letting the tea cool before she can take it into her mouth. Nevertheless Andrea's ardour seems no less fierce as he takes his drink. Treves filled the margins of the first proofs with question marks. D'Annunzio responded with a simple affirmation that every word was in the right place, that the novel was deeply spiritual, dolorous in the extreme, and highly moralistic.

One major preoccupation of Treves concerned a potentially explosive reference by the novel's protagonist, Andrea Sperelli. This concerned the demonstration by the Roman populace on 2 February 1887 in memory of Italian soldiers who, the week before on 27 January, had been slaughtered in Africa, at Dògali, during Italy's first, unsuccessful attempt to expand into Ethiopia and Somalia. In *Il piacere* (III. 3), Sperelli, observing the demonstration in the square beneath, describes the fallen heroes as 'four hundred brutes who died brutally'. Understandably enough, Treves, even leaving aside his legitimate fears of what critics might say about his new author, was fearful of reprisals from a fervently patriotic and excitable Italian public. Yet D'Annunzio persisted in his refusal to alter a word. His defence was reasonable: to begin with, he said, Treves should re-member that he had earlier written a celebratory ode for the fallen heroes, which had been published in February 1887; in it he had expressed sorrow at the tragedy of Dògali and pride in Italy's heroic soldiers. But what is most interesting in his defence to Treves is his statement that the phrase about the four hundred brutes, 'was spoken by Andrea Sperelli, not by Gabriele D'Annunzio, and it goes well in the mouth of that *monster*. Why should the critics go mad therefore?'.[23] Indeed D'Annunzio was a strong supporter of Italian expansion overseas, an attitude which became more and more evident as his activities expanded into the more purely polit-ical sphere. Andrea Sperelli, then, considered by all knowledgeable readers of *Il piacere* as being autobiographical, seems here to be denied by his creator, and, in that reference to him as a monster, rejected as a self-portrait. One answer to that apparent dilemma seems to be that here and in all the other early novels, the Dannunzian protagonist, however autobiographical and authentic the events which allow his character to develop, is meant to represent a mon-strous side of D'Annunzio, struggling against the Chimera of decad-ent self-indulgence and voluptuousness, and ultimately failing to overcome its temptation. It was an explanation which Scarfoglio tried to promote, but the truth is that, from these relatively inno-cent beginnings to the final drug-induced debauchery of his later years, D'Annunzio revelled in self-indulgence and voluptuousness; the last thing he desired, as a man or as an artist, was to overcome life's temptations. Nevertheless, fictionally, at least, his male prot-agonists invariably experience the conflict between sensual degrada-tion and heroic achievement.

A further explanation or elaboration of the dilemma of the licen-tious aesthete may be found during the course of *Il piacere* (II. 1), in a quasi-Swinburnian reference during the course of the novel to

---

[23] For the exchange and D'Annunzio's rejoinder see Masci, *La vita e le opere*, 84–5; D'Annunzio there adds, 'Give all your pity to Maria Ferres; she needs it!' There is further discussion of the episode in V. Salierno, *D'Annunzio e i suoi editori* (Milan, 1987), 29–33.

'Il Re di Cipro' (The King of Cyprus), a poem purporting to be written by Sperelli, in which the promises of the Chimera are offered
to the young libertine:

> Vuoi tu pugnare?
> Uccidere? Veder fiumi di sangue?
> gran mucchi d'oro? greggi di captive
> femmine? schiavi? altre, altre prede? Vuoi
> tu far vivere un marmo? Erigere un tempio?
> Comporre un immortale inno? Vuoi (m'odi,
> giovine, m'odi?) vuoi divinamente
> amare?

> [Do you wish to fight? to kill?
> to see rivers of blood?
> great heaps of gold? herds of captive women?
> slaves? and other, still other prey? Do you wish to
> bring a statue to life? to set up a temple?
> to compose an immortal hymn? Do you desire (listen,
> young man, listen to me!) do you desire
> to love divinely?]

The lines return as an epigraph to *La Chimera*, the newly rear-
ranged collection of 1890. At the end of the *Chimera* anthology,
D'Annunzio had included a poem, 'Al poeta Andrea Sperelli', which
he had previously published in August 1889 in the *Corriere di Napoli*
(the newspaper founded by his friends Matilde Serao and Edoardo
Scarfoglio). The title of that concluding poem was an obvious reference to the hero of *Il piacere*, and may be seen as connecting the
Chimera anthology and the poet–protagonist of the novel. The gist
of the poem suggested that the Gorgon–Sphinx–Chimera which
tempted the young man with voluptuous delights had been overcome by D'Annunzio's confession of the sterility of such achievements. Such, anyway, was the interpretation now openly put upon
the poem and upon *Il piacere* by the friendly and, it must be added,
naïve Edoardo Scarfoglio in his introductory notes to the piece
in the *Corriere di Napoli* of 15 August 1889. Scarfoglio decided that
the poem served as a retrospective comment on *Il piacere*, 'the
novel about the struggle between a monstrous aesthetic-aphrodisiac
chimera and the palpitating phantasma of life in the soul of man'.
All who admired the young poet, Scarfoglio thought, would have
been glad to see that, at least in his writings, 'the healthy change
had been completed'. The sentiments chime with Scarfoglio's regrets

that D'Annunzio's first experiences of Rome had turned his head away from the serious intellectual pursuits of which he was capable to the decadent trivialities which Scarfoglio regretted had characterized his first Roman compositions.[24] But here too, as in that earlier judgement, Scarfoglio was deluding himself. Almost simultaneously with the publication of *Il piacere*, D'Annunzio was taking notes for *Il trionfo della morte*, finally published in 1894, but before then serialized (as far as chapter 16) in the recently founded weekly, *La tribuna illustrata*, under the title of *L'invincibile* (The Invincible One). However, as will be seen, what he wrote in *L'invincibile* contained specifically autobiographical details of the period immediately following the completion of *Il piacere*, and those details gave the lie to Scarfoglio's hopeful statements of a reborn D'Annunzio. The projected publication of the first version of *Il trionfo*, however, came to a premature end in March 1890, not least because D'Annunzio finally had to perform his military service, beginning on 1 November 1889.

Il piacere was a great success with the Roman public. It was read as an autobiographical reflection of D'Annunzio's scandalous life as well as being a clear portrait of Roman society in the early 1880s (it has its declared beginning in 1884). The quality of the writing, the consistency of the plot, and the likeliness of its situations are variable. Undoubtedly, however, an important part of the novel lies in D'Annunzio's statements about artistic sensitivity and the supremacy of art over any other human joy or achievement:

Art! Art!—This was the faithful Lover, ever young, immortal. This was the Fount of pure joy, forbidden to the multitude, conceded to the elect; this was the precious sustenance which made man like a god. Having set his lips at that cup, how could he have drunk at any other? How could he have searched for other joys after tasting the supreme joy of all? How could his spirit have welcomed other distractions when it had felt within itself the unforgettable excitement of creative force? How could his hands have dwelt lasciviously on the bodies of women when once he had felt substance and form bursting from his fingers? In short, how had his senses managed so weakly and perversely to sink to such a low point of voluptuousness when once they had been illuminated by a sensitivity which could discern invisible outlines in the appearance of things, perceive the imperceptible, and guess the hidden thoughts of Nature? (*Il piacere*, II. 1)

---

[24] Scarfoglio's *Libro di Don Chisciotte* has more than one augury that D'Annunzio may renounce his more lubricious tendencies: see e.g. pp. 159–64.

A reading of the work which D'Annunzio was to produce in future years might initially reinforce the impression made by his statements here: that for the poet, Art would always triumph over Sex. This is an idealistic view, though it contains certain elements of truth. The reality was that, by natural processes, each of his sexual encounters lost its physical piquancy with the passing of time, whereas he continued to *write* about each new sexual experience long after the affair was over, thus giving the impression that the artistic process seemed to triumph; in fact by that time he would have moved on to fresh sexual conquests.

Nearly all critics have looked for biographical references in *Il piacere*, and have variously seen Elena as a representation of Barbara Leoni, with some shared characteristics of Olga Ossani, while Maria Ferres is viewed by some as having some of the kindly qualities of D'Annunzio's long-suffering wife. In his letters to Barbara D'Annunzio did write that he would immortalize in the novel the most sad and most divine aspects of their love; and she no doubt saw herself portrayed in various episodes; she was later to recognize other elements from their love affair when *Il trionfo della morte* was published. But as far as D'Annunzio's biography is concerned, the sexual gymnastics of the time are relatively trivial; they continued anyway in much the same guise for the next twenty years or more before giving way by 1920 to a straightforward combination of cocaine and prostitutes. If the biographer seeks in *Il piacere* important and lasting reflections of D'Annunzio's real life, they are to be found in Sperelli's meditations on aspects of literature and art, which closely mirrored D'Annunzio's now consistent attitude to his writing. One such concern was his view of the value of poetry:

Verse is everything. In the imitation of Nature no other artistic instrument is more alive, agile, acute, varied, multiform, plastic, obedient, sensitive, faithful. [. . .] A thought which is exactly expressed in a perfect line of poetry is a thought which already existed pre-formed in the obscure depths of language. Extracted by the poet, it continues to exist in the consciousness of men. The greater poet is therefore the one who can bring out a greater number of these ideal pre-formations. (*Il piacere*, II. 1)

Those sentiments were to dominate his life, and perhaps had already dominated him, to the exclusion of personal feelings or consideration for others. In the novel, Andrea Sperelli presents himself as an unscrupulous Don Giovanni figure, considering 'The motive for his power over women lay in the fact that, in the art of love, he felt no repugnance at being false, lying and deceptive.' All the evidence points to D'Annunzio's having similar attitudes, not only in his disloyalty to women, but also in his fidelity to his art; the most dramatic demonstrations of that dedication were produced when D'Annunzio rejected jaded personal relationships in favour of literary achievement. At times he would not spare even himself in his pursuit of his art, and in one particular case, when he was half-blinded during World War One, and in danger of losing his sight completely, his sufferings and his self-examination produced, in 1916, one of his most remarkable, and most wholly original, works of literature, *Il notturno* (The Nocturne).

It is interesting to note that the heavily bowdlerized version of *Il piacere*, translated as *The Child of Pleasure* by Georgina Harding in 1898, omits any kind of intellectual reflection on serious subjects. It was understandable that the sanitized version offered to the Victorian reading public would omit voyeuristic descriptions of the naked Elena being seduced by the libidinous Andrea; also understandably excised was any characterization of the sadistic and perverted tastes in literature and art of the noble Englishman, Heathfield. But to remove all reference to any intelligent debate inevitably reduced the novel to the level of the innocuous kind of work produced by Mary Braddon, Ouida, Marie Corelli, and other purveyors of similar sentimental fiction. It is worth remarking, however, that D'Annunzio's temporary popularity in Britain came about in large part because Miss Harding, constrained by contemporary censorship regulations and held back by a natural prudishness of her own, forced his work to harmonize with the literary fashions favoured by the majority at the time. Symptomatic of the bowdlerization was Orlo Williams's later review of D'Annunzio's *œuvre*, which congratulated the author on his depiction of Andrea Sperelli, opining that it would have done honour to the imagination of Ouida.[25] Williams, naturally, intended his remark as a compliment to D'Annunzio, but it did indicate the level at which the translation was rated by his contemporaries. Ouida herself declared that she felt D'Annunzio to be a soul mate, and translated certain tracts of *Il piacere* which, she said, she could have written herself.

[25] O. Williams, 'The Novels of D'Annunzio', *Edinburgh Review*, 218/443 (1913), 343.

But it is also true that she regretted his obsession with sex and with what she termed the 'mere filth' of some of his writing.[26]

The translations of his novels may have guaranteed D'Annunzio a certain popularity and a source of income (though in Britain his financial return was not as great as he might have hoped), but his merits as a creative writer were being judged by critics and littér-ateurs in Britain only from what they were able to read of him in translation. Very few could read him in Italian. That problem has continued until the present day, compounded most recently by the unscrupulous actions of the publishing house Daedalus. Following the expiration of copyright in 1988, Daedalus unloaded upon an unsuspecting Anglophone public the very translations which Miss Harding had bowdlerized in the late 1890s, without any open ref-erence to the original date of publication or to the omissions and changes which she made and which scholars have pointed out over the past century.

For D'Annunzio *Il piacere* marked a new move into European fashionability. In particular, there is much in the novel to link it with the European literary trend which came to be known as Decadentism. In the already cited letter of 14 November 1892 sent to his translator, Georges Hérelle, D'Annunzio remarked that he had crammed into *Il piacere*, 'as if to deliver myself of them, all my predilections for form and colour, all my subtleties, all my pre-ciosities, confusedly'.[27] The resultant *mélange*, 'all bursting with art' had perhaps, he added, some correlation with J. K. Huysmans's *A rebours*. In fact there seems to be no specific borrowing from Huysmans's novel (published in 1884), though the character of D'Annunzio's Sperelli has much in common with that of Huysmans's protagonist, Des Esseintes. Both have an exquisitely refined aesthetic sense, both are Anglophile, full of an élitist ambition to escape the mediocrity of bourgeois ideals, to shock the establishment. By tying himself to the methods of his Belgian contemporary in what was for him that rather unusual admission of affinity, D'Annunzio showed his further awareness of belonging to that new movement in Euro-pean literary activity under whose banner could also be counted Swinburne and Wilde in Britain and Hugo von Hofmannsthal in Austria. It was yet another literary direction for D'Annunzio.

---

[26] De la Ramée, 'The Genius of D'Annunzio', 350; cf. above Ch. 1 n. 47.
[27] See above, Ch. 2 at n. 49; here *Lettere a Georges Hérelle*, 60.

After his self-imposed retreat in Michetti's convent, D'Annunzio took Barbara to Albano for a week of love-making, which was later to figure as an episode in the *Trionfo della morte*. Meanwhile Michetti had rented for the two lovers a rustic cottage (the *eremo*) at San Vito Chietino, twenty miles from Pescara, perched high above the beach on a steep cliff. In the hermitage D'Annunzio intended to write *L'invincibile* (which he was to develop into the *Trionfo della morte*). Even nowadays the habitation which aficionados of D'Annunzio point out as being 'the hermitage of San Vito' has a primitively uncomfortable aspect, and the thought of that rugged provincial dwelling did nothing for his beloved's sophisticated spirit. At first Barbara, who had returned to Rome, refused to join him there, and D'Annunzio went back to Michetti, desperate for female company. Michetti, no doubt by this time tired of his house-guest, genius or not, left for Rome to persuade Barbara to join D'Annunzio as previously planned. He succeeded in his objective and for two months, from 23 July to 22 September 1889, she and D'Annunzio lived together in the cliff-top house at San Vito. The literary result of the quest by Michetti (his *ospite ammirabile*, admirable host) and of their renewed romance was the love story of Ippolita Sanzio and Giorgio Aurispa in the *Trionfo della morte*, and the *Libro segreto* continues at this point: 'Thus Barbara Leoni was given back to me by sadness and poetry, like a leaf, or a flower between the pages of a sculpted book. She became Ippolita Sanzio. The book was entitled *The Triumph of Death*, like the frescoed allegory of Orcagna in the cemetery at Pisa.'[28]

During the summer that the couple spent together, D'Annunzio also worked on the transformation of his *Isaotta Guttadauro ed altre poesie* into *L'Isotteo–La Chimera*. The vicissitudes of the anthology at this time must have reflected his experiences with Barbara. Initially D'Annunzio sent to Treves, along with the first pages of the definitive edition, his dedication 'To Donna Maria Gallese', but on 15 September 1889 he wrote again from San Vito, asking the publisher to suppress those words. A week later, presumably after Barbara's departure from San Vito, he returned the proofs of the

---

[28] A version of Michetti's bringing the two together, heavily romanticized by time and distance, is given by D'Annunzio in *Il libro segreto*, *Prose di ricerca*, ii. 675–6; Orcagna's frescoes survived a wartime bomb and are visible at Pisa, but their relevance to the novel (apart from the fact that death closes all) is not immediately obvious.

opening pages, reinstating the dedication to his wife. The dual volume came out in the following year, 1890.[29] Barbara must have suffered a similar disappointment when the *Elegie romane* were published in 1892 with a dedication not to her, their inspiration, but to the influential Nencioni, whose friendship would prove much more useful and certainly more durable than D'Annunzio's passion for Barbara.

The poet's attempts to postpone his military service had begun in 1883, when he had used the excuse of being enrolled as a student at Rome University. By 1889 he had no further excuse. Letters from him to Barbara, to Vincenzo Morello (shortly to become his new patron), and to Emilio Treves rail against the threat of a year or more in barracks (more if he were not counted by the authorities as a volunteer). 'It is certain suicide', he repeats to Barbara on 7 October 1889, continuing his futile protests. 'The barracks is death for me. Ariel a corporal! The delicate Ariel! Can you imagine it?', the self-pitying letter continues, but a month later, on 1 November, D'Annunzio was enrolled as a 'volunteer' in the Alexandrian Light Cavalry (Cavalleggeri d'Alessandria), and he entered military camp on 6 November. The first months of his service, stationed at Rome's Macao barracks, were no doubt a rude awakening for the delicate aesthete, who, in theory anyway, would be required to groom his own horse and help clean the stables of his cavalry regiment. 'My worst enemy could not have imagined a more ferocious, inhuman torture for me', he wrote to Barbara on 10 November 1889.[30] But within a couple of months he had invented sufficient excuses for absenting himself from the barracks. His influential contacts no doubt helped to secure him a more comfortable billet—an attendant, usually a concession only allowed to officers, was appointed to groom his horse. In February he was given a period of leave to go to the bedside of his sick father; he somehow succeeded in prolonging that leave until early March to enable him to visit the old fleshpots of Rome, and at the same time to join Barbara on several occasions; finally, instead of returning to duties, he reported sick at Rome's Sant'Antonio military hospital. From there he convalesced at Pescara between 5 and 23 April, before returning to the capital,

---

[29] For this succession of events and the notes to Treves, see Gatti, *GD'A* 98–9, and id., *Le donne*, 100–2.

[30] GD'A, *Lettere a Barbara*, 160 and 173–4.

where at the Macao barracks the sitting-room normally reserved for use by officers of the medical corps was put at his disposal. He used it as a venue to meet his friends, his wife, and his lover, and found enough spare time to compose poems for the journal *Nuova antologia* and to write the first sixteen chapters of *L'invincibile*.

The episodic publication of the new novel, the content of which reflected in particular the summer spent with Barbara at the hermitage of San Vito, appeared in *La tribuna illustrata*. This new journal was a lavish weekly magazine which began publication in January 1890 under the editorship of Vincenzo Morello, with the close collaboration of D'Annunzio and his painter friend, Giulio Aristide Sartorio. By 16 March the magazine had run into financial difficulties; between these problems and D'Annunzio's other occupations, including his attempts to avoid military duties, publication of *L'invincibile* was interrupted. It was to be 1894 before the book was transformed and published as *Il trionfo della morte*. In the meantime D'Annunzio decided to make his military service as comfortable as possible. He had rented an apartment on an upper floor in Via Piemonte, and had installed there Donna Maria with the family, who had moved up from Pescara to Rome in October 1889. He now rented separately a ground-floor apartment in the same building; there he would meet Barbara sporadically until May 1890, when she was, diplomatically, sent away by her family to visit relatives in Turin. Despite his irregular attendance in the barracks, D'Annunzio was mysteriously promoted corporal at the end of April 1890, the highest rank that a volunteer national serviceman could normally hope to reach during peacetime.

The following month, on 6 June 1890 to be precise, Donna Maria threw herself from the window of their apartment. No doubt D'Annunzio's shameless relationship with Barbara was a major factor in driving his wife to the edge, but there were many other reasons which might explain her desperate act, notably the poverty in which she was forced to live because of D'Annunzio's indifference to the family's material well-being and his frivolous profligacy whenever he did have money in his pocket. By scrimping and saving Donna Maria might relieve the household of the worst of her husband's debts. But then D'Annunzio himself, delighted at his wife's economical success, would go out to celebrate, 'light and gay as a little bird', she wrote, and return, after a visit to an auction, with some useless ornament (Donna Maria gave the example of a piece of jade), which had cost him several thousand lire.[31] Years later, talking of her fall from the window, Donna Maria told Guglielmo Gatti that her mood had also been affected when she was out walking with little Veniero and by chance met her now elderly father, Duke Giulio, who had refused to acknowledge her or her child. The positive indifference of her father, 'Who are you? I don't know you', added to D'Annunzio's complete lack of regard for anyone but himself, could have been the main motives for poor Maria's action. But the incident was further complicated by a rumour that Maria was being propositioned by Vincenzo Morello, and found it insulting that D'Annunzio should be so indifferent to this affront to her decency. Taken to hospital, she was found to be not gravely injured and, according to the usual medical prognosis, was expected to spend twenty days there. D'Annunzio was later to exploit the sensations and experiences of the attempted suicide and of his wife's recovery in evoking certain moods in his later novel, *L'innocente* (The Victim), published in 1892.[32]

Critics are strangely reticent about D'Annunzio's feelings at the time of his wife's attempted suicide. The newspapers suggested that Donna Maria's fall was accidental. In the correspondence with Barbara there is a gap between a letter of 21 April and the next of 17 June 1890. Piero Chiara reports that D'Annunzio wrote to Barbara on the very day of the suicide attempt, to inform her of the incident, and inviting her to rejoin him in Rome while his wife was away in hospital.[33] In D'Annunzio's opinion marital faithfulness (*la fedeltà*) was either hypocrisy or a widely diffused perversion of truth. In the *Libro segreto* he was to write:

Faithfulness has about it the sound of false chains on stage. The actor who appears to drag them after him knows how much more lubricious they are than those fetters simulating bondage, which lend lasciviousness to certain Malay dances. I mean faithful lovers—a non-existent genus. There is no couple faithful because of love. I am unfaithful because of love, because of the art of love when I love to the death.[34]

---

[31] Alatri, *GD'A*, 94 describes the situation.

[32] For these events see ibid., and cf. Gatti, *GD'A* 100–1. Gatti's report combines what Donna Maria told him personally concerning her father's snub, and what he says Barbara Leoni told Mario Guabello, the great collector of Dannunziana, forty-five years after the event.

[33] Chiara, *GD'A* 68.

[34] *Il libro segreto*, *Prose di ricerca*, ii. 681; for this passage and his comments upon it, see Gatti, *Le donne*, 16.

That kind of facile, sophistic self-justification can be seen at many points in D'Annunzio's life and *œuvre*. As a practical illustration of what he noted in the *Libro segreto*, the letters to Elvira that month are good examples. When Donna Maria came out of hospital she took her children and went to live at 9 Piazza di Spagna; D'Annunzio rented a large room in 5 Via Gregoriana.

His military service was still not complete. In his spare hours he studied Stendhal and began to read the great Russian novels, which were just then appearing in their French translations. If he were to hold his position in the forefront of fashion when he was demobilized from the cavalry, it would be necessary for him to concentrate his energies on keeping up to date with the latest masterpieces. A further spell in hospital with a mild bout of malaria ensured he had more leisure for reading during the heat of August, before he rejoined his regiment at Faenza; there the citizenry greeted him as a triumphant hero and he was permitted to lodge in the same hotel as the officers. On 19 October he took the necessary qualifying examinations to gain a commission, obtaining seventeen marks out of the possible twenty. Piero Chiara reports the story told by Giuseppe Fatini that when the examining colonel congratulated D'Annunzio on his good result, he added, 'Well done, Corporal D'Annunzio! Keep on studying. Perhaps one day you may become a writer, like Edmondo De Amicis. The raw material is there.'[35] We have to imagine D'Annunzio's reaction. He was promoted sergeant on 31 October, commissioned a month later as a sub-lieutenant in the Novara Lancers, and immediately given unlimited leave. Legally constrained to resign a year later, he was finally taken off the reserve in December 1902. He was to revive his commission when Italy entered World War One in 1915, but by then, as will be seen, he would be virtually in a position to create his own commission and rank. D'Annunzio returned to Rome the day after being commissioned and spent four days with Barbara at the Hotel Alibert, before leaving for his 'large room' in Via Gregoriana. Barbara, after a few weeks back with D'Annunzio, began to suffer attacks of her uterine illness, and needed medical treatment; she chose to be operated on at home by her gynaecologist. D'Annunzio visited her every day, took notes of the treatment carried out and the reactions of the patient; he later wrote up the episode for the operation

[35] Chiara, *GD'A* 71.

undergone by Giuliana Hermil, the female protagonist of his next novel, *L'innocente*.

Closely linked in mood to *L'innocente* was the long short story *Giovanni Episcopo*, which was serialized in the *Nuova antologia* during February and March 1891. D'Annunzio, ever in need of money, had written the story (and the subsequent *Innocente*) with undue speed in order to persuade his publishers to give him an advance. Both works were strongly influenced by his recent reading of the Russian classics, particularly Dostoevsky. The sombre plot of *Giovanni Episcopo* concerns the wretched Episcopo of the title, a modest clerk, abjectly in the power of his more vigorous friend Giulio Wanzer and of his wife Ginevra, who between them cuckold him. His one blessing or compensation in life is his 11-year-old son Ciro, whose silent suffering finally drives Episcopo to kill Wanzer. There is here a return to something of the crude naturalism of D'Annunzio's earlier short stories, with scenes reminiscent, for instance, of the brooding atmosphere of a particularly unpleasant murder in *La madia*.

D'Annunzio himself thought little of the book's artistic merit, and was later reluctant to accept it as part of his collected works. But his reflections upon the defects of the book and on the artistic climate in which it was written are important to show his development as a writer. When the story appeared as a separate volume in the following year, 1892, D'Annunzio included his thoughts in a self-deprecating letter of dedication to Matilde Serao, which prefaced (and prefaces) all subsequent editions.

Illustrious lady, my dear friend, this small book that I am dedicating to you has for me no artistic importance; but it is a simple literary document published to indicate the first instinctive effort made by a restless artisan of words to achieve a final renewal of his art.

He also noted in the dedication the realistic genesis of the story: that is, in company with Angelo Conti and Marius de Maria, he had actually met the alcoholic who was to provide the character of his protagonist, and subsequently he recalled lighting by chance on the title, *Giovanni Episcopo*, one evening while he was leafing through some of his old notes. Thus, he informed Matilde and his readers, the story, touched off by a combination of the name and his recollection of the earlier meeting, burgeoned suddenly in his mind. Next morning, and for the next few days he had worked with his usual unstoppable rhythm, until the story was completed. Having thus described the genesis of the new work in the dedication, D'Annunzio added a more important observation, ostensibly for Matilde Serao's personal information, that the book contained the elements of a renewal of his art, more rigorously pursued in *L'innocente*, with greater character-analysis and simplicity of style. 'The whole method consists of this formula:—One must study men and objects DIRECTLY, without modification of any kind. [. . .] Never before as today has the dilemma been so imperious—*Renew yourself or die*.' The dedication made clear, too, D'Annunzio's disappointment at the current state of Italian letters. There was, he feared, no one willing to study (indeed no one seemed to know the meaning of the word), no one willing to renew himself, to have faith in his own powers, to feel secure in his own sincerity. D'Annunzio considered himself to be guilty of similar irresponsibility, and in this new statement of authorial policy publicly renounced his own previous writings as vacuous and false, lacking in vitality; he declared instead his realization that he needed to find new inspiration.

The reflections are typical of this period in his life and work, and correspond to the famous page of criticism of two years before when, on 26 May 1888, one of his columns in the *Tribuna* had pronounced the naturalistic novel dead. Writers, in order to keep ahead of fashion, had tried to blend the old methods (exploiting external observation and exact description) with the new psychological interest which was sweeping Europe. The Naturalists failed, D'Annunzio argued, because 'their work lacked the ability both to analyse external sensations and logically to create interior situations'. In a word, their novels were incoherent: 'This fundamental literary error of self-reforming naturalist writers stems from a scientific error. They believe that exterior things exist outside of ourselves, independently, and that they must present the same appearance for all human spirits.' D'Annunzio's voracious reading of Tolstoy and Dostoevsky in 1890 seemed to indicate a solution to the literary and artistic dilemma which he himself faced. Throughout his life he was to use other men's works to inspire his own innovative writing (inimitable creation, he would call it). A good illustration of his emulative method is to be found in *Il piacere*, at the point where Sperelli–D'Annunzio describes how he uses a line or so from ancient sonneteers to inspire the first note of a new creation of his own:

Almost always, to begin composing, he would need a musical tone given to him by another poet; and he would take it, almost invariably, from the ancient versifiers of Tuscany. Half a line of Lapo Gianni, Cavalcanti, Cino, Petrarch, Lorenzo de' Medici, the memory of an ensemble of rhymes, the conjunction of two epithets, a harmonious grouping of beautiful, fine-sounding words, some rhythmical phrase, these were enough to open the vein so to speak, to give him, as it were the *la*, a note which could serve as the basis for the harmony of the first strophe. (*Il piacere*, II. 1)

When this 'method' became allied to his principle of dynamic imitation, that is, his habit of setting up great littérateurs as targets to be overcome, D'Annunzio would lay himself open to certain charges of plagiarism, which were to affect his reputation.

Giovanni Episcopo, denied as a work of art by its author was, then, a first step in the renovation of his style, acknowledged as such in the famous preface. The slim volume is also important as an example of a change in D'Annunzio's literary technique, from the lush and esoteric language of *Il piacere* to a more down-to-earth, everyday mode of expression. In *Giovanni Episcopo* the new style takes the form of a monologue, which ranges from broad choral descriptions of society to the minute analysis of an individual psyche, as Episcopo narrates his own lugubrious story. From its initial serialized publication, the monologue form indicated to D'Annunzio's adverse critics his source in Dostoevsky. Particularly obvious was the influence of the short story *Kròtkaja*, while the figure of Episcopo himself could be seen as derivative from Marmeladov in *Crime and Punishment*. There were many other accusations of plagiarism, well summed up in the excellent introduction to her edition by Clelia Martignoni;[36] those accusations were to be exhumed in the mid-1890s by Enrico Thovez.

Although D'Annunzio was proud of his ability to work long hours, concentrating only on the subject before him, the speed with which he wrote *Giovanni Episcopo* did little to help its artistic success; this was a speed dictated by the truly dire financial situation in which D'Annunzio now found himself. His room in Via Gregoriana had been besieged by creditors, who finally broke in and, at some time in mid-March 1891, carried away all his belongings to be sold at auction. He left Rome hurriedly and immediately took refuge again with Michetti in the Francavilla convent. To a Russian

---

[36] GD'A, *Giovanni Episcopo*, ed. C. Martignoni (Milan, 1971), pp. vii–viii.

friend, and potential patron, Katerina Pavlowna Tulinow, he sent apologies for not having seen her before leaving the city: 'It was not possible for me to come and kiss your hand; I could not delay my departure. I abandoned the house to its invasion of bailiffs, and I left, in despair, ill and weakened, in a gloomy dawn which reawakened the fever in my blood.'[37]

At the Francavilla convent D'Annunzio immediately began writing hard to complete his next novel, *L'innocente*. In just over four months, by August 1891, it was finished. As with *Giovanni Episcopo*, he deliberately changed his style from that of his earlier narrative prose, and the plot, like that of *Episcopo*, again consists of a confessional monologue. This time the confessant is the protagonist, Tullio Hermil, unfaithful husband of Giuliana. In the past Giuliana has always forgiven Tullio his betrayals, even consoling him for certain disappointments in his adulterous love, but Tullio is not so tolerant when one day he returns to find that Giuliana is pregnant, having herself, in her only moment of weakness, succumbed to a seducer. Despite Tullio's jealousy, the two determine to try to forget the grimness of the present by rediscovering their once passionate love for each other. But inevitably Giuliana's innocent baby is viewed continually as an intruder coming between the two as a living obstacle and a reproach (D'Annunzio approved the novel's French title, *L'Intrus*). Tullio plans to get rid of the child by exposing it to the cold air; his stratagem succeeds and the infant dies. The reader might expect remorse at the crime, and indeed Tullio's 'confession' which forms the subject of the story should have been born from his subsequent contrition, which superficially anyway is meant to supply the motive for his monologue. It may then seem inappropriate, that, while his words are a specious attempt to resolve the moral torment felt at his misdeed, his return to Giuliana simply enables him to exploit her sexually; any regret the reader expects to hear from him is grotesquely outweighed by his excited relief that the obstacle is removed, the child dead. All critics agree that Hermil is a self-contemplative, an egotist who seeks with his self-justification to put himself above the law of ordinary men. In

[37] Reported by Alatri, *GD'A*, 102; D'Annunzio's need for funds would dominate his existence. This seems to have been the poet's first experience of what would be a long series of evictions for debt. Prophetic of his letter to Treves and Mondadori, a missive of his written to a Tuscan bookseller as early as 1880 declared his urgent need for funds (he was then 17 years old); see Fracassini, *GD'A, convittore*, 88–9.

a brief epigraph to the novel, he imagines himself coming before a judge to confess, 'I have committed a crime. That poor creature would not be dead if I had not killed her.' But he then asks himself, 'Can I go before a judge? Can I speak to him like that? I cannot and will not. Man's justice does not touch me. No earthly tribunal could judge me.'

Critics, particularly left-wing critics, have seen in Tullio Hermil the germs of the Italian *Übermensch*, already discernible in the insuperable talents of Andrea Sperelli, and now more openly declared. Nietzschean phraseology accompanies Hermil's characterization of himself in the long preamble to the novel. Later (in chapter XIV) he talks of the excessive (*eccessivo*) development of his intelligence, his 'many-souled' qualities which nevertheless do nothing to modify 'the substantial basis of his being', the hidden substratum, in which are inscribed 'all the hereditary characteristics of his race':

In my brother, a balanced organism, thought was always an accompaniment to deed; in me thought predominated, without at the same time destroying my faculties for action, which, on the contrary, developed with extraordinary power. In short I was a violent and passionate intelligence, in whom the hypertrophy of certain cerebral centres rendered impossible the co-ordination necessary for normal spiritual life. A most lucid observer of myself, I had every impetus common to undisciplinable primitive natures.

In the novel, Giuliana's comprehension of his uniqueness allows Tullio to indulge in further self-justification, to such an extent that he is convinced that any action he performs will automatically be exalted, distinguished, or ennobled by the very uniqueness or rarity of his opinions and feelings. His wife's feeding of Tullio's ego and the protagonist's own self-justification could well have been a close reflection of D'Annunzio's personal life at the time. Infanticide may not have figured among D'Annunzio's personal shortcomings, though he was later to refer to his favourite child by Maria Gravina as their particular 'innocente',[38] but there is no doubt that *L'innocente* also made use of autobiographical elements from his life and experience. The good nature of Giuliana finds a ready parallel in the character of Donna Maria, and the egotism of Tullio compares closely with that of the poet himself. Even in Giuliana's momentary lapse there may be an echo of that rumour which suggested that Donna

---

[38] *Lettere a Georges Hérelle*, 85, cf. below pp. 109 and 131.

Maria had been the reluctant target of Vincenzo Morello's attentions at a time when D'Annunzio was using his friendship with Morello to ensure the publication of his work in *La tribuna illustrata*.

On 14 July 1890 D'Annunzio wrote to Emilio Treves to inform him that *L'innocente* was almost finished, and requesting an advance of 2,000 lire, and in August, apparently oblivious to the hallowed ritual of the Italian summer holiday, he sent Treves the manuscript of the novel. Treves ignored this for long enough to provoke a furious D'Annunzio to write demanding a decision. By way of reply Treves returned the manuscript (along with one of *Giovanni Episcopo*) with a rejection note, which also made it clear that he considered the novel 'highly immoral'.[39] The poet was briefly in Pescara that August, accompanied by his wife and family, socializing as well as he could. But as soon as he heard the news of his rejection by Treves, he left the Abruzzi, firstly for Rome (on 26 August) and, three days later, for Naples.

---

[39] The brief correspondence was published by M. Mosso, 'Le prime lettere di GD'A al suo Editore', *Illustrazione italiana* (6 May 1923); the circumstances of composition and publication are fully discussed in Sozzi, *GD'A* 128–9.

4

Naples and Beyond

D'ANNUNZIO had decided to travel south with Michetti, searching for amusement while at the same time looking out for someone to publish his new novel. They set out on 26 August 1891 with the original intention, at least notionally, of spending a few days in Naples, where Michetti had business to attend to, before possibly taking the boat for Sicily; instead, though Michetti speedily returned to Francavilla, it was to be a further two years before D'Annunzio left the old Bourbon capital. On the way to Naples he succeeded in breaking the journey for a three-day visit to Rome where Barbara Leoni had been notified of his advent. On 30 August he arrived in Naples, and there he found an immediate opening for his manuscript. He met at once with his old friends Edoardo Scarfoglio and Matilde Serao and presented them with the 900 manuscript pages of his *Innocente*. Subsequently, between 10 December 1891 and 8 February 1892, it was issued as a serialized appendix to the *Corriere di Napoli*, the newspaper which the husband-and-wife team were co-editing; after it had been offered again to Treves (and again rejected), Ferdinando Bideri offered to publish it in March as a separate volume. The contract guaranteed D'Annunzio 3,000 lire for the right to print 3,000 copies, the first 500 of which were to sell at 5 lire each, and the rest at 4 lire. D'Annunzio was subsequently to receive 20 per cent of the cover price of reprints.[1]

With a cover design by Aristide Sartorio, the novel carried a dedication to Maria Gravina. Maria who? His readers might well wonder. Therein lay another motive for his journey to Naples, because during the summer in Pescara he had met the statuesque Sicilian Princess Maria Gravina Cruyllas di Ramacca, a name as exotic as any that could have come from the pages of his *Piacere*. He had then visited her in Naples, fallen madly 'in love', and entered on a

---

[1] Letters to Ferdinando Bideri concerning these editions are published in A. Cappelletti, *Due carteggi dannunziani* (Naples, 1929): the contract in particular is at 5–6; other documents are available in Masci, *La vita e le opere*, 97–107.

relationship which was to have disastrous consequences for them both. However, before the wretched affair developed, D'Annunzio enjoyed a few months of publishing triumph. The new novel was having success, three reprints followed quickly after the first, a fifth was accepted by the wily Treves in 1895, after poet and publisher were reconciled, and a sixth reprint came out in 1896. *Giovanni Episcopo* was also published later, by another Neapolitan house, that of Luigi Pirro.

Naples, aware of its position as a former capital city, was a focal point of southern intellectuals; there D'Annunzio, thanks to Scarfoglio and his newspaper contacts, had an immediate introduction to the local society of writers and critics which included Salvatore Di Giacomo, Roberto Bracco, Ettore Moschino, Arturo Colaiutti, and Ferdinando Russo, as well as the peppery Matilde Serao. D'Annunzio began writing his usual gossip-column articles and more and more theatrical and artistic reviews, including an infamous attack on Pietro Mascagni.[2] But the power of the word, represented by the media, was something D'Annunzio had relished for years. And being in an ambience of artists and writers helped his own competitive genius for writing, stimulated at the same time by the inspiration which he gained from his new conquest, Maria Gravina. During these two years, apart from the publication of *L'innocente* and *Giovanni Episcopo*, he finished the composition of his *Elegie romane*, wrote the poems collected in the *Poema paradisiaco*, and, recalling his voyage on the *Barbarigo* and other naval experiences, completed his *Odi navali*, the poems in which he celebrated naval prowess.

Meanwhile Elvira Leoni, his darling Barbara, was being gradually marginalized, and in that context it may here be helpful to anticipate D'Annunzio's fictional deliberations concerning Ippolita Sanzio, the heroine of *Il trionfo della morte*, a novel which probably contains as much autobiographical detail as any other event in his life-as-art, art-as-life existence. In particular, certain reflections on Ippolita by the novel's protagonist Giorgio Aurispa undoubtedly represented D'Annunzio's diminishing passion for Elvira. There is, for instance, something approaching loathing in the words of Aurispa as he

---

[2] Copies of *Il mattino*, though rare, are available in the library of the Vittoriale; more accessible is G. Infusino's *D'Annunzio a Napoli* (Naples, 1995), which publishes D'Annunzio's main articles, here 147–52; for the attack on Mascagni see *Lettere a Barbara*, 404–5 and 462.

meditates upon the barren companion to whom he has taught the art of lubricious sexuality. The literal sterility of the very act of copulation with Ippolita is brought home to Aurispa with a force which shows him both the fruitlessness of his life, and the demise of his artistic aspirations, swamped as they are in a morass of debauchery.[3] D'Annunzio had seen Barbara–Elvira only infrequently during the period between his voluntary retreat to Michetti's convent and the publication of the *Innocente* which had been gestating during his seclusion at Francavilla. It was true that he had paused on his journey from Francavilla to Naples to spend three days with her, and she was later to come to see him in Naples, in February 1892, but the old fire of passion was no longer present. Nevertheless D'Annunzio continued to write letters to her, hypocritically protesting his undying love. 'I shall never be able to love another woman', he wrote as late as 24 April 1892:

You need have no fear of any rival. If all the women that Don Giovanni dreamed of were really to pass through my bed, you should be happy at the end, because all of them would *certainly*, *certainly* leave me a regret and a frenzied desire for you. But my bed is chaste, and the only visitations I experience are the images of past happiness.[4]

Guglielmo Gatti, who has investigated these matters more carefully than most, suggests that, in his far from chaste bed, D'Annunzio was being very profligate with his favours even while he was actually writing such passionate letters to Elvira Leoni. In particular, something stronger than rumour showed that, at the very time of writing that letter, he was involved in the intense affair with Maria Gravina: she was to give birth to their daughter, Renata, in January of the following year, 1893.

Barbara and D'Annunzio saw each other for the last time on 2 May 1892. Nevertheless D'Annunzio continued to assert his undying love for her alone in subsequent letters, though, to judge from his reactions, her own letters became more sceptical until his letter of 3 November shows that he knows that his secret is out. On 15 November D'Annunzio wrote his final letter to her, adding in one farewell paragraph, no doubt with an eye to future publications:

---

[3] See particularly *Trionfo*, V. 2.

[4] Barbara's attitudes have to be judged from D'Annunzio's reactions in the letters written during this final ten months, and some imagination is required to complete the picture; see *Lettere a Barbara*, 423–71.

I shall be very grateful to you if you will return all my letters to me instead of burning them. Fulfil patiently this last act; and send them to me intact. I shall read them often; and I shall remember with inconsolable regret, for ever, until death. A love like ours, even when extinguished, is enough for a whole lifetime.[5]

Most of the letters to his former lover over that summer and autumn are full of self-pity, often declaring that he is ill, sad, or uncomfortable. The tone is not unlike that which characterized his last letters to Giselda Zucconi, and the farewell letter of 15 November 1892 concludes not unlike one of his final letters to Giselda:

I pursue my blind and vertiginous course towards who knows what precipice. I shall not turn round, except to gaze, with eyes veiled with tears, at the great love which is past, the great love lost for ever.

Goodbye, Barbarella.

Ariel.

As a postscript to the affair it is interesting to see that fate dealt as consistently with Barbara as it did with D'Annunzio's other lovers: in 1949, after a series of disastrous attachments, she ended her days in dire poverty in a Roman *pensione* run by nuns; she was 86 years old. In 1935 penury had forced her to sell D'Annunzio's letters.

Barbara's successor, Maria Gravina, was the wife of Count Fernando Anguissola di San Damiano. Thirty-one years of age when she met D'Annunzio, she was already the mother of four children. The couple began their affair by meeting surreptitiously for a while in a small Neapolitan hotel until, in May 1892, Count Anguissola lost a large part of his fortune in financial speculation, and was forced to retreat from the relatively sophisticated luxury of Naples to his country estate. Maria Gravina refused to leave with her husband and rented herself a small apartment in Via Caracciolo, where she moved with her children and a maid. On 4 July she notified the growingly resentful Anguissola that she wanted a legal separation. This provoked him to increase his surveillance of the adulterous duo, and on 5 October 1892 he surprised them in the princess's rooms and brought a charge of adultery against both.[6]

At the same time, Maria Gravina's father cut off her personal income in order to prevent any more of it filtering though to her

---

[5] Ibid. 444.

[6] Gatti, *Le donne*, 110–43, documents these and subsequent events in Naples.

spendthrift lover; as a consequence she was unable to pay her rent. The feckless D'Annunzio, still combining indigence with extravagance, was unable to help financially, and, by 15 October, mother and children had been forced to leave Naples to retreat to the castle of Ottajano, where Maria Gravina's friend, the Princess Emma Gallone di Ottajano, took pity on her and gave her temporary accommodation. D'Annunzio then moved out of the city to a house at Resina, half-way between Ottajano and Naples, where he could certainly be nearer to Maria Gravina, but where he was also further from his many creditors. On 29 July 1893 D'Annunzio and Maria Gravina appeared in court, with their defence lawyer, Carlo Altobelli, to face the accusation of adultery; found guilty, they were condemned to five months in gaol.[7] The judgement of the court was confirmed after appeal, but in 1894, under one of the many amnesties granted by king and government, the sentence was lifted. The effect of the guilty verdict was to be felt later when D'Annunzio was elected member of parliament, but for the moment the two could go on living together as before.

In the meantime, true to form, the relationship was becoming artistically productive. Rather as the 'Peccato di maggio' had represented D'Annunzio's seduction of Donna Maria and foreshadowed the birth of their first child, so in the forced and rather gloomy 'La passeggiata' (The Stroll) of his next collection, *Il poema paradisiaco*, D'Annunzio described the elegant beauty of his latest Maria and, in the expert view of Guglielmo Gatti,[8] hinted at another 'sin', this time beneath the veiled skies of April:

> Non ad altro la nostra anima aspira
> che a una tristezza riposata, equale.
> Conosco il vostro portentoso male;
> e il dolore ch'è in voi forse m'attira
> più de la vostra bocca e dei capelli
>
> vostri, dei grandi medusèi capelli
> bruni come le brune foglie morte
> ma vivi e fieri come l'angui attorte
> de la Gòrgone, io temo, se ribelli,
> e pieni del terribile mistero.

---

[7] D'Annunzio's lawyer Carlo Altobelli was the same politician who was to reappear in 1887 as his political opponent for the constituency of Ortona a Mare.

[8] Gatti, *Le donne*, 119.

[Our soul aspires to nothing more
than to a constant restful sadness
I know your portentous troubles
and the grief which is in you perhaps attracts me
more than your sweet mouth and your hair,

that mass of Medusa hair,
dark as dark fallen leaves,
but vital and wild like the writhing
snakes of the Gorgon; I fear them rebellious
and full of terrible mystery.]

The poem continues with particulars of Maria's physical appearance, the red lock of hair which so distinguished her dark hair, for instance, increasing, like a fetish, his infatuation for the woman. It concludes with the allusion to the April affair and, in fashionable 'crepuscular' poetic vein, with a negative finale:

[. . .] Ed abbia i suoi
cieli velati Aprile, come ieri,

i suoi mari quieti, come ieri;
sí che possiamo noi recar lungh'essi
i lidi, o sotto gli alberi, sommessi
colloqui e sogni e taciti pensieri,
—o voi dal dolce nome che io non chiamo!—

perché voi non mi amate ed io non vi amo.

[[. . .] And let April
keep its skies veiled, like yesterday;

and its sea quiet, like yesterday;
so that along the shore and beneath
the trees we may continue in our hushed tones,
our talks and dreams and silent thoughts.
—Oh you of the sweet name that I do not invoke!—

For you love me not and I do not love you.]

The submissive tone of this and other contemporary poems may well also echo a mood dictated by the wretchedness of the situation in which the two found themselves. D'Annunzio had managed to persuade Maria Gravina to send her children back to their father's house, where at least they would be well looked after. Their absence also left the field clearer for sexual adventures. But there were other crises upon them. Among the letters exchanged between D'Annunzio and a rich Roman acquaintance, Pasquale Masciantonio, there is one which talks about the queues of creditors that were to become familiar to D'Annunzio, and to anyone in his vicinity, during the next twenty years:

Since this morning it has begun again, the lugubrious line of people to whom we owe money. Twenty times I've heard the door knocker, twenty times the uncouth voices, twenty times I have been suffocated by a suppressed and most bitter anger. Farewell. Whatever happens consider that I am simply the victim of a blind force, brutal and invincible. Farewell. I embrace you strongly. Your Gabriele.[9]

Yet Paolo Alatri reports that when Hérelle sent the poet 500 lire as an advance on the French translation of *L'innocente* (which was being serialized in *Le Temps* as *L'Intrus*), he spent the whole sum in one day on unnecessary luxuries. Amazingly D'Annunzio finds many defenders amongst his commentators, during the rather sordid affair with Maria Gravina, as though this great force of love, beyond his power to control, bringing in its train debts, hack work, and law-suits, were something to excite public compassion. For any reader in danger of succumbing to such compassion, it is worth recalling that, while his wife, Donna Maria Hardouin, was sitting in Rome with their three children, living a hand-to-mouth existence, D'Annunzio was not only declaring his indestructible new love for Maria Gravina, and simultaneously maintaining to Elvira that his bed would be eternally chaste for her, but there is also evidence that he was having an affair with another married woman, whom he called Moriccia, and with whom he was caught *in flagrante* by her husband some time in June.[10] And there were, according to Gatti, other women in the offing at the time.

However much his own shortcomings reduced him to poverty and wretchedness during these two Neapolitan years, and despite his complaints about the troubles which threatened to overwhelm him, those same self-inflicted crises allowed him, in his writings, to elaborate similar events in fictional form. In particular, as seen briefly in 'La passeggiata' he was able in the field of lyric poetry to develop themes which chimed with European Symbolism, and he thus foreshadowed the subsequently fashionable 'crepuscular' school

---

[9] G. Infusino publishes this and other relevant letters in his *D'Annunzio a Napoli*, esp. 80; the circumstances are discussed by Gatti, *GD'A* 119, and Alatri, *GD'A*, 109.

[10] Not much is known about Moriccia; Masci has a small note: *La vita e le opere*, 99; most biographers mention the affair, including Gatti, *Le donne*, 119.

of poetry in Italy. He was following the trend in Europe represented by the work of Maurice Maeterlinck and Catulle Mendès, as well as by some of the more submissive poems produced by Baudelaire, Rimbaud, and Verlaine. Regretful memories of serene days in the past are evoked in elegiac poems such as 'Alla nutrice' (To his Wet-Nurse), which opens the collection entitled *Poema paradisiaco*:

> Io forse piangerei ancora un pianto
> salùbre e forse ancora dal profondo
> mi sorgerebbe qualche antico e santo
> affetto, e mi parrebbe nel tuo canto
> ritrovar l'innocenza di quel biondo
> pargolo;—e lungi queste cose orrende!

> [Perhaps I would weep once more, health-giving
> tears, and perhaps once more some old and blessed
> affection would rise from somewhere deep within,
> and in your song I would seem to find again,
> the innocence of that fair-haired
> infant—and away with these horrors!]

That some of this poetry is more than usually fashionable (rather than felt or 'inspired') is clear from a poem such as 'Nuovo messaggio', originally published in Scarfoglio's *Mattino* on 16 April, at the precise time he was in triumphant mood after his successful assault on Maria Gravina's emotional defences:

> [. . .] Io mi sento
> morire. E' questa, è questa oggi la sola
> verità. Non so dirti altra parola
> che questa. Cade ogni proponimento,
>
> mi lascia ogni speranza. Tutto è vano.

> [[. . .] I feel myself dying. This, this alone
> is today the only truth. I can tell you nothing
> beyond this. All resolutions fall away,
>
> all hope abandons me. All is vanity.]

On 9 January 1893 Maria Gravina gave birth to a daughter, Eva Renata Adriana, to whom D'Annunzio added the pet names Cicciuzza and Sirenetta; the girl was to prove a great help to him in his later years, notably after the serious injury to his eye in World War One. In turn, though his attitude towards her varied according to his moods, D'Annunzio seems to have been more affectionate to Renata than towards any of his other relatives or dependants. His letters to her, sometimes enclosed with toys, biscuits, or sweetmeats, are dotingly ordinary; from the Capponcina he writes on 3 October 1898:

Dear, dear Cicciuzza,

Write a long, sweet letter to you poor Daddikins [*papaletto*] who is very sad and hasn't heard news of you for a long while.

What are you doing? How are you? Are you becoming prettier and prettier? Do you think of me?

What would you like me to send you?

Tell me if you would like me to send you another doll or some other toy. Tomorrow I shall send you a box of biscuits.

Kiss Mama for me. I send you so many, so many, so many kisses on your little flower of a face.

Your Daddikins.[11]

The child's first months of life caused him no little anxiety because of an illness, which he was to recall movingly a quarter of a century later in his *Notturno*.[12] While the sentiments here and in contemporary letters to Maria Gravina may seem tender it is salutary to recall that by October 1898 he was already in the middle of his passionate affair with Eleonora Duse.

To add to the melancholy experiences attaching to his 'grand' amore' for Maria Gravina, he was recalled to Pescara by the death of his father. For years he had been signing promissory notes or paying off debts incurred in his father's name. Francesco Paolo D'Annunzio was, after his own gross fashion, as dissolute as his son, and, in *Il trionfo della morte*, where life and fiction so often coincide, Gabriele seemed not only to recognize this, but also to acknowledge the fact that he had inherited his father's fleshly gene. Some commentators, including Guglielmo Gatti, have suggested that the personalized reference to a recognizably 'Dannunzian' family, made widely known by the serialization of the *Trionfo* in the *Mattino* after 12 February 1893, helped to bring on the heart attack which finished off Francesco Paolo.[13] In particular, the hateful description of Giorgio Aurispa's father, which Francesco Paolo had

---

[11] Raffaele Tiboni publishes other delicate letters of D'Annunzio to his little daughter, full of a rare if short-lived affection, and unlike anything else in D'Annunzio's work. See *Lettere di D'Annunzio a Maria Gravina ed alla figlia Cicciuzza*, ed. R. Tiboni (Pescara, 1978), here particularly 13.

[12] See *Notturno, Prose di ricerca*, ii. 404.   [13] Gatti, *GD'A* 127.

read that spring, might have seemed only too lifelike. Here, for example, is part of D'Annunzio's observation and description of the father-figure in that novel:

Flesh, flesh, this brutish thing, full of veins, tendons, ligaments, glands, bones, full of instincts and needs; flesh, sweating and stinking; flesh becoming deformed, sick, covered in sores, callouses, wrinkles, pimples, warts, hairs. This brute thing, flesh thrived in him with a sort of impudence, producing in his delicate neighbour at table an impression almost of revulsion. 'It wasn't like that ten, fifteen years ago, it wasn't like that', Giorgio thought. 'I well remember it wasn't. It seems as though this increase in latent brutality had been unsuspected, and had gradually come to fullness in his father. I, I am the son of this man!' (*Il trionfo*, II. 1)

The disdainful Giorgio Aurispa (the 'delicate neighbour at table') imagines his father struck by cardiac arrest, as though from the blow of some invisible hammer, wonders whether his mother would be sorry, meditates on the former youth and love of his parents, and declares his hatred for this man whose germ of sensuality he feels within himself. Not surprisingly, Georgina Harding would excise from her translation of the novel both the physical description and the Freudian reflections on the son's hatred for his father. That Oedipus complex manifested itself with variations in much of the poet's work during the remainder of his literary career.

Whatever the truth of Gatti's hypothesis concerning the possible provocation of the heart atttack, it is a fact that, despite a flood of telegrams warning of his father's imminent demise, D'Annunzio left Naples only after receiving the final communication announcing that his father was dead. A few years earlier it had required much less to recall him from the irksome duties of the Macao barracks to his father's bedside. In Pescara Francesco Paolo had been living in the Villa del Fuoco with a succession of mistresses, gradually spending not only the money he had inherited personally from Antonio D'Annunzio, the uncle who had adopted him and his family, but also the inheritance left to him in trust for his own two sons, Gabriele and Antonio. The portrait in *Trionfo della morte* continues remorselessly:

This father had a mistress, a hairdresser who had been in the service of the family, a lost woman, greedy in the extreme. For her and for their bastard children he dissipated all his substance without any restraint, neglecting his business, his lands, selling crops at a low price to the first comer, just to have ready money. He reached such a pass at times, reached such a pass, that the necessities of life were sometimes missing at home, and he refused to give a dowry for his younger daughter, who had been engaged for such a long time. He met every remonstration with shouts, insults and at times the most contemptible acts of violence. (*Il trionfo*, II. 8)

The passage is fictional, but the coincidences with reality are so strong that it is easy to believe that here, as in so much of D'Annunzio's work, the author is reflecting autobiographical experiences. The style of the passages concerning the father-figure is also a revelation. The repetition, for instance, of *giungeva*, 'he reached such a pass, reached such a pass', adds little to the objective description of the father, but it does show D'Annunzio's almost spluttering disgust at having to recall his character. The Villa del Fuoco and other family possessions had to be sold to pay off the dead man's debts. Only by using his mother's dowry was D'Annunzio able to prevent the sale of the family home in Corso Manthoné.

The harrowing situation was recalled by the poet many years later in his *Libro segreto*, where there are further regrets that the sale of the family properties also took with them 'images of childhood and adolescence'.[14] Yet, twenty years after the death of his father and the sale of the family goods, during a commemoration of his fellow poet, Giovanni Pascoli in 1912, D'Annunzio used the words *splendida miseria* ('poverty-stricken splendour') to describe the life he was living during these two years. That comment coincided with the famous account of his first meeting with his 'brother poet', when D'Annunzio was actually staying in the old harness room of the Villa Borghese, which his friend Adolfo De Bosis, as official receiver of the bankrupt Borghese family effects, had let him have as a *pied-à-terre*.[15] But it is difficult to see much splendour, poverty-stricken or otherwise, in the squalid and harassed existence D'Annunzio was leading. On 29 July came the joint sentence to five months in prison for adultery; later that year he was to be taken to court by his wife seeking legal separation and maintenance for their children; and Maria Gravina, no doubt with an eye to the future, also filed a paternity suit against him to safeguard Renata's (and her own) future.

[14] The description of his regrets becomes almost poignant in *Il libro segreto, Prose di ricerca*, ii. 898.

[15] The account of the meeting of the two poets and further details of D'Annunzio's poverty-stricken splendour in the vast harness room are given in his *Contemplazione della morte, Prose di ricerca*, iii. 216–17.

Not for the first time D'Annunzio's creditors besieged his house at Resina, and on 6 October D'Annunzio wrote again to Pasquale Masciantonio to say that the bailiffs had taken all his possessions and sold them to pay off his debts.[16] Simultaneously, Maria Gravina was undergoing various nervous crises (one of which involved her in a suicide attempt), not least since she suffered from what Paolo Alatri calls morbid jealousy, because of what she suspected were her lover's other affairs.[17] D'Annunzio's friends were urging him to distance himself from Gravina, not only because they generally disliked her, but also because, at least without D'Annunzio's presence, Maria Gravina's family might have helped her in her destitution. Gatti has published a letter revealing that D'Annunzio was desperate enough to have to ask his former mistress Olga Ossani for a hand-out to assist him in some of his financial difficulties:

My situation is most grave. There is a lady here stressed by all kinds of adversity and unrelenting struggles, and there is a poor child, not many days old, whose mother gives a milk to which oftentimes grief adds a bitter taste. And I am here, constrained to continuous effort, which causes me no little amazement, while my sensitivity, already morbid, has sharpened so much that at times fear of sudden madness assails me.[18]

Left with only the clothes they stood up in, the two lovers had to make a swift decision. On 11 December D'Annunzio departed from Resina for Pescara, and Maria Gravina took Renata to live in Rome, in an apartment belonging to Pasquale Masciantonio. Their woes were far from over.

During the two years spent in Naples, D'Annunzio's rate of composition had slowed a little. Nevertheless he had written the *Odi navali*, composed most of the poems which make up the *Poema paradisiaco*, and written a good part of the *Trionfo della morte*, which was launched by Treves in March 1894. Apart from these three

[16] The letter is reported by most of his biographers: see Gatti, *GD'A* 131; Masci, *La vita e le opere*, 105–6, lists and summarizes several other documents of the time reflecting D'Annunzio's wretched situation.

[17] Alatri, *GD'A*, 124; Alatri's account includes most previous references to D'Annunzio's disastrous domestic arrangements at the time. It might be added that, months before, a letter from the poet to Hérelle, dated 18 Jan. 1893, seeks to excuse his failure to work on *La nemica* (The Enemy)—an enterprise which was subsequently amalgamated into the *Trionfo della morte*—by reference to his unnerving domestic circumstances and to the bitterness of his 'friend' (Maria Gravina), who had just given birth to their own 'intrus', Renata; see *Lettere a Georges Hérelle*, 85–6.

[18] Gatti, *GD'A* 125; Gatti does not give the source of the undated letter.

works he was also engaged on the kind of journalism which had paid so well in Rome, though in Naples he was rewarded with only 20 lire per article (which he pretentiously insisted on referring to as *venti Luigi* (20 louis)). But, more than this, he was consolidating his previous work. Partly to make a little money, for instance, he put out a popular paperback edition of short stories selected from the original *San Pantaleone* volume; at the same time he was also concerned to produce definitive editions of *L'innocente* (written earlier at Francavilla), *Giovanni Episcopo* (produced initially at Rome), the *Elegie romane* (of which a few later poems were written in Naples), and the *Intermezzo di rime*, which in April 1894 followed the publication of the *Trionfo della morte*.

Under the direction of Edoardo Scarfoglio and Matilde Serao, *Il mattino* had a right-wing bias. For the most part D'Annunzio's articles were politically anodyne, but in 1892 the increasingly fashionable philosophy of Nietzsche, which had already been present in the serialized *L'invincibile*, influenced him to publish an item entitled 'La bestia elettiva' (The Elective Beast) which both chimed with the Scarfoglio line and presented a garbled version of Nietzschean and Darwinian ideas. In view of D'Annunzio's later political career, within and outside parliament (in 1897 he would be elected member of parliament for his local constituency), it is important to examine what his opinions were at this time. It should also be noted that these ideas became fundamental to his thinking and did not simply form part of his hack work for *Il mattino*; so much may be deduced from the way they influenced the immense poetic labour of the *Laudi*, which began to germinate in his mind after 1894.

'La bestia elettiva' appeared in *Il mattino* on 25 September 1892.[19] Democracy, in the author's view, was anomalous, since it tried to depress to the lowest common factor those virtues and privileges which had been legitimately acquired by an élite few. It was fortunate, he declared with some irony, that universal suffrage ensured that the state was not only an ignoble, but also a precarious, edifice. Statements of this kind may have been intended by D'Annunzio merely to shock his readers, since a form of democracy seemed manifestly to be working in other countries, but in Italy it was true that

---

[19] The article is available in Infusino's *D'Annunzio a Napoli*, 153–62; extracts keeping alive the controversial opinions were published in GD'A, *Pagine disperse*, ed. A. Castelli (Rome, 1913), 544.

democracy was still in its infancy. Corruption had already begun to enter the system and formed a major item of debate in newspapers of both right and left tendencies, as well as in the fiction of such leading authors as Luigi Capuana and Federico De Roberto. The theme had also been taken up by the disreputable Pietro Sbarbaro, whose novel *Regina o Repubblica* (Queen or Republic) had portrayed parliament as a sink of iniquity, controlled by a combination of bully-boys at the head of a crowd of rabble. Sbarbaro's book sold in massive numbers. From Carducci onwards powerful voices had been railing against the decline in morals and patriotic sentiment which had come about since unification. The corollary of such impressions and beliefs was that Italy needed strong guidance to lift her from the slough into which she had fallen following the glory, heroism, and enthusiasm which had brought about her unification.

D'Annunzio's views in 'La bestia elettiva' were not far removed from such nationally accepted opinions. Other ideas from his essay were to recur in his political speeches and writings, particularly in the five years preceding the turn of the century:

Men will be divided into two races. To the superior race, which shall have risen by the pure energy of its will, all shall be permitted; to the lower, nothing or very little. The greatest sum of well-being shall go to the privileged, whose personal nobility will make them worthy of all privileges.[20]

D'Annunzio here makes a clear distinction between the hereditary nobility, the 'loinless heirs', of ancient, decadent families, pointing instead to an 'interior sovereignty' which guarantees personal liberty. The true nobleman, in D'Annunzio's sense, would never soil his hands with a voting slip, and so for the moment had to renounce his right to rule. The rather sinister declarations are left thus suspended, presumably in the expectation of greater days to come. As for the populace, he continues, their position would remain as it had always been. 'The plebeians remain slaves, condemned to suffer, as much in the shadow of the feudal chimney stacks of the modern factory as in the shadow of ancient feudal towers. They will never feel at their shoulders the sense of liberty.' The sentiments would recur on a wider canvas later in D'Annunzio's literary as well as his political career.

[20] Infusino, *D'Annunzio a Napoli*, 158.

In spite of D'Annunzio's view that the chosen few were worthily destined to dominate, there are curious anomalies in his reasoning. It has been noted that *Il trionfo della morte* was imbued with Nietzschean ideas; alongside them in the novel, as a kind of leit-motiv filling the background of the 'hermitage' of San Vito, is the music of Wagner, appropriately his *Tristan und Isolde*, which was in great vogue at the time. *Il caso Wagner* was the title of a series of three articles which D'Annunzio published during July and August 1893 in the *Tribuna*. D'Annunzio was undoubtedly influenced by Nietzsche's pamphlet of the same title, a French translation of which had been issued in 1893. But whereas Nietzsche criticized Wagner for descending from heroic and aristocratic tones (in *Siegfried*) to democratic and socialist music (in *Parsifal*), D'Annunzio defended Wagner on the grounds that the artist necessarily expressed the spirit of his time. And herein lies what seems to be an inconsistency in D'Annunzio's views. Where one might expect him to have asserted the directive authority of the master spirit, he declared instead that it was the mood and habits present in a given epoch which deter-mined a work of art:

The century puts its stamp on all its artificers. It is not possible to resist the pressure of the public spirit. The general state of the customs of a society determines the species of its works of art, by tolerating only those which conform to it and eliminating the others by interposing a series of obstacles, renewing its assaults at every step of their development.[21]

Although the sentiments expressed seem contrary to D'Annunzio's apparent ambition to be always in the forefront of fashion, there may in fact be discernible here an unconscious admission, a truth which may also explain the frequent accusations against him of plagiarism. That is, while following fashion (or what he called the spirit of the times), he was attempting in his work to go beyond the current artistic ideal. Throughout his literary career D'Annunzio would set up great literary figures as targets, and he made no excep-tion for the fashionable authors who sped like comets across the skies of late nineteenth-century Europe. They, too, were fair game; he would write in their mode, but always tried to carry their skilled accomplishment one stage further with the aim of surpassing their achievements. In this attitude he was following the principles which

---

[21] The three articles on *Il caso Wagner* were published in the *Tribuna*, 23 July, 3 and 9 Aug. 1893. The quotation is taken from the last of these essays.

he had derived from Renaissance theories of imitation. In particular he seems to have been impressed by the kind of dynamic imitation or emulation advocated in the first decade of the sixteenth century by Cardinal Pietro Bembo in his *De imitatione*, and exemplified in such works as Bembo's *Asolani* and the *Prose della volgar lingua*. D'Annunzio admired the way that the Venetian scholar, faced by a crisis in Italian language and letters at the end of the fifteenth century, had proposed to raise vernacular culture to new heights by a dynamic imitation of the great writers of the past. Bembo's theory had been that, by first raising one's technique to the level of the best model available, it might be possible to push one's talents even further to new peaks of literary and linguistic achievement.[22]

One area in which D'Annunzio appeared to follow that humanist principle was in his emulation of the French Symbolists during the composition of *Il poema paradisiaco*, the collection which chronicles episodes in his affair with Maria Gravina. The poems take up where the *Elegie romane* left off, the waning of the affair with Barbara Leoni shading elegiacally into the submissive tones of the fundamentally unhappy association with Maria Gravina. The *Poema paradisiaco* is a collection which has puzzled critics since its inception. Was it merely an attempt to emulate the Symbolist poetry in vogue at the time? Or were the subdued tones of the poems a true reflection of D'Annunzio's state of mind, torn between his sexual drives (or what he termed his 'love'), and the emptiness which resulted from such self-indulgence? At the same time awareness that he was falling short of his artistic aims and ambitions depressed the mood of particular poems which apologized for his art. How far were those poems simply meant to be fashionable? Croce would argue, with justice, that this mattered little as long as their artistic merit was great enough. Nevertheless it is impossible not to address the question of 'sincerity of expression' if we are looking for authentic biographical traces in such poetry; equally, critics who mistakenly see autobiography in every line need to ask the same question.

If we consider some of the journalistic writings contemporary with the *Elegie*, where the arguments about sincerity may not be so controversial, it is possible to see moods not of humility and

---

[22] In the vernacular Bembo's principal models were Petrarch for verse and Boccaccio for prose; P. Bembo, *Prose della volgar lingua*, ed. C. Dionisotti (Turin, 1960), is the best edition of Bembo's works with a classic introduction by the editor.

submissiveness, but of anger and irritation with the world and D'Annunzio's fellow men. His expression in these slight essays is not on a Nietzschean scale, but often betrays petty annoyance with the Neapolitan scene. His articles in *Il mattino* have at times an irrationally polemical approach; one such was the review in that newspaper inspired by Pietro Mascagni's *Cavalleria rusticana*. D'Annunzio's attacks on Mascagni in the by now notorious article entitled 'Il capobanda' (The Band-master), which characterized the composer as a buffoon, dressed as a chocolate soldier, always well distanced from the world of art, seem to have been dictated by dyspepsia, rather than by any desire to write a critique of the opera. The review was published on 3 September 1892 and provoked an outcry, particularly, D'Annunzio mentioned in a letter to Barbara ten days later, in the city of Venice, where there were demonstrations of popular protest. The same letter contained a cutting of his review: 'I send it to you to give you a laugh', D'Annunzio continued. That this was meant to hurt Mascagni could have been predicted from the content of an earlier letter, to Barbara Leoni, dated 3 December 1891, and written after the first night of Mascagni's *Amico Fritz*.[23] D'Annunzio seems to have been jealous of Mascagni's popularity: 'Modern art', he wrote, in that letter of 13 September 1892, 'is religious; it requires humble and patient worshippers'; he declared himself happy at what he said was a disdainful reception by the Neapolitan audience, 'happy at this castigation, inflicted on a bestial artificer by the very bestial public which raised him to the stars a few months ago'. D'Annunzio boasted in the letter of his 'ferocious propaganda which had contributed heavily to the fall of Mascagni's gross opera'.[24] There is an ironic footnote to the incident: somehow reconciled with D'Annunzio, Mascagni was, twenty years later, employed by the poet on the desperate task of putting to music the unproducible play *La Parisina*. According to Aldo Rossi, Mascagni went to it with a will ('setting even the commas to music', D'Annunzio said), and producing a marathon score. Subsequently, in an erudite article which Mascagni wrote on the adaptation of the piece, he pointed out that the play was unperformable as an opera lasting from four to five hours. Indeed, when *Parisina* was put on at La Scala, Milan on 15 December 1913, the performance ended at three in the morning; it was, to the author's great regret, produced

[23] For these letters, see *Lettere a Barbara*, 404–5 and 462.   [24] Ibid. 462.

in a form abbreviated by the deletion of the final act.[25] The critical reception of *Parisina*, according to Gatti, was not warm, though later the text without music had a good welcome from the audience in Rome's Teatro Argentina. Giuseppe Sozzi remarked that the inevitable comparisons with Mascagni's *Cavalleria rusticana* were made during and after the performance, the very opera which, after its brilliant success in 1890, first provoked D'Annunzio's irrational attacks on Mascagni.[26]

Signs of irritability are visibile, too, in the many allusions in his correspondence to what he considered the mean-minded Neapolitans, an attitude which culminated in his attempt to impose the title *Margheritae ante porcos* (Pearls before Swine) upon the new anthology, which was, in fact, to come out as *Poema paradisiaco*. Emilio Treves refused to use a title which would, he observed, simply antagonize potential readers. In a letter of 3 May 1893 to Georges Hérelle, announcing that he would send the Frenchman a copy of the poems, D'Annunzio dwells scornfully on the publisher's 'fastidious insistence that he change the title, which Treves considered too injurious to the reader'.[27] That attitude may well have been genuine. On the other hand, verse from the *Poema paradisiaco*, such as the above-mentioned 'Nutrice', regretting his lost innocence and infancy, must be regarded more cynically by the side of the final poems of *Elegie romane* written contemporaneously and containing a wealth of sensuality.

There were other moods to his compositions at the time: on 26 November 1892 Admiral Simone Pacoret de Saint-Bon died in Rome, and D'Annunzio seized the occasion to put into verse some of the enthusiasm he had earlier devoted to the essays in *L'armata d'Italia*. His six *Odi navali*, published to commemorate the admiral, were supplemented in the following year by four other poems and

---

[25] Pietro Mascagni's essay was entitled 'Come nacque *La Parisina*' and appeared in *La lettura*, 14/1 (Jan. 1914), 15–24; to this should be added his interestingly analytical letters: 'Mascagni, Parisina e D'Annunzio', ed. A. Lualdi, *Quaderni dannunziani*, 30 (1965), 67–100. Cf. A. Rossi, 'D'Annunzio giovane, il verismo e le tradizioni popolari', in E. Tiboni and L. Abrugiati (eds.), *D'Annunzio giovane e il verismo* (Pescara, 1979), 41–58; Mascagni cut the final act, but Rossi argues that he would have done better to omit the first, which D'Annunzio plagiarized from Carducci's edition of *Cacce in rima* (Bologna, 1896). Other details of the relationship with Mascagni are discussed in G. Celati's *Il vate e il capobanda: D'Annunzio e Mascagni* (Rome, 1992).

[26] See Gatti, *GD'A*, esp. 280, and Sozzi, *GD'A*, 256.

[27] *Lettere a Georges Hérelle*, 98.

published along with the *Poema paradisiaco*. Differences in tone between the two disparate collections show again that D'Annunzio's search for humility and goodness in the lyrics of the *Poema paradisiaco* was fashionable rather than deep-rooted. By contrast, for instance, the *Odi navali* have an understandably nationalistic flavour, with asides such as the following from '26 novembre 1892':

> Marinai d'Italia, giustissimo orgoglio del sangue
> nostro, eletto fiore di giovinezza cresciuto
> lungo i lidi ove i padri legarono l'alte galee
> vittoriose, udite, marinai d'Italia, speranza
> prima!

> [Italian sailors, most justly the pride of our blood,
> chosen flower of our youth, raised along the shores
> where our fathers tied the tall victorious galleys,
> hear my voice, sailors of Italy, first hope of us all.]

Less dogmatic but more original are his admiring descriptions of individual ships. Exhilarating, for instance, is the ode dedicated to 'Una torpediniera nell'Adriatico' (A Torpedo-Boat in the Adriatic), which has about it something of the vitality of Carducci's steam engine in the ode to Satan:

> Naviglio d'acciaio, diritto veloce guizzante
> bello come un'arme nuda,
> vivo, palpitante
> come se il metallo un cuore terribile chiuda;

> tu che solo al freddo coraggio dell'uomo t'affili
> come l'arme su la cote,
> e non soffri i vili
> su la piastra ardente del ponte che il fremito scote.

> [Craft of steel, straight, swift, skimming
> lovely as a naked weapon,
> alive, quivering,
> as though the metal enclosed a terrible heart;

> sharpened on man's cold courage alone,
> like a weapon on the whet-stone,
> you suffer no coward on the burning plates
> of the bridge, which throbs with the pulsations.]

When D'Annunzio came to sail in torpedo-boats during World War One, the evocation of that original vessel must have returned to him, as it certainly did on 21 July 1915, when he quoted the poem during an address to the survivors of the *Amalfi*, torpedoed by the Austrian navy off the mouth of the River Isonzo. The words also foreshadowed his later delight in the speed of the MAS, the torpedo-boat given him by the Italian navy after his retirement to the Vittoriale in 1922.[28]

D'Annunzio, having been driven from Resina by his creditors, retreated back to Michetti's convent home in January 1894. Once there, contemplating Maria Gravina's invidious situation, he suspected that she would have a miserable time in Rome, not least because of society gossip, and the enmity of her own class. His few visits to her in Masciantonio's apartment confirmed his fears and, perhaps out of some rare feeling of compassion, at some time between mid-April and May 1894, Maria Gravina and Renata were invited to join him in Francavilla where they were to remain until the autumn of 1897. By the time of their arrival in the Abruzzi, D'Annunzio had written the final pages of *Il trionfo della morte*, the novel which had been on the stocks for the previous five years, first as the serialized novel *L'invincibile*, commissioned and encouraged by Vincenzo Morello for his *Tribuna illustrata*. The original had been interrupted at chapter 16 in 1890, partly, as has been noted, because as a conscript D'Annunzio was too distracted to continue the work, partly because its host, the *Tribuna illustrata*, was about to fold,[29] but also because his passion for Barbara Leoni, which filled the original sixteen chapters, had changed. Ippolita Sanzio, the new heroine of the *Trionfo della morte* would evolve into a composite being, made up of Barbara–Elvira and Maria Gravina, and the tone of the completed novel would show a development from the abandoned passion of those earlier experiences to the final suicidal outcome which was probably a closer reflection of the more doleful events associated with his Neapolitan years.

The psychology underlying the *Trionfo* had also undergone several changes in the intervening five years; in particular, D'Annunzio had concentrated for a while before September 1893 on a kind of Darwinian notion of the ineluctability of hereditary characteristics (hence the increasing self-hatred visible in his portrait of the father). A further 'solution' to the problem of the sterility and futility of

[28] See below pp. 308 and 367 for further details; see also Plate 17.
[29] See Morello, *GD'A* 55–6; Morello also publishes an interesting series of letters to himself from the poet which illustrate well D'Annunzio's mood of melancholy at the time of writing *Il trionfo della morte*.

social relationships, suggested in earlier drafts, was a return to his native, vigorous roots in the countryside, which in the case of his protagonist, Giorgio Aurispa, also happened to be the Abruzzi; that theme, too, had a strong part to play in the final version. But most importantly of all, in summer 1893 D'Annunzio became more closely acquainted with the doctrines of Nietzsche, which seemed to offer his hero, Aurispa, a way out of the labyrinth of sterile voluptuousness which he had at first entered willingly and joyfully.

Ultimately, in *Il trionfo della morte*, Aurispa fails as a 'superman' because sensuality eventually triumphs, Tristan overcomes Zarathustra; but in the next two novels, *Le vergini delle rocce* (The Virgins of the Rocks) and *Forse che sí forse che no* (Maybe, Maybe Not), Nietzschean ideas are more fundamental to the logic of the plot. It is therefore useful to observe at this stage that D'Annunzio's prefatory letter to the *Trionfo* is lightly imbued with Nietzschean reflections and, further, that as an epigraph to the whole book he quotes a famous aphorism from the German philosopher. The prefatory letter, it should be explained, is in effect a dedication to Michetti, whom he addresses throughout as 'Cenobiarca' (Ruler of the Convent). 'We bend our ear to the voice of magnanimous Zarathustra, O Ruler of the Convent; and we prepare in our art with certain faith, the advent of the *Übermensch*, the Superman. (From the Convent of Santa Maria Maggiore. Calends of April, 1894.)' The concluding aphorism, reproduced in the original German, is taken from Nietzsche's *Jenseits von Gut und Böse* (Beyond Good and Evil), and suggests that certain books have a dual interpretation, a dual effect which offers opposing values depending on whether the books serve the ignoble soul (lacking verve), or the noble soul (possessing a great vital inner force). 'In the first case those books are dangerous, corrosive and unhinging, in the second they are heraldic peals which invite the most valorous to give proof of their courage.'

More important to D'Annunzio than the superficial attention he paid to Nietzschean ideas is the stress which that prefatory letter laid on two technical or stylistic aspects of his own writings. The first is his rather vague statement, much quoted by subsequent critics of his work, that it was the function of language in the book 'not to imitate but to *continue* Nature' (*non imitare ma* continuare *la Natura*), a view which becomes clearer in the images and language of his better lyric poetry, as may be seen when *Alcyone* is considered. The second point is a corollary of this, and one which smacks of his Bembist imitative principles: he intends to create a new prose which will be worthy of the great language of Italy, traceable back through its Latin roots to Livy, and exalted by the great medieval writers, not least of whom was Giovanni Boccaccio. Implicit in his purpose was a nationalist bias, a desire to raise the language from the slough of decadence into which it had fallen. Those ideas were to be elaborated in the next four or five years and given form in his powerful and fashionable prose and verse. Osbert Sitwell was not alone in believing that D'Annunzio was during his lifetime 'the man who had done more for their language than any writer since Dante'. Indeed Italy's most venerable academy, the *Crusca*, guardian of the national language, would honour the poet in 1915 by offering him membership.[30]

Autobiographical details from D'Annunzio's recent past were incorporated at various levels in *Il trionfo della morte*; their fictional translation is, as ever, intriguing. The actual plot of the novel is distinguished by three main themes: first, the sensual love of Giorgio Aurispa for the beautiful but barren Ippolita Sanzio, married to an odious and despised husband; second, the frustrated attempts by Giorgio, after the sophisticated emptiness of Rome, to reintegrate himself into his provincial environment; and finally the Nietzschean theme, visible in long interior monologues which reinforce the conflict in the protagonist between his will and his periodic abandonment to instinctive sexuality. The second theme is rendered turbulent for the hero by contrasts between traditional peasant wholesomeness and the immoral decadence typical of his urban experiences, as well as in his being assailed by resentful thoughts that he has inherited his father's lubricious genes. The three motifs are bound together in the figure of Ippolita Sanzio. By the end of the novel she has become the symbol of sterility and carnal obsession, selected and trained for libidinous exploitation by Giorgio, and finally overshadowing his life to such a degree that his only way of self-assertion is a suicidal plunge over the cliff which has dominated their idyllic stay in the Abruzzi. As a background to the action, it should be added that there are periodic glimpses of Wagner's influence (through the atmospheric music of the recently published *Tristan und Isolde*) blending ideas of Romantic love with Nietzschean heroism.

---

[30] O. Sitwell, *Noble Essences* (London, 1950), 114; Sitwell exaggerates, probably because he was unaware of other Italian writers, notably Alessandro Manzoni, but the effective point is made.

Although the Nietzschean search for a heroic solution does not in *Il trionfo della morte* resolve Giorgio Aurispa's dilemma, the text contains many allusions to the German philosopher which emphasize the concept of the hero as a being free of ordinary restraints, the view expressed in germ in *Giovanni Episcopo*. It is not difficult to see D'Annunzio applying the same ideas to his own life. There is, for instance, a striking episode in *Il trionfo della morte* where his *alter ego*, Giorgio Aurispa, meditates on the rural beauty and the glorious luminosity of the harvest festival, coming so soon after the heat, sweat, and dust of the grotesque pilgrimage to Casalbordino (which has about it something of the grimness of Zola's *Lourdes*). Thought is now interwoven with the pastoral images before him, and, dazzled by the beauty of the sunset, Giorgio allows his thoughts to wander to the ideal hero who wrests from life only what he desires:

Where breathes the human being to whom the whole day, from dawn to dusk, is a festival, consecrated by a new conquest? Where lives the dominating hero, crowned with the crown of laughter, that crown of smiling roses of which Zarathustra spoke? Where lives the strong, tyrannical dominator, free from the yoke of any false morality, sure in the feeling of his own power, convinced that the essence of his person overcomes in value all accessory attributes, determined to raise himself above Good and Evil by the pure energy of his will, capable of forcing life to maintain its promises to him? (*Il trionfo*, V. 3)

Other passages harp upon the superiority of the Word of Zarathustra and the philosopher's innate wisdom concerning such details as 'the laughable and wretched feminization of the ancient European soul, the monstrous reflorescence of Christianity amongst the decrepit races'. Giorgio Aurispa himself lends an ear to the axioms which affirm Life, or consider grief as the discipline of the strong, axioms which repudiate all faith, especially moral faith, and proclaim instead the justice of inequality, glorify the instinct for struggle, domination, and power, and finally exalt the forces which operate for generation and fecundation, 'all virtues of the Dionysiac, the victor, the destroyer, the creator'.

Ippolita, by contrast, 'feminizes' Giorgio. Her barren womb is a deadly furnace in which his seed is destroyed, his energies which should be directed towards higher spiritual ambitions are absorbed instead by her sensual embraces. But more than this, the instinct for self-perpetuation seems to Giorgio to be the only true motive for sexual love; simply to enjoy Ippolita as a sex object calls into question their entire relationship:

Why was he then tied to the barren woman by such a strong bond? Why did the terrible 'will' of the Species persist in him with such ferocity as to demand that he tear the vital tribute from that womb, already devastated by disease and incapable of conceiving? His love lacked its first *raison d'être*: the affirmation and development of life beyond the limits of the individual existence. (*Il trionfo*, V. 2)

To the modern reader, these unspoken thoughts begin to have about them the tone of a papal encyclical against contraception. Nevertheless the love affair continues, until Aurispa's failure to break the spell leads to the suicide which concludes the story. D'Annunzio did not commit suicide (if anything Barbara Leoni might have been the more likely to kill herself), but psychologically autobiographical elements in the novel are clear on every page. In particular the aspirations of the rich and independent Giorgio Aurispa (untroubled by such petty debts and preoccupations as those which afflicted Gabriele D'Annunzio) were manifestly the same aspirations to which D'Annunzio would have liked to devote himself had he had the freedom to do so. To this extent the Nietzschean reflections were an accurate representation of D'Annunzio's attitudes at the time and a forecast of his future development.

The novel was D'Annunzio's first real breakthrough into the British market, and it is interesting to consider the original English translation in its strange role as the vehicle for such popularity. In the version of the novel done by Georgina Harding in 1896, all references to Nietzsche and Nietzschean philosophy were excised, as were references to Ippolita's illness, to her role as a sex object, to Aurispa's father, and to Ippolita's husband (largely unnoticed anyway in the original). Add to this the fact that Miss Harding also avoided any translation of the word *gamba* (leg), *letto* (bed), and a dozen other less frequently used words which might have had any physical or olfactory quality,[31] and the extent of the bowdlerization becomes clearer. Her efforts had reduced *Il trionfo della morte* to little more than an innocuous romance. In the late nineteenth century such bowdlerization undoubtedly helped Heinemann in his

---

[31] Even the breeze which seemed to blow through the very *pori del legno* (the pores of the wood) had to have the image of the pores omitted in Miss Harding's translation; this is the impoverished version which regrettably was foisted upon an unaware public in 1988.

sales, and so popularized D'Annunzio's name for a brief time in Anglophone circles, but the bowdlerized version which reduces the complexity of the plot to suit the lowest common intelligence had less appeal for more discriminating readers, and certainly, apart from its curiosity value, it has no appeal in its modern resuscitation.[32]

In its time *Il trionfo della morte* enjoyed good sales, and helped to spread D'Annunzio's fame in Europe. In particular he enjoyed a better reputation in France, where, as has been noted, his novel *L'innocente* had been translated by Georges Hérelle. After the publication of *Il trionfo della morte*, Hérelle was to enter D'Annunzio's sphere of influence more frequently, and, in view of his value from this point onwards as a biographical witness during the next decade or so (when an epistolary argument finally demolished friendship and co-operation), it may be useful to understand his situation.[33] Georges Hérelle taught philosophy in a secondary school at Vitry-le-François; he was also a great Italophile, and during a holiday in Naples in 1891 regularly took as his daily newspaper the *Corriere di Napoli*, in which he was able to read the serialization of *L'innocente*. Enthused by the story he began to make a translation for his own amusement, and, preparatory to returning to France, he took out a subscription to the newspaper. He must have written to D'Annunzio communicating these details in or before December 1891; there is extant an encouraging letter from D'Annunzio, dated Christmas 1891, requesting examples of Hérelle's work.[34] By 14 February 1892, D'Annunzio had declared that he 'could not have desired a more penetrating, more faithful or more sensitive translator'.[35] He was soon to become obsessed with the possibility of new fame, in France; and the completed translation of *L'innocente* began to appear in serial form in *Le Temps* after 24 September 1892, with its new title, *L'Intrus*. In 1893 the novel was published as a separate volume by Calmann-Lévy, a publishing house which maintained its Dannunzian interests until after World War Two.

[32] The reworking of the *Trionfo* has been discussed at some length in J. R. Woodhouse, 'La fortuna inglese del *Trionfo della morte*', in E. Tiboni and L. Abrugiati (eds.), *Il trionfo della morte* (Pescara, 1981).

[33] Information about Hérelle is available in G. Tosi's edition and translation of the correspondence between D'Annunzio and his French translator, *GD'A à Georges Hérelle: Correspondance* (Paris, 1946). An interesting account, which also includes letters exchanged by the four, is available in R. Giglio, *Per la storia di un'amicizia: D'Annunzio, Hérelle, Scarfoglio, Serao* (Naples, 1977).

[34] *Lettere a Georges Hérelle*, 35.   [35] *GD'A à Georges Hérelle*, 113.

During the next four years Hérelle translated all of D'Annunzio's major prose fiction into French; after 1897 Hérelle's translations of the poet's theatrical work were also published in major French journals, notably the *Revue de Paris* and *Revue des deux mondes*. From the outset, French reviewers were kind to D'Annunzio; two critics in particular, Eugène-Melchior de Vogüé in the *Revue des deux mondes* (in January 1895) and René Doumic in the *Revue blanche* (the following March) praised him to the heights. That welcome publicity became the basis for D'Annunzio's later penetration of France and French society following his exile from Italy in 1910. More immediately, and more importantly, considering the dire financial situation in which he and his relatives and dependants were floundering, a steady trickle of money began to arrive from French publishers.

D'Annunzio wrote assiduously to Hérelle during the three years following the Frenchman's original enquiry of December 1891. After D'Annunzio's reply from Naples, offering Christmas greetings for the season, Hérelle was bombarded with pages of self-centred information, not all of it accurate, often on notepaper headed QUALIS ARTIFEX VALEO ('What a worthy craftsman I am').[36] In the famous letter of 14 November 1892, for instance, D'Annunzio keeps up the pretence of having been born on board the brigantine *Irene* in the waters of the Adriatic. Even his date of birth, possibly to increase his reputation as an infant prodigy, is there given by D'Annunzio as 1864. The letter itself was sent from 'The Medici Palace' at Ottajano, and its contents range from a description of the poet's status as that wonder child, to his deification after publishing *Canto novo*: 'Success was rapid and widespread; my name was on everyone's lips. Everyone sought me out, presented me with incense, proclaimed me god [mi proclamavano dio]. Women especially were very moved by it all.' The letter ends with a plea for royalties to be forwarded to him as soon as possible: 'The summer yachting has completely exhausted me.' The outrageous self-publicity becomes more understandable when one juxtaposes the names of Hérelle and an influential friend of his, Amédée Pigeon. In what is essentially the final paragraph of the letter, D'Annunzio sends his salutations to Pigeon and asks Hérelle to pass on his biographical details. Pigeon

---

[36] The words are D'Annunzio's variant on the Emperor Nero's dying words 'Qualis artifex pereo' (What a craftsman the world loses in me).

was thus presented with all the material for the brief critical bio-graphy of D'Annunzio which he published in the *Revue hebdomadaire*. It was for D'Annunzio a great public relations (or propagandistic) coup.[37] By 1894 the poet and Hérelle were on good terms and D'Annunzio, despite one or two quibbles about Hérelle's French, seemed at the time satisfied with his new-found fame in France. When the Frenchman decided to holiday in the north of Italy dur-ing the summer of 1894, D'Annunzio arranged to meet him early in September in Venice.

The poet's life with Maria Gravina was at the time full of nerv-ous crises; she was increasingly unpleasant to his friends and relat-ives, particularly to his sister Anna and to Michetti, who in turn continued to urge D'Annunzio to end his friendship with the woman. D'Annunzio had moved out of the convent to be with his new family in a nearby house, the Villa Mammarella, but his domestic situation during the period immediately before he left to meet Hérelle in Venice is visible in phrases such as 'I do not wish to talk about myself today. This is one of my days of black sadness.' In the same letter, of 6 August 1894, he refers to himself as 'a tormented man', in need of Hérelle's 'good and compassionate words'.[38] In the next letter, dated 18 August 1894, D'Annunzio describes his new friend as a Messiah bringing profound words and consolatory ges-tures. He is ready to confess his troubles to this 'unseen friend': 'These last weeks, my dear friend, have been very hard to me:— alone, face to face with a creature suffering from terrible nervous attacks which almost make her demoniacal, a being who wishes to possess me entirely, like a inanimate object, and whom I no longer love.'[39]

To add to the tale of woe, D'Annunzio also complained to Hérelle that the air was full of the continuous monotony of bells as Francavilla celebrated its saints' days. By contrast, thoughts of the peaceful canals and the harmonious squares of Venice 'remind him nostalgically of the vestibule of a paradise made from marble and gold'. In an earlier letter of 30 June 1894, D'Annunzio had

---

[37] See *Revue hebdomadaire* (24 June 1893), 596–613, where Pigeon's sketch is a word-for-word translation (there acknowledged as such by Pigeon) of D'Annunzio's letter; five days later D'Annunzio was able to write to Emilio Treves to underline the quality of Pigeon's article and the great success which *L'Intrus* was having in France.

[38] *GD'A à Georges Hérelle*, 191.   [39] Ibid. 192.

announced that he and Scarfoglio had acquired a fifty-three-ton yacht, and that he would be obliged to his French translator if he could forward an advance of his *droits d'auteur* for the work he had already published, implying that the money was needed for his new extravagance. The request was repeated in his following letter of 30 July 1894, where D'Annunzio also bemoans the presence of Maria Gravina: 'I'm not here alone; I'm with an invalid. She's almost insane and passes her time torturing me with unfeeling ferocity.'[40]

Scarfoglio had in fact purchased a yacht, though the impecunious D'Annunzio had no money of his own to put into such an enterprise. In response to his letters, Hérelle managed to send 150 lire in July 1894, to which D'Annunzio was able, at the beginning of September, to add an advance of 1,000 lire from Emilio Treves. This windfall, surprisingly sent without demur by the publisher, followed a typical begging letter from D'Annunzio which held out the prospect of a new novel, *Le tre principesse* (The Three Princesses). D'Annunzio told Treves that the work was nearing completion (and in fact under the new title of *Le vergini delle rocce* it was ready for publication nine months later), but Treves was, no doubt, also impressed by his author's spreading fame. D'Annunzio's self-publicity was paying off in all directions.

The poet and Hérelle must have arrived in Venice at more or less the same time, in mid-August. Leaving unpaid debts on all sides, D'Annunzio lavished luxurious hospitality on his French guest; Hérelle, in turn, introduced him to such French society and culture as there was to be found in Venice. During the many parties and social occasions which formed their round, D'Annunzio also met again Eleonora Duse, at that time occupied with her long affair with Verdi's librettist, Arrigo Boito. Letters from her to Boito show that she was an enthusiastic reader of D'Annunzio's, requesting copies of his latest works from the bookshops.[41] Those two new Venetian encounters, with Hérelle and Eleonora Duse, were to have lasting consequences for the poet's life and art.

Hérelle, not being a Nietzschean superman, had to return to his school-teaching and left Venice on 20 September 1894. Only three

[40] *Lettere a Georges Hérelle*, 152–8.
[41] P. Nardi, *Vita di Arrigo Boito* (Milan, 1942), 605 and *passim*, reproduces the atmosphere of La Duse's first requests for D'Annunzio's works; for her particular request see also E. Duse and A. Boito, *Lettere d'amore*, ed. R. Radice (Milan, 1979), 831.

days later, on 23 September, and again on 30 September, just two hours before finally leaving for Francavilla, D'Annunzio wrote affectionate letters to his new-found translator-friend. His mood was now more serene than before, a serenity which continued in the letters written following his return to Francavilla. There, back at the Villino Mammarella, D'Annunzio began to work seriously on his next novel, earlier announced to Treves as *Le tre principesse*. In fact, however, it was his wealthy friend Adolfo De Bosis who began to publish the renamed version, *Le vergini delle rocce*, in his glamorous new review, *Convito*, which, at 30 lire per volume (perhaps £75 at today's prices), was one of the most extravagant of the genre, containing illustrations by leading artists and contributions from Italy's most well-known littérateurs.[42] D'Annunzio was a leading light in promoting the journal, and rejoiced in the luxury of the thick, opulently designed, and richly illustrated tomes. It was he who wrote the *proemio* to the first volume, which came out in January 1895. In that proem he praised the journal's renewed vision of beauty and of Italy's grand tradition, which so contrasted with the philistinism and vulgarity which had spread over what he termed the great and privileged land where Leonardo and Michelangelo had once created their masterpieces. Dominant here amid the pleas to restore Beauty are strong nationalistic tones, both in oblique references to Italy's great artistic past and in the evocation of her 'Latin blood and Latin soil', of the 'hidden virtues of the race', of the 'ascendant force of ideals transmitted from our fathers', which D'Annunzio hoped might stem the barbaric flow ruining contemporary culture in the Peninsula.[43]

De Bosis's new journal was an important manifestation of high bourgeois culture, typical of its time, in much the same way as Sommaruga's journals had typified Rome's 'Byzantinism'. The sumptuous new volumes were, however, only sporadically or irregularly published. It was true that by June 1895 the *Convito* had fully serialized D'Annunzio's *Vergini delle rocce*, but Books X and XI (De Bosis insisted on calling the large fascicules 'books'), which should

[42] For a discussion of the birth of the *Convito* see E. Scarano, *Dalla 'Cronaca bizantina' al 'Convito'* (Florence, 1970); G. Gatti discusses the special role of D'Annunzio on the *Convito* in his 'Il *Convito* di Adolfo De Bosis', *Quaderni dannunziani*, 8–9 (1958), 41–6.

[43] The *proemio* is also available, in a slightly revised form, in *Prose di ricerca*, i. 453–8.

have been issued at the end of that year, took a further two years to produce, and finally came out in January 1898. The next volume, the twelfth, proved to be the last, taking a further ten years in the making; De Bosis, probably for want of other contributions, was by then reduced to printing an issue consisting solely of his own poetry. The volumes were too thick and lavish to be sustained, despite the fact that some very famous names were recruited as contributors to the first books. By definition, too, they were in all senses élitist tomes: they were expensive, directed at a limited readership, the thought behind the publication was the chauvinistic ideology expressed in D'Annunzio's *proemio*, and the contents were nationalistic, if not absolutely imperialistic. Typically, for instance, two famous explorers, Vittorio Bottego and Guido Boggiani (an ethnologist as well as a painter), contributed their experience of the kind of imperial exploration to which the British were more accustomed at that epoch; both were to die on expeditions, Bottego in Africa, Boggiani slain by Indians in South America.

The loss and dissipation of the artistic and intellectual talents of the *Convito*'s original contributors was exaggerated in its effect because those cultural pioneers had also found other activities with which to occupy themselves: Sartorio and Michetti had larger canvasses to fill, Giovanni Pascoli, after publishing in *Convito* his massive pioneering essay, 'Minerva oscura', was launched upon a career which would lead him to Bologna and Carducci's important Chair of literature, while Carducci himself, despite his support for De Bosis, was ageing rapidly and no longer able to contribute weightily to any journal. Not least of the distractions for D'Annunzio (though potentially he had whole volumes with which to feed De Bosis's presses), was the famous and inspirational voyage to Greece conceived by Scarfoglio for the autumn of 1895; Scarfoglio was to be accompanied by Pasquale Masciantonio, Guido Boggiani, D'Annunzio himself, and D'Annunzio's guest, Georges Hérelle. The sometimes bizarre journey and its consequences would divert D'Annunzio's literary attention and ambitions for the next decade.

But before leaving for Greece and the Aegean, D'Annunzio supervised the publication as a separate volume of *Le vergini delle rocce*, which had had a run in *Convito*. The new novel, published by Treves in July 1895 (with a publication date of 1896) was of a different order from his previous works. On 18 June 1895, during a dinner in Pescara, D'Annunzio had proposed a toast to contemporary political putrefaction, judged by the newspapers to be an unfortunate choice of subject. His brief discourse mentioned Charles Darwin and the profusion of life, 'and there is no more fervid and violent manifestation of life than putrefaction'. D'Annunzio therefore drank to contemporary decay and dissolution, 'from which will emerge the most splendid flowers! I drink to the roses which will flower from the blood.'[44] The new novel and D'Annunzio's burgeoning political aspirations accorded with the words of his brief toast to the company.

Indeed, the protagonist of *Le vergini delle rocce*, Claudio Cantelmo, in whom it is easily possible to see yet another side of D'Annunzio, is a more positive hero, with none of the inner turbulence, psychological or sexual, which helped to destroy Sperelli, Aurispa, or Hermil. Two aphorisms from Leonardo da Vinci, whose painting gives the book its title, introduce Book I of the novel: 'There can be no greater sovereignty than that over oneself', and 'Thou shalt be alone, thou shalt be wholly thine own'. Cantelmo, having left behind the youthful disorders of his earlier life, declares his awareness of his semi-divine mission:

The world is the representation of the sensitivity and thought of a few superior men, who have created, amplified and adorned it during the course of time, and who will continue to amplify and adorn it more and more in the future. The world, as it appears today, is a magnificent gift donated by the few to the many, by the free to the enslaved, by those who think and feel to those who have to work. And thus I recognized that my highest ambition lay in the desire to bring some ornament, to add some new value to this world of humanity which is eternally increasing in beauty and grief. (*Le vergini*, I. 1)

In short, Claudio Cantelmo sets himself a threefold mission: to achieve in his own person an ideal of a Latin *Übermensch*, to create a supreme work of art, and to father a messianic child who might carry his own potential as a 'Dominator' into the future. The child will be 'the King of Rome', 'He who must come' (*Colui che deve venire*). Another quotation from Leonardo helps his thinking: 'The receptacle of virtues shall be full of dreams and vain hopes.' And so most of the novel is spent by Cantelmo looking for a suitable vessel in which to plant his super-seed. He, in fact, returns to his roots in southern Italy, to court Violante, Massimilla, and

---

[44] The dinner and D'Annunzio's toast is reported by C. Antona-Traversi, *GD'A: Curriculum vitae*, i. 18.

Anatolia, the three beautiful daughters of Prince Capece-Montaga, last remnant of a decaying local aristocracy. The atmosphere of the old family palace is full of moral decadence and physical decay. In that environment, the prince has unlikely conversations with his guest, which help to reinforce Cantelmo's mad thesis, notably concerning the fall of the Bourbons, and the role and mission of the aristocracy. Continuing his quest for an adequate 'vessel', Claudio eventually rejects Massimilla (who becomes a nun), is rejected by Anatolia (strong in her own mission to protect her decaying house), and is about to launch his assault on the exquisite Violante, when the novel ends.

His readers might justifiably have felt cheated by the fragile quality of the plot and the bathos of the novel's finale, but D'Annunzio, true to his method of thinking in terms of a series of literary works, had in mind a cycle of three novels, and Cantelmo's adventures were to continue in the unwritten sequels. To the proposed trio he gave the overall title of *I romanzi del giglio* (The Novels of the Lily) in order to suggest their aspirations to pure, heroic love. *Le vergini delle rocce* was to be the first, to be followed by *La grazia* (Grace), and *L'annunciazione* (The Annunciation), 'which will be published in 1896'.[45] In *La grazia* he intended Anatolia to die and Violante to go mad, coming out of her madness towards the end of the book to give birth to The One, and then herself dying in the sequel, *L'annunciazione*. But there were no more novels of the lily, and the superman's plans, for the time being at least, were left on the shelf. Nevertheless, Claudio Cantelmo stands out amongst D'Annunzio's earlier protagonists as possessing new vitality, while at the same time proposing a more openly declared Nietzschean design for the future of the world, which undoubtedly represented the poet's own attitude at the time.

In view of D'Annunzio's imminent entry into national politics, which came just two years later, in 1897, it is important to consider the type of ideology which motivates Cantelmo's statements; that kind of philosophical idea would be incorporated into D'Annunzio's political speeches and writings during the next two years, and would

---

[45] Morello, *GD'A* 60–5; a facsimile of the important parts of the letter is reproduced at pp. 66–73. It should be added that much of the correspondence with Hérelle at the time is concerned with his abortive tripartite scheme; D'Annunzio's final form of the project is discussed in letters of 12 and 14 Nov. 1894: *GD'A à Georges Hérelle*, 211–18.

continue to influence him for the next two decades. D'Annunzio's traditional, and by now not unexpected, tendency to foster the interaction of life and art, fact and fiction, is nowhere more striking than in *Le vergini delle rocce*. Familiar by now is the apparent paradox that the fact of a state's being founded upon popular suffrage and social equality is gratifying to the hero (at least it gratifies the indomitable Cantelmo), because such popular institutions guarantee precariousness in the organization of the state, and clear the way for such a one as he: 'The task will not be very difficult to bring the herd to obedience. The plebs will always be slaves, with an innate need to hold out their wrists to the fetters. They will never have in them, even to the end of time, the sentiment of liberty' (*Le vergini*, I. 1). The multitude would inevitably profane the altars of Thought and Beauty, and finally reduce civilization to a new darkness, but then, appalled by what it had done, the rabble would feel the necessity for Heroes, 'and will again invoke the iron rods which will discipline it once more'. When Vincenzo Morello criticized the novel in his review as a reactionary negation of the progress that science and reason had clearly made, D'Annunzio responded that it was the 'synthetic representation of a current of ideas and feelings which today is running through Europe'. Paolo Alatri agrees that D'Annunzio's view was unfortunately correct.[46]

With these undemocratic notions fermenting in his mind, D'Annunzio prepared to relax, after the exertions of completing the novel, by taking up Scarfoglio's offer to accompany him on the long-awaited trip to Greece. His correspondence at this time with Georges Hérelle became more copious, particularly concerned as he was with the translation into French of *Il piacere* (*L'Enfant de volupté*), but he was also constantly proposing new translations, new cycles of novels for Hérelle to consider, and presumably to put before Calmann-Lévy and others. It was becoming more and more important to him to publish in France, not only because of the income which he could derive from the translations of his works (on 4 February 1895[47] he acknowledged receipt of 6,000 lire from Hérelle in a single payment), but also because he had found that, following the earlier surprise advance on royalties, Emilio Treves was more willing to send him further sums, persuaded by thoughts

[46] For Alatri's trenchant thoughts on these political developments see his *GD'A*, 162.

[47] *GD'A à Georges Hérelle*, 225.

of the wider readership which now seemed to be awaiting any new volume published.

On 5 May 1895 D'Annunzio suggested to Hérelle that he really ought one day to join him as his guest in the Abruzzi.[48] Two months afterwards, in a long letter of 11 July, D'Annunzio proposed that Hérelle join the merry company, as his guest on the yacht *Fantasia* which was, he said, about to sail for Greece and the Aegean. (He still maintained the charade that the yacht belonged jointly to himself and to Scarfoglio.) He also asked Hérelle to obtain for him an advance of 2,000 lire from Ferdinand Brunetière, editor of the *Revue des deux mondes*, which was currently publishing a serialized version of *Il trionfo della morte*. In the same letter D'Annunzio stressed the informal nature of the holiday-voyage, telling his friend that at the most he needed just a dark suit ('like the one he'd worn in Venice'), in case they had a guest on board; they would not be accepting invitations ashore. In the next letter D'Annunzio requested that Hérelle bring him the most recent translations of Homer, Hesiod, and Euripides, and two copies each of his own translations, *L'Enfant de volupté* and *L'Intrus*. With that the correspondence closed for a couple of months, the interval which marked the duration of Hérelle's sea voyage, though not, at the end, in company with D'Annunzio, who would cut short his own journey.[49]

Hérelle stayed four days with D'Annunzio and Maria Gravina at the Villa Mammarella in Francavilla, before leaving with the poet on 29 July 1895 to board the yacht on the southern tip of Italy, at Gallipoli. From the notes which Hérelle now began to take of his latest Italian adventure it becomes clear that D'Annunzio took the opportunity to confide in his new friend, using him almost as a psychiatrist:

Those who know me simply through my books imagine that I am a man of no morals, unscrupulous, capable of committing a crime to satisfy my passion or even my curiosity, but those who really know me know that my consciousness of my responsibility is very much alive.

To Hérelle D'Annunzio admitted that he was the deliberate cause of Maria Gravina's downfall, and that she had no moral or material resources, despised and rejected as she was by all. And herein lay his consciousness of his responsibility:

---

[48] *Lettere a Georges Hérelle*, 175–6.
[49] For the two letters concerned see ibid. 175–6 and 181–5.

I know all that, and this is the reason I continue to live with her. And yet living with her is an unimaginable torture. I no longer love her. Last year before I left for Venice I had endured torments to which I would have preferred any other affliction. June, July and August were a hell for me.[50]

The journey to Greece had its unsettling moments for Hérelle. But the beginning seemed propitious enough—a fine ship of thirty-six metres, not fifty-three tons as D'Annunzio had first told him, but ninety (as Hérelle found out from Scarfoglio),[51] with, the Frenchman reported, an excellent cook, and a crew of nine, plus captain. Among the disturbing incidents Hérelle's account of the journey showed that he was somewhat disconcerted by D'Annunzio's nude swimming and sunbathing, as well as by his prurient humour and the pornographic jokes he exchanged with his Italian companions. As for what D'Annunzio had referred to as informality at dinner and on social occasions, Hérelle's diary of the journey reveals his discomfiture at discovering that D'Annunzio had brought with him a dinner-jacket, six white suits, thirty or forty shirts, and eight pairs of shoes. Furthermore, formal invitations were extended and accepted at various ports of call, despite D'Annunzio's previous assertion that they would not be.[52]

D'Annunzio had told his translator that they would be able to work together on board, discuss the latest translations, and spend their leisure time reading in what, for such a small boat, was an extensive library. Instead, Hérelle's account shows his disappointment that D'Annunzio seemed intellectually inert, both on board and at the sites which they visited, and the journal is full of adverse criticisms of D'Annunzio's attitudes or, better, of the poet's seeming indifference to the glorious ruins of ancient Greece. He appeared to the Frenchman to be apathetic to the history which surrounded him, for instance at Olympia or Eleusis, more interested still in what Hérelle observed were 'pornographic conversations' with his companions. D'Annunzio slept for much of the time when the travellers had to take trains to reach various sites, and so, too, on the boat;

---

[50] Hérelle's diaries, still in manuscript in the Bibliothèque Municipale de Troyes, have been made available in an Italian translation entitled *Notolette dannunziane*, ed. I. Ciani (Pescara, 1984); here Hérelle reports the exchange at p. 30. His *Journal de Bord* has been partly published by G. Tosi, *D'Annunzio en Grèce et la croisière de 1895* (Paris, 1947), which will here also be used as a source for Hérelle's experiences.

[51] If any doubts remain a good photograph of the *Fantasia* is reproduced by Morello in his *GD'A*, facing p. 81.

[52] See Tosi, *D'Annunzio en Grèce*, 36.

if aroused from his snooze, says Hérelle, he seemed not to want to see things, even covered his face with a silk handkerchief. He inserted pornographic topics even into conversation at the highest level. Hérelle noted one such discussion on art, theatre, and opera, interspersed with dirty stories, which D'Annunzio carried on with the noble Salvatore Contarini, Italian ambassador in Athens, adding, 'There is really something puerile about Gabriele D'Annunzio'.[53] The reported conversation with Contarini recalls that D'Annunzio was perhaps genuinely unable to distinguish pornography from high culture, lacking a sense of the appropriate, as well as social decorum. Hérelle's anecdote recalls vividly the conversations which D'Annunzio describes in *Il piacere* as occurring during certain soirées in the noble salons of Rome. The occasions are settings for the super-artist, Andrea Sperelli, after due tribute has been paid to his exquisite taste and incredible cultural talents. Significantly, the conversations involved are among the many excisions made in Georgina Harding's English translation, and concern such details as the underarm hair of one of the female guests, the peculiar smell of another, the shape of 'the most beautiful belly in Christendom' displayed by another. With an apparent lack of artistic discretion, Sperelli–D'Annunzio was willing to insert such details into his companions' high thoughts on art and poetry. Strangely Miss Harding's bowdlerized translation added to the verisimilitude of Sperelli's artistically sensitive character: that he should, even in his role as insensitive womanizer, talk like a prurient schoolboy, or participate laughingly in similar puerile vulgar discussions, seems as inappropriate in the context of the novel as the indecorous stories told to the noble Salvatore Contarini at the embassy in Athens.

Hérelle must have grown in self-confidence since his first meeting with his peculiar host, and, as the voyage wore on, his down-to-earth remarks come ever closer to contempt for D'Annunzio's shortcomings. But his narrow-minded prurience caused his remarks to take on a peculiar hilarity of their own when he contrasts D'Annunzio and company's evident enjoyment of their bawdy entertainment with the solemn atmosphere which Hérelle thinks they are ignoring. A typical instance is his stolid, puritanical condemnation of the Italians' preference for what he calls the raddled meat of prostitutes in the Piraeus and the squeaking of a bad pavement orchestra:

[53] Ibid. 43–6.

Undoubtedly the bizarre eroticism of my companions, the excitement inspired by the presence of these awful women, these sailors' women, gets on my nerves and seems to me very uncouth. I cannot understand how in Greece, in the Piraeus one can waste time so foolishly with this rotten merchandise.

The Frenchman's comments present a cartoon image of himself, perched uneasily on his café chair, presumably trying to make urbane conversation amidst this coarse ribaldry.[54] On occasions Hérelle evidently made his feelings felt; he reports, for instance, D'Annunzio's reaction to one of many rebukes concerning his indifference to the magnificent or venerable surroundings. D'Annunzio had responded, 'I am always thinking: I am always working mentally, to fix in my soul the spirit of things, to seize their internal truth.' Stubbornly, Hérelle added at once, 'But he doesn't look at anything in the whole of this time', and later, 'In short his impressions are much more literary than real, much more bookish than alive'. Guy Tosi, the leading expert on the relations between D'Annunzio and Hérelle, has a telling note on his fellow Frenchman's observations. He was, Tosi writes, a dilettante criticizing a creative artist, and though 'probably Hérelle's observation of his surroundings may have been better, D'Annunzio's observation was, as it could only be, different'.[55]

In fact D'Annunzio's sensitivity to his environment in Greece, and his memory of events, even the most trivial and unimportant, must have astonished the mundane Hérelle a few years afterwards. By 1903 the poet's thoughts reflecting the experiences of Greece were transferred to the pages of the vast poem *Maia*, subtitled *Laus vitae* (Praise of Life), the first of the cycle entitled *Le laudi* (The Lauds, or Poems of Praise). More immediately the tragedy, *La città morta* (The Dead City), inspired by the ruins of Mycenae (where D'Annunzio had read Sophocles and Aeschylus under the Lion Gate) was written in 1896 and accepted by Sarah Bernhardt. So many were the actress's commitments at the time that D'Annunzio had to wait until January 1898 before *La Ville morte* was put on in Paris and in French. The vicissitudes of the play will be discussed in their turn, but worth noting at this point is the interesting omission from the playbills of the name of a translator (in fact, still the faithful Georges Hérelle). That omission gave the impression to the French public that *La Ville morte* was D'Annunzio's first play in

---

[54] See Tosi, *D'Annunzio en Grèce*, 99.   [55] Ibid. 44–5.

French, an impression which contributed not a little to admiration for his work. In a letter of 19 October 1896, D'Annunzio attempted to justify himself to Hérelle for having omitted his name: 'In the theatre this word *translation* already seems to put a veil between the work and the audience. When one listens to or reads a translation, one thinks instinctively of what the original text might have been. And there is, as it were, a diminution of pleasure.'[56]

Some of Hérelle's reactions to the voyage to Greece have already been noted, but the most astonishing use made of his Greek adventure by D'Annunzio is further illustrated in Guy Tosi's volume *D'Annunzio en Grèce*. There the French critic reproduces Hérelle's banal or prosaic observations of the everyday, and demonstrates the imaginative leap which D'Annunzio made to create a poetic apotheosis of the same event. For example on their first landfall, at Patràs, Hérelle wrote, 'After dinner Scarfoglio and D'Annunzio wanted absolutely to celebrate their arrival in Greece with an evening of love [*par une soirée d'amour*]'. But on the failure of their first attempts to use as their pandar a certain Bertucci, a local but ineffectual dragoman, the whole party went off into the town, making their way down sordid, narrow streets:

In the end Bertucci takes us to a house out of the centre where we climb a wooden external staircase. Upstairs we find a female, completely dressed in white, neither young nor beautiful, who soon disgusts everyone. After exchanging a few words we turn our backs to leave, at which point, from a neighbouring room comes a very old woman, also dressed in white and with white hair, who asks us for money. We give her a few drachmas and leave. Going down the staircase a wooden tread broke and Boggiani was almost thrown to the ground.[57]

By contrast, the episode is transformed, in *Maia*, into a vast recreation of an ancient myth. The prostitute becomes for D'Annunzio a once fair woman from Pyrgos, reduced by the years and by her profession to 'a small, fat creature, like a pregnant goat with many teats, redolent of her odoriferous bridegroom'. The old, white-haired woman becomes Helen of Troy, aged by the centuries (and by centurions). D'Annunzio poetically imagines Helen's decline, from the perfumed beauty who left Sparta for Troy, to her present condition. Brought back to Greece from the glories of Asia Minor, she is reduced, after being ravished by whole armies, and following

---

[56] *Lettere a Georges Hérelle*, 210.   [57] Tosi, *D'Annunzio en Grèce*, 66–7.

aeons suffering the most sadistic humiliations, to the task of cleaning chamber-pots in a brothel. She breaks her last tooth on a bone among the scraps she has to wrest from the establishment's scabby dog. In a brief hundred lines of verse, D'Annunzio's ability to evoke centuries of classical myth and history, following his banal visit to 'the ancient city of the Achaeans', is truly remarkable. And Boggiani's accident on the decayed tread of the staircase is not forgotten:

> E noi scendemmo la scala
> di putrido legno. Cedette
> un de' gradi all'urto del piede,
> s'infranse con gemito. Oh dolce,
> dalla soglia del lupanare,
> mirar le stelle.

> [And we descended the stair
> of putrid wood. One of the treads
> yielded to a blow from a foot, and
> broke with a groan. How sweet,
> from the brothel's threshold
> to see the virgin stars.]

> (*Maia*, 1318–23)

The final line is an echo of Dante's famous image as he expresses his relief on emerging from each of the three realms during the epic journey of his *Divine Comedy*.

The small episode is a good example of one way in which D'Annunzio could 'continue the work of nature', in this case by turning reality into poetic dream. The episode in Patràs also illustrates many facets of the poet's skill which will be examined in due course. But it would not be out of place here to mention an aspect of D'Annunzio which is not commented on by any critic: his sense of humour. D'Annunzio is regularly criticized for lacking this, and it is certainly true that he took himself so seriously that humour is rarely present in his work, though his life presents the biographer with many unconscious examples. Lack of a sense of humour was an apparent failing which helped particularly to increase the prejudice against him of English critics. Here, although in the rather grim circumstances of the brothel visit humour is bound to be at best sardonic, there is laughter present when one of the party (evidently D'Annunzio), in deliberately pompous tones (and with an allusion which would have baffled many a professor of Classics), asks the younger prostitute 'whether she had once bathed her youthful limbs in Homer's Minyeius, the dismal River Anigrus'.

> Ella gustar l'attico sale
> non seppe, e scagliò contra noi
> l'ingiuria e i sandali. Allora
> ci ritraemmo, con nari
> occlusi, giù per la scala
> di putrido legno.

> [She could not taste
> the Attic salt, and against us
> hurled insults and sandals. So
> we withdrew, holding our noses,
> down the stair of rotting wood.]

> (*Maia*, 1171–6)

D'Annunzio did, in fact, keep a detailed diary of certain aspects of the journey, which he then transcribed into further *taccuini*, from which he worked up his epic poem.[58] But by 16 August D'Annunzio had had enough of the heroic voyage. On that day the jovial sea-farers were to have left the Piraeus for Constantinople. A storm blew up, D'Annunzio was violently seasick, and the yacht put back to Phaleron, where D'Annunzio and Masciantonio disembarked to catch the ferry back to Brindisi, after a rapid excursion to visit Eleusis. Hérelle and the rest continued their journey, not to their original destinations in the eastern Mediterranean, but to Milos, and then back to Italy, calling at various ports on the way, until Hérelle left the boat at Naples on 24 September; by 26 September he was safe home in Paris.

---

[58] See e.g. his notebooks for 1895: *Altri taccuini*, 5–19. The journey to Greece formed the subject-matter of the centennial conference at the Centro Studi Dannunziani in 1995, the proceedings of which were published as E. Tiboni (ed.), *Verso l'Ellade* (Pescara, 1995).

5

The Poet as Playwright:
On Stage with Eleonora Duse

ANOTHER phase in D'Annunzio's life was about to start. He had already written to influential friends indicating his enthusiasm for *La città morta*, the new tragedy, the outline of which he had been inspired to sketch after the impact upon him of the magnificent Achaean treasures and the awesome atmosphere of the Greek remains at Mycenae. On 23 September 1895 an affectionate letter to Hérelle urged him to prepare the *Revue de Paris* to receive the drama, which, he wrote, would be finished by the end of the year.[1] He had never written a play, and, coincidentally with the new Mycenean inspiration, his path was very soon afterwards to cross that of Eleonora Duse. It was she who provided the new interest in the poet's life, new inspiration for his creative writing, and new finances for his princely life-style. At the same time Hérelle seems to have noticed a further change in D'Annunzio following the Greek escapade. D'Annunzio had returned briefly to Francavilla to sit for one of Michetti's most famous portraits. Hérelle's verdict on the new face which stared at him from the canvas is significant in view of D'Annunzio's less caring attitude after this date.

Now the Gabriele D'Annunzio represented by that pastel is a completely new individual, seemingly having nothing in common with the previous portraits. In those the physiognomy is sweet, the eyes cast down a little, the moustaches modest, and the smile is vaguely melancholic. By contrast, in the pastel, his lineaments are harsh, his moustaches rise like long hooks, his pointed beard is threatening, his eyes are aggressive, his brows somewhat furrowed. That pastel is certainly the first portrait of D'Annunzio 'superman'.[2]

Soon after writing the letter to Hérelle D'Annunzio returned to Venice. There, by what seemed an extraordinary coincidence, he

---

[1] *GD'A à Georges Hérelle*, 255.   [2] Tosi, *D'Annunzio en Grèce*, 173.

and Eleonora Duse met one day as dawn was breaking; D'Annunzio suddenly appeared, stepping out of a gondola; they talked about art and discussed the wretched state of the theatrical profession at the time. No mention was made of any emotional commitment, but some sort of silent pact was agreed between them.[3] The 'pact' was to lead to a new career as a dramatist for D'Annunzio, and, ultimately, to humiliation for the self-sacrificing Eleonora, who was exploited more heartlessly than any of his women to date. For his brief sojourn in Venice, D'Annunzio had this time chosen Venice's best, the Royal Hotel Danieli. In an apocryphal note in his *taccuini* dated 26 September 1895, he writes 'Sacred to Love and to Grief'. The words, which became the title of a sonnet published in 1905, after the break-up of their association,[4] are generally regarded as the beginning of more intimate physical relations between the two lovers, who had already encountered each other briefly on earlier occasions. They had already spoken, for instance, at a meeting arranged by Angelo Conti and Adolfo De Bosis during the journey which D'Annunzio had made to Venice in 1894 in order to acquaint himself better with Georges Hérelle.[5]

Between 1896 and 1904, for the eight years that their affair lasted, Eleonora sacrificed her health, substance, and dignity to promote what she saw as D'Annunzio's literary genius. Her influence, indeed, led to continuing attempts on his part to write a dramatic master-piece, though it must be said that his need to write quickly and for profit led during the following twenty years to only indiffer-ent artistic success. But Duse's reputation as Italy's leading actress, rivalling Sarah Bernhardt in her European fame, also helped to spread his name on a world-wide scale. Within Europe D'Annunzio's standing was enhanced by Eleonora's performances in his dramas

[3] For a discussion of the episode and its consequences see E. Mariano, 'Il patto d'alleanza fra Eleonora Duse e GD'A', *Nuova antologia*, 86/1801 (Jan.–Feb. 1951), 3–16.

[4] '*Amori et dolori sacra* * 26 settembre 1895. Hôtel Royal Danieli Venezia', in *Taccuini*, 77. The sonnet is available in GD'A, *Versi d'amore e di gloria*, ed. E. Bianchetti, 2 vols. (Milan, 1940), i. 1016.

[5] In the naïve posthumous memoirs of Benigno Palmerio, D'Annunzio's major-domo in Settignano, D'Annunzio is said to have confessed that as a 23-year-old reporter in Rome's Teatro Valle he had gone to La Duse's dressing-room between the acts of *La Dame aux Camélias* and greeted her with the words 'O grande amatrice'. The major-domo has other more or less reliable memories of the two in B. Palmerio, *Con D'Annunzio alla Capponcina* (Florence, 1938), 26 and *passim*. G. Damerini, *D'Annunzio e Venezia* (Milan, 1943; repr. Venice, 1993), has overly romantic views of the lovers' meetings in Venice.

on the stages of London, Paris, and Berlin; he began thus to consolidate his reputation with littérateurs of the importance of Anatole France, Romain Rolland, Jean Moréas, and J. K. Huysmans; even James Joyce made the tedious journey from Dublin to London in 1900 to see Duse perform, and for many years afterwards was captivated by D'Annunzio's literary ability.[6] Duse also took his plays to the United States, to Russia, to South America, and to Egypt, where in 1898 she invited D'Annunzio to accompany her on his second, rather more luxurious, cruise towards the eastern Mediterranean. This more comfortable experience of classical Greece also helped to bring to completion the poetic concepts which Greece had inspired in D'Annunzio during the adventure with Scarfoglio in 1895.

Eleonora, or Ghisola as he soon rebaptized her, was 37 years of age in 1895, five years older than D'Annunzio. Countless photographs of Duse allow readers to form their own view of her beauty or attraction, but it would not be unjust to say that by 1895 any sylph-like figure she might have had as a girl had matured considerably; by then, too, she possessed what seems to have been D'Annunzio's preferred jaw-line, which repeated that of Elda Zucconi and Maria Gravina, tempered in Eleonora's case by soulful eyes, generous lips, and a noble brow. But for D'Annunzio she brought a new fascination: the glamour of an international reputation. The name of Eleonora Duse was by then known throughout the world and her brilliant acting had acquired for her a host of admirers in many countries. The gap in their ages was to be a key element in D'Annunzio's portrait of the actress, not only in the plot of the notorious semi-autobiographical novel, *Il fuoco*, but also in his other work, including the story-line of the second play destined for Eleonora, the *Sogno d' un tramonto d'autunno* (Dream of an Autumn Sunset). The way he exploited in the novel the theme of an older woman falling for a younger man was one of the implicit reproaches which was to break up their relationship in 1904. D'Annunzio's true feelings for her are perhaps unconsciously revealed in Palmerio's account of a meeting the poet said he had with Eleonora in Paris in January 1898. D'Annunzio's description of the meeting to Palmerio

---

[6] S. Joyce, *My Brother's Keeper*, ed. R. Ellmann (New York, 1958), 147; J. Joyce, *Letters*, ed. R. Ellmann (New York, 1966), ii. 85; cf. R. Ellmann, *James Joyce* (Oxford, 1982), 266.

reports the 'loving voice with which Duse addressed him, albeit with a maternal intonation to it'.[7]

Eleonora had been born into poverty on 3 October 1858 in Vigevano, a small town in Lombardy, the daughter of strolling players, Vincenzo Duse and Angelica Cappelletto.[8] Her own stage career had taken off in 1878, when she became popular with impressive performances in front of the normally uncompromising Neapolitan theatre audiences at the Teatro dei Fiorentini. It was coincidentally in Naples that D'Annunzio's old friend, Matilde Serao, came to know Eleonora well; she was to remain supportively by the actress's side in her moments of greatest distress. When acting in Naples as a fragile 20-year-old, Duse's character had been genuinely unsophisticated; indeed, that childlike innocence was said to have been a major feature in creating a new style of 'natural' acting which so impressed the critics. But, in view of D'Annunzio's later treatment of his new patroness–lover, it is worth noting that by 1895 Eleonora had acquired a notoriety of her own, and had been toughened by some harsh experiences. In Naples she had been seduced by Martino Cafiero, a wealthy newspaper proprietor, who left her pregnant and alone to have her child in the distant sea-front village of Marina di Pisa.

By all accounts the actress, still naïvely in love with Cafiero, was hopeful that he would stand by her, even though the baby died shortly after birth. Her disillusionment was great.[9] As a reaction to what proved to be Cafiero's indifference, she dedicated the next three years completely to her art, and by 1881 was being well received on all the national stages. That year she married Tebaldo Checchi, a minor actor in the company; a daughter, Enrichetta (later to spend most of her adult life in Britain as the wife of a Cambridge academic), was born the following January. Biographers have described the marriage as loveless, at least on Eleonora's part, but Checchi looked out for her interests and by all accounts was a good-natured individual. Enormous popular success followed Duse's performances, and Checchi continued loyal, even when he became

---

[7] Palmerio, *Con D'Annunzio*, 26.

[8] There are at least forty major biographies of the actress; for further information and bibliography see G. Pontiero's very readable *Eleonora Duse: In Life and Art* (Frankfurt, 1986).

[9] Ibid. 31; Pontiero has an excellent note on the mysterious episode: see pp. 308–9 n. 21.

aware of affairs with her leading actor Flavio Andò and, some gossip columnists added, with the juvenile lead Arturo Diotti, all of which led to scandalous reports in the national newspapers. But after one tour in South America, in 1885, Checchi could take no more infidelities, and, good-natured as ever, left Eleonora to her own devices and stayed behind in Buenos Aires when the company returned to Italy.[10]

Throughout the turbulent period after 1883, and again in the years following the actress's final break with D'Annunzio, the name of Arrigo Boito stood out amongst Duse's friends and admirers, as a guarantee of solid, undemanding support. In his fine biography of the composer and librettist, Piero Nardi has shown how deeply Eleonora relied on Boito before and after her relationship with D'Annunzio.[11] Boito is best known as Verdi's librettist, but as a member of the Milanese 'Bohemian' group La Scapigliatura (The Dishevelled Movement) he had been a good minor poet in his own right; as one of the *scapigliati* he had helped revolutionize the lethargic poetry of the second phase of Italy's Romantic movement, against which the less uninhibited Carducci had also railed for many years in his neo-classical poems and polemics. In his turn D'Annunzio's outrageous attitudes owed something to the voice of protest of the Milanese revolutionaries. From Nardi's account, and from the correspondence between Duse and Boito, it becomes clear that even before meeting D'Annunzio the actress would write to Boito, giving him her emotional, if not passionate, reactions to reading the poet's work. On 8 June 1894, for instance, she wrote to Boito from London, referring, among other things, to D'Annunzio's *Trionfo della morte*:

The other evening I went to hear *Falstaff*. God-Arrigo forgive me, but it seemed such a . . . melancholy thing, that *Falstaff*! Despise deeply, but . . . that's it! . . . And . . . something else! That *infernal* D'Annunzio! That book, I've finished it . . . all the enormous anguished sacrifice which *living* is, is destroyed in that book. No! No! No! Despise, but neither *Falstaff* nor D'Annunzio, that is no; D'Annunzio, I detest him, but I adore him.[12]

---

[10] For the breakdown of the marriage with Checchi (the strange stage name of Tebaldo Marchetti), see ibid. 58–60.

[11] Nardi, *Vita di Arrigo Boito*, 538, 713, and *passim*.

[12] Duse and Boito, *Lettere d'amore*, 831; it should be noted that many of Duse's letters and comments are characteristically incoherent—many exaggeratedly theatrical—both in their language and in their calligraphy, at times producing incongruities which editors and printers have found it difficult typographically to represent, though they may reflect accurately her breathless moods.

This was the woman who was to provide D'Annunzio with much of his psychological material and inspiration for the next eight years.

In his letter of 23 September 1895, D'Annunzio had told Hérelle that he would be 'travelling here and there for about a month, having to do a number of things'.[13] His vagueness, as so often, covered the banality of his activities. In fact, he had to take his son Mario to Prato on 4 October for the opening of the new school term at the Cicognini, where the boy was to follow in his father's footsteps. The experience of accompanying his son, D'Annunzio remarked in a letter to his friend Angelo Conti, he found strangely disquieting, so unused was he to the role of father: 'I can't tell you how painful I find contact with this tiny soul in these circumstances. The sentiment of paternity always makes me suffer when it is revealed to me.'[14]

But while he was in Florence staying at the Hotel de Russie Eleonora came to visit him. Thereafter they met on a regular basis in what their champion, Frances Winwar, called 'amenable settings for their love'.[15] Eleonora was often accompanied by a beautiful young woman, Giulietta Gordigiani, the 20-year-old daughter of the Florentine painter Michele Gordigiani, one of Duse's portraitists. Giulietta was, during the poet's affair with Duse, to provide him with the youthful presence, if not actually the physical gratification, which he so often implied and declared was missing after the first passionate impetus of his relationship with Eleonora. As usual, however, in D'Annunzio's relationships, both women were to provide him with more than sex (or, in the case of Eleonora, more than sex and money): they were to be two of the major characters in the next of his novels, *Il fuoco*, which portrays Eleonora with particular and pitiless accuracy. As will be seen, Eleonora, Giulietta, and D'Annunzio are represented respectively as the ageing beauty, Foscarina, the young singer, Donatella Arvale, and the vibrant composer, Stelio Effrena.

D'Annunzio had committed himself to giving a speech at the closure of the first Venetian international art exhibition, nowadays universally known as the Biennale of Venice. He returned to Francavilla to prepare for what was to be his first public discourse, and by 8

[13] *GD'A à Georges Hérelle*, 255.
[14] Reported by Masci, *La vita e le opere*, 130–1. D'Annunzio went on to write 'I shall also have to look with an intent gaze on this zone of my inner life'.
[15] Winwar, *Wingless Victory*, 147.

November 1895 he was back in Venice for the occasion. The speech was in effect a paean of praise to the traditions of Venice, celebrating her former imperial power, the beauty of her artistic heritage, and her reputation as a vast and glorious cathedral to pleasure. Soon afterwards the lecture was published in Florence by Roberto Paggi, initially as an appendix to add bulk to 'L'allegoria dell'autunno' (The Allegory of Autumn), an incomplete poem in ten stanzas, describing a neo-classical hunting procession, and written in Venice in 1887;[16] Venice seems to be the only connecting link between poem and speech, but the discourse has since then often been incongruously attached to that work. The speech is best viewed in the context of *Il fuoco*, where it reappears in Book I, reproduced almost word for word as Stelio Effrena's rousing oration in the great Council Room of the Doge's Palace. The discourse is full of erudite historical allusions to the Middle Ages and Renaissance, to the artistry of Giorgione, Tintoretto, Carpaccio, and Veronese, and to the famous political leaders that Venice had produced in the past. Despite its erudition and its appeals to support the cause of 'beauty', D'Annunzio's rhetoric is generally, and with some justification, regarded, in Paolo Alatri's words, as 'a series of digressions, a sprint through illustrious and banal themes—the Venice of Veronese, the *Concerto* then attributed to Giorgione, pleasure as a means of knowledge connected by only the slightest correlation between them'.[17]

Following D'Annunzio's speech at the Biennale, it was to take a further four years before the new novel, *Il fuoco*, appeared in the bookshops, but the harangue in Venice was important for two main reasons. First, and more immediately, it showed D'Annunzio that he could use his voice to command the attention of an audience, and control them, with a vocal power similar to the influence of the printed word which in earlier years he had felt able to exert over bourgeois readers of his gossip columns. Secondly, the oration provided him with further material for the character of Stelio Effrena, who in the main themes of his fictionalized speech in the first book of *Il fuoco* prefigures D'Annunzio's own political appearances and speeches. Indeed, during the two years preceding his election to parliament in 1897 excerpts from the speeches in *Il fuoco* provided D'Annunzio with ready-made copy for newspaper articles

---

[16] This peculiar composition is available in the appendix to D'Annunzio's *Versi d'amore e di gloria*, i. 1035.

[17] Alatri, *GD'A*, 166.

of a political bent. In the novel, Stelio concentrates on the heroic pursuit of beauty, betrays a thinly disguised contempt for the multitude, and expresses an élitist philosophy shading into nationalism. And, despite the strictures of critics concerning the incoherence within the novel's plot of Stelio–D'Annunzio's performance as orator-cum-demagogue, its importance for the future lay, not so much in its style, but in the effect which D'Annunzio felt it should be having on his public. The reader of *Il fuoco* is permitted an insight into that effect when Stelio's thoughts on audience reactions are allowed to interrupt his flow of words, and in particular allow him and, by implication, his autobiographical creator, to comment at several points in Book I on the power of the orator:

He was amazed at that unknown force which converged in him, abolishing the confines of the particular individual and conferring on a solitary voice the fullness of a chorus.—So this was the mysterious serenity which the revelation of Beauty could offer the daily existence of the weary multitude. [. . .] In that hour he was simply the go-between, the means by which Beauty presented to people gathered together in a place consecrated by centuries of human glories, the divine gift of forgetfulness.

Later, during his two political campaigns, D'Annunzio was to be referred to as the 'Candidato della Bellezza' (Candidate for Beauty), his political affiliation unclear or non-existent, so that, for instance, although in the constituency of Ortona a Mare in 1897 his opponent, Carlo Altobelli, was a Republican (and possibly of Socialist inclinations), it would be difficult to infer this from any of D'Annunzio's esoteric pronouncements. As will become clear, it would prove impossible to categorize D'Annunzio's political programme or such political beliefs as he might hold in the years ahead. Stelio Effrena's speeches are as vague as D'Annunzio's own political views.

D'Annunzio now prepared to devote himself wholeheartedly to writing his play, *La città morta*, and in October 1896 actually interrupted the composition of *Il fuoco* to complete the drama in the course of the following month. There are many possible explanations for his enthusiastic dedication to the new genre, not least his desire to excel in another sphere of literary activity. The play was directly inspired by his visit to Mycenae during the expedition to Greece with Scarfoglio and company, and D'Annunzio genuinely shared Europe's wonderment at the opening up of the site, his enthusiasm for the great *Oresteia* myth being further whetted by the dazzling archaeological discoveries by Schliemann. Could the fifteen skeletons found at Mycenae possibly be Agamemnon, Cassandra, and other members of the royal entourage, slaughtered by Clytemnestra and Aegisthus? To add to the attraction of a new venture, there was no doubt that the possibility of an association, professional and otherwise, with one who was arguably the world's greatest actress sharpened his desire to experiment with another genre. But, equally importantly, I believe that the experience of his speech at the Biennale had also given him a lively sense of the way in which the spoken word launched from a stage could have an immediate effect upon an audience. There are clear parallels between his attitude at the time and certain elements in the plot of *Il fuoco*, which was being completed simultaneously with *La città morta*. Stelio Effrena's contemplation of the impact on the audience of his oratory is no more than a thinly disguised reflection of D'Annunzio's own feelings, while Stelio's oration is more of a dramatic performance than a political discourse; significantly, the memory of the speech and of its effects remains with him throughout a large part of the novel. The juxtaposition of poet, orator, and warrior in a dramatic context was important: it prophesied a specific role for D'Annunzio himself, and a future change of direction for the political attitudes of the nation. Those new dramatic skills in particular were to prove of almost utilitarian benefit in view of the course that the poet's career would take from that point onwards. Luigi Russo, one of the most percipient and unusually objective of critics in the immediate pre-1939 period, significantly entitled his first section on D'Annunzio's theatre and politics 'An Aesthetic Colloquy with the Crowd'.[18]

D'Annunzio had such a power of imagination that he often allowed himself to be guided by illusion rather than by reality itself, and in the theatre, too, as will be seen in the case of *La città morta*, his dreams of moving an audience with his dramatic creations were nurtured more by the strength of his own convictions than by the actual responses of his theatre-going public. Indeed most Italian critics who have judged the play objectively imply that it is too static a drama, mitigated only by one or two efficacious scenes and some beautiful tracts of lyric poetry. The plot of the play is, however, more ingenious than D'Annunzio is sometimes given credit

---

[18] L. Russo, *GD'A* (Florence, 1939), 53.

for. He took the newspaper stories of Schliemann's discoveries of a few years previously, added his own reaction to the priceless finds (which he had been able to examine in the Archaeological Museum at Athens), and transferred all of these elements to a contemporary archaeological dig. The team-leader of D'Annunzio's fictional group of archaeologists is a poet, Alessandro, married to the blind Anna, but in love with the chaste Bianca Maria. The hypersensitive Anna intuits their love, and her consequent emotional suffering adds to the pathos of the story; the passionate turmoil is further deepened by the remorse and the compassion of Bianca Maria, who has in her turn fallen desperately in love with Alessandro. Anna goes off, planning to drown herself, in the hope of cutting short her own suffering and leaving the path open to the two lovers. In the meantime the professional archaeologist Leonardo, Bianca Maria's brother, directs the excavations which bring to light the Mycenean tombs. Those discoveries infect him with a germ of ancient voluptuousness; he is driven to an incestuous passion for his sister, and, partly to prevent her from falling into Alessandro's bed, partly to free himself from his illicit love, he kills her.

Although some of these themes appear outlandish to a modern audience, there is no doubt that D'Annunzio's plot reflects obliquely the tragic history of the ancient Mycenean dynasty. To that mythical and classical lore, he fashionably attached Europe's then current fascination with the new and barely credible archaeological discoveries; he also inserted a prophetic theme (later to be borne out by the legends surrounding Lord Caernarfon's discoveries in Egypt): the theme of the intrusion of the inquisitive present into a solemn and untouchable past, with the baleful consequences that such desecration brought in its train. Against these curious novelties, almost every Italian critic adduces the lack of action as a major defect in the play. It is true that the murder of Bianca Maria, the only violent action, takes place offstage, though it was probably better thus, and possibly more in keeping with the way D'Annunzio was thinking at the time about the Orestes myth, which is also present here in ghostly form. In his later plays, as will become clear, D'Annunzio would not be so hesitant about allowing onstage violence.

If we view the play as indicative of autobiography, it has other interesting facets. Alessandro seeks, through his love for Bianca Maria, to achieve happiness, and the creation through poetry of an ideal beauty. Leonardo, the physical *alter ego* of Alessandro, is desirous of asserting himself, freeing himself from his turbulent passion for his sister, even though this means killing her. The self-sacrificial Anna ('What am I for Alessandro if not a heavy chain, an intolerable restraint?') is seen by some critics to be a representation of Eleonora Duse, ready to sacrifice herself for the greater glory of the poetic duo Alessandro–D'Annunzio:

You realize what a deep aversion he has against every inert kind of grief, against every useless suffering, against every impediment, every hindrance which may interrupt the ascent of noble forces towards their supreme status. You realize with what assiduous vigilance he casts around to absorb everything which can increase and accelerate the active virtue of his spirit through the task of beauty [*per l'opera di bellezza*] which he must accomplish. (*Città morta*, Act III, sc. ii)

Alessandro and Lorenzo fit into the mould of the earlier protagonists of D'Annunzio's novels, either as supreme aesthetes, such as Sperelli or Aurispa, or as more active, but no less cultural, all-rounders, such as Hermil or Effrena.

There was no doubt that Eleonora Duse had conceived an irrepressible passion for D'Annunzio. Although the two were able to meet on various occasions during the following months, the actress had theatrical engagements in northern Europe and Russia between the winter of 1895 and August 1896. She knew that D'Annunzio was working on a drama and was looking forward to being given the lead role. But in February 1896 an apocryphal note in a letter of D'Annunzio's to Hérelle reads 'Adieu, dear friend. I shall talk to you about the *Città morta* on another occasion. I am already plotting for its performance. In Rome Giuseppe Primoli and I have woven a frightful conspiracy.'[19] The conspiracy was Byzantine in its intricacy; at its heart was a contract requiring the play to be staged in Italy by 15 November 1896, even though D'Annunzio did not begin writing the opus until 30 September 1896 (it was to take him forty days). But in a letter received by Hérelle on 9 July D'Annunzio announced, 'Sarah Bernhardt has accepted for the Renaissance immediately and "with enthusiasm", my *Città morta*, and is insisting on having the manuscript as soon as possible.'[20] During July he signed a contract with the French actress, inserting a clause restricting her performance to France, and simultaneously sent a proposal offering Eleonora the possibility of a performance in Italy before

---

[19] *Lettere a Georges Hérelle*, 190.   [20] Ibid. 204.

15 November. Without immediately knowing of the contract with
Bernhardt, Duse wrote to D'Annunzio regretting that in the brief
time available she was unable to put together the necessary company and make adequate preparations. This gave D'Annunzio the
excuse he needed to offer the play elsewhere, to one who had the
resources for an immediate production. As soon as Eleonora learned
that her rival had been offered a contract, she must have realized
that this had simply been D'Annunzio's method of ensuring that
Bernhardt had the opportunity to give the first performance. She
therefore broke off all contact with the poet, renewed her friendship with Boito and left again for a tour in Berlin, Moscow, and
St Petersburg. D'Annunzio was then free to launch on the wider
Parisian stage his first tragedy, apparently, as has been shown, composed in his own French. The famous (or infamous) letter to Hérelle
of 19 October 1896 had also spoken of his original intention to
attempt to write the play directly in French; he would simply rely
on Hérelle to revise the text.[21] In Hérelle's next letter, perhaps written three days later on 22 October 1896, the Frenchman passively
offered his services virtually free of charge:

Allow me to offer you without any fixed remuneration the translation of
the *Dead City*. Subsequently, according as the piece is more or less successful and has brought you in more or less money, I will accept, as a gift
between friends, whatever you think it proper to send me. And since we are
not dealing with a fee but with a friendly gift, I shall employ the sum by
putting it at the disposal of our friendship. I shall use it to make another
visit to you or to accompany you on some pleasant journey you may like
to make with me.[22]

In Paris Sarah Bernhardt was too busy with her other commitments to be able to put on the *Città morta* as quickly as D'Annunzio
wanted. Indeed he had to wait more than a year before she was able
to give its first performance at her own Théâtre de la Renaissance,
on 21 January 1898. But before then reconciliation between Eleonora
and D'Annunzio was at hand. First, their mutual acquaintance,
Adolfo De Bosis, acted as go-between to engineer a surprise meeting between the two, and Eleonora, after the added intervention of
Giuseppe ('Gégé') Primoli, was persuaded to sign a contract for the
exclusive performance in Italy of the *Città morta*. That was at the

---

[21] Ibid. 209; cf. above pp. 134–5.   [22] Ibid. 214.

end of March 1897.[23] At the same time her friend, the impresario Joseph Schurmann, had succeeded in persuading Bernhardt to lease the Renaissance to the Italian company. Eleonora agreed to the venue at the beginning of April 1897, somewhat hesitant at the thought of performing in her rival's theatre, and in front of the traditionally chauvinistic Parisian audience. It was while she was discussing her dilemma with Primoli that D'Annunzio walked in on their conversation. Primoli recorded the meeting with dramatic concision: Duse suggested that D'Annunzio might resolve the dilemma by writing a play for her: 'You cannot be serious; in one week! It's madness.' 'Then create the role of a madwoman for me.'[24] D'Annunzio immediately withdrew to Albano, one of their old retreats, and there in ten days, between 13 and 23 April 1897, he composed for Eleonora his *Sogno d'un mattino di primavera* (Dream of a Spring Morning). The première of the *Sogno* in Paris on 16 June 1897 was not well received, though Duse was applauded for her personal performance; later, during productions of the play in Italy, it had a similarly disappointing reception. One reason for its lack of success, and for the similar fate of its partner, *Sogno d'un tramonto d'autunno*, probably lay in the intricacy of the plots, which involved the audience in difficult calculations and hypotheses following action offstage (and, in the case of the first play, by their having to intuit what had happened before curtain-up). Nevertheless the two plays require a mention at this point because of their significance for the biographer interested in D'Annunzio's psychological make-up at the time, and in the lack of judgement which allowed him to create such unacceptable spectacles. The themes, for such slight offerings, were over-complex (and unduly morbid and bloodthirsty, to the extent that the first play was banned from the London stage). Brief examples of these everyday stories of family life may suffice to explain their unpopularity with audiences. In the *Sogno d'un mattino di primavera*, for instance, Giuliano, the adulterous lover of Isabella, is murdered by Isabella's husband. After hugging Giuliano's dead body all night and getting thoroughly drenched in his blood in the process, Isabella rises, the morning afterwards, insane. Her sister, Beatrice, is in love with Giuliano's brother Virginio, who, however, prefers the mad Isabella, and

[23] Pontiero, *Eleonora Duse*, 144.
[24] Ibid. 146. The actress waxed lyrical about the new play in a long letter to Boito of 4 Apr. 1897: Duse and Boito, *Lettere d'amore*, 914.

impersonates the dead Giuliano in an attempt to collaborate with her doctor in order to shock her out of her insanity. But Virginio's scheme fails, and Beatrice in turn is left desolate at the end. In the second *Sogno*, written in 1898 but not performed until 1905, the ageing Dogaressa Gradeniga, in order to further her adulterous affair with a younger man (unnamed), kills her husband the Doge, only to see her lover fall into the arms of the young courtesan Pantea. She casts a spell on Pantea's ceremonial barge, the *bucintoro*. The curse is worked out when the noble Priamo Gritti and others in rival groups attack the barge, which, set ablaze, incinerates Pantea and her lovers. In the second 'idyll', critics were not slow to see the association between the ageing Duse–Gradeniga, the younger D'Annunzio, and the even younger Gordigiani–Pantea.

The themes of murder, eroticism, cruelty, and madness, along with hints of incest and necrophilia, were to continue in various guises throughout D'Annunzio's literary career, particularly in his tragedies. Although by modern standards they seem to constitute a bizarre mixture, D'Annunzio was consciously trying to break the mould of contemporary Italian drama by creating what were undeniably revolutionary if outlandish plots with overstated characters. And while it was true that Duse made her reputation by playing traditional parts with a new naturalness, she wrote to Boito from Rome on 9 April 1897 to say that she was 'terrified of taking up her so-called work again with the eternal *Dame aux Camélias*; my very mouth by now refuses to say those words! Boredom, boredom, more deadly to the artiste than any physical danger'.[25] The theme is continued in a letter of 8 May 1894, this time written during her spring tour in London:

That so-called work taken up again yesterday evening seemed more than ever the phenomenal absurdity and pettiness of my life and of human life in general. What an offence to the soul to ape life. And I see around me, amongst those papier mâché trees padded with green canvas, people clinging to the chimera of chimeras.[26]

There are further hints at D'Annunzio's new ambitions as a playwright in the contemporary *Fuoco*, where he makes Stelio Effrena talk of creating a new drama, 'a new form, by obeying only my

---

[25] Ibid. 907.
[26] Ibid. 815; Nardi, *Vita di Arrigo Boito*, 606, picks up the point about Duse's disillusionment.

instinct and the genius of my race', and parallels that ambition with the results obtained by the Greeks 'when they created that marvellous edifice of inimitable beauty which was their drama'. D'Annunzio's effects depended rather more on the cruel folklore and fierce traditions of his native province, which he believed chimed with the bloodthirsty quality of the myths underlying Greek drama; these comparisons are revealed in Stelio's further reflections to Daniele Glauro in the second book of *Il fuoco*:

Just as the creatures of Aeschylus carry within them something of the natural myths which spawned them, I wish my creatures to be felt to be palpitating in the torrent of savage forces, grieving from their contact with the earth, and, in their pathetic struggle against a Fate which has to be overcome, pulsating in their communion with the air, water, fire, mountains and clouds, and I want Nature to surround them as it was seen by the ancient patriarchs, Nature, the passionate actress in an eternal drama.

Curiously, at this point in the plot, reminiscences of the journey with Scarfoglio to Mycenae also enter Stelio's discussion with Glauro, including the story of his reading the *Oresteia* under the Lion Gate there, blended with recent archaeological discoveries; in effect Stelio gives a thumbnail sketch of the main themes of the *Città morta*.

The period was a busy one for the bard from Pescara, and his life was further complicated at the beginning of 1896 by the irritating intervention of a young Turinese critic, Enrico Thovez. During early January and late February of that year, Thovez wrote three articles in *La gazzetta letteraria* accusing D'Annunzio of plagiarism.[27] The titles of the articles were meant to be ironically insulting: 'Signor D'Annunzio's Art of Composition', 'The Secret Sources of Signor D'Annunzio and the Mystery of the New Renaissance', and, following a response from D'Annunzio in *Le Figaro*, 'Crumbs from the Superman'. Thovez demonstrated clearly that D'Annunzio had plundered the work of his contemporaries for themes, phrases, and ideas, from which, Thovez alleged, he had created what he would like to think of as a monument of pure Italianness. D'Annunzio had, indeed, taken such themes and ideas. Guy Tosi has shown that when *Il piacere* was translated for his French audience, many cuts had to be made in those sections which a French reader would immediately have recognized as coming from certain French Decadent writers, and in particular from the fashionable if scurrilous pen of

[27] Later reprinted in E. Thovez, *L'arco di Ulisse* (Naples, 1921).

Joséphin Péladan.[28] Thovez added the name of Guy de Maupassant, four of whose short stories, he said, D'Annunzio had disguised by dressing them up in Abruzzese rags; he made many other adverse criticisms. For D'Annunzio any publicity was good publicity, and he would no doubt have been content to let his name become associated with this other scandal; he was, anyway, too busy with his other literary work and erotic activity to be distracted by a young critic on the make.

The open letter containing his apologia in the *Figaro* of 1 February 1896 was squeezed out of him by friends who said that he *must* defend himself, particularly if he was to safeguard his reputation in France. In it D'Annunzio pointed out the right of creative spirits to take their advantage where they could (*Tous les grands ouvriers de prose e de poésie ont pris leur bien où ils l'ont trouvé*); Molière, he said, had made a similar defence. It was also true that D'Annunzio had not been concerned with excising simply those citations which might be potentially embarrassing; he had himself made certain cuts, but other obvious echoes still remained.[29] D'Annunzio's general defence against Thovez in *Le Figaro* was published in Italian eight days later in the *Illustrazione italiana* of 9 February 1896, to the delight of his friends. Their supportive attitude and some of the flavour of the polemic can be gathered from D'Annunzio's secretary, Tom Antongini. In his biography of D'Annunzio, Antongini gives a scornful account of Thovez, whom he calls a 'covert poet', and of the *Gazzetta letteraria*, which he terms a *giornaletto* ('a petty journal'); he pours ridicule on Thovez's attempts to cast doubt on D'Annunzio's originality, and exults in the way that D'Annunzio's friends had clustered round to protect him and 'immunize D'Annunzio for ever against the attacks of the little reptile that had attached itself to his heels'.[30]

Although the incident was trivial seen in the light of the massive literary enterprises and the cataclysmic events in which D'Annunzio was soon to be involved, I believe that the way in which Thovez

---

[28] Thovez had already pointed this out in the *Gazzetta letteraria* (29 Feb. 1896), cf. his *Arco di Ulisse*, 67; Tosi discusses this aspect in the introduction to his edition of *GD'A à Georges Hérelle*, esp. 94–5.

[29] E. De Michelis, *Ancora D'Annunzio* (Pescara, 1987), 66–7 and 233–4, has clearly shown that D'Annunzio's excisions were not necessarily concerned with avoiding accusations of plagiarism and that many relics of Péladan and others remain; he also considers D'Annunzio's openly stated need for inspiration from others.

[30] Antongini, *D'Annunzio*, 55.

was subsequently silenced had a wider significance. The importance of D'Annunzio's counter-attack was threefold: it showed D'Annunzio's method of working, it demonstrated the power of the press under his manipulative skill, and it proved to him, if he needed reminding, how easy it was to gull an Italian public. If he could bring about a successful outcome of the contest with Thovez, his enemies would be hesitant in future about calling him a liar; the power to intimidate, which he had also experienced as a writer of gossip columns, would grant him immunity from similar attacks, and in future he would thus be allowed greater creative scope in the use he made of other men's names, reputations, and work. It has already been seen that as a schoolboy, twenty years before the polemics of Thovez, D'Annunzio was not averse to deceiving his teacher Angelo Tonini with essays copied from established writers, for which he was awarded encouragingly high marks. His first major reviewer, Giuseppe Chiarini, had pointed to the many echoes from other poets in D'Annunzio's first collection *Primo vere*, and Chiarini was not slow to point out other similar borrowings in D'Annunzio's later, more mature work. D'Annunzio was accustomed to using imitative techniques and was indifferent to the adverse criticism which arose when his borrowings were uncovered.

After Thovez's first two articles an anonymous well-wisher sent the Turinese critic a selection of Rossetti poems, not then generally known in Italy, pointing out obvious similarities between the Rossetti and some of the poetry in D'Annunzio's latest successful anthology, the *Poema paradisiaco*, particularly the poem 'Consolazione'. Thovez leapt at the new evidence and published his third article, throwing into relief the alleged plagiarism.[31] So blatant did the borrowing now seem that the *Corriere della sera* took up a strong anti-Dannunzian stance, reproaching him for such unashamed copying. At that point D'Annunzio, alone or in concert with others, responded in *Marzocco*, the new journal which had started publication in Florence on 2 February 1896. On 5 April its editorial pointed out that the Rossetti poems were spurious, and that D'Annunzio's poems could not therefore be derivative of them. The style of the piece was deliberately insulting and provocative:

[31] In the *Gazzetta letteraria* of 4 Jan. 1896; Thovez there has a good turn of phrase: he imagines D'Annunzio 'composing his poetic mosaics with a pen in one hand and the fingers of the other between the pages of some author' (see *L'arco di Ulisse*, 45).

A journal, unworthy of being named here, which each week proceeds through the public places of Italian literature, collecting garbage, like the stinking cart dragged by donkeys through the grimy suburbs, wheels squeaking, surrounded by the howls of hungry dogs, the usual journal, in a word, some days ago, printed on its usual first page, open for every excretion, a collection of its usual fragments, with which a certain G. B. Mazzoni wanted to demonstrate that the marvellous 'Consolation' of Gabriele D'Annunzio was simply an able paraphrase of two of Rossetti's sonnets.

The day before D'Annunzio had written to Treves to tell him to contact Achille Torelli Viollier, publisher of the *Corriere della sera*, and obtain a retraction ('and I hope there will be no need for litigation').[32]

At this point it is useful to consider an important aspect of D'Annunzio's method of composition. If Thovez had been more of a comparativist, instead of a rather puritanical Carduccian, he might have realized the danger he was running, and particularly so if he had studied D'Annunzio's style a little more carefully. Best of all he might have read two of D'Annunzio's earlier publications. The first of these was, at first glance, a slight offering, written during D'Annunzio's *Tribuna* period, and published in that journal on 8 October 1887. The article depended heavily for its success upon its readers being ignorant of, or held in awe by, D'Annunzio's insouciant use of non-Italian sources. Under the title 'Un poeta d'autunno' (A Poet of Autumn), the piece purported to be a review of an anthology of poetry which had allegedly landed recently on D'Annunzio's desk. The author of the collection was said to be a certain Adolphus Hannaford. D'Annunzio's 'review' summed up Hannaford's qualities in terms of English Romantic and post-Romantic writers: thus this poet of autumn was said to be the last in the school of poetry which included in its ranks Byron, Coleridge, Keats, Landor, Shelley, Swinburne, Tennyson, and Wordsworth. Hannaford also seemed to combine in his person the aesthetic sensibilities of another octumvirate, this time in the visual arts; here D'Annunzio included the names of Joshua Reynolds, Alma Tadema, Leighton, and Dante Gabriel Rossetti; also thrown in were the ideals of the pre-Raphaelite Brotherhood and the art criticism of

[32] Amusing details of the affair, along with the letter to Treves, are published in Gatti, *GD'A* 160–1.

John Ruskin.[33] Tenuously, from these elements D'Annunzio managed to build up a portrait of his new poet: 'He is well thought of and enjoyed by that very choice group of poets and critics who follow the so-called Aesthetic School founded in England around 1848.' The only artistic movement to which D'Annunzio could be referring was the pre-Raphaelite Brotherhood, and sure enough, another of D'Annunzio's later inventions, exploited above all in his novels, is his personalized version of pre-Raphaelite aesthetics and poetics.

The result of his Hannaford spoof, added to derivative assertions in *Il piacere* and several other pieces in *Tribuna*, was to make him appear an authority on much of the latest fashionable poetry in Britain. It was a part-substitute for D'Annunzio's not being able to read the originals, since his English was never very good. At the same time, it should be added that Giulio Aristide Sartorio, the poet's artistic friend and collaborator, had been to London several times between 1890 and 1895, had met William Morris, Burne-Jones, Arthur Hughes, and William Michael Rossetti, and had published essays on the pre-Raphaelites in *Convito* during the period 1895–6. There was material on the subject for D'Annunzio to peruse; whether he did so with much attention is doubtful, since Sartorio had cleverly made clear a three-stage development in the pre-Raphaelite movement, which rendered meaningless any talk of a unified aesthetic school.[34] For his own review in *Tribuna*, D'Annunzio helpfully 'translated' a couple of Hannaford's poems into Italian, but, far from revealing a poet of an English autumn, the result came out as a very 'Mediterranean' and very Dannunzian autumn:

> Il vino è pronto. O artefice, tu scegli con ogni diligenza un marmo
> senza difetto per farne un bel vaso.

[33] D'Annunzio's artist friend Giulio Aristide Sartorio was one of the few experts on the subject; in 1895 he had regretted the confusion surrounding a definition of pre-Raphaelitism in Italy; see his 'Nota su D. G. Rossetti pittore', *Il convito*, 2 (1895), 211.

[34] I am grateful to Giuliana Pieri for information to appear soon in her thesis 'The Pre-Raphaelites in Italy'; she there notes an unpublished letter of Enrico Nencioni, to Ferdinando Martini, dated 30 Apr. 1882, in which Nencioni confessed his ignorance of D. G. Rossetti's work; two years later D'Annunzio, in a letter of 15 Feb. 1884 to Nencioni, expressed a similar ignorance and declared himself eager to read the latter's article, 'Le poesie e le pitture di Dante Gabriele Rossetti', in the *Fanfulla della domenica* of the same date. Much of D'Annunzio's knowledge may therefore have stemmed from that article and his acquaintance with the critic.

Ricerca a lungo la sua forma e non vi rappresentare in giro misteriosi
   amori né pugne sacre.

[The wine is ready. Artificer, choose diligently marble without
   imperfection to create a fine vessel for the vintage.
 Work hard on its form, and around it carve no mysterious loves nor
   sacred battles.]

Hannaford, in short, was D'Annunzio's own creation and the qualities revealed by his analysis of the former's poems, had been offered
to his *Tribuna* readers as authentic characteristics of the so-called
new aesthetic school in England. The spoof is betrayed at several
points, notably when he treats Joshua Reynolds (whom we know
was Dante Gabriel's *bête noire*) as though he were a pre-Raphaelite.
It comes as no surprise that the qualities revealed by D'Annunzio's
analysis of Hannaford were, *mirabile dictu*, close to the techniques
which D'Annunzio himself used in his latest poems.[35] So when
he went on to create a pre-Raphaelite heroine in the poem 'Le
due Beatrici', the image could now appear something more than a
superficial and modish imitation. And in a novel such as *Il piacere*,
his pre-Raphaelite heroines are described as if they were recreations,
in Walter Pater vein, of Rossetti portraits.

   A similar spoof, which had wider repercussions for his art, was
the creation of his own 'Shelley', a figure that had haunted him all
his creative life. When in 1892 D'Annunzio had written a commemoration of the poet, he had included many characteristics which
were more his own than Shelley's, so that when later he came to
write in Shelleyan vein in *Alcyone* and elsewhere, his reading public could be convinced that he had mastered the techniques of yet
another genius, when in fact the techniques were personal to him,
and foisted on the long-dead Shelley. One of the most interesting
features of that Shelley *Commemorazione* was a quotation from the
latter's *Prometheus Unbound* which concerns Asia, the venerable
and ancient daughter of Ocean. Shelley calls her the 'Child [that
is, 'daughter'] of Ocean', but D'Annunzio mistranslated 'Child' as
'figlio', *figlio dell'Oceano* ('the son of Ocean'). The Chorus greets
Asia with the words:

Sconosciuta nel mondo dorme una voce non rivelata. Soltanto dal tuo passo
può il suo riposo essere turbato, figlio dell'Oceano!

---

[35] The poems also have something about them of the French Parnassian school;
cf. the creation of the marble wine-cup and Théophile Gautier's *L'Art*.

In the world unknown
Sleeps a voice unspoken
By thy steps alone
Can its rest be broken
Child of Ocean.[36]

D'Annunzio's translation of 'Child of Ocean' as a masculine *figlio* was more consonant with his own attitudes to myth and nature, as he formed a mental picture of a Pan-like being, able to mediate between Nature and Art. Such a being was to become the protagonist of 'Il fanciullo' (The Young Boy), the second poem of *Alcyone*, and it is *his* free spirit which animates the poetry of most of that particular collection. The happy error of translation did lead to some inspired lyric poems. It may well be that D'Annunzio genuinely thought that he was outdoing Shelley at his own poetry, but it is more probable that he knew he was substituting a Shelley of his own making for a Shelley he could never properly know.[37]

In *Il piacere* of 1889 D'Annunzio's *alter ego*, Andrea Sperelli, consciously uses a line or a theme from earlier poets to give him the initial inspiration for his own work. In recent years Aldo Rossi and Pietro Gibellini have shown how D'Annunzio used dictionaries and thesauri to obtain material, sometimes from banal and prosaic sources, and with it created some diaphanously beautiful poetry.[38] Mario Praz concentrated his investigative energies on the 'creative' use made of other men's work, and has pointed out, at times over-obsessively, D'Annunzio's presumed literary sources. Praz was particularly alert to the influence of the English Decadents, whom D'Annunzio so often read through the medium of translations, notably those of his French acquaintance, Gabriel Maurey. At times D'Annunzio absorbed not only the atmosphere of a Swinburnian poem, but also the gaffes which his French translators might have made. Nevertheless, Praz is the only critic before Paolo Alatri clearly to show that D'Annunzio had constructed from his borrowings a new European poetic amalgam possessing a character and

---

[36] GD'A, *Commemorazione di P. B. Shelley*, *Prose di ricerca*, iii. 365–72, here 369.

[37] For further details of these spoofs, see J. R. Woodhouse, 'Curiouser and Spuriouser: Two English Influences on D'Annunzio', *Italian Studies*, 42 (1987), 69–80.

[38] Rossi, 'D'Annunzio giovane'; P. Gibellini,'Fiori di carta: La fonte della flora di *Alcyone*', in E. Tiboni and L. Abrugiati (eds.), *Natura ed arte nel paesaggio dannunziano* (Pescara, 1980), 41–50.

an atmosphere of its own, which could be nothing other than Dannunzian.[39]

In these and other cases, it might well be argued that D'Annunzio was no more plagiaristic than any other writer, Dante and Shakespeare included; his proximity in time to ourselves makes the borrowings seem more obvious. It would, however, leave questions unanswered simply to pass on from the area of D'Annunzio's so-called plagiarism without mentioning that in his work there were more glaring examples of rather less creative borrowings, assimilated less artistically into some inferior pieces. The most shameless instances were those which D'Annunzio found necessary to incorporate in order to meet a publisher's deadline. For example on one particular occasion in 1912, oppressed by creditors, he needed rapidly to finish the first act of *Parisina* in order to obtain the publisher's advance. The task took him only three days, thanks largely to the fact that he had copied most of it from poems lifted from Carducci's obscure edition of fourteenth- and fifteenth-century lyrics (*Cacce in rima de' secoli XIV e XV*), with further details lifted from another obscure poet, Panfilo Sasso, edited in 1882 by Severino Ferrari. And Aldo Rossi has shown how the poet took books from the Marucelliana library in Florence, the Vittorio Emanuele in Rome, and the Estense library in Ferrara, scoring them heavily in the margins in order to pinpoint ideas and information which he then lifted for his *Francesca da Rimini* in 1901.[40]

Much more could be written about D'Annunzio's so-called plagiarism, but, as ever, he had the last word. During the period of controversy D'Annunzio was also engaged on *Il trionfo della morte*, which contained much philosophical speculation deriving, at times line for line, from his recent reading of Nietzsche. In the novel D'Annunzio's prefatory letter to Michetti contained the declaration that he was preparing the way for the Superman, and many of the concepts in this and other writings, for instance the conflict between sensation and spiritual aspirations and the sterilizing effect of the sex-drive on magnanimity and artistic creativity, may be said to be among the ideas taken from Nietzsche, just as he borrowed material

[39] GD'A, *Poesie, Teatro, Prose*, abbr. and ed. M. Praz and F. Gerra (Milan and Naples, 1966), is thick with footnotes showing D'Annunzio's sources or presumed sources, as well as the gaffes he sometimes made.

[40] I am grateful to Aldo Rossi for this information; see also Ch. 4 n. 25 above, and Rossi, 'D'Annunzio giovane', 54.

from other writers for other themes. But what he undoubtedly took over from the German philosopher were certain ruthless tendencies or instincts, which he saw were present in his own make-up. One such tendency was Nietzsche's view of the predatory genius. In D'Annunzio's library at the Vittoriale there is an edition of Nietzsche in Henri Albert's translation; one of the apophthegms (no. 100) has been particularly noted in the margin. In it, Nietzsche discusses the predatory genius, particularly in art, which is capable of deceiving the most subtle of intelligences and which is born when a person unscrupulously considers as his prey any property not protected by the law. In the margin D'Annunzio had written large: EGO. It is a fact that his predatory forays gave him the material to forge some inimitable work. And some of the work will stand comparison with the masterpieces, which, in the best Renaissance and Bembist tradition, he had both emulated and gone beyond.

Marzocco, the journal which D'Annunzio used to demolish Thovez and temporarily humiliate the *Corriere della sera*, was to have a long and prosperous future; the driving force for its early issues was summed up in the *Prologo* of that first number, published on 2 February 1896, jointly written by D'Annunzio and Giuseppe Saverio Gargano: 'To strive towards a purer and higher art', and 'to oppose any literary or artistic work which had its origins outside pure beauty'. Such slogans as these became part of D'Annunzio's idiosyncratic political programme for years to come and, while the views may seem vague, even absurd to the modern reader, they echoed similar ideas put forward by aesthetes from Dante Gabriel Rossetti onwards. Almost contemporaneously, for instance, Frederick Stephens, one of the original Pre-Raphaelite Brethren, in his biography of Dante Gabriel described how he and the others founded their brotherhood: 'What might be called a League of Sincerity with loftier aims than artists generally cared for, a leading principle of which implied that each confessor should paint his best with due reference to nature, without which there could be no sincerity.'[41] The two concepts were not far distant from each other, and were reflected even more closely in the creed of the artists working for the group In Arte Libertas, after 1887. The ideas propounded for *Marzocco* were

---

[41] F. Stephens, *Dante Gabriel Rossetti* (London, 1894), 17; cf. D'Annunzio's views in the letter to Matilde Serao prefaced to *Giovanni Episcopo*, see above, p. 92.

not as entirely impractical or romantic as might nowadays be imagined. Not long after the journal's foundation in 1896, during speeches to essentially unlettered and uncultured electors, D'Annunzio was to have the multitude wild with enthusiasm for the beauty of his descriptions of golden ears of wheat or the blueness of a cornflower. Evidently what Italy actually needed were radical reforms of suffrage and education, and the creation of new agricultural and manufacturing enterprises to offset the poverty of constituencies such as D'Annunzio's and those of the deprived south in general. What D'Annunzio offered was a series of beautiful concepts. Stelio Effrena, the orator–composer of *Il fuoco*, had been the prototype for such an aesthete–demagogue. And when, in *Alcyone*, D'Annunzio makes poetry out of the political experiences of the years following 1886, he rejoices in the fact that the *bestia elettiva*, the elective beast, despite shortcomings such as its collective stench of sweat (and its failure to re-elect him in 1900), could be provoked to appreciation of his glorious dicta thanks to the shafts of gold launched by his oratory into its apparently insensitive flanks.

The importance of the *Marzocco* lay in the fact that it soon became one of Italy's most authoritative journals, and, as far as D'Annunzio was concerned, it lent him its unqualified support for the rest of his creative period as a writer, until, indeed, it folded in 1932. It had some first-class contributors and editors, and appeared to have a solid academic base, unlike many of the rather more ephemeral journals founded later in order simply to provide literary claques which supported intellectually fragile or ideologically oppressive points of view. Nevertheless Paolo Alatri for one, always alert to symptoms of the political mayhem which was to break on the world, sees in *Marzocco* the political implications of the triumph of élitism, of self-indulgent caprice, rather than the old Carduccian asceticism, and of voluptuousness and passion rather than reason.[42] Another effect of the support for a Dannunzian political aesthetic was to make such attitudes fashionable and so imitable by lesser followers. D'Annunzio undoubtedly made many thousands of Italians proud to be Italian; his patriotism seemed beyond question and his charisma was as great inside the Peninsula as that of any of his predecessors or contemporaries. Thus if Dannunzianism was the

---

[42] Alatri, *GD'A*, 175.

'contagion' which some critics (particularly political critics) believed, the fact that he should have a large following of enthusiasts who believed that they were all, in their own ways, facsimiles of the master, could only be seen as a danger by proponents of a more egalitarian view of society. The *Marzocco* was one of those elements which helped play a part in the dissemination of the myth.

6

The Poet as Politician

IT was inevitable that the blend of aesthetics and politics, discernible in D'Annunzio's self-assertive attitudes before 1897, should find another and different outlet. Between March and July of that year the opportunity arose. A by-election was announced to replace the traditional Liberal member of parliament for Ortona a Mare, Filippo Masci, whose election the previous March, by a fifty-vote majority over his more radical Republican if not Socialist opponent, Carlo Altobelli, had been declared null and void by parliament on 2 July 1897.[1] On 16 July 1897 D'Annunzio wrote from Venice to a local lawyer, Francesco Ercole, who was to become one of his strongest supporters, confirming his willingness to accept nomination as candidate for the constituency of Ortona a Mare, the coastal area which comprised Pescara, Francavilla, and Ortona itself. Umberto Russo has shown through a study of the previous contender's election promises and statements that Filippo Masci, a professor of philosophy and the rector of Naples University, was too idealistic, too concerned with wider social reforms, to be acceptable to his political grouping. Furthermore, Masci was unpopular with the electorate because of his refusal to offer patronage to clients. D'Annunzio had no such scruples, but he had supported Masci in the previous election against the Republican Altobelli and he could legitimately now take the wise precaution of consulting with Masci before accepting the definitive nomination. Russo publishes an important letter sent by D'Annunzio from the Grand Hotel in Venice to Francesco Ercole in Francavilla concerning the conversation:

---

[1] Masci, *La vita e le opere*, 137 (see Ch. 1 n. 11 above on these homonyms). Why the election of Masci was declared void has never been made clear; Chiara, *GD'A* 109 mentions 'formal errors in the election process', and U. Russo, 'L'avventura elettorale: 37 lettere inedite di GD'A', *Oggi e Domani*, 6/3–4 (Mar.–Apr. 1978), 35–41, like most other commentators, speaks of a failure by parliament to ratify Masci's election; perhaps the victory by only fifty votes was suspicious.

After a loyal and cordial talk in Rome with our friend Filippo Masci I am resolved to accept the candidacy in the College of Ortona, as long as the illustrious Member and his electors trust in the good fortune of my name and are willing to help me sincerely [*francamente*] in the enterprise.[2]

There was some irony in D'Annunzio's opposing Carlo Altobelli, since, it may be recalled, the latter had been his defence lawyer in the adultery case brought by Maria Gravina's husband, the Count Anguissola, but there was never any question that D'Annunzio was a lifelong Monarchist, and thus radically opposed to Altobelli's republicanism.[3] There was, however, no small risk in a Superman's standing for election in Ortona, since the constituency had been evenly split during the elections earlier that year and it could have been unbearably humiliating for D'Annunzio to be rejected by the electorate. Courting Francesco Ercole, by all accounts a man of imposing personality, strong intellectual ability, and high principles, was one of the first steps he took to ensure that no such defeat was possible; in particular, Ercole was to be a powerful advocate in the influential ward of Francavilla a Mare. D'Annunzio's letter to him goes on to speculate, 'How do the voters of Francavilla feel? I hope that they are willing to consider me as one of them, since on their delightful hill was born the better part of me—the whole of my life's work.' D'Annunzio is there alluding to the novels, plays, and poems written in Michetti's convent, as well as in his love-nest, the Villa Mammarella, but he also had relatives in the area, and, perhaps above all, he was willing to cultivate the favour of individuals, a ploy unacceptable to Masci, by promises of preferment after he had been elected.

The *taccuini* of this period are full of strange jottings, no longer the typically inspirational notes for his literary work: hints that for one constituent he can obtain remission of a gaol sentence, obtain a scholarship for the education of another voter's daughter, ensure a job as a prison warder for another ('which', he notes, 'would bring in its train four further votes').[4] Private letters of the time

[2] Russo, 'L'avventura elettorale', 40.

[3] One of D'Annunzio's most famous publications in Britain was his piece, 'The King of Italy', which came out in the *Daily Telegraph* on 3 Jan. 1916. His enthusiasm is reproduced in translation in S. Laredo De Mendoza's *GD'A, fante del Veliki e del Faiti* (Milan 1932), 21–5 ('Il Re d'Italia'); for his ode 'Al Re giovine' (To the Young King), see below p. 194.

[4] *Altri taccuini*, 72, 83, and *passim*.

show how his pledges and promised favours were in some cases later carried out. Other constituents, he noted in the *taccuini*, could be brought over by the gift of a signed copy of one of his works. It was to convince his publisher Treves of the need for such free presentation copies that one of D'Annunzio's most famous letters was written:

I have just come back from an electoral trip; and my nostrils are still full of an acrid smell of humanity. This enterprise may seem stupid and extraneous to my art; but to judge my aptitude it is necessary to await the effect towards which my will is bent directly. Victory meanwhile is assured. The world, my dear fellow, must be persuaded that I am capable of everything.[5]

The stench in D'Annunzio's nostrils might well have been due as much to concessions to clients as to the physical atmosphere of a nineteenth-century crowd in August. His publisher responded with free copies of D'Annunzio's most recent publications and with complimentary election posters printed on the Treves presses.

Then, as now, it was obviously useful to have the support of the news media. D'Annunzio's main propaganda outlet in the province was the weekly *La Provincia di Chieti*, which was under the editorship of another ally, Vincenzo Vicoli. D'Annunzio, being a nationally recognized figure, had the advantage of being able to reproduce in the *Provincia* eye-catching snippets from the national press concerning his more wide-ranging activities. These were often incestuous pieces, since D'Annunzio himself solicited from journalistic friends items to which he added, anonymously, linking comments of his own to be republished for local consumption. The campaign was not always fought courteously, particularly in the local newspapers. On 20 July 1897 the *Provincia* declared, quite unjustifiably, that Altobelli intended to withdraw his candidature and leave the field open to D'Annunzio. Altobelli's side in turn gave their candidate strong support through the newspaper *Lo svegliarino*; the opposing press campaigns produced at times nothing less than hilarious results. Naturally enough, D'Annunzio's private morality (or his lack of it) came in for some harsh criticism, and, on a more practical plane, he was castigated for his indeterminate political views. The *Svegliarino* may have come close to the truth when it

[5] Reported and commented upon by Sodini, *Ariel armato*, 368.

tried to explain away D'Annunzio's candidacy as no more than a further means of collecting different material for a new book.[6]

Among D'Annunzio's most influential and enthusiastic supporters was Giuseppe Antonio D'Alessandro, a local general medical practitioner, whose family home was located centrally in the constituency, at Ari, and whose practice took him far afield by carriage and on horseback. In a constituency of just over 3,000 voters here was evidently a host worth cultivating, and his name figures large, along with those of other members of D'Alessandro's family, in the *taccuini* of the time.[7] Despite the obvious political advantage to be derived from the doctor's acquaintance, there is some evidence that D'Annunzio did also have a genuine affection for the man. D'Alessandro's speeches also acted as a warm-up for some of D'Annunzio's own orations. The two men evidently saw eye to eye, for instance, on policy matters, especially on the decadence of the current parliament. An anti-intellectual policy, according to D'Alessandro, had brought the state to its knees:

And while this theory triumphs we have a House which has trampled on national dignity, corrupted its character in every fibre. This is because dignity and character, the sense of our most austere duties and the courage of daring and noble achievements, are also composed of poetic qualities; they are fragments of lyric and epic in action.[8]

The words could not have been chosen more appropriately to introduce D'Annunzio's own politics of poetry, particularly as expressed in a famous speech which he gave in Pescara on 22 August 1897, the 'Discorso della siepe' (Discourse of the Hedge). Hard-headed commentators, Anthony Rhodes for one, have spoken ironically of the associations which D'Annunzio made in the speech between himself and various aspects of Abruzzese life and nature.[9] The sentiments D'Annunzio expressed certainly justify his title of *il candidato della bellezza*, but there is a recognizably joyful inspiration in his phrases which allowed them to produce a more substantial

---

[6] For a discussion of this part of the campaign, see J. R. Woodhouse, 'D'Annunzio's Election Victory of 1897: New Documents, New Perspectives', *Italian Studies*, 40 (1985), 63–84.

[7] See *Altri taccuini*, 81.

[8] For further details of D'Alessandro's speeches and general support, see Woodhouse, 'D'Annunzio's Election Victory of 1897', here 70–1.

[9] A. Rhodes, *The Poet as Superman: The Life of GD'A* (London, 1959), 80.

effect on an audience than we might imagine from reading Anthony Rhodes's account:

The gleam of a blade of straw in the dust helps me to uncover the harsh aspect of a truth. Illumined thoughts are generated in my head by the gesture of the baker as he draws from the oven the smoking, risen, golden bread which fills the house with the joy of its perfume.[10]

From his self-identification with the wholesome genius of the people, D'Annunzio is led to a vision of the ideals of Italy's Risorgimento, reduced by anti-intellectual materialism to what he describes as a 'thick grey slime where an ignoble multitude tosses and turns and traffics as in its natural element'. Italy was the genetrix of beauty, and it was the duty of all, particularly the poet, to revivify that ancient tradition, 'The fortune of Italy is inseparable from the fate of beauty, of which Italy is mother.'

There is evidently little here of the conventional political harangue, and most of D'Annunzio's statements would have been above the heads of his audience, but the concluding part of the speech becomes a Darwinian–Nietzschean statement of evolutionary survival, while a final agricultural metaphor, urging his hearers to cultivate the hedge which surrounded their own plot of land, would have been clear enough to any bucolic mind: 'I tell you, Farmers, that the hedge which encloses the fertile soil broken by your steel and watered with your sweat is never sufficiently thick and stubborn and thorny and vigorous. Strengthen it more; make it put out more powerful roots, more fierce thorns.' Sentiments of that kind have always been taken over and exploited by critics of D'Annunzio's political views in order to bolster one or other party viewpoint. It is not difficult to do so. Yet his words contained a novel and different element which might here usefully be emphasized: despite the agricultural and other associations, D'Annunzio makes clear to his audience the distance which separates them from him:

Welcome me as you would a purer, more limpid brother. For just one day at least, allow to shine on yourselves the cloak of light which I have woven for you. Consider, you workers, that there is no disharmony between the works in which you exercise your strength and the divine hopes for which I am fashioning my wings.

[10] The 'Discorso della siepe' is available in *Prose di ricerca*, i. 464–76, under the title of 'Laude dell'illaudato'; quotations here are respectively from pp. 464, 473, 474, and 475–6.

Notes for this and other orations were jotted down in the *taccuini* for the period; many variations there on the same theme bear out D'Annunzio's later declaration that he had made twenty different speeches adapted to the diverse aspects of local life and industry which corresponded to the various areas of the constituency.[11] Some of the atmosphere is captured by the *Provincia di Chieti* in a report on the poet's visit to the tiny village of Ari on 20 August 1897:

An imposing demonstration of solidarity awaited the illustrious poet on the provincial road. Youthful groups waved the tricolour, and some copies of the *Mattino* containing D'Annunzio's speech had been fixed to poles, serving as flags [. . .]. The band intoned the National Anthem, and to cries of 'Viva D'Annunzio! Viva the Abruzzi poet!' the procession moved off towards the house of the egregious Doctor Giuseppe D'Alessandro, a most likeable gentleman and very cultured [*gentiluomo simpaticissimo e assai colto*].

Local dignitaries and their wives contended to secure a mention in the paragraphs of the *Provincia*.

D'Annunzio's son Mario, who thirty years afterwards had the experience, with Mussolini's help, of winning a parliamentary election of his own, has described in vivid terms the interminable meetings, dinners, receptions by local mayors, parades with village bands, and the rest. Surrounded by a motley retinue of cat-calling, cart-wheeling urchins, the official group of mayor, dignitaries, and candidate would get down from their improvised transport, usually a wine-cart, and step out on to the dusty road:

The candidate, hat in hand, even in cold weather, as if he were going to a funeral, turned to right and left, looked up and down so as not to disappoint anyone, thinking of future elections, and fixed his face in a stereotyped, cinematographic smile which gave the impression to anyone who did not know him that he was a cretin (even though basically he wasn't).[12]

Then would follow the speeches from a town-hall balcony, or similar vantage-point. Each of D'Annunzio's many election meetings must have compounded his irritation and discomfort. Hastily written notes to Giuseppe D'Alessandro give some idea of the agitated nature of the different venues, 'I'm sending a cyclist to give you

---

[11] The relevant entries in the *Altri taccuini* follow 71; Masci, *La vita e le opere*, 138, mentions the many harangues; D'Annunzio himself spoke at length of the variations in an interview with Edmondo De Amicis published in *Tribuna*, 10 June 1902.

[12] M. D'Annunzio, *Con mio padre sulla nave del ricordo* (Milan, 1950), 46.

warning. Don't prepare dinner; we shall have to return to Francavilla before nightfall.' Another such arrived on 23 August 1897,
a pencilled note on one of D'Annunzio's visiting-cards, informing
D'Alessandro that their carriage had broken down on a mountain
road, on their way to an important venue at Ari; their horse was
lame; the driver refused to go on; another carriage which had come
to their aid was unserviceable, and there were now nine people in
their one vehicle. D'Annunzio promised to send another runner in
the morning.[13]

In 'Della mia legislatura' (On my Period in Office), a long front-
page article published in *Il giorno* on 29 March 1900 D'Annunzio,
reflecting on his time in parliament, ignored the dust and sweat and
discomfort to describe his candidature in terms which make his
efforts seem more heroic or idealistic:

The sentiment which drove me to enter the conclaves of my adversaries
does not contradict in any way the doctrine to which I give life in my artistic work. [. . .] Among all human attitudes I love that of the one who
bends the bow; among all manly enterprises I admire that of the one who
breaks the law imposed by others in order to establish his own law.

These are the feelings which animate the protagonists of his novels,
and, sure enough, the early prognosis of the *Svegliarino*, that the
election was a pretext for D'Annunzio to collect more material for
further publications, was partly borne out with the launch three
years later of *Il fuoco*, the novel which marked the transit from the
mystical and unattainable aspirations of Claudio Cantelmo, protagonist of *Le vergini delle rocce*, to the poetically rhetorical politics of
the new hero, Stelio Effrena. Effrena is aware of the barbarity of
his fellows but feels that he has the unique responsibility, proper
to the artist, of using the multitude as a means of self-exaltation
and fulfilment. His fictional words are exactly foreshadowed in the
Giorno article of 29 March 1900:

It seems to me that the word, addressed orally and directly to a multitude,
must have as its only purpose action, violent action if necessary. Only with
such an implicit understanding may a somewhat fierce spirit, without self-
diminution, communicate with the mob by way of the sensual qualities of
voice and gesture.

[13] These notes and other valuable material were deposited in Oxford's Taylorian
Institute Library by Camillo Talbot D'Alessandro, Giuseppe D'Alessandro's son;
several are published in Woodhouse, 'D'Annunzio's Election Victory of 1897'.

With this might be contrasted the decadent nihilism of the views expressed in Book I of *Le vergini delle rocce* concerning the vanity and grief of all efforts: 'Renunciation, complete unconsciousness, the dissolution of all dreams, absolute annihilation—that is the ultimate liberation.'

It is illuminating to trace a line of development between the language and nihilism of D'Annunzio's writings before 1897 and the poetical idealization of language and ideas which followed soon afterwards in the *Laudi*, especially in *Alcyone*. The line runs through the election campaign itself, particularly the 'Discorso della siepe' and the subsequent opinions put into the mouth of Stelio Effrena by D'Annunzio in *Il fuoco*. As will be seen from the *Laudi*, the chimera–mob depicted in the opening poem of *Alcyone* and the multitude addressed or described in *Il fuoco* and 'La siepe' are as one. Thus Effrena in the first chapter of *Il fuoco* declares:

There was, then, in the multitude, a hidden beauty from which only poet and hero could draw flashes. When that beauty is revealed by the sudden clamour which arises in the theatre, in public squares or in the trenches, then the orator feels his heart swollen with the joy of knowing how to arouse that beauty with his verse, his harangue, the sign of the sword. The word of the poet, communicated to the crowd was, then, an action, like the gesture of the hero.

Those words are lifted almost verbatim from the 'Discorso della siepe'. There are many similar auto-quotations, revealing that life and art were even more indissolubly intertwined at this stage in D'Annunzio's career. The sentiments expressed by him in these articles and speeches, fictional or otherwise, are also remarkably prophetic of his demogogic harangues to the Roman mobs on the eve of Italy's entry into World War One in 1915. In *Il giorno* D'Annunzio admitted the technique: Effrena 'repeats still more fiercely what I said in the meeting of citizens and farmers'. But there is, too, a new regret in Effrena's triumph. The need to humiliate himself before the electorate is something dishonouring: 'Let each one of you consider the element of humiliation for me contained in the honour for which I am marked out, consider the uselessness of my next effort.'

The election took place on 19 August 1897. Final numbers vary, but according to the figures published by Umberto Russo, whose expertise and objectivity concerning the campaign are undeniable, out of a possible 3,743 voters 2,919 votes were cast, 1,427 favouring D'Annunzio, 1,262 Altobelli; the other votes were void. Although D'Annunzio was a clear winner his election was not ratified immediately by parliament. The earlier condemnation for adultery made it possible for his fellow Deputies to declare his election invalid, and they were not slow to do this. It should also be remembered that, apart from his new amorous escapades with Eleonora Duse, he was still seen to be cohabiting with Maria Gravina, who on 2 May 1897, just three months before the election, presented him with another son, Gabriele Dante. D'Annunzio, who suspected Maria Gravina of having affairs of her own, always refused to recognize the child as his. Long after the deaths of all parties, as late as the 1970s, an unsuccessful court case was brought by an indignant descendant of Gabriele Dante in order to assert D'Annunzio's paternity of the boy.[14] It took the new member of parliament a further nine months of lobbying and cajoling, until 26 April 1898, when his colleagues finally allowed him to take his seat in the House.

D'Annunzio's feelings about the humiliation of having to submit himself to a plebeian electorate find some reflection in Filippo Masci's chronological study, particularly where Masci reports that D'Annunzio had noted that the 'first contacts with the electoral beast had made his hair stand on end. The enterprise, which had from a distance seemed tempting, now disgusted him.'[15] Further, on 5 September 1897 Masci notes D'Annunzio's malaise, despite his victory: 'D'Annunzio curses the hour in which he allowed himself to be drawn into politics. His poor mother is assailed by anonymous letters which threaten him, and she seems out of her mind. D'Annunzio is afflicted and furious at himself and at everyone else.'[16] No doubt Masci was, like so many commentators on the event, prejudiced in his own way. It is difficult to believe that D'Annunzio did not feel a sense of achievement at his ability to control the crowds he harangued. However, in part-confirmation of Masci's comment, it is fair to note that D'Annunzio reported the news to Hérelle in a very subdued tone ('after much struggle I have triumphed'), and the same letter went on to mention that his

---

[14] The case was against the editor of the Pescarese journal *Oggi e Domani*, which had published an article alleging that the descendants of this love-child were not of D'Annunzio's blood. The proceedings were indefinitely postponed as unprovable (DNA testing was not then available!).

[15] Masci, *La vita e le opere*, 137.   [16] Ibid. 138.

mother was a nervous wreck and showing all the signs of dementia, 'shocked by anonymous letters with threats against my life'.[17] It is also true that, outside of the sphere of his erotic fancies, D'Annunzio always felt a sense of fulfilment at his ability to dominate his own emotions, seeing it as a variety of Franciscan self-control, a kind of sadomasochistic triumph akin to his later boasts that he was unafraid of sharp or explosive objects or of physical hurt. Yet all the indications are that D'Annunzio derived little positive pleasure and small satisfaction either from the campaign or from his victory. Inevitably, the motive for his standing as a candidate must puzzle the curious, and when one considers his subsequent actions (or rather his total inaction) in parliament, alongside the fact that he was willing to change his allegiance and stand as the Socialist candidate in Florence during the next parliamentary elections of 1900, great doubts must remain about his political sincerity or his commitment to the democratic process.

The period between the unification of Italy and the candidacy of D'Annunzio for Ortona a Mare is littered with works by minor Italian writers—novels, short stories, eye-witness accounts—concerned with the fledgling parliament.[18] The majority of those impressions of parliamentary life are negative. Ferdinando Petrucelli della Gattina set the tone for many in *I moribondi di Palazzo Carignano* (The Moribund of Carignano Palace). The book represents the views of a disillusioned Republican who still believed in the principles of parliamentary democracy, but who saw too well the failings of the new assembly. Writing with the bright illusions of the struggle for independence just behind him, Petrucelli decided that even the most energetic and conscientious individual would be rendered inert after a three-year stint at the tedious round of an MP's life.[19] D'Annunzio was rarely in danger of being rendered inert by conscientious parliamentary work. 'Not very assiduous' is the massive understatement used by Mario D'Annunzio to describe his father's presence in the political sphere after his

[17] See *GD'A à Georges Hérelle*, 323.

[18] A critical summary and anthology of such literature, including excerpts from D'Annunzio's own work, has been published by A. Briganti, *Il parlamento nel romanzo italiano del secondo 800* (Florence, 1972); for other such details, see n. 19 below.

[19] F. Petruccelli Della Gattina, *I moribondi di Palazzo Carignano* (Milan, 1862); for an account of the many disillusioned MP–novelists in the following thirty years, see G. Caltagirone, *Dietroscena: L'Italia post-unitaria nei romanzi di ambiente parlamentare 1870–1900* (Rome, 1993).

victory.[20] That verdict is confirmed by all who have written of the episode. But D'Annunzio's absence from both constituency and Chamber must have alarmed his supporters in the Abruzzi. Umberto Russo has published the text of one letter dated 2 June 1898 written by D'Annunzio to Francesco Ercole in which he reveals a defensive attitude:

My dear Ciccillo,
  Forgive me if I reply with some delay to your wise and affectionate letter. I am oppressed by work and distressed by my anxiety to finish it before coming home to my sweet shores (bitter-sweet, perhaps!) and returning to the service of my political friends. I asked for a respite, after a not easy victory, because it had become a pressing necessity for me to take up my work again actively and vigorously.[21]

The 'respite' which he took from his constituents and from parliament formed the subject of the opening poem of *Alcyone* ('La tregua'), one of the first creative pieces to come out of the experience of his election; it will be discussed in due course.

  The title of Petrucelli's satire concerning the moribundity of parliamentary life was echoed by D'Annunzio some two years later when on 24 March 1900 he made his dramatic move in parliament from extreme right to extreme left, the famous *salto di quinta* (switch—literally leap—of wings). He had noted three evenings before, 'After today's spectacle I know that on one side there are many dead men, howling, and on the other a few men alive and eloquent. As a man of intellect I advance towards life.' Earlier he had disdainfully turned down the request by an usher to make up a necessary quorum, with the well-known riposte, 'Tell the President I am not a number'. The account of that switch of allegiance, along with other ironic comments on the workings of parliament, appeared in *Il giorno* on 26 March 1900.[22] His indifference to the whole parliamentary process was summed up in his lack of

---

[20] M. D'Annunzio, *Con mio padre sulla nave del ricordo*, 48; Mario D'Annunzio here explains his father's absences by the repellent quality of his fellow MPs and the counter-attractions of the elevated cultural life of the capital.

[21] Russo, 'L'avventura elettorale', 40.

[22] It is reported by all his biographers; perhaps most amusingly of all by his confidant and secretary at the time, Benigno Palmerio, *Con D'Annunzio alla Capponcina*, 174–6: 'With the agility of a goat he jumps from bench to bench, advancing to the benches on the left.' The *salto di quinta* is sometimes called the *salto di siepe* (leap of the hedge) because of a strange association with D'Annunzio's speech 'Discorso della siepe'.

commitment in the 1900 compaign (standing, as it were, for the opposition) and in his final disgusted withdrawal from democratic politics, when, after constant obstruction from officials and opposition from newspaper editors, the Florentine electorate rejected him in favour of an aristocrat with a double-barrelled French name, the lawyer Tommaso Cambray-Digny.[23]

Not entirely unexpectedly, the vital response of audience to orator, noted so often in his references to public oratory, coincided with D'Annunzio's new ventures into the theatre. *Il sogno d' un mattino di primavera*, as has been shown, was written to mollify Eleonora Duse after D'Annunzio had given *La città morta* to her rival Sarah Bernhardt. The theatre must have seemed the apotheosis of the election address, ideal in the sense that D'Annunzio did not have to submit himself in person to the same humiliation that political candidates often endure, though it is true that audiences were not slow with cat-calls and insults if the performance was poor and they knew that the author was present. Indeed at the beginning of his career as a dramatist D'Annunzio tried to attend as many performances as possible of his plays in order to ensure a full audience, aware that the public was likely to be entertained by his presence if the play failed. Mario Giannantoni captures well that relationship of orator–poet and constituency–audience:

Art and politics are perfectly fused in the poet's mind; they have one and the same identical finality: the thought, by now matured in him, of no longer wishing to be the lonely ascetic proponent of Beauty, but one who desires to descend to the masses so that they may follow him and ascend to his visionary forms of poetic life. [. . .] He considers dramatic work as the only vital form with which poets may show themselves to the multitude, offer them the revelation of beauty, communicate to them the virile, heroic dreams which transfigure life.[24]

Drama now occupied D'Annunzio's attention more and more, the presence of Eleonora Duse acting as a stimulus to generate plays written specifically with her in mind, following on the example of the *Sogno d'un mattino di primavera*, performed by her company in Paris in July 1897. D'Annunzio had been unable to attend that particular first night, committed as he was at the time to his own

---

[23] See below, pp. 192–3.
[24] M. Giannantoni, *La vita di GD'A* (Milan, 1933), 154–5; Giannantoni grasped D'Annunzio's insubstantial message with the fervour of a religious convert.

performances at the hustings. By the end of August, however, he was free to indulge his new hobby; indeed, he began to talk about a grandiose plan to build an open-air theatre, like the Roman theatre at Nîmes, but reserved for the privileged élite who could appreciate the Beautiful. It was an idea which later provided a motif for *Il fuoco* and another passionate purpose in life for Foscarina, his actress–protagonist in that novel, to work towards the building of the fictional Theatre of Apollo. As usual, fiction was not far from truth: Eleonora was enthusiastic about D'Annunzio's actual theatrical project and set about raising funds, helped by a committee of noblewomen recruited by D'Annunzio's friend Count Primoli. Even Gordon Bennet, wealthy proprietor of the *New York Herald*, visiting Venice at the time, declared that he was ready to underwrite a substantial number of shares in the scheme. In the end nothing came of the idea, though in *Il fuoco* D'Annunzio did fictionally build his theatre on Rome's Janiculum Hill. The scheme was no doubt undone by such cynical spoil-sports as the Marquis Alessandro Guiccioli, who noted in his diary for 13 October 1897:

At the Exhibition we met Countess ***, who, along with Princess *** and others helps constitute the fanatical throng of initiates in the new Dannunzian aestheticism. The rumour is that they intend to construct on the banks of Lake Albano what was done at Nîmes: an open-air theatre to put on the pseudo-classical idylls written by D'Annunzio on the basis of cerebral eroticism. Those gentlewomen and their intellectual acolytes will end up coupling in the bushes shading the lake, like old nymphs with old fauns. But the lake won't be surprised; in its many-centuried and agitated life it has seen far worse.

But then Guiccioli was probably jealous.[25]

Shortly after the election campaign, on 10 September 1897, as if to emphasize the Franciscan streak in his character, D'Annunzio left the constituency to go off to Assisi with Eleonora Duse; there they enjoyed a romantic celebration of his electoral success. Later hints of the legend of St Francis and Santa Chiara were to be a feature of their life together in Tuscany, where D'Annunzio renamed Eleonora's house La Porziuncula, after St Francis's first sanctuary. But the holiday in Assisi also marked the definitive break with Maria Gravina: after that September of 1897 D'Annunzio was not to return

---

[25] The entry is published as A. Guiccioli, 'Diario del 1897', *Nuova antologia*, 76/1657 (16 Apr. 1941), 385.

to Francavilla while she was there. With her two children Maria Gravina later left the Abruzzi for Rome and oblivion, though not before causing D'Annunzio certain further inconvenience. In May 1903, for instance, he told Treves that he had had to intervene to prevent her from being convicted for swindling a jeweller; he also went to some trouble to rescue his daughter, Cicciuzza, from the squalor of Maria Gravina's house. Later Eleonora offered to pay for the girl's education at the prestigious Collegio di Poggio Imperiale in Florence, and gave D'Annunzio the 5,600 lire (£13,000 crudely translated into modern terms) necessary for the four years' tuition. According to a late newspaper article by Guglielmo Gatti, who is usually more sympathetic to D'Annunzio, the poet used the money a few days later to buy himself a horse in Milan. Gatti alleges that the situation was saved when D'Annunzio's agent, Marco Praga, took the sum from the poet's royalties and sent it direct to the school, resigning from D'Annunzio's service immediately afterwards.[26] Maria Gravina, more and more marginalized, now faded from the picture. Gatti is strangely silent about her ultimate fate; D'Annunzio's French biographers relate that, after other disastrous affairs, she ended her days keeping a second-rate boarding-house in Monte Carlo.[27]

Eleonora meanwhile, in July 1897, had rented a modest villa on the hillside of Settignano, a few minutes' drive from the centre of Florence in that select area of the periphery near Fiesole where Boccaccio had set his *Decameron* five centuries earlier. D'Annunzio was to sense the literary vibrations of the place, and in March 1898, carrying with him debts amounting to 76,000 lire (some £190,000 in modern terms), rented La Capponcina, a fourteenth-century villa which had during the Renaissance belonged to the ancient and noble Capponi family. Coincidentally it was contiguous with Eleonora's property, linked by a narrow path between hedges and a wicket gate. The building was let furnished, but D'Annunzio set

[26] G. Gatti, 'Dopo una lite D'Annunzio non volle più vedere la figlia', *Il resto del Carlino* (31 Jan. 1966); Eurialo De Michelis, D'Annunzio's most constant critical ally, seems to accept the story of the way the poet squandered Eleonora's cash: see De Michelis, *Ancora D'Annunzio*, 168–9.

[27] P. Jullian, *D'Annunzio* (London, 1972), 351; Jullian's biography lacks footnotes or secure source material and quotes from his colleague André Germain, whose *La vie amoureuse de GD'A* (Paris, 1954) is treated with caution by most critics; see also E. De Michelis's severe but hilarious review of Jullian, 'Un biografo ameno', in his *Roma senza lupa*, 82–91.

about converting the property to his own tastes, spending thousands of lire buying antique furnishings and copies of works of art, just as he was later to do at the Vittoriale. He also began structural alterations, brought his horses and dogs from Francavilla and put them into sumptuous stables and kennels, and employed a permanent veterinary surgeon, Benigno Palmerio, who also acted as his very efficient estate manager and in that role, for a while at least, even succeeded in keeping the creditors from the door. The structural alterations alone, according to his secretary Tom Antongini, raised the value of the property from an estimated 25,000 lire when he first rented it in 1898, to 300,000 lire when he was driven out by his creditors twelve years later, and those figures take no account of furnishings and zero inflation.

In view of D'Annunzio's mania for redesigning rented properties according to his own sometimes grotesque tastes, and his habit of surrounding himself with antiques and reproductions from what seem the remains of charity auctions, it is worth recalling Antongini's wry definition of D'Annunzio the home-maker:

Normally, and for most people, to 'create' a house means to build it; to 'destroy' it, means to pull it down. But, in fact, D'Annunzio has never thought of either process. He has contented himself always with redecorating and refurnishing, to his own fancy, the furnished houses which he has rented. Such improvements have usually cost three times the original value of the house; and then, after one, two or ten years, as the case might be, he has calmly abandoned all the objects accumulated during his tenancy when financial or moral reasons have induced him to change his abode.[28]

In a letter received by Georges Hérelle on 12 January 1898, D'Annunzio announced his arrival at the Hotel Mirabeau in Paris to attend the first night of Sarah Bernhardt's production of his *Città morta* on 20 January.[29] Bernhardt's performance seems to have been received politely by her French supporters, but the Parisian newspapers next day gave the play only faint praise, and after only a dozen performances Bernhardt stepped down and thereafter eliminated it from her repertoire. Perhaps more interestingly, at the house of Count Primoli in Rome a group of D'Annunzio's friends, including Eleonora, had gathered to hear news of the play's reception as

[28] Antongini, *D'Annunzio*, 146.
[29] The events which follow are documented in *GD'A à Georges Hérelle*, 324–9; see also n. 31 below.

telegrams reporting on audience reaction arrived during intervals in the drama. Ugo Ojetti witnessed the reactions of Duse as news came through of what the telegram declared to have been a successful first act:

Then came other telegrams. The success, it seemed, had been a great success. Duse had sat down. Her eyebrows were raised half-way up her forehead; her nostrils flared like wings. Her lips were white but her broad Slavic cheeks, the wild part of her anxious features, were flushed red as though with fever.[30]

There to comfort her was Matilde Serao, who with the others persuaded her, as dawn was breaking, to leave for her own apartment. Ojetti later noticed that the flowers in a vase next to Duse's armchair had had all the petals stripped from them.

The same letter to Hérelle announcing his descent upon Paris carried another chore for his translator, the manuscript of a new drama, the *Sogno d' un tramonto d'autunno*, the twin to Duse's recently performed *Sogno d'un mattino di primavera*. D'Annunzio told Hérelle that the manuscript was the work of a copyist and full of errors, and since D'Annunzio himself had no time to go over the text, he would rely on Hérelle's discernment to review and correct the play during the process of translation. He also added a note which might have consoled Hérelle, 'It is probable that Edoardo Scarfoglio will come to Paris with me. We have a plan this summer for a grand voyage on the new yacht *Tartarino*. You will be our sweet companion.' It was the prelude to a traumatic time for the Frenchman and for their semi-professional relationship. Further communications and letters followed, encouraging Hérelle to join the new yacht at Naples in July. He in fact arrived in the port on 6 July 1898 and installed himself first in the Hotel de Genève and then in a cabin on board the *Tartarino*, only to receive, on 22 July, a telegram from D'Annunzio, surprisingly still at his new house in Settignano, 'Greetings to the mariner shipwrecked in port. You will receive a letter tomorrow. Tender embraces. Gabriele.' The morrow's letter informed Hérelle that 'the boat had had to be changed' and that voyage had been put off until later. 'It is a necessity which Edoardo suspected from the first moment and which I considered

---

[30] Ojetti, *Cose viste*, vi. 20.

inevitable.' Hérelle waited another six weeks. The excuse was a lie; Scarfoglio had been sentenced in his absence to eight months in gaol for sedition during anti-government disturbances that year, and his newspaper and yacht were forfeit. Hérelle found out about this much later, though D'Annunzio had already known of the circumstances at the time of the première of *La città morta*; the Frenchman did not take up D'Annunzio's alternative invitation, made in the same letter, to visit him at the Capponcina, and for the disappointed Hérelle a second expedition with Scarfoglio never took place.[31]

The non-event helps to explain later developments in the relationship with D'Annunzio's French translator, but the anticipated pleasure of a cruise in the Mediterranean may also have whetted D'Annunzio's appetite to accompany Eleonora on a tour to the Middle East in December 1898. He had not been idle in his new 'rinascimental' surroundings at the Capponcina. He took up again the text of *Il fuoco* which had been laid aside in deference to his new dramatic interests, and began to publish episodes from it in paying journals, along with other prose essays, such as *La cicala vespertina* (The Evening Cicada) and *Il venturiero senza ventura*, which were destined initially to make further pin-money. Apart from the *Sogno d' un tramonto d'autunno*, he wrote another play, *La Gioconda*, specifically for Duse, and began to compose his finest poetic work, *Le laudi*. There are many testimonies to D'Annunzio's tough working schedule at this time, most of which make use of an article written by his son Gabriellino, who was for a time with him at the Capponcina. Seen only at mealtimes, the poet seemed to live the life of a Trappist monk: servants went around on tiptoe; visitors were politely turned aside by Rocco Pesce, the poet's faithful Abruzzese servant. The frugal evening meal was followed by a short period of relaxation, sometimes ending with D'Annunzio falling asleep, only to awaken and work until dawn.[32]

No doubt visitors, including the infatuated Eleonora, were anxious not to interrupt him, and it is interesting to see how D'Annunzio (condescendingly with hindsight) describes her arrival in the memoir *Il secondo amante di Lucrezia Buti*:

[31] The accounts published by Guy Tosi in his translations of the relevant letters are confirmed by Hérelle's own notes for the period, in *Notolette dannunziane*, 81–3.

[32] Good accounts are given by Giannantoni, *GD'A* 202–5, and Gatti, *GD'A* 194–5. Both utilize G. D'Annunzio, 'Ricordi dannunziani', *La lettura*, 12/11 (Nov. 1912), 989–96.

Sometimes I would hear a gentle rustling at the door . . . It was the dress of the pitiful one. It was the pitiful one come to eavesdrop [*origliare*]. I felt so pale; yet I seemed to grow paler [. . .] I open the door. I say: 'Come in'. She comes into my room and into my soul just as a beautiful thought enters the mind, as though I were the place of her devotion and she in me served my noblest poetry. [. . .] Sometimes I think she is tuning some admirable instrument.[33]

Eleonora's tuberculosis occasionally required that she spend time in more salubrious climates, and the trip to Egypt fulfilled a professional as well as a convalescent purpose. She had already left for her tour when D'Annunzio decided to join her, taking the boat from Naples to Alexandria on Christmas Eve 1898. D'Annunzio's accounts of his experiences in Egypt, many described in the *taccuini* and later written up for the *Faville del maglio*, show them to be, for him at least, almost all pleasurable. Eleonora, delighted to see him, had prepared a splendid welcome, and his first experiences in Alexandria, where he arrived on 27 December 1898, after three days of inevitable seasickness and fasting, had a dreamlike quality. The hallucinatory effect was no doubt helped somewhat by a warm bath, the glass of champagne which he drank on an empty stomach, and the 'abandonment of his naked body to voracious caresses'; the world outside, he wrote, seemed to disappear as he felt 'confusedly the indefatigable search of the warm mouth'. He concludes that particular *taccuino* with an injunction in the second person plural: 'Weaken your body, exhaust it with an orgy, with lack of sleep— then on this horrible weariness pour strong wine. Marvellous effects.' Half a lifetime later, in 1930, he is still following his own advice, 'After the orgy and a long period without food [. . .] I ask for a glass of Mumm Champagne.'[34]

The Pyramids, the Sphynx, the boats on the Nile, all the usual tourist sites were visited. A newly opened tomb gave D'Annunzio the startling opportunity to see honey still glistening in a jar until then unopened for a thousand years. He recalled the incident years afterwards in the *Secondo amante di Lucrezia Buti*, reminded of it by the beauty of Eleonora Duse's hands. The honey had attracted a bee, which stung the fourth finger of Eleonora's right hand as she tried to keep the insect away.[35] The beauty of Duse's hands was

[33] *Prose di ricerca*, ii. 173–4.
[34] *Taccuini*, 294 and 302; and cf. GD'A, *Di me a me stesso*, 107.
[35] *Prose di ricerca*, i. 179–80.

legendary, and Frances Winwar, recalling the incident, thinks that the bee-sting may have inspired the scene in *La Gioconda* where Silvia sacrifices her beautiful hands as she tries to save her husband's masterpiece.[36] No doubt D'Annunzio used the episode for one or other of his later inspirational creations, as he was to use another more startlingly realistic experience for one of the most powerful images of his career. It served to illustrate the piteousness of Eleonora's infatuation for him and was probably the major cause of their separation when transposed into the fiction of *Il fuoco*. The episode took place in the Khedive's garden in Cairo, more precisely in the labyrinth, where Eleonora succumbed to a panic attack when she found herself alone and unable to find the way out. It is interesting to see the incident from Eleonora's point of view as she described it to one of her company, Augusto Jandolo: finding herself alone, the dense green walls, the silence, the fear of being lost, 'Look at these scratches on my hands; I pushed them uselessly through the myrtle hedges. And I kept crying in distress: Enough! Enough! I can't bear it any longer! D'Annunzio!'[37]

D'Annunzio, unknown to her, was just around the corner taking notes, and the episode, in particular the distress of the hysterical woman, is pitilessly exploited in *Il fuoco* where he uses the very words: 'Enough! I can bear no more, Stelio . . . I'm fainting away'. There, in Book II of the novel, the scene takes place in the labyrinth of the Villa Pisani on the Brenta where the young Stelio plays a cruel game of hide-and-seek with Foscarina, getting sexually aroused as he senses her distress, transfiguring himself mentally into a mythical priapic figure: 'He needed at that moment a creature like himself, a fresh breast to which he could communicate his laughter, two swift legs, two arms ready for combat, a prey to grab, a virginity to storm, a violence to accomplish.' But in place of a young she-goat, the ageing actress Foscarina appears, and falls helpless to the ground; the rest of the episode reflects the youthful virility of the faun-like Stelio and the worried, hysterical woman, anxious not to lose her young lover.

From Egypt the two went on to Greece and Athens, where Duse recited scenes from *Sogno d'un mattino di primavera* and D'Annunzio

---

[36] Winwar, *Wingless Victory*, 180, and see below, p. 184.
[37] The incident is analysed by Gatti, *GD'A* 172–3; he takes much of his material from Augusto Jandolo's memoirs: A. Jandolo, *Le memorie di un antiquario* (Milan, 1938).

gave a panegyric on the splendours of Greek civilization and Europe's debt to the ancients. He and Eleonora then retreated to Corfu, where, between February and March 1899, he wrote the tragedy *La gloria*. On 27 April the play had one disastrous performance at the Mercadante theatre in Naples, where it was howled off stage; D'Annunzio withdrew it from his repertoire, though elements of it later resurfaced in *La nave*, the Swinburnian tragedy staged in 1908. The journey to the eastern Mediterranean also served to reawaken positive memories of his earlier expedition with Scarfoglio and company, and some of the earlier jottings concerning Athens and the Acropolis, Eleusis and its bas-reliefs, amalgamate with many other aspects of Greece, mythical and real, and are repeated in the *Laudi*.

What had all this to do with D'Annunzio the politician? His constituents were asking the same question. His brother-in-law, Antonino Liberi, must have voiced some of the doubts of D'Annunzio's unfortunate clients in a now lost letter, to which D'Annunzio replied on his return from Greece. He had, he said, been reduced to skin and bone by the tough work of recent weeks; he had written a national tragedy (*La gloria*), 'Which will cause a great noise amongst the frogs of this putrid marsh which is today our native land.'[38] In addition to these exertions, he wrote that he had been engaged on foreign affairs:

I was able to study at close hand during my travels the big questions of the Mediterranean. In Egypt, in Crete, all over the place our policies are carried out with ignominious ineptitude. We are heading for every kind of humiliation, degradation and ruin—inevitably. The hardest of hearts is torn at such a spectacle. I shall soon have occasion to say publicly what I think.

One conclusion for his constituents to draw was that if the name of Italy meant anything D'Annunzio himself deserved some of the credit, 'thanks to my art, my stubborn efforts and my indomitable faith'. He warned Liberi against mentioning these qualities to the electorate, for whom such things had such little value. D'Annunzio followed this with the wonderful protestation, 'I tell you that I do not understand how the constituents can complain about negligence on my part'. D'Annunzio was evidently indifferent to the feelings of his brother-in-law and of electors alike:

---

[38] The letter to Liberi is published in *Lettere di D'Annunzio a Maria Gravina ed alla figlia Cicciuzza*, 22–4.

For the rest, my dear Antonino, since it seems that the electorate is not content with me, I am considering sending a letter to their leaders to ask whether they think it opportune that I tender my resignation. Thus I shall be in order, and the disagreements will be smoothed out definitively.

The dismissive attitude to politics and electorate alike was typical of that stage in his development. He treated his election as a member of parliament as another acquisition, another obstacle to be overcome, another target to aim at, just as he had aimed at literary targets in order to achieve and go beyond them. In a similar way he 'acquired' heroic actions during World War One, and tried to obtain more medals for bravery than any other combatant, not only from Italy but from all the Allies, soliciting them when they were slow to be offered. It was a habit, not unlike his habit of acquiring antiquarian bric-à-brac, romantic conquests, houses, boats, and other more obvious collectibles. It was the apotheosis of one-upmanship, and he believed that all such achievements helped add to his uniqueness and inimitability.

Another preoccupation mentioned in that important letter to his brother-in-law concerned the welfare of Cicciuzza, his daughter by Maria Gravina, a concern indissolubly linked with the problems of the various domestic crises he had escaped from in Francavilla: 'The thought of Cicciuzza produces dark melancholy in me. But it is all finished as far as I'm concerned. I shall never again go back to the house at Francavilla. I know things which would make you blush. I shall make provision soon.' Here was his first declaration that he was leaving Maria Gravina, and also the hint that her sexual mores and appetites had become as questionable as his own (the son he refused to acknowledge was alleged to have been sired by Maria Gravina's groom or coachman, or by D'Annunzio's own faithful henchman Rocco Pesce). One statement in the letter to Liberi was accurate enough: D'Annunzio never returned to Francavilla while she was there. When Maria Gravina realized that he was not coming back, she took the contents of the Villa Mammarella and left for Rome. It was from Rome in 1901 that D'Annunzio 'rescued' Cicciuzza, who for a while joined him and Duse before being sent to the boarding-school at Poggio Imperiale in Florence.

As D'Annunzio had told Liberi, he was preoccupied with the production of two plays. Predictably, the plot of the first, *La Gioconda*, reflected D'Annunzio's life and attitudes at the time and was put on by Duse's company in Palermo in 1899. In the tragedy, Gioconda Dianti is the beautiful young model and mistress of a sculptor, Lucio Settala, who is married to the conventional but loving Silvia. Lucio has some of the characteristics of earlier artistic supermen such as Andrea Sperelli, seeing himself as being above the laws of normal mortals, and considering it his duty and function to create beauty:

Do you really believe that illumination has to come to me through goodness and not from that deep instinct which whirls my spirit precipitously towards the most superb manifestations of life? I am born to make statues. When a substantial form has come from my hands with the imprint of beauty, the duty assigned to me by Nature is, for me, completed. I am within my own law, beyond goodness though it may be. (Act II, sc. i)

Nevertheless Lucio is torn by the emotional conflict between feelings of tenderness for his devoted wife and his sexual passion for the girl who at the same time provides him with his necessary artistic inspiration. Along with his Sperellian characteristics, Lucio also has in him the self-immolatory germs of Giorgio Aurispa from *Il trionfo della morte*, and, true to form, tries to kill himself. Nursed back to life by the loving Silvia, and faced again with the choice between the two women, he chooses Gioconda. In an argument between the two women, Gioconda pushes over one of Lucio's heavy statues and Silvia, the victim in this drama, has both hands hideously crushed in an attempt to save the work of art.

　It is not difficult to see autobiographical details reflected in the triangular relationship. Silvia is the artist's past inspiration, still infatuated with Lucio–D'Annunzio, while Gioconda is the present stimulus, who, if we may imagine an unending sequence to the drama, would presumably spiral down to take the place of a Silvia and, in her turn, be replaced by a further more youthful inspiration. Not without significance is the dedication of the play, 'To Eleonora Duse of the beautiful hands', perhaps confirming Frances Winwar's thoughts about the incident of the bee-sting to Eleonora's finger during the visit to the Egyptian tomb. Reception of the play in Palermo's Bellini theatre was mixed, not least because the Sicilian audience had their own ideas about what they considered D'Annunzio's mistreatment of his 'Sicilian' princess, Maria Gravina. A rowdy audience was, by all accounts, won over by the acting of Duse, in the role of Silvia, and by the sentimentality of Sirenetta, the waif in the last act, played by a very young Emma Gramatica, who was later to make her own name as a national celebrity.[39]

La gloria, the second play of the season, was the drama which he had told Liberi was destined to rouse the frogs in the putrid bog which was Italy. It proved to be a kind of political counterpart to the artistic *Gioconda*. It was also wonderfully prophetic of the state of Italian politics under Mussolini. If *La Gioconda* is linked with the artistic supermen of *Piacere* and *Trionfo*, *La gloria* reflects the ideas expressed by the political superman Claudio Cantelmo of *Le vergini delle rocce*. The plot describes the competition for power between the old conservative politician Cesare Bronte and the bright new political orator Ruggero Flamma, eager to reconstruct the city, the fatherland, and a Latin vitality or 'force'. The setting was D'Annunzio's contemporary Rome, corrupt and decadent, and the play's two politicians were generally considered to represent the old statesman Francesco Crispi and his rival Felice Cavallotti. Flamma succeeds in usurping not only Bronte's political power but also his beautiful, passionate, and above all ambitious mistress, Comnena. Following the decline in Bronte's influence, Comnena (with Flamma's connivance) poisons Bronte and spurs Flamma on to achieve his goal. But her aspirations and her sexual prowess are too overwhelming for the new lover, who sees that he is falling short of his political dream and losing both the support of his party and the favour of the people. With a death-wish akin to that of Aurispa in *Il trionfo della morte*, Flamma finally begs Comnena to kill him; she obliges, stabs him to death, and leaves his body to the hostile mob.

Critics are unanimous in judging *La gloria* as the worst of D'Annunzio's plays. D'Annunzio is said to have revealed before the performance, with a mad lack of diplomacy, that he intended the character of Bronte to resemble that of Crispi. That guaranteed a politically hostile audience at the Mercadante theatre in Naples, where the play was barracked throughout, and where the evening ended with cries of 'Down with Rapagnetta' and 'Death to Rapagnetta', adding the insult of the former plebeian family name to the injury of their barracking. It was not performed again. But the play is remarkable for certain semi-prophetic statements; one

---

[39] Gatti, *GD'A* 169, sees Maria Gravina also reflected in the play as Lucio Settala's sacrificed spouse. Eleonora Duse commented favourably on the run of *La Gioconda*: see Pontiero, *Eleonora Duse*, 175, which reports a letter of hers on the subject, sent on 19 May 1899 to Adolfo De Bosis.

such is made by Bronte just before he dies, when he suggests that he would die happy if he could see amongst his fellow politicians, 'a true man, suited to the great emergency, a vast, free human spirit, a son of the earth, rooted deeply in our soil'. And in response to those sentiments one of Flamma's acolytes, Giordano Fauro, declares that he believes Flamma to be that man:

I and my comrades, leaving behind the solitude of our studies and our workplaces, have entered the struggle with the premonition that soon would appear a dominant and creative idea which we would willingly serve as obedient and clear-headed instruments for the reconstruction of the City, the Fatherland and the Latin Force. (Act I, sc. ii)

The patriotic mission, the power of rhetoric, and the blind faith of acolytes were concepts which had already been expressed in D'Annunzio's own political life, and which would reappear with Mussolini. Flamma also relies on mob violence, as well as on his own powers as an orator, to achieve his ambitious ends, spends lonely hours working on his political schemes, and could well prefigure, ten years before its appearance on the political stage, the character of Mussolini. Later, Flamma's political slogan, 'Chi si arresta è perduto' ('He who stops is lost') was by a remarkable coincidence adopted by Mussolini. *La gloria* was set aside by D'Annunzio as a literary curiosity, with a dedication 'To the cypresses of Mamalus', which perhaps only La Duse would recognize as an allusion to the village in Corfu where they had retreated after the tour in Egypt, and where D'Annunzio had written the play. Other critics associated the cypresses with cemeteries and saw the dedication as a cryptic reference to his burying the tragedy for ever.

During the autumn of 1899 Duse and D'Annunzio were staying in Zurich while she played *The Second Mrs Tanqueray*. In the same hotel were Romain Rolland and his wife, who were to prove useful witnesses of the painful relationship which the two lovers were evidently experiencing on the eve of publication of *Il fuoco*, prior to the break-up of their relationship. Eleonora must have known the contents of the novel, and must have been able to recognize the humiliating references to the ageing actress Foscarina *vis-à-vis* her younger paramour Stelio Effrena. Possibly to save face, La Duse told Rolland that D'Annunzio had denied that he had portrayed her in the novel. The novel had taken D'Annunzio four years to write (six if his original conception of the theme in 1884 is taken

into account). *Il fuoco* was the first and only volume in a projected
cycle of *Romanzi del melograno* (Novels of the Pomegranate), the
overall title which was meant to imply regality and joy. Both themes
are clearly signalled in the lovers' farewell scene in the final chapter
of *Il fuoco*, and throughout the novel Foscarina characteristically
loves the bitter-sweet taste of pomegranates, which were also significant for D'Annunzio himself (to this day a sculpted bowl of
the fruit stands in the entrance to the Vittoriale). Another theme,
implied in the title of this first novel of the cycle, is the destructive
and potentially re-creative power of fire. That is true enough, but
it also has more complex undertones. The phrase which stands as
the epigraph to the novel 'Fa come natura face in foco' (acting like
nature does in fire), is a direct quotation from Dante's *Paradiso* (IV.
77). There Dante is drawing a parallel between the natural tendency
of flame to rise (no matter what turbulence affects it) and the natural tendency of the will not to be deflected from a firm resolution.
There is also an inevitable allusion to the power of fire to change
and remould. All this is reflective in turn of the ability of his new
superman, Stelio Effrena, to mould and create artistically. Effrena,
protagonist of the novel, is a poet and composer acclaimed as their
master by a unanimous chorus of disciples; he is also conscious of
his own superhuman talents. Venice the dominant and Dionysiac
city described in the Biennale speech, is part of Stelio's stimulus to
action, as is the heroic figure of Wagner, another triumphant genius,
who died in Venice in 1883, and the female inspiration of Foscarina,
the great actress who not only collaborates with Stelio's dramatic
genius but also gives herself to him as a woman. At the same time,
the presence of the young singer, Donatella Arvale, tempts Stelio
away from the fading charms of the actress. The body of the plot
is concerned with Foscarina's jealous inner torment, which is compounded by an altruistic determination to give up her love in order
to allow Stelio's genius its freedom. Thus Foscarina plans to leave
for an overseas tour which may generate the necessary funds to
complete the building of a grandiose Teatro di Apollo which would
provide the worthy setting for Stelio's creative and nationalistic
drama. The funeral of Wagner at the close of the novel provides a
severe example of artistic devotion and an inspiration for Stelio.

Stelio Effrena is another artistic superman, but this time having
the power to stir audiences with his operas, and with his oratory.
His regality is undisputed, and his ambition is 'to create joyfully'.

The figure is evidently as idealistically autobiographic as D'Annunzio's other heroes. Stelio, like Aurispa before him, was an admirer of Wagner and of the theatre which the 'Great Barbarian' had created at Bayreuth, as D'Annunzio hoped to create his own Theatre of Beauty at Albano. But Stelio is more patriotic than Aurispa; his dream is to create a Latin theatre and drama, based on the great Greek tradition, and by definition turned away from the Teutonic exemplars of Wagner. The grandeur of Venice supplies a large part of the Latin inspiration for Stelio's new drama, which he intends to be interpreted by Foscarina, pet-named Perdita, the greatest of all tragic actresses. Between her jealousy for Effrena's passion for the young soprano, Donatella Arvale, and her feeling of inferiority in the presence of her younger lover, Foscarina decides that Effrena belongs to his art. The novel closes on 13 February 1883 with an account of the death of Wagner on the Venice water-bus, and the great man's final journey from boat to train, when, in a dramatic scene, Stelio and four of his followers, having obtained permission from Wagner's widow, take the composer's coffin on their shoulders, and bear it to the train.

Stelio Effrena is the first superman without any of the defects of his predecessors. At the end of the book, the sensuality which usually defeats D'Annunzio's supermen is symbolically left behind, when Foscarina–Perdita, though still infatuated with Effrena, realizes that his art is greater than their voluptuous affair, and retreats voluntarily from the scene to collect money for his great dream. Meanwhile Wagner is dead and the sprays of laurel placed on his coffin have been specially picked on the Janiculum; the boughs brought thence by two workmen from the works recently initiated in Rome on the great new national Apollo Theatre. That scene, too, has obvious symbolic undertones, and while Stelio's admiration for the German composer never lessens, just as his flawed passion for Foscarina never dies, the reader is left in no doubt that the Latin genius is about to take over from the Teutonic. Strangely, D'Annunzio puts the contrast between old and new into the hands of the powerful and handsome young workmen brought from the site of the new theatre. In the final pages of *Il fuoco*, they carry the laurel boughs (which the six aesthetes then place on the coffin), summing up in their persons a physical ideal of youth which Stelio–D'Annunzio hopes to control with his oratory: 'Sinewy and powerful, chosen from the strongest and best, they seemed to be forged from the ancient mould of the Roman race. They were grave and serene, with the savage freedom of the common Roman homeland in their eyes veined with blood.' Their noble profiles recall those of ancient consuls; their attitude, 'shorn of any servile obsequiousness, made them worthy of their burden'. Even the laurels are 'most noble Latin laurels' cut on Rome's hill, where once the eagles brought portents and where 'Garibaldi's legionaries had recently spilled their blood for the beauty of Italy'. 'While Italian laurels made their way towards the Bavarian hill, still asleep in its ice and snow, the illustrious trunks of those laurels had already begun to put out new shoots in the light of Rome, to the sound of hidden springs.' Thus endeth *Il fuoco*. The autobiographical quality of the novel is self-evident. The oratory typical of Stelio had already been seen in the run-up to D'Annunzio's election in 1897, and D'Annunzio's awareness of his personal ability to sway a crowd had been long ago brought home to him; here in *Il fuoco* that ability is visible in an idealized way in Stelio's skill at writing musical drama and, simultaneously, in D'Annunzio's new penchant for the stage.

It was the very autobiographical quality of the book which caused such a scandal when it was published. Duse had been ill during the winter of 1899/1900, allowing D'Annunzio the leisure to devote himself full-time to finishing the novel, and *Il fuoco* was published by Treves in March 1900; in May it was serialized in the *Revue de Paris*. It immediately aroused storms of protest for its humiliating treatment of the character of Foscarina–Perdita–Duse. D'Annunzio was not often shaken by adverse criticism. His defence of the novel was similar to that offered years earlier when he had been vilified for allowing Andrea Sperelli to talk of the dead Italians at Dògali in terms of 'brutes killed brutally'. His defence then was that this was fiction, and he offered the same justification now, in a letter to Romain Rolland which he hoped would somehow filter through into the French press:

They insist on seeing in a work of *pure invention* a kind of biography! And they misunderstand the true essence of the book, which is no more than a celebration and an exaltation of the loftiest human sentiments, an act of gratitude toward a heroic and solitary soul. I don't know of any character in modern fiction who can compare with Foscarina for moral beauty.[40]

---

[40] Quoted by Frances Winwar from an unpublished letter in the Vittoriale: *Wingless Victory*, 187.

Famous enough was the scene in the labyrinth, but there were other incidents where it was easy to recognize, in the rapport between Foscarina and Effrena, a similar relationship between the poet and Eleonora, always to the detriment, in some way, of Eleonora's character. Whereas Stelio Effrena lives in an ethereal realm of his own making, and can afford to treat lesser mortals as passing fancies, Foscarina, for one, is limited by her human passions and emotions, and suffers bitterly from his indifference to what becomes for her a disproportionately loving infatuation. He is young and vigorous; she is fearful of losing his affection. That kind of contrast is constantly made, the painful effect being increased by the stream-of-consciousness technique which allows the reader to see her most intimate thoughts (obviously thoughts created by Effrena–D'Annunzio), and her feelings of frustration and despair; in a typical passage from Book II, she muses:

And she wanted to stop him, hold him, possess him! There was in him an ever-present yearning for unconfined living, as if every second seemed to be his last. [. . .] And she wanted to attract that insatiable ardour to feed on her alone. What was she, then, for him except one aspect of the 'Life with a thousand and one aspects' [. . .]? She was a motive for visions and fictions, like the hills, the woods, the rains. He absorbed from her mystery and beauty as he did from any other form in the Universe.

Looking back on the furore which the novel aroused, D'Annunzio wrote defiantly in the *Libro segreto* concerning his personal reaction; in particular he attacked what he called the reptilian baseness of a few English, German, and French females for their insinuations that he was cheapening the reputation of La Duse.[41] And, as if to defend himself against the charge that this was a betrayal, he stresses that Eleonora 'lived alongside my work; sitting on a pew she read one by one the still hot pages', as though she were well aware of the contents and gave them her tacit assent.

The imminent prospect of the publication of *Il fuoco* had depressed Eleonora, and D'Annunzio wrote a famous letter to Angelo Conti concerning her changing moods and increasing depression. The letter, while it did not mention publication of the new novel, might have been a hint at what passed for guilt feelings in

---

[41] *Il libro segreto, Prose di ricerca*, ii. 678–9.

D'Annunzio, though these lasted but a short time.[42] The fact is, however, that Duse had had ample warning of the contents of the book and had refused to take any steps to prevent its publication. During the trip to Egypt and Greece D'Annunzio had allowed her agent, José Schurmann, to read those pages of the novel which he had already written. Schurmann rushed immediately to La Duse and begged her to intervene and dissuade D'Annunzio from publishing; she had thanked Schurmann without responding further, but later sent him a note:

A short while ago I did not tell you the truth. I know the novel and I have authorized its printing because my suffering, no matter how great, counts for nothing when it comes to giving Italian literature another work of art. And then, I am forty years old . . . and in love.[43]

She was also present when D'Annunzio wrote much of the rest of the work at the Capponcina and was able to read it there. When the novel was published, those critics, theatre-goers, and littérateurs who admired the divine Duse were soon up in arms, and polemics begun in 1900 have continued until the present day.

D'Annunzio was occupied briefly fending off the irritating critics, in particular with an article in *Le Figaro* of 31 May 1900, in which he both defended his novel and hinted at heroic dreams for the future of Italy. The defence of his most recent work (in part another symptom of what passed for conscience) was interrupted by the dissolution of parliament and the proclamation of new elections for 30 June. The Socialists, mindful of D'Annunzio's swing from right to left, offered to promote him as their candidate in Florence and, while accepting their support, D'Annunzio stood under the banner of the Union of Popular Parties. Indeed, on 29 March 1900 he published in *Il giorno* the article 'Della mia legislatura', followed on 21 May 1900 by 'Della coscienza nazionale'; in view of the fact that *Il giorno* was to be his main support during the Florentine campaign, his statements there are strangely right-wing and nationalistic, many

[42] Frances Winwar discusses D'Annunzio's apparent pang of conscience and the letter to Angelo Conti: *Wingless Victory*, 184; for the text of the letter see 'Lettere al "Dottor Mistico" (Angelo Conti)', ed. E. Campana, *Nuova antologia*, 74/1603 (1 Jan. 1939), 27–8 (letter XXXVII, dated 24 May 1899).
[43] Cf. Pontiero, *Eleonora Duse*, 178, and see O. Signorelli, *Eleonora Duse* (Rome, 1955), 213.

of them quotations from Claudio Cantelmo in *Le vergini delle rocce*, and from Ruggero Flamma, protagonist of *La gloria*. His main claim was that during his time in parliament he had saved the Italian language and brought back respect to the national literature; that was evidently aimed at the Florentines' pride in being the guardians of the true language of Italy:

And this is my political action, in the purest sense of the word; this is the reason why I consider myself a 'representative' man in my country [. . .] This is my praise, as I told the people who gave me their vote; like water and like bread the figures of my style contribute to perpetuate the life of our people.

In the same newspaper, on 9 June 1900, his addresses 'Agli elettori di Firenze' (To the Electors of Florence), are full of erudite references to Florence's great past, to Machiavelli, Leonardo, Michelangelo, and to their great works. The electorate in Florence were not so easily won over by his purple prose and his defence of their linguistic inheritance (though, as I have noted, the ancient Florentine Accademia della Crusca, later nominated him to membership).[44] In addition his opponents had powerful means at their disposal. His conservative opponent, Tommaso Cambray-Digny, had much influence with the local bureaucracy, which at times put obstacles in D'Annunzio's way; thus he was locked out of buildings where he was booked to give a speech, and ultimately he was prevented from hiring halls to harangue his potential electors. A letter to the mayor of Florence complains about the 'mysterious embargo' on him, the man who had, alongside the same mayor inaugurated the annual Dante readings in the church of Or San Michele. The mayor failed to reply and D'Annunzio was forced to make his major speech in a hall at the local laundry.[45] The opposition newspaper *La nazione* was also much more sophisticated and had more power than the parochial journals which had opposed him in the Abruzzi. *La*

[44] S. Parodi, *Catalogo degli Accademici della Crusca* (Florence, 1983), 339, reports his nomination to the Crusca of 24 Nov. 1914, though D'Annunzio seems never to have responded, except with an etching by his friend Adolfo De Carolis of a head of Dante, which he sent to the Academy in 1921 (ibid.); in earlier years D'Annunzio had made fun of the Crusca for what he considered its pedantry: see Andreoli, *D'Annunzio Archivista*, 226–9.

[45] B. Palmerio gives an excellent account of D'Annunzio's trials and tribulations during this election, including the text of his final oration to the Florentines: *Con D'Annunzio alla Capponcina*, 177–90.

nazione's editor, Ettore Barnabei, was particularly offensive in his attacks on the poet–politician. So tense did things become that D'Annunzio challenged the editor to a duel, which, unusually, he won, wounding his opponent near the left eye. Despite his best, if oft-frustrated efforts (which he later played down in interviews), on 30 June 1900 D'Annunzio was easily beaten by Cambray-Digny. This chapter in his life and his parliamentary career was finished.

7

The Tuscan Idyll

IMMEDIATELY following his stormy election campaign and his ensuing defeat at the polls, D'Annunzio left with Eleonora for the cooler breezes of the Tyrrhenian sea, comfortably shielded from the public by the pine grove surrounding the villa he had rented near the seafront not far from Viareggio, at the point known as Il Secco. Eleonora was away from Viareggio for long spells, particularly during 1900, when she had a successful tour in Switzerland and Germany (where D'Annunzio joined her briefly in May of that year). It was at Il Secco during his hours of greater leisure that he found inspiration for some of his most sublime poetry, including 'La pioggia nel pineto' (Rain in the Pinewood), published as the collection of lyrics which made up the third book of the *Laudi*, entitled *Alcyone*. For the moment, however, politics continued to interrupt his retirement, as certain cataclysms or solemn events forced D'Annunzio to take up a prophetically nationalistic stance, and spend much time travelling around Italy. At Monza on 29 July 1900, King Umberto I was shot dead by the anarchist Gaetano Bresci, and D'Annunzio used the occasion to publish the ode to Vittorio Emanuele III, 'Al re giovine' (To the Young King).

> Tu non dormirai
> se degni sieno i tuoi occhi
> di contemplar l'orizzonte
> che il Quirinal discopre
> al dominatore;
> tu non dormirai
> se le tue mani sien pronte
> alle lotte e all'opre,
> alla spada e al martello [. . .].

> [You shall not sleep
> if your eyes are worthy
> to contemplate the horizon
> which the Quirinal reveals

> to the dominator;
> you shall not sleep
> if your hands are ready
> for the struggles and for the deeds
> for the sword and for the hammer [. . .].]

At times his tone becomes hectoring:

> T'elesse il Destino
> all'alta impresa combattuta.
> Guai se tu gli manchi!

> [Destiny elected you
>   to the high fought-over enterprise.
>   Woe betide you if you fall short!]

There follows a prophecy of Latin glories to come. But in addition to this, and impertinently in the circumstances, D'Annunzio looks forward to a new role for the poet himself, and hints at his own heroism as a potential saviour of the Italian race:

> Ché se il danno e la vergogna duri,
> quando l'ora sia venuta,
> tra i ribelli vedrai da vicino
> anche colui che oggi ti saluta,
> O tu che chiamato dalla Morte
> venisti dal Mare,
> Giovine, che assunto dalla Morte
> fosti re nel Mare.

> [For if ruin and shame endure,
>   when the hour comes
>   you will see close at hand amongst the rebels
>   him who today greets you,
>   O you who, called by Death,
>   came from the Sea
>   Young man, appointed by Death
>   you were king on the Sea.]

The assassination of King Umberto had further repercussions of a nationalistic character. A wreath sent in the name of those Italians claiming independence for the Austrian Trentino was removed from the royal tomb by the Italian authorities themselves, on the grounds that it might provoke a diplomatic incident with Austria. D'Annunzio seized this other opportunity to write the stirring ode 'Alla memoria di Narciso e Pilade Bronzetti' (To the Memory of Narciso and

Pilade Bronzetti), celebrating in part the martyrdom of two famous sons of Trento who had died fighting for the independence of the region forty years previously. But the 'pure wreath of flowers', which had been 'swept aside from the Roman temple by a thug', was merely a minor slight to the patriotic ideal; D'Annunzio went on to list the many territories, which were Italian in anything but name, still suffering under the Austrian yoke: Trieste, the Quarnaro, Istria. Giuseppe Garibaldi, the Omnipotent Duce, would rise again to save them, the barbarians would be swept aside and the sacred mountains of Trento would be redeemed:

> Non piangere, anima di Trento,
> la tua calpestata corona.
> Ribeviti il tuo pianto amaro.
> Dimentica il male se puoi
> Non fare lamento. Perdona.
> Prepara in silenzio gli eroi.
>
> [Weep not, soul of Trento, for your
> trampled wreath.
> Take back your bitter tears, drink them.
> Forget the offence if you can.
> Do not lament. Forgive.
> Silently prepare your heroes.]

The black and yellow flag (of Austria) would be torn from the sacred mountain; Italy's lands would be redeemed. When Cesare Battisti tried to publish the ode in Trento, the Austrian authorities, understandably, restrained him; that enthusiasm for D'Annunzio's new nationalism was important, and foreshadowed events and attitudes which dominated the politics of north-eastern Italy for the following twenty years. Battisti's name adorns piazzas in every Italian city and is synonymous with patriotism and *irredentismo*, the view that all Italian-speaking areas should be under Italian rule. When he was elected member of parliament for Trento, he proved an even more powerful advocate of Italian freedom, and was among the dignitaries who would be at Genoa to welcome D'Annunzio back to Italy on 4 May 1915 after his exile in France. Coincidentally with D'Annunzio's most powerful anti-Austrian actions at the Front in 1916, Cesare Battisti was caught and hanged by the Austrians, providing a further martyr to the Italian cause.

Those patriotic odes, of political rather than poetic importance, were followed soon afterwards by other nationalistically inspired poetic statements. In August 1900 an ode, 'Per la morte di un dis-truttore' (For the Death of a Destroyer) commemorated Nietzsche, and simultaneously praised the ancient Greek origins of European civilization, a tradition D'Annunzio always considered as being the specific heritage of Italy and a view which was to underlie the myths of his collection *Elettra*. In September he composed the ode 'Per i marinai d'Italia morti in Cina' (For Italian Sailors Dead in China) where fatherland and heroism again assumed their predictable im-portance; finally that year he wrote an ode to Rome, which exalted Rome's imperial position as the head of a new Italy. The jingoistic series went on for a further month or so. At the beginning of January 1901, his ode 'Per la morte di un capolavoro' (Death of a Masterpiece), regretted the deplorable state of another great Italian work of art, Leonardo da Vinci's *Last Supper*, which he had seen during a visit to Milan in December 1900. At the Teatro Regio in Turin on 25 January 1901 he declaimed his recently composed ode to Garibaldi, 'La notte di Caprera' (The Night of Caprera), com-prising over 1,000 patriotic lines. The recitation went on for an hour and a half, was received with enthusiastic applause, and, almost as important to D'Annunzio, brought in over 3,000 lire from the paying public. For a poetic performance of an hour and a half, this was certainly a remarkable financial triumph; the sum involved would amount to some £8,000 sterling in modern terms, six times his monthly salary at the *Tribuna*. In addition it was a dramatic propaganda coup for his nationalistic ideas.[1] When Giuseppe Verdi died on 27 January 1901, national mourning inspired another hymn, 'In morte di Giuseppe Verdi', not only exalting the greatness of the composer but also the grandeur of Italy; this, too, was declaimed in public at the invitation of the student body of the University of Florence on 27 February. D'Annunzio was fulfilling the role of Stelio Effrena and Ruggiero Flamma: he was the *poeta–vates*, the self-appointed Bard of Italy, he had become Gabriel of the Annuncia-tion, and above his master-chair in the Capponcina was the device *Nobiscum Angelus Dei* (With us the Angel of the Lord), undoubtedly regarded as a blasphemous statement at that time.[2] His views and

[1] For further details of these *tours de force*, see Antona-Traversi, *GD'A: Curriculum vitae*, i. 31–2, where Antona-Traversi also includes newspaper reports as well as dra-matic telegrammed accounts of the events.

[2] Benigno Palmerio omits this detail from his description of the dining-room in his *Con D'Annunzio alla Capponcina*, as does Tom Antongini, *D'Annunzio* (and *Vita segreta*). Masci, *La vita e le opere*, 140, adds this and other items to the inventory.

mode of expression, between the composition of *La gloria* and the group of patriotic odes, were remarkably prophetic of the political events which were to come after 1914.

Between 1896 and 1902 D'Annunzio had been publishing in reviews and newspapers some of the lyric poetry which was later to be issued in the collections comprehended under the title of *Laudi* (Lauds). The Istituto Nazionale edition of D'Annunzio's published work also contains a facsimile of a long catalogue of proposed productions, including such non-existent works as *La vittoria dell'uomo* (The Victory of Man) and *Trionfo della vita* (Triumph of Life), the two novels which, along with *Il fuoco*, were meant to make up the trilogy of the pomegranate. The list in the Edizione Nazionale also includes the titles of seven books of *Laudi*, which were meant to correspond to the names of the seven Pleiades, that group of stars which Greek mythology had named after the seven daughters of Atlas and Pleione. The comprehensive title of *Laudi* had undertones of the *Laudes creaturarum* of St Francis, thanks and praise, that is, for the beauty of creation. Some of the poems, particularly in *Alcyone*, are praises of humble aspects of nature: the ear of corn and the olive are deliberately singled out for such attention. D'Annunzio does carry his own exultation a little further than St Francis. His concentration on more sensual aspects of the joy of life and on prodigality, rather than austerity, becomes more comprehensible when one considers that he believed in only five of the sins punished in Dante's *Comedy*; lust and avarice–prodigality were not part of his canon.[3] The list contains two final books of *Laudi*, complete with dates, but never written; for the record these were *Taigete* (dated 1921) and *Celeno* (dated 1927). The remaining five books included *Merope*, a small group of poems written in 1911 and published in 1912, largely to celebrate the Italian invasion of Libya, and *Asterope*, published in 1916 to commemorate and justify Italy's entry into World War One. These last two collections were on a different (and much slighter) scale from the trio of volumes written at the opening of the century, and their Pleiadic titles were probably opportunistic additions to anthologies of poems published in newspapers and journals which would have been written and collected

[3] A famous inscription in the Stanza delle Reliquie at the Vittoriale parallels the five fingers of the hand with the five sins: 'Cinque le peccata cinque le dita'; perhaps in similar vein William Blake saw Dante's giants around the well of Cocytus as representing 'the five sins'.

anyway, with or without the preconceived scheme of the seven Pleiades.

The first three volumes of *Laudi* stand by themselves, indeed are, in all senses, in a class of their own: they do have some unity of conception, and their tone and period of composition were close, though *Maia* was written after the other two and deliberately placed as their vast prologue. At the head of each of the three volumes, D'Annunzio had added the general subtitle *Laudi del cielo, del mare, della terra e degli eroi* (Praises of Sky, Sea, Earth, and Heroes) and *Maia* has the further subtitle *Laus vitae* (Praise of Life). The nature of a biographical study of this kind prevents a detailed analysis of the lengthy and complex *Maia* (8,400 lines) and *Elettra* (4,600 lines, distributed in ninety-six major poems of varying lengths). Nevertheless, precisely because of its autobiographical implications, as well as its beauty and grandeur, the poetry of *Maia* deserves comment. It is a reflection of the poet's life in two senses: firstly, it is a chronicle of D'Annunzio's cruise to Greece with Scarfoglio and company in the summer of 1895, and of his later journey with Eleonora Duse to the eastern Mediterranean and Greece in 1898, and at the same time of his constant awareness of the continuation of the wonders of Greek civilization, which now resided in the Rome he knew so well; secondly, *Maia* records that period of his existence when he was preparing himself for what can only be described as his personal transformation of literature into life.

Greece and the Greek islands were the cradle of European civilization, and more immediately of the Roman and Latin civilization which had inherited that grandeur. The first part of D'Annunzio's poetic odyssey, which takes him through Greece to Delphi, centre for the worship of Apollo, god of poetry, is, then, a voyage to discover a source for his own poetic regeneration, to rediscover the civilizing forces which inspired and inspire Europe. It has already been seen how, during the actual journey with Scarfoglio, D'Annunzio's hyperactive imagination transformed the ordinary into the epic: the chambermaid of the Phrygian prostitute met in sordid circumstances in Patràs becomes Helen of Troy in old age, and the contrast between Georges Hérelle's prosaic account and D'Annunzio's poetry serves to throw into relief the poet's inventive brilliance. Another notable incident of the same kind is the encounter with Ulysses in the waters off Leucas, in fact a Greek fisherman alone in his boat. The splendid description begins at line

631, when they first see the man. By line 679 D'Annunzio calls out
to him: 'O Laertiade' (O son of Laertes):

> 'Re degli Uomini, eversore
> di mura, piloto di tutte
> le sirti, ove navighi? A quali
> meravigliosi perigli
> conduci il legno tuo nero?
> Liberi uomini siamo
> e come tu la tua scotta
> noi la vita nostra nel pugno
> tegnamo, pronti a lasciarla
> in bando o a tenderla ancora.
> Ma, se un re volessimo avere,
> te solo vorremmo
> per re, te che sai mille vie.
> Prendici nella tua nave
> tuoi fedeli insino alla morte!'
> Non pur degnò volgere il capo.

> ['O King of Men, destroyer
> of city walls, pilot through all
> dangerous shallows, whither sailest thou?
> To what marvellous hazards
> dost thou drive thy black bark?
> Free men are we,
> as thy grip holds the tiller,
> our fist holds our life,
> ready to abandon it
> or tense it more tautly.
> But if we needed a king
> thee alone we would want
> for ruler, who knowest a thousand ways.
> Take us into thy vessel,
> thy faithful unto death!'
> He deigned not to turn his head.]

The poem is full of such flights of fancy, as reality becomes subsumed into D'Annunzio's recreated neo-classical world, though, as
here, his sublime images are sometimes tinged with the ridiculous.
Helen, Pericles, Themistocles, and other famous personages also
provide him with imaginative encounters, as do famous sites of the
classical Greek past: Parnassus, Olympia, Delphi, Mycenae, and many
more. The second stage of his itinerary takes in the inheritance

by Italy of the virtues of Greece, summed up superbly by an
elegant poetic passage which moves from the Roman countryside
to Michelangelo's paintings in the Sistine Chapel, themselves a
record of man's civilizing achievements. Inspired by his experiences
D'Annunzio hopes that his poetry will spur on the people to greater
political deeds under his heroic leadership. But the third part of *Maia*
implies temporary disappointment; he withdraws disillusioned but
prophet-like to the wastes of Libya where the purity of the desert
provides him with personal liberty and serenity.

   Although it was written after the other two books of *Laudi*, *Maia*,
almost entirely taken up with the epic journey of *Laus vitae*, was
published first. It has an openly political programme, albeit of a
peculiarly Dannunzian kind. From the beginning, after an invocation to the Pleiades and to the Fates, the poem's symphonic prelude, 'L'Annunzio', plays on the archangelic annunciation and on
D'Annunzio's name:

> Udite, udite o figli della terra, udite il grande
> annunzio ch'io vi reco sopra il vento palpitante
> con la mia bocca forte!

> [Listen, listen, sons of earth, listen to the great
> annunciation which, with my strong mouth, I bring to you over the
> pulsing wind.]

Grande annunzio, the great annunciation, links the tone of *Maia*
with D'Annunzio's current demagogic-patriotic mood. The vast poem
ends with two well-delineated episodes, both having political undertones: the first celebrates the fame of another poet inspired by
Graeco-Roman civilization, Giosuè Carducci, acknowledged here by
D'Annunzio as his forerunner in the role of heroic national poet,
the second prays to immortal Nature to help him prepare for further conflict:

> [. . .] 'Su, svegliati! E' l'ora.
> Sorgi. Assai dormisti. l'amico
> divenuto sei della terra?
> Odi il vento. Su! Sciogli! Allarga!
> Riprendi il timone e la scotta;
> ché necessario è navigare,
> vivere non è necessario . . .

> [Up, awaken! It is the hour.
> Arise. Thou has slept thy fill. Hast thou

become the lover of the earth? Up! Unfurl! Increase sail!
Hear the wind. Take up the tiller and the line;
for it is necessary to sail,
to live is not necessary . . .]

The closing lines echo chiastically the famous phrase of Plutarch, said to characterize the vitality and daring of Pompey the Great,[4] and the cover which D'Annunzio's usual designer Adolfo De Carolis devised for the *Laus vitae* contained a sailing-ship with a motto taken from the saying, *navigare necesse est*. During the course of the poem, D'Annunzio had, in the steps of Blake, created his own, tenth, muse, Energeia, inspirer of inventive energy, to drive him on Ulysses-like to new discoveries. The idea is not unlike the picture of Dante's grandiose sinner in the infernal circle of fraudulent counsellors, as Dante, ignorant of the ending of Homer's epic, completed his personal version of the *Odyssey* with the wonderful account of Ulysses sailing beyond the pillars of Hercules, 'to the world without people'. It was an imaginative leap which briefly links both poems.

Indeed, the achievements of the two poets must have been linked in D'Annunzio's mind at the time; certainly the pride he felt at his achievement in *Maia* was great, and a parallel seemed appropriate. In the preface to his tragedy *Più che l'amore*, produced in 1906, he noted, with what he called 'Franciscan modesty', that 'from my furnaces has come the only poem of total life, the true and proper Representation of Soul and Body that has appeared in Italy since the *Divine Comedy*'.[5] The poem was certainly a *tour de force*, the first half written almost without pause as he stood at his 'writing' lectern in the Capponcina, the second part delayed until some six weeks later after he fell ill in Milan. One dominant theme and idea here is precisely the notion that D'Annunzio was a master of language, and that the Italian language was one of the great bonds which had held the nation together and glorified it over the centuries, and which could be revivified to recreate a greater Latin fatherland.[6] The underclass, the 'slaves, intent on ladling their slops in old stone bowls, like blind Scythian servants, know nothing of the power and

[4] Plutarch, *Life of Pompey*, 50, available in Plutarch, *Lives* (London, 1939), ii. 431; it is also noteworthy that Pompey's disdain for a storm at sea on that occasion was inspired by his desire to bring necessary supplies to Rome.

[5] That Franciscan modesty is repeated in a note in GD'A, *Di me a me stesso*, 214: 'Italian poetry begins with 200 verses of Dante and—after a long interval—continues in me.'

[6] See above Ch. 6 n. 44 for the honour offered to D'Annunzio by the Accademia della Crusca for his services to the national language.

splendour of words', whereas the poet has restored these signs of Italianness to their virginal glory:

> Io vi trassi con mano
> casta e robusta dal gorgo
> della prima origine, fresche
> come le corolle del mare
> contrattili che il novo lume
> indicibilmente colora.
> Io vi disposi nei modi
> dell'arte cosí che la vita
> vostra rivelò le segrete
> radici, le innumere fibre
> che legano tutta la stirpe
> alla Natura sonora. [. . .]
> Splendete e sonate, o parole,
> in questo Inno che è il vasto
> preludio del mio novo canto.
> Converse v'ho novamente
> in sostanza umana, in viva
> polpa, in carne della mia carne,
> in vene di sangue e di pianto

> [With chaste but robust hand
> I drew you forth
> from your first beginnings, fresh
> as the contractile corollas of the sea
> coloured by first light, ineffably.
> I disposed you in the ways
> of art so that your life
> revealed the secret roots,
> the countless filaments
> which link the whole race
> to sonorous Nature. [. . .]
> Shine, ring out, my words,
> in this Hymn, which is the vast
> prelude to my new song.
> I have converted you again
> into human substance, into living pulp,
> into the flesh of my flesh,
> into veins of blood and tears.]

And, forecasting great triumphs to come, the poem ends with the 'Saluto al Maestro', the greeting to Carducci, who preceded him along that particular road.

Elettra, the second volume of *Laudi*, has no pretensions to epic unity, but it is the volume which venerates heroes, and that celebratory theme, potentially so rich in nationalistic undertones, functions as its unifying element. Electra's legendary or historical significance lay in her role as the mother of Dardanus, founder of Troy; it was the Trojans, under their leader Aeneas, who were traditionally the carriers of civilization from the eastern Mediterranean to Rome. The relevance to D'Annunzio's spiritual journey is evident, and is reinforced by the individual poems, written for specific occasions or to celebrate specific men, places, or events, all having consistent inspiratory themes: the awareness of Italy's contemporary decadence, the need for political revival, and the exaltation of Rome and of a greater Italy. The opening poem, 'Alle montagne' (To the Mountains), is an invocation to the traditional dwelling-place of mystics and prophets, and a prayer that they may send a heroic poet–prophet. The next, 'A Dante', sees Dante as a prophet of Italy's revival; it is significant that Dante is to recur in D'Annunzio's work as a political rallying-point, until indeed his august name serves to help justify the invasion of Fiume in 1919, on the grounds that seven centuries earlier he saw and, in his divine poem, set the north-eastern boundaries of Italy.

Praise of heroes and famous men (not always Italians) and exaltation of Rome and Italy fill other compositions in *Elettra*, including the patriotic group of odes written in 1901 (many of them declaimed that year in theatrical performances) and here republished. The book ends with two poems which look to the future: the first, 'Canto di festa per Calendimaggio' (Song for the Mayday Holiday), is an appeal to Italians, particularly those of the working class, to aspire to freedom from false doctrines (especially those of Socialism), which weaken them; at the same time the ode calls upon them to fight for individual liberty and national greatness. The final poem, 'Canto augurale per la nazione eletta' (Song of Augury for the Chosen Nation), is divided into three lyrical sections which describe legendary Italians distinguished in fighting, international figures famous in philosophy and the arts, and, finally, the future heroism inherent in Italy's great cities already demonstrated by the past heroism of their citizens. Critics ever alert to discern the germs of future fascist and imperialist developments in Italy are not slow to see in the two volumes of *Maia* and *Elettra* prophetic references to the period leading up to the fascist revolution of 1922.

Alcyone, the third book of the *Laudi*, differs from the other two. *Maia* was written in one continuous process, *Elettra* was largely a collection of occasional poems, composed over a period of several years. In *Maia* people whom D'Annunzio had met, including such creations as 'Helen' and 'Ulysses', served to symbolize or evoke historical personages; in *Elettra* historical personages, events, and places were chosen to symbolize the virtues he wished to promote: Garibaldi becomes heroic patriotism, Rome becomes nationalistic glory. And both works, deliberately or otherwise, illustrate D'Annunzio's by now recognizably personal blend of politics and poetry, physical and imaginative energy. By contrast *Alcyone*, originally published in the same volume as *Elettra*, was the product of a period of tranquillity, introduced by the poem 'La tregua' (The Respite), the title which implied a truce from the political conflicts of the previous five years. Here the epic note is no longer dominant; even in the most heroic self-portraits of *Alcyone*, Glauco in 'Ditirambo II' and Icaro in 'Ditirambo IV', there are elegiac overtones. Glaucus is stripped of his immortality and plunges into the sea; Icarus, it is true, rises level with the chariot of the sun to challenge Apollo, but he dies in the attempt, and, though his fame is immortalized, it is because of the name of his watery grave. The poems here are no longer committed poems, and in 'La tregua' D'Annunzio pleads with his guardian daemon to allow him to feel the grass beneath his naked feet, feel young again:

> Despota, or tu concedigli che allenti
> il nervo ed abbandoni gli ebri spirti
> alle voraci melodie dei venti!
>
> Assai si travagliò per obbedirti.
> Scorse gli Eroi su i prati d'asfodelo.
> Or ode i Fauni ridere tra i mirti,
> l'Estate ignuda ardendo a mezzo il cielo.
>
> [Despot, now concede that he may slacken
> his bowstring and abandon his elated spirit
> to the voracious melody of the winds.
>
> He travailed hard to obey thee,
> saw Heroes on their asphodel meadows,
> now he hears Fauns laughing amongst the myrtles,
> as naked summer blazes in mid-heaven.]

Poetically speaking the respite allowed him to enjoy physical relaxation after his election defeat of 1900, and spiritual repose after the heroic efforts of *Maia* and *Elettra*. In *Alcyone* D'Annunzio came close to the mysteries of nature, sleeping beneath the stars, observing deer in the forest, listening to the rain in the pinewood, riding his horse along the sea-shore, and all the time contemplating the ever-changing miscellany of nature's beauty.

In *Maia* D'Annunzio had said that the characters immortalized in the ancient myths were more alive than the contemporary Greeks met during his journey. So, in *Alcyone*, as he listened quietly to the rustlings in a wood, or silently witnessed the passage of some wild creature, he felt he was better able to understand the feelings of wonder which had, in classical times, peopled the woods and streams with legendary creatures. Hence many of the poems of *Alcyone* are full of the atmosphere of myth: Pan, the rural deity of the ancients, seems present in the Tuscan countryside, audible in the sound of the cicada. Galloping hooves as the poet waits in a thicket remind him of the mythical centaur, symbolic blend of strength and intelligence. Conical fishing-nets swung out over the river sparkle iridescently as water drips from them, like giant exotic flowers in an enchanted landscape. A fall from his horse, as he gallops along the beach near where the sea cast up Shelley's body, inspired him to turn the episode into the story of the nymph Undulna, while his youthful identification with the life and art of the English poet motivated several semi-mystic evocations of Shelley's legendary death and the cremation of his remains at the point on the Versilia coastline known as Il Gombo.

The structure of *Alcyone* is not over-formal; the poems up to the first 'Ditirambo' are concerned with late spring in the area around Florence and Settignano, often seen realistically from his vantage-point in the Capponcina. The majority of poems precede the fourth 'Ditirambo', and are concerned with summer in Tuscany. The final group of poems, which comes after that 'Ditirambo', introduced symbolically by a personified Tristezza (Sadness), herald of the coming autumn, witnesses the gradual passage from heat to mellow fruitfulness and decay. D'Annunzio captured the mood of the seasons and observed, with splendid linguistic precision, all the subtle and varied aspects of nature. He did more: with his vivid imagination he *continued* the work of nature, as he had promised to do in the preface to *Il trionfo della morte* years before. 'La morte del cervo'

(Death of the Stag) is one of the best examples of his method of blending accurate observation with fertile imagination. As the poet lies in wait in a dark section of the pinewood near the riverbank, the image of a swimmer and the sight of deer in the wood inspire in him the twin vision of a centaur (its bestiality for the moment hidden beneath the surface of the stream), and a stag, the king of the herd. In his fantasy the two creatures meet and fight for supremacy, the strength and human intellect of the centaur eventually triumphing over the mere animal power of the stag. D'Annunzio's innovations were exciting; at the same time the new poems were also accessible, their language, though sometimes recherché, appealed to a wide public. Many of the poems of *Alcyone* have passed into Italian folklore, so memorable that, for generations of middle-class Italians, their verses became as familiar as certain lines of Dante. Much of the impact of these poems depends upon the musicality of D'Annunzio's language and verse and they defy translation. 'La sera fiesolana' (Evening at Fiesole), is a typically evocative lyric poem, which it is useful to include here to demonstrate the strong contrast with the heroics of earlier collections. Here is the first stanza:

> Fresche le mie parole ne la sera
> ti sien come il fruscio che fan le foglie
> del gelso ne la man di chi le coglie
> silenzioso e ancor s'attarda a l'opra lenta
> su l'alta scala che s'annera
> contro il fusto che s'inargenta
> con le sue rame spoglie
> mentre la Luna è prossima alle soglie
> cerule e par che innanzi a sé distenda un velo
> ove il nostro sogno si giace
> e par che la campagna già si senta
> da lei sommersa nel notturno gelo
> e da lei beva la sperata pace
> senza vederla.

> [May you find my words in the evening
> fresh as the rustle of mulberry leaves in the hands
> of their silent harvester, lingering over his slow task
> on the high ladder which grows black against the tree. Its
> trunk and naked boughs turn silver, as the Moon
> approaches the threshold of the sky, holding out, it seems,
> a veil before herself, wherein our dream finds rest.
> The very countryside already seems to feel submerged

beneath her rays invisible in the evening's cool, soaking up
the longed-for peace,
not seeing her.]

The form of individual poems varies enormously in *Alcyone*.
D'Annunzio exploits, for instance, many different types of metrical
form: sapphics, blank verse, madrigals, ballads, sonnets, *terza rima*,
and three variants on the hendecasyllable. Yet, recalling his irritation at any constraint upon his creative powers, readers must not
be surprised if those metres are by this time not always strictly dis-
ciplined. Gone now is the punctilious attention to metrical detail
which characterized Carducci, but which simply hampered the new
D'Annunzio's freedom of thought and expression. Preoccupied, too,
with musicality and spontaneity, D'Annunzio is much more concerned with assonance, onomatopoeia, alliteration, and rhyming
plays. There was no lack of critics to point out an obvious danger:
that the freedom with which he wrote verse after 1895 would allow
him to ramble, and replace linguistic artistry with verbiage or oratory. He was certainly prone to that tendency, even in *Alcyone*, in
a poem such as 'L'onda' (The Wave), where he attempts to capture
linguistically and rhythmically the shape, sound, colour, size, movement, in short the essence of a wave. The later poems, reflecting the
autumnal season, are particularly evocative; one poem 'I pastori' (The
Shepherds) is especially relevant in its memories of D'Annunzio's
home province, where the herders take their flocks down from the
high pastures in preparation for the coming winter. Here are the
two final verses:

> E vanno pel tratturo antico al piano,
> quasi per un erbal fiume silente,
> su le vestigia degli antichi padri.
> O voce di colui che primamente
> conosce il tremolar della marina.
>
> Ora lungh'esso il litoral cammina
> la greggia. Senza mutamento è l'aria.
> Il sole imbionda sí la viva lana
> che quasi dalla sabbia non divaria.
> Isciaquio, calpestio, dolci romori.
>
> Ah perché non son io co' miei pastori?
>
> [They follow the ancient drovers' path to the plain,
> 　as though beside some silent grassy river,

on the traces of their early fathers,
Oh, the voice of him who first knew
the trembling of the seascape.

Now along the shore trots the
flock. The air is still;
the sun so gilds the living wool
it hardly differs from the sand.
Sea-washing, trotting, sweet sounds.

Ah, why am I not with my shepherds?]

All things considered, *Alcyone* was a triumph, the work by which he wished to be remembered if all else were destroyed. Even hostile critics such as Natalino Sapegno had to admit the merits of the collection; Sapegno's statement that no important Italian poet since the publication of *Alcyone* had been free of its influence, was echoed by Montale's similar remarks concerning the whole of D'Annunzio's output.[7]

During the period that he was engaged on the *Laudi*, D'Annunzio spent much time travelling with Eleonora on various tours, which involved him in journeys to Germany and Switzerland, as well as northern Italy. By October 1901 he had also written a new play, *Francesca da Rimini*, a dramatization of the events which Dante had made famous in *Inferno* V. Published in 1902 by Emilio Treves, the opening page of the volume made it clear that this was to be the first in a trilogy of plays entitled *I Malatesti*, of which only one other, *La Parisina*, was ever written, more an opera (set to music by Mascagni) than a play; a third tragedy, *Sigismondo Malatesta*, remained only a title. Benigno Palmerio entertainingly describes the first reading of *Francesca* to a select group of friends and actors chosen for the first performance; Eleonora, to whom the work was dedicated, was the second luminary at the soirée, draped in her most precious jewellery, and radiantly reconciled for the various slights suffered over the *Città morta* and the humiliating revelations of *Il fuoco*.[8]

---

[7] N. Sapegno, *Compendio di storia della letteratura italiana*, 3 vols. (Florence, 1946), iii. 388, a section which advances largely adverse criticism of D'Annunzio, not least because of Sapegno's post-war Socialist view of previous literature; see also his 'D'Annunzio fu più retore che poeta', *La Stampa* (17 Apr. 1963), though even here he accords due praise to *Alcyone*. For Montale's remarks see his *Prefazione* to the poems of Lucio Piccolo, *Canti barocchi* (Rome, 1956).

[8] Palmerio, *Con D'Annunzio alla Capponcina*, 127.

The theme of the latest drama was provided by the well-known episode of Paolo and Francesca in the second circle of Hell, though in D'Annunzio's play, to which he referred as his epic of blood and lust, there is none of the finesse of Dante. *Francesca*, then, was D'Annunzio's version of the adulterous, if humanly justifiable, love of Francesca for Paolo, the discovery of their love by Paolo's grotesque brother, Gianciotto, aided by an Iago-like figure, Malatestino, and the couple's bloody deaths impaled upon Gianciotto's sword. The tragedy was meant to break new frontiers in D'Annunzio's revolutionary new verse drama, and for once a Dannunzian play did receive a less hostile reception from an Italian audience, at its première in Rome's Costanzi theatre on 9 December 1901. Reading the unperformable work nowadays it is difficult not to agree with De Michelis's verdict that this is typical of one of D'Annunzio's pieces of archaic inspiration, containing the usual superabundance of *ad hoc* erudition which fills scenes with technical descriptions of medieval accoutrements, 'a fake antiquity which can be tied in with the bric-à-brac of *Piacere*'.[9] The staging of the play cost more than any previous production on the Italian stage, and its very sumptuousness may have astonished the audience into taking a more positive attitude. Critics were divided in their judgements, though most thought it a medieval pastiche.

D'Annunzio, despite his many other literary occupations at the time, is said to have devoted much effort to the documentation of the new play, in order to guarantee its authenticity. Strangely enough, one of the most unlikely and incomprehensible elements was the language, which reflected the difficult, recherché, and often hypertechnical terminology relating to twelfth-century customs and objects. So exaggerated were these technicalities that Emilio Mariano has been led to defend the poet from accusations of pretentiousness by claiming that he intended some of the allusions to have a comic purpose in the plot. Editions of the play owned by Italians invariably have their margins heavily paved with glosses explaining some of the specialized vocabulary which D'Annunzio excavated during the period he was 'researching' the play's background.[10] There

[9] De Michelis, *Tutto D'Annunzio*, 225; for some of the technicalities see n. 10 below.

[10] E. Mariano, 'La *Francesca da Rimini* e i suoi significati', *Quaderni del Vittoriale*, 24 (Nov.–Dec. 1980), 101–16, responds to some adverse criticism of D'Annunzio's specialized vocabulary, which included such technicalities as camlet (*cambellotto*),

1. D'Annunzio's mother, Luisa De nedictis. ('Weep no more. Your eloved son is returning home.')

2. D'Annunzio's father, Francesco Paolo Rapagnetta-D'Annunzio

. Maria Hardouin, duchessa di Gallese, nd their first-born, Mario

4. Maria Gravina Cruyllas di Ramacca and their daughter Eva Renata Adriana (Cicciuzza)

Alla Gloria
questa figura della mia
più lontana malinco-
nia. "Primo vere", 1878.

5. The 15-year-old author of *Primo vere*. ('To Glory,
this image of my most distant melancholy.')

6. The Cicognini pupil before his assault on Rome
in 1881

7. The Michetti portrait of 1895 (Hérelle's new image of the superman)

8. The Commandant at Fiume in 1920. ('To Captain Sovera of Ronchi—his faithful comrade.')

9. Giselda Zucconi (Elda, Lalla)

10. Elvira Natalia Fraternali-Leoni
(Barbara)

11. Alessandra di Rudiní-Carlotti (Nike)

12. Eleonora Duse (Ghisola)

13. The Villa Cargnacco before restructuring in 1921

14. The transformation into the Prioria, the main entrance to D'Annunzio's dwelling in the Vittoriale

15. The biplane of the record-breaking
flight over Vienna, suspended from the
auditorium of the Vittoriale

16. The warship *Puglia* in the garden of
the Vittoriale, overlooking Lake Garda
300 metres below

17. The MAS (Anti-submarine Boat) of Buccari

18. The Fiat Tipo 4 of the invasion of Fiume, restored
in 1997 to its former glory

19. Nathalie de Goloubeff (Donatella) and greyhounds at St Cloud

20. Olga Levi-Brunner (Venturina)

21. Luisa Baccara (Aloisia/Luisetta)

22. Amélie Mazoyer (Aélis)

is no doubt that he pulled down many volumes to ascertain the historical period. Aldo Rossi has checked the books which at the time of composition D'Annunzio took out of several public libraries and treated as though they were his personal property. Rossi's account includes other less than endearing facets of the poet: the blue and red pencil-marks scored by him alongside passages later used in the play, notes scribbled in the margins along with signatures and dates, and, in the case of two particular books describing the history of the period, pages torn out.[11]

The difficulty of comprehending the play's meaning could well have been overlooked by an emotional audience eager simply to join in the spectacle and be overwhelmed, as D. H. Lawrence later noticed, by the sheer musicality and exoticism of the sounds of D'Annunzio's language.[12] There is, however, another shock in store for the reader who expects something of the subtlety of Dante's heroine and her delicate love affair. The play is not lacking in Swinburnian touches of the sadistic and the grotesque: thus we are shown Francesca's almost depraved interest in such things as Greek fire and its effect on various commodities, including human flesh. The tower-keeper's confirmation of the perilous nature of Greek fire is followed at once by Francesca's playing with what by then she knows to be a dangerous substance, almost provoking a general conflagration. Such behaviour might have been justified had D'Annunzio added his usual psychological *deus ex machina*, a heroic madness, but Francesca does not have this excuse for her unlikely behaviour. Duse regarded the tragedy as making up for her loss of *La città morta* to Bernhardt, and for the time being, at least, it also helped to avert the potential rift caused by her portrait in *Il fuoco*. She also paid most of the expenses of the production.[13]

grogram (*grossagrano*), and tamin (*stamigna*), while other lexical items require the expertise of the British Museum's fabric experts: *camuccà*, *cataluffa*, *paracani*, *zetani*, and dozens of other which have no obvious translation in English.

[11] Rossi, 'D'Annunzio giovane', 54; it might be added that it was not permitted to take out on loan books from the public libraries concerned.

[12] 'Bosh' is the term Lawrence used in his *Twilight in Italy* (London, 1960), 69, in order to describe D'Annunzio's compositions. Lawrence, despite his constant castigation of D'Annunzio, borrowed much from him; see Woodhouse, 'GD'A e la cultura anglosassone', esp. 636–41; for further information on Lawrence's attitude see below, Ch. 8 n. 15.

[13] The cost of production, 400,000 lire, beat all records at the time; at current actuarial rates of exchange it would have been the equivalent of forty years' salary in 1900 for a top civil servant.

During their sojourn together at Settignano, D'Annunzio continued to enjoy the company and favours of other women, particularly during intervals in his horseback rides around the Capponcina; two women in particular he described as 'experts in perverse games'. On one particular occasion, returning from such an expedition, he responded to Duse's questions with 'Don't ask', the reply with which, as Silvia in *La Gioconda*, she had fobbed off Sirenetta; D'Annunzio recalled the line as he leapt down from his horse at the Capponcina to greet her.[14] Eleonora was regarded with increasing pity by the theatre-going public, to whom she was by now a national institution. At the end of March 1902 she went on tour in Austria and Germany with exclusively Dannunzian drama in her repertoire, returning briefly to Tuscany before leaving for her third tour of North America, where she performed in *La Gioconda*, *La città morta*, and *Francesca da Rimini*. The plays were not to the liking of her conservative American public and audiences were small. Most critics agree that Duse sent back to D'Annunzio regular payments of royalties based upon her playing to full houses.[15] When she returned to Europe early in 1903, it was for further performances in Vienna before being reunited with D'Annunzio in the Villa Borghese, not far from Anzio, at the time when his daughter Renata–Cicciuzza also joined the household.

A more successful play from every point of view was the second major tragedy of this period, *La figlia di Iorio* (Iorio's Daughter), written in just over a month during the summer of 1903, and generally regarded as D'Annunzio's masterpiece. A letter to Benigno Palmerio of 3 September notified his major-domo that he had terminated his latest offering, 'which seems to me the most profound of my compositions so far. Writing it I have felt my roots in my native soil.'[16] Set in an undefined but remote period of time in the countryside of D'Annunzio's native Abruzzi, it makes use of the superstitious lore and primitive instincts of a tribal community. The drama was also inspired by a real incident, witnessed by Michetti and D'Annunzio twenty years before at the village of Tocco

[14] D'Annunzio's daily horseback riding took him to various assignations in the neighbourhood; in the *Libro segreto*, *Prose di ricerca*, ii. 682–3, he mentions the episodes described here.

[15] Typical of such comments are those of Pontiero, *Eleonora Duse*, 190–1.

[16] Palmerio, *Con D'Annunzio alla Capponcina*, 148; a very similar letter was sent at the same time to F. P. Michetti, mentioning the artist's masterpiece; see Gatti, *GD'A* 199.

Casauria, the painter's birthplace. There one summer's day they had seen a dishevelled but beautiful young woman running across the square, pursued by a group of lecherous, half-drunk peasants. Michetti later used the incident as inspiration for his best-known, and prize-winning, canvas, exhibited at that first Venice Biennale in 1895; there was an undoubted artistic cross-pollination of ideas between play and painting.

The plot of *La figlia di Iorio* depends upon D'Annunzio's distantly remembered folklore, the reality of primitive villages in the mountains of the Abruzzi, and upon his great imaginative gifts. Aligi, the protagonist, a shepherd newly betrothed to a decent local girl approved by his family, has saved Mila di Codra, Iorio's daughter, from a crowd of drunken, lustful yokels and has given her sanctuary in his family home. In the primitive, superstitious atmosphere of the time, Mila's presence is seen as a profanation of Aligi's betrothal rites and a source of dishonour for the house. Aligi's gifts as a wood-carver set him apart from his cruder fellow villagers, while his disregard for their superstitions marginalizes him even further. He breaks his vows and leaves home for a cave in the hills where he and Mila live a wholesome, apparently sexless, existence. When his enraged and overbearing father Lazaro arrives to have his way with Mila, by then regarded even more as a public woman, Aligi uses his sculptor's axe to kill him. The final act sees Aligi condemned to a barbaric death (his hand is to be severed and he is to be thrown into the river, bound in a leather sack with a vicious dog). He is saved when Mila declares to Aligi's accusers that she had bewitched him and that it was then she who had killed Lazaro. She leaps into a convenient funeral pyre, and the play ends.

The drama was an immediate success at its première on 2 March 1904 at the Teatro Lirico in Milan. Naturally enough, there were few peasants in the audience; the Milanese bourgeoisie found in that cruelly primitive world a picture of southern peasant life which they suspected was not far removed from late nineteenth-century reality. Audiences in Italy still regard the play as reflecting some of the primitive quality of life in southern villages; such a feeling at the turn of the century would have been much stronger. It was at that time possible to witness the self-torment of religious fanatics on cruel pilgrimages to local shrines, as it is nearly a century later in certain areas of Asia and South America. Michetti's photographs, still available to us today, graphically capture the reality of events and illustrate the fanatical mentality. In *Francesca da Rimini*, the violence and sadism had been buried in what seemed falsified medieval history, something *fasullo*, bogus, like the plaster casts with which D'Annunzio filled his dwellings. In *La figlia di Iorio* there was the smack of authenticity, and the effect was helped by brilliant costumes and settings painted by Michetti, and not least by the outstanding performance of Irma Gramatica in the role of Mila. Irma had had to stand in for La Duse, who at the last minute had fallen ill with a recurrence of her tuberculosis, which perhaps may have been a diplomatic illness, since it was clear that Mila di Codro would be more appropriately played by a vigorous young girl. D'Annunzio refused to put off the opening night to accommodate Eleonora, who spent the night coughing blood at the Hotel Eden in Genoa, comforted by Matilde Serao.[17]

It is usually advisable to take D'Annunzio's drama at face value, to enjoy the rhetoric and display, and often the bravura of the actors; but in the case of *La figlia di Iorio*, despite its apparent parochialism, its enduring success has also depended upon more universal ideas. D'Annunzio is reported as saying that the substance of the characters depicted is the eternal human substance of today and of 2,000 years ago. Thus Aligi is the outsider pitted against physical and psychological opponents; the conflict between him and his father, Lazaro, recalls the antagonism which D'Annunzio felt for his father, as well as the unconcealed fictional contempt he put into the character of Aurispa's father in *Trionfo della morte*. Here the conflict is different; the soft, fleshy corruption of the father in *Trionfo* is replaced by the sinewy patriarch, with power of life and death over his family, and the right, should he demand it, to use his son's shin-bone as a handle for his axe. And there are other conflicts which D'Annunzio would recognize: his own constant battles with conformity and ritual, the inner struggle, which he had long before resolved in his own life, between conscience and principles of conduct accepted by his fellows.

The success of the play no doubt fed D'Annunzio's ego more than anything he had so far achieved. It may also have increased his disregard for those who had previously been his great defenders and supporters. In particular there seems to have been a cooling of

---

[17] Serao's account is available in her 'La figlia di Iorio', in L. Vergani (ed.), *Eleonora Duse* (Milan, 1958), 178–85, esp. 182–5.

the relationship with Michetti, who over the years had taken on many of D'Annunzio's financial burdens, putting him up in his most desperate times at the Francavilla convent, finding him the love-nest at the Villino Mammarella (and enduring for years the tantrums of Maria Gravina), loaning him cash, and carrying out at his own expense design work such as that for *La figlia di Iorio*. Guglielmo Gatti indicates that Michetti resented D'Annunzio's failure to reim-burse him for the materials and services used for the settings of the play.[18] While Michetti had been living a sober family existence, his savings had been used to subsidize a life-style of princely luxury, and the stable of horses and racing greyhounds which D'Annunzio kept at the Villino were living reminders, if Michetti needed them, of D'Annunzio's extravagances. After the Milan production their friendship was never the same.

The play also signalled the end of the relationship with Georges Hérelle. The years immediately preceding *La figlia di Iorio* are full of requests from D'Annunzio for speedy translations of the works he was almost simultaneously producing in Italy. What must have proved increasingly irritating for Hérelle was his position not only as translator, but as a kind of unofficial agent running between D'Annunzio and the two most important publishers of his work in France, Ferdinand Brunetière and Louis Ganderax. Hérelle's papers are at this time full of copies of his letters to D'Annunzio sent for information to the two editors; he also had to parry demands which, experience told him, D'Annunzio would have treated with derision, such as Brunetière's request that *Il trionfo della morte* should have footnotes added. At one point during an earlier and particularly dense period of correspondence, on 18 May 1900, Hérelle told D'Annunzio bluntly:

Either I cease to put my name to the translations, and in that case, as far as I'm concerned, there is no obstacle to printing them in the state in which your corrections, however infelicitous, have left them;—or else you will find another translator, who may be easily more pliable, but who could never be more conscientious.[19]

D'Annunzio took two months to reply to this missive, regret-ting that his friend had taken his disapproval so much to heart,

---

[18] G. Gatti, 'Un contrasto nell'amicizia fra D'Annunzio e Michetti', in his *GD'A, Studi-Saggi* (Bologna, 1959).

[19] *GD'A à Georges Hérelle*, 352.

but reiterating the kind of criticism he had made earlier.[20] In the particular case of *La figlia di Iorio*, on 4 January 1905, after an exchange concerning the translation, D'Annunzio wrote a letter which described Hérelle's work as a 'black betrayal'.[21] The pun on *traduzione* and *tradimento* is a cliché, and the first lines of the letter may not have had much immediate impact, even though this was already the Frenchman's second attempt at translating the play, but D'Annunzio proceeded in the rest of the letter to decry Hérelle's best efforts. Already the two had had disagreements, and the correspondence during this period reveals some tense exchanges. Hérelle would put into his perfect French D'Annunzio's extraordinary Italian, thus reducing it, in D'Annunzio's view, to the level of bourgeois literature. D'Annunzio, with an exaggerated opinion of his own ability to use French, insisted upon keeping close to the Italian text, even to the extent of using non-existent expressions 'You use barbaric constructions', objected Hérelle, 'which make the French text look like the translation of a badly trained schoolboy'.[22] In short the Frenchman refused to go further, appended a disclaimer to his translation of the play, and simultaneously truncated correspondence and translation. In the letter of 4 January D'Annunzio responded: 'All, or almost all of your corrections are far worse than the first version. The whole work is *banalisée* because it is *francisée*. Your concept of translation is, in my view, completely mistaken.'[23] In spite of such fierce strictures, D'Annunzio's letter went on blithely as though he had written nothing untoward, and concluded with remarks about the weather (was it sunny at Bayonne? the Arno had frozen over) and 'with a very affectionate embrace' ('Vi abbraccio con grande affetto').

By 1905, however, thanks to Hérelle's not inconsiderable help, D'Annunzio enjoyed an established reputation in France and was happy to replace Hérelle with André Doderet;[24] thereafter, with a few erratic exceptions, the correspondence ceased, though D'Annunzio, in exile in France after 1910, tried to renew his acquaintance. Hérelle in fact was to undertake further sporadic translations during the next

---

[20] *Lettere a Georges Hérelle*, 248.   [21] Ibid. 275.

[22] The letter quoted here is one of 18 May 1900, which has further references to 'phrases gauches, mal costruites, des impropriétés d'expression, et même des barbarismes': *GD'A à Georges Hérelle*, 349–50.

[23] *Lettere a Georges Hérelle*, 275–9.

[24] Hérelle's successor left his own account of a less than idyllic relationship in A. Doderet, *Vingt ans d'amitié avec GD'A* (Paris, 1956).

ten years, but their formerly regular exchange of news and views
virtually ceased until D'Annunzio took up residence at Arcachon.
In his notebook the Frenchman makes no mention of their dis-
agreement, though there is a note written in 1900 which might
obliquely reflect his growing disillusionment. There he mentions a
speech by Ferdinand Brunetière at the Académie Française, which
adversely criticized those novelists who set themselves at the centre
of their novels, defining them as *exhibitionnistes*, a noun which in
the original context had undertones of indecent exposure. 'The
works of D'Annunzio must irritate you at times, then?' he asked
Brunetière. 'Often', was the reply, 'but D'Annunzio is a great writer
[. . .] and in my heart the masterpiece prevails over theory.'[25]

When D'Annunzio was forced by his creditors to flee to France
in 1910, he went to meet Hérelle at Bayonne, where the latter had
been assigned a new teaching post. In 1912 Hérelle published a selection of D'Annunzio's lyric poetry, and D'Annunzio wrote him a
complimentary letter in return.[26] The praise seems to have gone to
Hérelle's head: seemingly reduced to sentimentality, he translated
D'Annunzio's epic poem *Maia* in 1913; a letter of D'Annunzio's
acknowledges receipt of the hefty notebooks concerned: 'C'est par-
fait, et même étonnant', D'Annunzio wrote to him on 26 March
1912.[27] Hérelle hastened to finish the translation, completed it, revised
it, made a fair copy (120 pages in all), and sent it off to Arcachon:
'From that moment I've never heard another word about it', he
noted in his journal. After 1913 D'Annunzio no longer wrote to his
old translator, despite the occasional letter to him from Hérelle.
Apart from sending a copy of *Il notturno* to Hérelle in 1921, and
brief greetings in 1931, D'Annunzio made no other contact. Hérelle
sent a note of sympathy when D'Annunzio fell from an upper
window in the Vittoriale in 1922, a word of congratulation when
D'Annunzio was created Principe di Montenevoso in 1924, and a
final isolated letter of 1931, when Hérelle was 74 years of age, in
which he recalled with pleasure the exciting moments that he and
the poet had spent together.[28] D'Annunzio's exploitation of his
French translator seems in that last missive to be countered by
the experiences which the latter, at least in retrospect, treasured,
and without which one suspects his life would have been more

[25] Hérelle, *Notolette dannunziane*, 113.   [26] *GD'A à Georges Hérelle*, 403.
[27] Ibid. 409.   [28] *Lettere a Georges Hérelle*, introduction, particularly 28.

restricted and provincial. In the archive at the Vittoriale a sad note from Hérelle's housekeeper informs D'Annunzio that Hérelle had wanted the poet to know of his death on 15 December 1935. He was 87 years old.

The most profound, if least unexpected, break with the past came when Eleonora Duse was jettisoned in favour of a younger lover. Duse was still hurt at D'Annunzio's insistence on producing *La figlia di Iorio* without her, but this was nothing compared to what was to ensue. D'Annunzio had been unfaithful to her on many occasions since their cohabitation began. De Michelis defines their relationship as a marriage of convenience because of their mutual interest in the theatre, and he adduces evidence to show that Duse, who addressed him in her letters as 'my son', regarded D'Annunzio with maternal affection after their initial sexual encounters.[29] She returned from her various tours of the United States and Europe in 1903, and for the summer holidays that year the couple spent their time at the Villa Borghese near Anzio, along with the 10-year-old Renata, at that time awaiting the beginning of the new school term. It was at Anzio during August 1903 that he composed *La figlia di Iorio*. The relationship continued until after the production of the play, though at that precise time Duse was living apart from D'Annunzio, convalescing from her bronchial problems. She continued her recovery on Capri during March and part of April 1904, before returning to Rome and then to Settignano for the summer. One day she left the Porziuncula and went unannounced to the Capponcina where, in the guest bedroom, she found hairpins belonging to a blonde. Palmerio describes the drama of the situation as Eleonora first planned to burn the house to the ground, only to be gradually calmed by him and led outside.[30]

Among the few scraps of correspondence which Piero Nardi was able to collect in 1975 is a letter dated 17 July 1904 from D'Annunzio to Duse shortly after the breakdown in their nine-year relationship:

The imperious needs of a violent, carnal life, of pleasure, of physical risk, of happiness, have kept me from you. And you, who at times have been moved to tears by an instinctive movement of mine, just as you are moved

---

[29] E. De Michelis, *D'Annunzio a contraggenio* (Rome, 1963), 144–54; cf. ibid. 137–43, where De Michelis also tries his best to justify D'Annunzio's apparently callous treatment of Eleonora.

[30] Palmerio, *Con D'Annunzio alla Capponcina*, 205–8.

ν the hunger of an animal or the efforts of a plant to climb a gloomy
 ιll, can you cry shame on me for these needs of mine?[31]

 ɔt content with that particular piece of egoism, D'Annunzio com-
 ımented Eleonora on being the only woman worthy of revealing
 ʌhat a great poet could do, 'and since I am a great poet, it is necessary, in the sight of the great laws of the Spirit, that you give your
strength to my strength'. Eleonora seems to have made an attempt
to reply equally rhetorically to D'Annunzio's farewell letter, but
pathos was the main message of her response, except for a couple
of phrases which have the smack of sincerity.

Do not speak to me of the imperious 'reason' of your 'carnal' life, of your
thirst for 'joyous existence'. I am tired of hearing these words. I have heard
you repeat them for years now: I cannot entirely go along with your philosophy nor entirely understand it [. . .]. For what love can you find which
is worthy or profound if it lives only for pleasure?[32]

As the note reveals, Eleonora had sacrificed everything for D'Annunzio.
She had now to begin her attempt to build up her finances, reputation, and resilience to the point they had been at nine years previously. She succeeded, but only in part. In 1909 D'Annunzio asked
her to play Phaedra in the play of that name which he had just then
written. She refused, and her letter, after so many years of separation, showed her deep hurt: 'You classified me as an instrument of
art, which you can take up and throw away [. . .]. I have already
given you everything, I have nothing else left.'[33] D'Annunzio wrote
to her periodically, perhaps in periods of melancholy when he required a confessor or an hour of nostalgia; in particular during the
final years of World War One, when he wrote more frequently.

The mystery of the missing correspondence between the two
lovers had not been solved at the time of the centennial conference
at the Vittoriale in 1963. In that year Roberto Weiss made a journey to Cambridge to look for the letters, and the paper he read as

[31] *Carteggio D'Annunzio–Duse*, ed. P. Nardi (Florence, 1975), 69; Nardi died just
before the publication of this his last book and Vittore Branca prefaces Nardi's
introduction with a useful obituary of the critic and a history of the documents
he edited.

[32] Ibid. 81 and 83–4; these are notes for a letter replying to the preceding communication from D'Annunzio, though there is no specific letter from Duse in the
Vittoriale to which the notes correspond.

[33] Her words are taken from what seem to be notes for a reply held in the
Fondazione Cini; see Nardi's introduction to *Carteggio Duse–D'Annunzio*, 31–2.

a consequence declared that Duse's family had burned the corres-pondence.[34] Six years later Vittore Branca published an important article in the *Corriere della sera*,[35] in which he revealed that Duse had entrusted the letters to Teresa Giacosa, who had solemnly prom-ised to destroy them in the event of her friend's death. Duse's last wish appears to have been carried out except for the scraps which remained with her daughter Enrichetta; at the latter's death they were consigned to the Fondazione Cini by Enrichetta's own daughter, the Dominican nun Suor Maria di San Marco. The outcome of Branca's revelations and of Nardi's subsequent edition of those fragments from the Fondazione Cini forces a revision of their relationship, at least in epistolary terms, after their final break-up. The group of notes, postcards, and telegrams, the last dated 22 May 1923, show that after some five years of silence (1904–9) the two were in con-tact for many years, until indeed the year before Eleonora's death. In 1922 they were reported to have met by chance in the vestibule of the Hotel Cavour in Milan, and in 1923 D'Annunzio was said to have sent her 30,000 lire to alleviate her financial plight. She died the following year in Pittsburg during yet another tour in America.

[34] Weiss, 'D'Annunzio e l'Inghilterra', 468.

[35] Under the title 'La scrittrice Eleonora Duse', 19 Apr. 1969, now repr. in *Nuova antologia* (Apr. 1991), 282–6, under the new title 'Vocazione letteraria di Eleonora Duse'.

8

From Dalliance to Exile

IN OCTOBER 1904 D'Annunzio installed Eleonora's successor in the Capponcina. He had encountered Alessandra di Rudiní a year before, when, by what for her turned out to be a stroke of ill fortune, he had been asked to be best man at the wedding of her brother Carlo. Since that first meeting he had by various ruses convinced the statuesque widow to fall for his charms; his campaign was launched with a persuasive letter in which he wondered why she did not wish to become the 'great love' of his life:

There exists in your soul an entire, immense zone of sensitivity, unexplored and unknown even by you. Anyone listening to you realizes that, and at times even succeeds in perceiving it as an instinctively musical rhythm emerging from strident discord. My ear is fine, Nike, my blonde miracle, and I am so thirsty to let my soul be cradled to that lullaby. I love you, Nike. I love you. I love you. And I am crazed and dizzy with this love. Gabriele.[1]

Alessandra's reply declared her desire to be left alone in her solitude, protested that she did not wish to be his 'great love', asked what he meant by Nike (a 'victory' for her or for him?), and stressed, 'I love horses, dogs, hunting and all those things which give me the opportunity of proving to men that not all women are animals to be preyed upon'. But the conclusion of the letter left the door open for D'Annnunzio to press his court further:

I am used to looking things squarely in the face and, I confess to you, the memory of certain things you said disturbs me overmuch [. . .] I know too much about you; too many women have loved you, too many, having loved you, curse you. [. . .] And yet, it is no secret, even for me that you are bound by powerful ties. So what can *I* be for you?

---

[1] G. Gatti, *Alessandra di Rudiní e GD'A, da un carteggio inedito* (Rome, 1955), 10, publishes a series of previously unpublished documents, including this letter and the reply from Alessandra which follows.

D'Annunzio's emotional bonds with Eleonora were evidently the 'powerful ties' to which Alessandra referred. But by 13 November he had seduced her, and on 14 November 1903 she can write to him acknowledging that he has shown her what love is, her mind, heart, senses are full of him and she is anxious to be again by his side. On 19 November Guglielmo Gatti notes with a smile ('ci fa sorridere') a letter which Alessandra wrote to her priest, a Monsignor Serenelli, speaking of the tumultuous state of her being, and thirsting to spend a few days in the quiet atmosphere of a convent.[2]

Alessandra was the daughter of one of the most ambitious and successful politicians of the time: at the age of 26 Antonio Starabba di Rudiní had become mayor of Palermo; he was then elected parliamentary deputy, chosen as cabinet minister, and finally succeeded Francesco Crispi as premier[3] in 1896. Alessandra had been married off at the age of 18 to the ageing Marchese Carlotti del Garda who, in 1900, had died of tuberculosis after five years of marriage, leaving Alessandra with two sons, the family estate overlooking Lake Garda, a stable of fifteen horses and her hounds, together with a house in Rome. Her mother had died in an asylum for the insane while Alessandra was still a child, and rumour had it that insanity ran in the family (her brother Carlo was to commit suicide in 1917). Her penchant for masculine clothes, her athleticism, and her love of fox-hunting and steeplechasing meant that in Roman society Alessandra was regarded as eccentric. D'Annunzio gave her the pet name Nike, the Greek word for victory, probably on the grounds of her powerful figure and noble deportment, though some commentators recall appositely that there were carved statues of Winged Victories on either side of the foot of the bed at the Capponcina. Tom Antongini also reminds his reader that D'Annunzio was fond of the classical masterpiece, the *Victory of Samothrace*, and he adds, 'A wit might have found further justification for the name in the fact that the poet had clipped her wings and caused her to lose her head'.[4] By the winter of 1903/4 their

[2] G. Gatti, *Alessandra di Rudiní e GD'A, da un carteggio inedito* (Rome, 1955), 11.

[3] Francesco Crispi was Presidente del Consiglio dei Ministri, but in the present volume, in order not to burden the text overmuch and at the same time to avoid possible confusion with the post-1946 title of 'President of the Republic', this and future references to leaders of the Italian government during D'Annunzio's lifetime, will use the titles of 'prime minister' or, as here, 'premier'.

[4] Antongini, *D'Annunzio*, 332.

secret was known to the press corps in Rome. On 21 February 1904 the hard-headed Alessandro Guiccioli noted in his journal that any conversation in Rome's Grand Hotel, where he had been invited for lunch by Alessandra, was ruined by her brother Carlo's resentment at her affair with D'Annunzio: 'Poor Sandra, beautiful, good, profoundly honest at heart but with such a terribly eccentric character; I feel so sorry for her. A widow at 26, with two children, trapped in that mess, in the worldly society of Rome she is destined to God knows what sad end.'[5] Like Maria Gravina's family before them, Alessandra's relatives succeeded both in reducing her allowance to a minimum (to prevent its possible dissipation by her extravagant lover), and in having her parental authority over her children taken away when she went to live with the poet in Settignano in October 1904.

Unlike D'Annunzio's other women, Nike lived up to her nickname for a while. She was more of an equal than his other conquests. Antongini noted that 'What D'Annunzio loved in Nike, apart from her physical and intellectual qualities, was her fiery horsemanship and especially her love of hunting and her manly courage'.[6] Nike was also as extravagant in her tastes as was her lover. The number of personnel at the villa rose from five to twenty-one, six more horses were bought to add to D'Annunzio's pair, thirty-five greyhounds were acquired to add to the four already there as pets. Alessandra ordered clothes from Parisian couturiers, including, Palmerio tells us, six blouses which cost 900 lire 'In great agitation I rushed to Gabriele with this bill and put it under his nose without a word. (In reality my face said it all). Gabriele gave a glance at the account, smiled and said, "It's all right. Pay it if you can".'[7] D'Annunzio made frequent trips to Florence where, Antongini wrote, he acquired priceless articles of every kind, which were added daily to the collection already made during La Duse's period as his consort:

Money was spent on so incredible a scale both by D'Annunzio and by his adorable companion that it looked as if they were trying to compensate

---

[5] A. Guiccioli, 'Diario del 1904', *Nuova antologia*, 78/1699 (1 Jan. 1943), 12.

[6] Antongini, *D'Annunzio*, 332.

[7] Palmerio, *Con D'Annunzio alla Capponcina*, 210–11. These details and other facts are confirmed by Tom Antongini's account; 900 lire at today's prices would be something over £2,500, not much in modern terms for Parisian fashions, but astronomical for 1904.

themselves in one wild fling for the austerity and reasonableness of some previous existence. I once saw with my own eyes D'Annunzio and Nike's favourite horses bedded down on Persian carpets, belonging to her.[8]

Palmerio also mentions how, on Alessandra's insistence, a blacksmith, along with his assistant, was summoned once or twice a month from Milan to shoe her horses. D'Annunzio, had he been in the slightest bit worried about such expenses, might have taken warning from the cautionary tale told about Alessandra's previous reclusive husband. One day a chimney fire at the Villa Carlotti on Garda caused the alarm to be sounded; the old marquis, forced out of his study, was delighted to find so much goodwill and so many friendly neighbours so speedily at hand to help put out the flames. Unknown to him at the time, however, the multitude of helpers were servants in the house and estate workers, hired by Alessandra and living at his expense.[9]

During the spring of 1905 Alessandra had to undergo three life-threatening operations. D'Annunzio stayed by her side for the height of the crises, and seems to have been genuinely worried about her welfare. In September he travelled to Switzerland with Tom Antongini to consult a lawyer, a certain Maître Giron, about the possibility of taking out Swiss citizenship as a preliminary step towards divorcing Donna Maria Hardouin and marrying Alessandra. Nothing came of this, probably, as Gatti suggested, because of an interview in Berne with a group of Swiss journalists, in which D'Annunzio gave divorce as his main reason for wanting to obtain Swiss citizenship.[10] In between convalescence and periods of good health, Alessandra was ill for some two and a half years.[11] It was unfortunate that she had begun to inject large quantities of morphine and by late 1905 must have been addicted; on 17 September 1905 she wrote a desperate note to D'Annunzio from the Capponcina: 'Nike has succumbed to her despair and has injected enough morphine to forget for an hour the torment of having Gabri far away from her. Send me a little word and as quickly as you can. Bisi.

---

[8] Antongini, *D'Annunzio*, 332.   [9] Winwar, *Wingless Victory*, 204.

[10] Gatti, *GD'A* 214, and id., *Le donne*, 207. Tom Antongini, who went with D'Annunzio to Switzerland, remarks that he did not know why the plan foundered, but he does note that Nike's recovery from her operations coincided with D'Annunzio's recovery from his passion: *D'Annunzio*, 334.

[11] Antongini, *D'Annunzio*, 333, confirms this chronic illness.

Bisi. With infinite tenderness. Nike.'[12] The poet's inspiration and his normally hyper-industrious efforts at publication were reduced after he met Alessandra. Most commentators echo Gatti's view that her effect upon his literary work was negligible;[13] nevertheless, during their sporadic affair, between 1904 and 1907, D'Annunzio did succeed in composing three plays, *La fiaccola sotto il moggio* (The Light under the Bushel), *Più che l'amore* (More Powerful than Love), and *La nave* (The Ship). He also wrote the unreadable *Vita di Cola di Rienzo* (Life of Cola di Rienzo), meant to be the first in a new series (which, typically, never went any further) of 'biographies of illustrious and obscure men'. The first of these four compositions, *La fiaccola sotto il moggio*, deserves a mention here because it was a vehicle to show off D'Annunzio's familiarity with Abruzzese folk-lore, blending what is potentially a contemporary situation with the passion and superstition which are associated with the more remote parts of the Abruzzi where the action takes place. The story has something of the atmosphere of the classical Clytemnestra–Electra conflict: Angizia has, unknown to all, killed the first wife of Tebaldo de Sangro in order herself to marry him and become the mistress of the house where she was formerly a servant. At the same time she is carrying on an affair with Tebaldo's brother Bertrando. Gigliola, Tebaldo's daughter, provokes Angizia into confessing to the murder, resolved at the same time to avenge her mother by slaying Angizia, and then to commit suicide. Gigliola plunges her hands into a basket of snakes, intending, while the poison is working, to kill Angizia, before she herself dies, but she makes the mistake before-hand of telling Tebaldo of the affair that Angizia is having with Bertrando. The furious Tebaldo then anticipates Gigliola's scheme by himself killing Angizia before committing suicide. Gigliola is mean-while dying from the inevitable end she has prepared for herself.

Although the atmosphere is more melodramatic than a Renaiss-ance horror tragedy, the staged drama has a strange power and fas-cination which maintains its commercial appeal even nowadays. D'Annunzio did his research well in the area where the action takes place, and understood the primitive mentality of the place and time.

---

[12] Gatti, *Alessandra di Rudinì e GD'A*, 20. Elsewhere Gatti suggests that Alessandra's drug habit was more to do with D'Annunzio's indifference than with a need for painkillers after her operations; see Gatti, *GD'A* 217.

[13] Gatti, *Le donne*, 291.

For anyone doubting the authenticity of the atmosphere, a trip to Cocullo on the feast of St Dominic is recommended. There, on the first Thursday of May, local snake-catchers such as the Serparo, the renegade father of Angizia in the play, bring in from the fields a rich harvest of serpents, both to display proudly to their colleagues and fellow citizens in the main square and also to adorn the statue of St Dominic, patron saint of the village. Decorated in this bizarre way, the plaster saint stands during the mass before the high altar writhing with snakes before being carried out into the square at noon to be shown to the people. The serpent lore of the region, noted centuries before by Virgil in his *Aeneid*, which D'Annunzio puts into the mouth of the snake-catcher is still very much alive in the final years of the twentieth century.[14] *La fiaccola sotto il moggio* had a mixed reception on the first night at the Teatro Manzoni in Milan on 27 March 1905, but it went on to better things. Contemporary critics, including the father of Futurism, Filippo Tommaso Marinetti, present at the first night, recalled that the first two acts went well, until D'Annunzio's son, Gabriellino, who, under the sobriquet of Gabriele Steno, played Simonetto, the ailing son of Tebaldo, became too hysterical, letting out bizarre cries and making mad gestures. The audience, with an obvious allusion to the relationship between Gabriellino and D'Annunzio yelled, 'Patricide! Patricide!'[15]

Dramatically speaking the second play, *Più che l'amore*, plumbed the depths of *La gloria*; D'Annunzio declared that none of his plays had been greeted with such vituperation. But it had the merit of attracting full audiences, who went to see how bad the thing could

[14] For a further examination of the phenomenon, including the Virgilian echoes from *Aeneid*, VII. 750–60, see J. R. Woodhouse, 'La fortuna inglese della *Fiaccola sotto il moggio*, in E. Tiboni, M. Rapagnetta, and U. Russo (eds.), *La Fiaccola sotto il moggio* (Pescara, 1987), 219–34. D'Annunzio's fondness for the ceremonial is visible in 1911 when he prefaced his edition of *Le Martyre de Saint Sébastien* with a dedicatory letter to Maurice Barrès in which the snake ceremony features as an opaque but inimitable and intriguing introduction.

[15] Some of the atmosphere was conveyed next morning in Giovanni Pozza's review in *Corriere della sera* (28 Mar. 1905); cf. D. Oliva, *Note di uno spettatore* (Bologna, 1911), 408–16. It is interesting to see that D. H. Lawrence wrote three 'reviews' (variations, rather, on the first review) of D'Annunzio's play *La fiaccola sotto il moggio*, his opinion growing less favourable until the final judgement in *Twilight in Italy*. His crabbed views and at the same time the debt he owed to D'Annunzio have been further studied in Woodhouse, 'La fortuna inglese della *Fiaccola sotto il moggio*', esp. 266–7.

be and to invent new methods of barracking the performance. In this play the theme of the superman returns, when Corrado Brando, an explorer who has already shown his courage by resisting torture by African tribesmen, plans a new expedition to the Dark Continent. While making his plans Brando impregnates the girl, Maria, sister of his best friend, Virginio Vesta. She it is who insists that he follow his great vocation as explorer, ignoring her pitiful state; unfortunately Corrado does not have the wherewithal to pay for his great new venture. However, reasoning that as a superman he is above all morals, he kills his gambling companion, the money-lender Paolo Sutri, and steals the necessary cash. Above morality or not, Brando is detected by the police, and the curtain falls on the heroic explorer and his faithful retainer as they load their African hunting guns ready to do battle with the forces of the law.

D'Annunzio did make an attempt to lend a Nietzschean verisimilitude to the play; thus the faithful Virginio defends the explorer with statements supporting the view that Brando is the new great exemplar about to reappear from the deep roots of his race. However, to any objective reader or spectator Brando simply gives the impression of being a squalid little criminal, insensitive to the wrong he is also doing to Maria, and seemingly motivated by personal and trivial ambition. But perhaps in that very insensitivity, and in his lack of awareness that in Corrado he had simply created a mean criminal, D'Annunzio is betraying his attitude to the world during the period at the Capponcina, and in particular to Alessandra di Rudiní. D'Annunzio began to spend more and more time away from Nike, inevitably aggravating her psychological malaise by his absence from her side; despite her promises to break the drug habit, it was evidently impossible. The two spent some time at the villa of Count Digerini Nuti, near Forte dei Marmi, where in fact D'Annunzio wrote *Più che l'amore*. Their affair was to drift on for a further year, even though by April 1906 D'Annunzio had other prey in his sights; three years of nursing his sick paramour had been enough. Gatti reports their final meeting at the Capponcina, when Nike saddled Malatestino, one of D'Annunzio's most powerful (and most valuable) horses, and galloped off in grief and despair, only to lose control of the beast; D'Annunzio followed on his own favourite horse, Malatesta, and took her back to the Capponcina. Next day she wrote a strangely abject letter apologizing for the 'unfortunate incident yesterday evening; my nerves overcame me':

The thing in itself has no importance, but what is grave is that [. . .] the life we lead in common has become a weight upon you. I feel it, I see it in a thousand little signs: your complete lack of trust in me (you never speak to me of anything which interests you)—your frequent deaf irritation (as last evening when you took my horse in hand)—and more, your words (like yesterday), cruel disenchanted, tired words which reveal your boredom.[16]

Alessandra's letter continues with generous statements about the joys that D'Annunzio's love had given her, and her willingness to walk out of his life to prevent his making any greater sacrifices on her behalf.

Alessandra then moved to Rome, first to the Hotel Boston, and then to an apartment in Palazzo Zuccari, which had, coincidentally, been one of the decadent settings for *Il piacere*. D'Annunzio visited her there and for over a year continued to write affectionate letters, several of which were probably intended to divert her from a possible return to Florence, where his next affair was proceeding apace. He had set up another *pied-à-terre* in Florence itself and there had already arranged meetings with Giuseppina Mancini, the plump wife of a rich and rather dissolute wine-merchant, Count Lorenzo Mancini, who was as keen as his wife to take D'Annunzio into his house to increase his social cachet, but more than this to obtain D'Annunzio's praise and approval for his own poetic compositions, which D'Annunzio lauded shamelessly. Gatti has shown very convincingly that Mancini was a coarse individual given to adultery and alcohol, who at some time passed on a serious venereal disease to his wife.[17] By February 1907 D'Annunzio felt confident enough to take his new lady with him to the Capponcina, and, though this was to be a relatively brief affair for him, in future years he would recall 11 February, their first night together, at key moments in his life until, indeed, his final days at the Vittoriale, where he noted less than a month before he died: '11 February 1938: O sweet

---

[16] G. Gatti, *Alessandra di Rudiní e GD'A*, 21. The Irish grey, Malatesta, which D'Annunzio rode to Alessandra's rescue on that occasion, recurs in a sad footnote to Benigno Palmerio's memoirs, when the creature ends its life impaled on a stanchion as it drags sand from the bed of the Arno; see *Con D'Annunzio alla Capponcina*, 254; the incident is also mentioned by Antongini, *D'Annunzio*, 193; see below, Ch. 9 n. 12.

[17] The sordid details are available in G. Gatti, 'Lo scandalo della bella Giusini', *Stampa sera* (2 Aug. 1959); in brief, Giuseppina had to disclose her condition in 1928 in order successfully to contest the will of her late husband, who had left his inheritance to his latest mistress, Adele Schöltzel.

and lacerating memories! . . . And it was my last happiness.'[18] One particular *taccuino* dated 20 July 1907 describes a night of naked passion at the Aquila Romana, a small inn at Borgo San Donnino, where the two paused for an hour before D'Annunzio returned his terrified charge to her home at Salso. The bill for the room is still kept in the Vittoriale archive.[19]

The period that Nike was at the Capponcina was a disappointing one from the viewpoint of D'Annunzio the littérateur, though *La nave*, the play which she was copying for him in their final few months together, would restore and enhance his reputation. Indeed, after Carducci's death on 16 February 1907, the king's presence at the opening night of that new play set D'Annunzio in the forefront of Italy's writers, as uncrowned poet laureate. It is significant that what, for D'Annunzio at least, had been a relatively barren period in his creative writing had also contained what he considered heroic moments, such as his epic endurance in looking after Nike during her hospitalization. Again in this context it is possible to see how D'Annunzio treated life as fiction and how fiction became part of his life. For instance when Nike was being operated on for an ovarian tumour, D'Annunzio's notes contain a dramatic build-up to the occasion, with technical descriptions of the scalpels, surgical instruments, chloroform pads, bandages, the 'articulated contrivance for holding limbs splayed out', the operating table, the heat of the evening, the dimmed lamps, the surgeon's eyes avoiding D'Annunzio's enquiring gaze. Three times this ghastly event took place over a period of six weeks, while the poor Alessandra was reduced three times to what D'Annunzio described as a deathbed agony. However, looking back on their relationship in his later autobiographical reminiscences, D'Annunzio saw the experience as a minor epic for himself, judging the long sleepless hours spent at the invalid's bedside as marks of his own fortitude, in much the same way as he frequently described his endurance at his writing lectern as an example of heroism. So the notes he made concerned only in a minor degree Alessandra's own great physical triumph at coming unscathed out of a horrifying experience at a time when surgery was in its infancy. Instead this is how he describes the main event:

[18] *Prose di ricerca*, iii. 837; the anniversary is recalled in 1917, and at other times (ibid. 834–5). For these and other anniversaries of 11 February see Gatti, *GD'A* 226.

[19] The episode is described fully in *Taccuini*, 513–15. D'Annunzio noted 'how little a night of inebriated passion and anguish cost' (21 lire), ibid. 514.

June.

I do not know what inebriation of the will is inflaming and multiplying my strength. The doctors are astonished at my endurance. For six weeks I have been awake every night. For the third time I have held in my hands the hands of the victim while her soul plunged into the dark abyss under the chloroform mask; and I seem to have been present at three death agonies [. . .]

August.

I have overcome. Convalescence begins. She lives, she will live.[20]

The doctors had told him that a miracle had been required to save her. D'Annunzio declared that he believed in the miracle, ('Credo nel miracolo'), and considered that his heroic presence there had brought it about.[21]

It is useful to reflect that D'Annunzio often made very similar statements concerning his ability to endure long hours at his desk, as for example in those letters of his to Elvira–Barbara, written to excuse his absence in Francavilla, where he was writing *Il piacere*. 'Art is long and painful', he had written on 11 September 1888, and, detailing his labours on 22 September, 'I work all day, indefatigably. Yesterday, after working five hours in the morning I remained seven hours uninterruptedly at my desk without getting up. When I stopped I was dying of tiredness.' And the epic struggle continued in another letter of 30 September 1888;[22] the tone there and elsewhere was prophetic of his attendance at Alessandra's bedside.[23] The sentiments were repeated a few months after his separation from Nike, when he wrote to Countess Nathalie De Goloubeff (who was later to turn out to be the successor to Alessandra's successor); in that letter, written twenty years after his earlier communication with Elvira Leoni, the same observations recur, as the much slighter effort involved in writing his new play *Fedra* in 1908 evokes similar remarks, 'I have worked eighteen hours without a break and without moving', he wrote on 11 December 1908, and,

---

[20] Taccuini, 630.

[21] D'Annunzio wrote up the events in 'Dell'amore, della morte, del miracolo', in *Il compagno dagli occhi senza cigli, Prose di ricerca*, ii; here the incidents are described at 628–9 (*Il compagno* is, incidentally, dedicated to Eleonora Duse).

[22] *Lettere a Barbara*, here 82, 84, and 87 respectively.

[23] 'Assiduous at the sick-bed' was how Tullio Hermil described himself in a reflection during the preamble to *L'innocente*, which fairly represents D'Annunzio's ghoulish interest in these things.

on 29 January 1909, 'I take up my work again. Truly I am a hero, and there is no wrought iron, forged and cold, which is comparable to the toughness of my spirit.'[24]

Alessandra–Nike was left writing sorrowful letters from Rome for a while, before giving up the unequal struggle to secure D'Annunzio's attention; his affection was long gone. As a postscript to their relationship it might be added that Alessandra appears a couple of years later to have overcome her morphine habit.[25] She then reverted to the childhood Catholicism for which her mother, before being certified insane, had been renowned. In October 1911 she took the veil, joining the sisterhood of Carmelite nuns, and as Sœur Marie de Jésus became well known for her practices of austerity and mortification of the flesh, not least after the illness and death of both her sons within two months of each other in 1916, and the suicide of her brother Carlo in the following year. The money and property left to her by her wealthy politician father was used by the Carmelites to build further convents in France, including a reconstruction of the old Carthusian Chartreuse du Reposoir in Savoy, on which Nike–Marie de Jésus was said to have worked as supervisor in all weathers. Requiring a further surgical intervention, she made over her estates to the Order and died undergoing her final operation on 2 January 1931; she was then 55 years old.

At the same time as D'Annunzio was writing what he knew to be his final, but still loving, letters to Alessandra, he was using similar phraseology to encourage Giuseppina Mancini to fall into his clutches. To her, in time-honoured fashion, he gave pet names, including Amaranta, the red amaranthus flower, in a reference to her auburn hair. Giuseppina, or Giusini as he also called her, was an enthusiast for the fashionable horseless carriage, and for the recently invented flying machine. The pair went to the first Coppa Florio, at the new motor-racing circuit at Brescia. La Mancini's enthusiasm for racing-cars, along with the passion and literal insanity of their love, would be echoed in the new novel *Forse che sí forse*

[24] Reported and commented on by Alatri, *GD'A*, 291–2; for Nathalie de Goloubeff, see below, p. 240.

[25] L. N. Prario, *Tre abiti bianchi per Alessandra* (Milan, 1954), 178–94, suggests that Alessandra, after a winter of suffering in 1907, managed to recover from her morphine addiction by March 1908; a less emotional account is given by G. Moncalvo, *Alessandra di Rudiní dall'amore per D'Annunzio al Carmelo* (Milan, 1994), in this context see esp. ch. 14, pp. 259–74.

che no, published in 1910. In the meantime D'Annunzio carried on his new affair at various venues, including the Villa di Giovi at Palazzetti, Count Mancini's country estate, where the poet was introduced surreptitiously at times by Giusini's servant, but where he was also invited to join the family for more legitimate occasions, such as the grape harvest in September 1907. It was there that he wrote the first draft of *Il secondo amante di Lucrezia Buti*, the long biographical memoir which also contains many vivid, and innocent, allusions to his time at Palazzetti. He brought with him the manuscript of *La nave* for Giuseppina to read, and, as a present, *Quattro canzoni di Amaranta* (Four Songs of Amaranta), which Francesco Paolo Tosti had set to music. As a thank-you offering for the Mancini hospitality D'Annunzio dedicated to the count 'a farewell garland' of nine sonnets, which now close the first volume of his *Faville del maglio*. Mancini was well satisfied by the compliments which D'Annunzio paid his poetry and happy at being so fashionably included as a dedicatee of the great man.

Much of D'Annunzio's time was spent away from the Capponcina in these years, not least because he was under continual siege from his creditors. But he was also keen to produce his new drama, *La nave*. In October he made the long journey across the Adriatic to the Italian-speaking port of Fiume, a name which he later caused to resound around the world; there a reading of the play was given to a tiny audience at the repertory theatre. On the evening of 11 January 1908 the drama, launched in Rome at the Teatro Argentina, was received with great enthusiasm: the king and queen were there, and invited D'Annunzio into the royal box; three days later D'Annunzio was guest of honour at a banquet at the Caffè Faraglia where other guests included government ministers and officials, among them the minister of education, Luigi Rava. D'Annunzio proposed an elaborate and controversial toast, which linked together his recent trip to Fiume, the success of his new play, and his ambitions for the lost 'Latin' territories of Dalmatia and Istria. His words could bring only embarrassment to the Italian Establishment and to the government representatives present in the restaurant. He began by recalling the Venetian traders whose custom it was to take their bee-skeps with them on board ship, so as to reach new feeding grounds and increase the sweetness of their honey. Thus, for his friends and companions that day, his ship (*la nave*) was laden with a different kind of honey; he savoured it with joy and hoped for active ferment thereafter; he concluded with the toast: 'This faithful water-drinker has infused one drop of wine which he would trust was born of the purest and most profoundly rooted vine of Latium, and in the company of good Italians from every land, he drinks from Rome to the Most Bitter Adriatic.'[26] D'Annunzio later explained that it was clearly obvious to all good Italians remaining in Italy that the bitterness referred to was the sick left lung of the country, which was permanently ruining the health of Italy's eastern seaboard. It was an allusion which would recur again and again after the end of World War One.[27] By all accounts the enthusiastic audience present that night in the Faraglia, notwithstanding the embarrassment of the government politicians, responded with waves of applause. Meanwhile Austria grew increasingly alarmed at D'Annunzio's ambitious views; rumour had it that the Austrian naval minister kept a volume of *La nave* on his desk as a permanent warning of potential dangers ahead from that quarter. Significantly, too, according to Mussolini's *Popolo d'Italia*, during an anti-Italian demonstration by Croats in Fiume thirteen years later, the insurgents took a copy of the play from the town library and burnt it publicly.[28]

The mood and theme of the new play at last caught the mood of D'Annunzio's audience, which was nationalistic and imperialistic, a factor that undoubtedly explained the initial enthusiastic reception. In addition the play, despite its length, kept the excitable audience's attention by virtue of its many extraordinary sado-masochistic episodes. An Anglo-Saxon (or Anglo-Celtic) contrast is amusingly provided by that great Italophile Ernest Rhys, founder of Everyman Books, who went to the spectacle years later (with Mussolini in the seat of honour), and was forced by exhaustion to leave at 2 a.m., after five hours of a performance which seemed likely to continue its magnificent progress well into the morning hours.[29] In light of future political repercussions, which reflected views expressed in the drama, it is useful to know something of the plot of this influential offering. Significantly *La nave* has its setting in Venice in the year AD 552, at a time, that is, when the city was attempting to assert its independence from the Byzantine empire. The proud sea-going

[26] The speech was published in *L'illustrazione italiana* of 26 Jan. 1908.
[27] The 'sickness' was caused by the presence of Austria; for these allusions, see S. Ghelli, *Austria nemica* (Milan, 1916), 116.
[28] The incident is reported in Mussolini's *Popolo d'Italia* for 15 Sept. 1921.
[29] E. Rhys, *Everyman Remembers* (London, 1931), 307.

people of this 'island in the Venetian estuary' are building a great ship; in the community itself, the reins of power are held by the two Gratico brothers, Marco and Sergio, the first a tribune, the second a bishop, who between them have broken the imperial power of Byzantium by slaughtering and maiming the powerful Faledro family, supporters of the emperor. The scene in which this is done is worthy of the worst (or most successful) Renaissance horror-tragedy: the four rival brothers are blinded and have their tongues torn out. The beautiful Basiliola, survivor of the family feud, appears as an avenging angel, or demon, causes the two Gratico brothers to fall in love with her, and incites them to a duel in which the jealous Marco kills Sergio. To expiate his sin Marco decides to take the great ship and sail into exile where he will perform heroic deeds (among them the transportation to Venice of the body of St Mark) which would at the same time add glory to his native city. Realizing too late how Basiliola has tricked him, Marco has her arrested and in the final scene of Act (or 'Episode') III is about to have her nailed to the prow of the ship in lieu of a figurehead, praising God ('Praise be to thee, O Lord') for having revealed this splendid way of punishing the wanton:

> [. . .] O compagni,
> eccola! Ce l'ha data il Dio tremendo.
> Eccola. E' bella. Noi la inchioderemo
> fra le due cubie.

> [[. . .] O comrades,
> Behold her! Awesome God has given her to us.
> Behold her. Beautiful she is. We shall nail her
> Between the two mooring holes.]

Freed temporarily from her ropes, Basiliola hurls herself, not unlike Mila di Codro in *La figlia di Iorio*, into the flames of an altar.

Basiliola, in particular, is a nightmarish *belle dame sans merci* who causes men to burn with masochistic desire to have her plunge her jewelled sword between their ribs, or to die from the arrow to which she has given a final kiss. Mario Praz shows the parallel between these actions and the more appropriate actions of Swinburne's sado-masochistic men, from whom D'Annunzio seems to have taken some of his material.[30] Add to these episodes Basiliola's striptease,

---

[30] M. Praz, *The Romantic Agony* (London, 1962), 292.

which finally entraps the Gratico brothers, and other interludes more or less shocking in those Edwardian days, and some of the popularity of that first performance is explained; the production was also one of the most lavish ever seen in Italy. All these factors helped, as ever, to compensate for D'Annunzio's uncompromising use of technical and sometimes archaic language, difficult to comprehend, even for a sophisticated Italian audience; they also helped to mitigate the difficult metrical form of the play, written in hexameters, not a metre natural to Italian, and heavily dependent upon the declamatory abilities of the actors. But, as D. H. Lawrence was later to discover when he saw provincial productions of D'Annunzio's plays, it was the sound of the words which produced the successful effect.[31] The tragedy ran from 11 January to 1 March and was then taken to other Italian cities, including Venice and Fiume, where its nationalistic message had a profound effect on the local populace. In Rome alone the run produced 110,000 lire, an enormous sum for the time, and a useful boost to D'Annunzio's crumbling finances.

D'Annunzio's brief affair with Countess Mancini was soon to come to a disastrous end, though she and her husband were also present at his great triumph on that opening night in the Teatro Argentina. In Rome D'Annunzio had by now met the Russian countess, Nathalie De Goloubeff. As usual in his relationships, he took good care to document as many details of the affair as possible. The *taccuini* of 1907 and 1908 are full of scattered references to Giuseppina Mancini, including what in retrospect may seem rather unfeeling sketches, which rehearsed material which he was later to incorporate into his novel *Forse che sí forse che no*. Federico Roncoroni's investigations have shown how D'Annunzio recorded some of the more dramatic moments of their relationship, many of which remained as unpublished loose sheets in the archive at the Vittoriale.[32] But, more substantially, the love affair between D'Annunzio and La Mancini was to produce the intriguing diary, *Solus ad solam* (A Man Alone to a Woman Alone), in which D'Annunzio noted down an account of their meetings as well as related memories of their moments of passion, which he recalled along with other of his experiences at the time. The strange title might seem

---

[31] See above, n. 15.
[32] *Taccuini*, 481–587; F. Roncoroni's excellent edition of D'Annunzio's *Solus ad solam*, (Milan, 1979), contains many reflected biographical details in the introduction.

to indicate that he was unwilling to allow the private details of their affair to become public property. Indeed, when, several years later on 25 August 1912, he wrote to Giusini to tell her of the existence of the manuscript, he also assured her that 'no one had ever violated its four volumes'.[33] It was true, however, that he incorporated massive parts of the diary into the plot of his final novel *Forse che sí forse che no*, and, according to Tom Antongini, both he, Antongini, and Emilio Treves had read the more intimate diary in 1919.[34] After making extracts for the novel, D'Annunzio took the manuscript with him on his enforced exile to Arcachon after 1910, only to hand it personally to Giuseppina in 1915, when he returned to Rome to rouse the sleeping citizenry to interventionist fervour in World War One. Although he subsequently borrowed it from her, probably for further extracts to be made, he soon sent back the document, which she kept until the year after his death. She then gave it to a friend, Iolanda De Blasi, well known in her time as a D'Annunzio specialist, with the request that De Blasi publish it with Sansoni in Florence. The tale of the manuscript does not end here. According to La Mancini's relatives, moral scruples about the content of the diary drove Giuseppina to ask Pope Pius XII what she should do with the manuscript. He was said to have advised her to burn it. These were some of the vicissitudes of the text which Federico Roncoroni has edited so well.

The circumstances of composition of the diary are reminiscent of earlier morbid, if not grotesque, episodes in D'Annunzio's love life, all concerning his self-analysis at the bedside of a sick woman. The main examples of this to date had been Barbara Leoni's uterine problems and Alessandra di Rudiní's ovarian cysts; now, in the case of Giuseppina Mancini, it was her decline into clinical insanity. D'Annunzio, despite his customary avowals in correspondence and notwithstanding the plangent notes which recur in *Solus ad solam*, treated Giuseppina with greater nonchalance than he did his other women, and had other relationships even during the brief period which saw the height of his passion for her. One such affair, with Luisa Casati Stampa, pet-named Corè, whom he had met in 1903, was later immortalized in both the *Notturno* and the *Libro segreto*. Isadora Duncan's autobiography describes her experiences of

---

[33] The letter forms part of an appendix to E. Bianchetti's edition of *Solus ad solam* published in *Prose di ricerca*, iii. 830.

[34] Antongini, *D'Annunzio*, 336.

Marchesa Casati's strange life-style at a time when D'Annunzio was trying to seduce both women in the Hotel Regina in Rome.[35] Left alone in the marchesa's suite Isadora was driven from room to room by the menagerie of strange pets which made startling and unexpected appearances from various points in the apartment: a bulldog, a snake, a monkey, and a parrot, all untethered. Isadora herself managed to make her escape both from Casati's pets and from D'Annunzio's embraces. Later Lucio Ridenti was to devote an intriguing chapter to Corè and to the effect which she had upon D'Annunzio. He confirms that she kept parrots, peacocks, monkeys, and various dogs, and tells how she kept a boa constrictor which she would wear on occasions, draped around her shoulders. Another bizarre part of her furnishings was a wax statue, life-size, which she would dress in her own clothes and put to sit at table with her guests.[36] In the *Libro segreto* D'Annunzio describes, in seven pages of dense French, his affair with La Casati Stampa, under the part-title of 'Notes pour la figure de cire'. The events described there are among the most sensual in the *Libro segreto*, and give a strange impression of the relationship which was to continue sporadically for another decade or more between Florence, Paris, and Venice.[37]

Meanwhile the break-up of the affair with Giusini was as dramatic as it was later to be revealed when written up for *Solus ad solam*, and the web of events was to provide material not only for this but for other semi-fictional accounts. If it is legitimate to reassemble events from notes of D'Annunzio's in the Vittoriale (evidently made for future incorporation in a fictional work), it is possible to speculate that on 1 September 1908 Giuseppina left her husband at the Villa di Giovi having decided to make a permanent break with her former life.[38] According to Guglielmo Gatti, she was minded to free herself from both husband and lover and seek sanctuary with friends in Venice. Her husband Lorenzo had been receiving anonymous letters concerning his wife's infidelity, and pressure had also built up against her from her own family, particularly

---

[35] I. Duncan, *My Life* (London, 1968), 272–4.

[36] L. Ridenti, 'D'Annunzio a Parigi', in *La Belle Époque* (Rome, 1966); evidently not so impressed with the marchesa as was D'Annunzio, Gilbert Adair has described the anorexic Corè as looking like a thermometer in a cloche hat (*Guardian*, 14 Nov. 1991).

[37] See *Il libro segreto*, *Prose di ricerca*, ii. 750–7.

[38] For the reconstruction of these events see Roncoroni's introduction to his edition of *Solus ad solam*, 20–2, and Gatti, *Le donne*, 240–1.

from her father.[39] Before leaving home, she had left a note for her husband. A crisis of conscience must have made her stop some ten miles from Florence, at the village of Compiobbi from where, according to the notes in the Vittoriale unearthed by Roncoroni, she telephoned D'Annunzio at the Capponcina. On the way to meet her his car broke down, and in the hot and dusty main square of the little Tuscan town, her reactions to the sun, the curious peasants, and the feeling of isolation had brought on a nervous attack. D'Annunzio eventually came to her rescue aboard the local butcher's cart, the only transport available. On 5 September she spent the day at the Capponcina, and in *Solus ad solam* D'Annunzio recalled their last scene in the bedroom there, and particularly Giuseppina's anxiety to get home. She did return that evening to the family's town house in Florence, and next morning D'Annunzio left for Bologna. At 2.30 p.m. Giuseppina sent an urgent telegram to him, 'Dying of grief and love. Come, come, come, for pity's sake. Alis.'[40] D'Annunzio's car would not start (Gatti surmises that he spent the night with another mistress),[41] and next day several other minor breakdowns delayed him further. By the evening of 7 September Giuseppina, who had been wandering the streets in a demented fashion all day, was confined to a psychiatric clinic, and D'Annunzio saw no more of her for years. She did not recover her sanity until three years later, in 1911.

Solus ad solam is in effect a diary of Giuseppina's illness between 8 September and 4 October 1908, or, better, an account of D'Annunzio's emotions, probably fictionalized, as he wallowed in reminiscences and sensations evoked by the tragically romantic circumstances. Many of the interesting episodes in the work, including the farewell scene at the Capponcina noted in the account of 8 September 1908 ('Nativity of Our Lady') were later transported bodily, word for word, into the text of his next novel *Forse che sí forse che no*; the madness of his heroine in that book owes its origins to what he knew of Giuseppina's illness. The protagonist, indeed the sufferer, in *Solus ad solam* is, throughout, not Giuseppina

---

[39] D'Annunzio came to know of the anonymous letters: see his letter of 7 Aug. 1908 to Noemi Gaspari, published in Damerini, *D'Annunzio a Venezia*, 167.

[40] Alis was a secret sobriquet (with D'Annunzio's own mysterious meaning attached) agreed between the two lovers (Adel was another), and Giuseppina's frequent signature for these love-letters.

[41] Gatti, *Le donne*, 241–3.

Mancini but D'Annunzio, and, not surprisingly, at the climax of the diary there is an allusion to his latest heroic effort in writing *La nave*: 'I had worked twenty-two hours in a row, in the final surge, from nine a.m. on Tuesday until seven a.m. on Thursday, without any respite, drinking an egg or two and eating some fruit on the same table as the joyous torment.'[42] D'Annunzio's attitude to Giuseppina Mancini finally broke Guglielmo Gatti's usual reserve concerning the poet's sexual excesses. Normally sympathetic to D'Annunzio's amorous adventures, Gatti surmised that D'Annunzio wrote *Solus ad solam* 'To delude poor Giusini, in case their affair could have continued'. Further, Gatti reports, two days before the diary ends, D'Annunzio was already having meetings with the Swedish artist Agata Wegerif Gravenstein, followed just three days later by Nathalie De Goloubeff, who came to join him in Florence, initiating a passionate affair which continued, with other bizarre interludes, until May 1915.[43]

By 1907, when Carducci died, D'Annunzio was incontestably Italy's best-known littérateur; indeed, to celebrate his new literary status, the university authorities at Bologna offered him the Chair of literature which Carducci had immortalized as the most distinguished professorship in Italy. D'Annunzio refused the honour. He may have desired the position and influence of a Carducci, but on his own terms and certainly without having to breathe the dust of academe. He already considered himself, anyway, to be Carducci's *de facto* successor as Italy's new *Poeta–vates*, the new national bard. On 21 February his ode on the tomb of Carducci celebrated the great man's 'Romanity', and was crammed with imperial allusions to Italy's great pagan past. As usual, the blend of poetry and civic history was a platform for D'Annunzio's most cherished political views. The effect which D'Annunzio and his writings had been having for thirty years on the Italian people had made it obvious to him that, however irrational (even incomprehensible) his poetic oratory might be, he was usually successful in whipping up enthusiasm for his 'cult of beauty', the strange politics of poetry, literature, and culture which had most recently formed the basis of Stelio Effrena's rhetoric in chapter 1 of *Il fuoco*: 'The Fortune of Italy is inseparable from the fate of Beauty, of which she is the Mother.'

---

[42] *Solus ad solam*, in *Prose di ricerca*, iii. 803 (entry for 4 Oct.).
[43] Gatti, *Le donne*, 241–3.

For D'Annunzio such oratory was easy, much easier than having thanklessly to dispense knowledge at Bologna, and it had an immediate and visible effect on audiences which not only included students, but also embraced a vast section of the middle classes. Politically he appealed to fashionable aspirations to nationalism and imperialism, but more and more he appealed to another side of society's cravings. His dissolute life-style, his irresponsible attitude to authority and convention, his apparently effortless access to money and possessions, and his manifest ability to enjoy and then jettison women made him the envy of the average Italian male. For almost thirty years not a week had passed without D'Annunzio's name appearing in the newspapers, and for almost as long his name had been held before the public thanks to the undeniable fact that his works had been on display in the windows of every bookseller in Italy. By 1907 it was fashionable to aspire to a life-style which mimicked what people knew of D'Annunzio and what they could read of the tastes and habits of his heroes, beginning with Andrea Sperelli. D'Annunzio's influence had reached its highest point so far when, that evening of 11 January 1908, Vittorio Emanuele invited him into the royal box at the curtain of *La nave*; the play summed up so many of D'Annunzio's political ideals as well as the revanchist ambitions which were to be realized during World War One. Here he was being applauded for them by the highest in the land.

Even before Giuseppina Mancini lost her sanity in Florence during September and October 1908, D'Annunzio was deeply involved with his new passion, the Countess Nathalie De Goloubeff, the pair having first met the previous March in Rome, at the house of D'Annunzio's friend Count Gégé Primoli. Frances Winwar has demonstrated with fair accuracy that the poet and his new mistress had a passionate encounter in May 1908, probably, Winwar surmises, 17 May.[44] D'Annunzio, true to habit, renamed Nathalie with the sobriquet Donatella, after the singer in *Il fuoco*, and began to sign his letters to her with the pseudonym Stelio. However disastrously their affair was to turn out for La Goloubeff, this was to be one of D'Annunzio's luckiest encounters, particularly when he fled penniless to France two years later. The countess was married to the very wealthy Russian diplomat, Count Viktor Golubev,[45]

[44] Winwar, *Wingless Victory*, 230.
[45] Her name is invariably given in its French form.

who, following a civilized agreement that their marriage was no longer viable, had granted his wife her freedom, though out of respect for his diplomatic position and perhaps for the sake of their children the two continued to share the same house. Count Viktor had made his wife a generous personal allowance which would continue until the 1917 revolution ruined him, along with others of his ilk, but by then D'Annunzio was well out of the picture and had seen Nathalie for the last time. His new conquest would ensure an essential financial guarantee for the early period of his exile in France, but, equally importantly, his new-found sexual passion immediately inspired the not unexpected literary by-product. In a letter of 19 November 1908 it is possible to see how Nathalie's slim body and long legs had him fantasizing about St Sebastian bound to a tree, while he sat nearby forging new tips for his arrows.[46] Nathalie was to be the catalyst for his last drama, *Le Martyre de Saint Sébastien*, though this would take several years before its completion in 1911 at Arcachon, and by then Nathalie would be replaced in his imagination by Ida Rubinstein as protagonist of the new play.

More immediately he took advantage of Nathalie's temporary absence during her return to Paris between December 1908 and February 1909 to write *Fedra*, his final Italian tragedy, a reworking of the classical Phaedra theme. From this time dates the famous letter to Nathalie concerning the heroic assiduity of his writing and the wrought-iron toughness of his spirit.[47] As a reward for his efforts, on 18 February 1909 he was invited to join her on the French Riviera at Cap Martin, where he read the play to her, prior to negotiating for its performance in Milan that April. Superficially the play follows the classical myth of Queen Phaedra in love with her stepson Hippolytus, who rejects her advances and whom she falsely denounces to her husband, Theseus; the latter believes her, curses his son, and calls upon Poseidon to avenge his honour. The god hears Theseus' prayer and causes Hippolytus' horse to rear up, throwing its rider prior to attacking him; Phaedra in turn is slain by the arrow of Artemis, Hippolytus' guardian goddess. If, on the

---

[46] Winwar, *Wingless Victory*, 232–4, a section which has a full account of these events, as well as a good discussion of the true identity of Nathalie De Goloubeff, otherwise known as Donatella Cross.

[47] See above p. 231 and n. 24; the most interesting account of his relationship with Nathalie is that of P. Pascal, *Le Livre secret de GD'A et de Donatella Cross* (Padua, 1947), preface.

surface, the plot conforms to tradition, D'Annunzio reworks it in his own inimitable way, introducing a new sensuality and certain sado-masochist elements. Phaedra, for instance, declares her love (and kisses Hippolytus) without inhibition; when rejected, she challenges him to split her body with his battleaxe and reveal her heart, burning with passion for him. In Act III, the messenger's speech describing Hippolytus' death engenders greater horror by its account of the way the horse bites and tears at Hippolytus' body 'and tore out his innards'. When Phaedra is finally slain, she dies heroically, affirming her will, proclaiming her superiority to the forces which have destroyed her, and triumphantly claiming the dead Hippolytus as her own in death. Once more, as with Basiliola in *La nave*, D'Annunzio's superman is replaced by a superwoman. The play received only poor notices and continues to be viewed with scepticism even by critics who admire D'Annunzio. Nathalie, who with the help of Charles Mueller and D'Annunzio translated the play into French, was expecting to get the part of Phaedra, but she was doomed to disappointment. D'Annunzio, indeed, had his sights fixed on better-known stars. It was for the part of Phaedra that D'Annunzio attempted to persuade Eleonora Duse to return, during the exchange when she wrote her famous letter refusing to be treated as a mere instrument of his art to be picked up and thrown down as it suited him.[48] The performance would have seemed almost incestuous if Eleonora had accepted, since D'Annunzio's son, Gabriellino, played the part of Hippolytus, his final appearance on stage before leaving to make a career as director–administrator first in the cinema and then as part of Mussolini's artistic bureaucracy.

Almost contemporary with *Fedra* was D'Annunzio's *Forse che sì forse che no*, the new novel, which had as its background the so far untried experience of flying. Giuseppina Mancini had been enthusiastic about the new flying machines and was said to have made flights before she knew the poet; D'Annunzio had accompanied her on visits to early air shows. The new novel had been in his mind for several years, and its progress through notes and diaries is documented in extraordinary detail: in a *taccuino* dated 25–6 May 1907 he had sketched out ideas later to be elaborated and inserted into

---

[48] See above, Ch. 7 nn. 32 and 33; Renata recalled in an article for *Il tempo* on 8 Jan. 1950 that her father had asked her to write to Eleonora in the hope of persuading her to play the part of Phaedra.

the plot.[49] Those dates coincided with his visit to Mantua, where, in the desolate ducal palace, he noted the smell of old mortar, the crumbling decorations of the rooms, including the ceiling with the painted labyrinth and the motto *Forse che sí forse che no*, which was to provide him with his new title; the notes on the palace and the sixteenth-century court of Isabella Gonzaga were to supply the background to the whole of chapter 1.[50] In September of the following year, 1908, a visit to Florence brought him to the church of Santa Fiorenza, where the ancestors of the Mancini family lay, and where D'Annunzio noted the tomb of Lorenzo Mancini, grandfather of his recent host, Lorenzo, and translator of Homer and Milton. Further notes in the *taccuini* at this point would later bring back memories of Giuseppina Mancini's madness which broke out on the steps of that very church, and thus provide him with another episode to be worked into the plot of the new novel.[51] The new material had its artistic apotheosis in the study of the madness of Isabella Inghirami, one of the female protagonists of *Forse che sí forse che no*, which also took much from the highly personal observations of *Solus ad solam*. What is technically and structurally striking is that in the *taccuini*, at a distance of several years from the publication of the completed novel, are to be found descriptive passages of this kind, which were later worked up, almost without disturbing their original order of composition.

His new enterprise brought D'Annunzio during the spring of 1909 to the airfield of Centocelle near Rome, where he spent long periods absorbing the technical terminology, as well as the atmosphere necessary to give a likely background to the novel. Six months later he was at Brescia for the first air display put on in Italy, and his notes again come thick and fast: technical details, names of parts of the aircraft, and of aerial manoeuvres, the greasy-armed mechanics leaning on the wings, the grip on a propeller to start the engine, Louis Blériot's strong jaws, aquiline nose, full moustache, and rebellious hair, and the aviator's big-bosomed wife, large straight nose, deep furrows where she smiled, good teeth. At Brescia he was able to meet such pioneers as Blériot himself, Glenn Curtiss, and Mario Calderara, and with these last two took his first flight, regretting that it was not in Blériot's more graceful craft which reminded him of the eagle in ancient Egyptian paintings.[52]

---

[49] *Taccuini*, 503–5.   [50] Ibid. 537–8.   [51] Ibid.   [52] Ibid. 542–8.

His notes on the experience and on the sensations it provoked in him predictably found a place in the new novel, which he began to write in earnest in August 1909 while staying in Marina di Pisa; he had taken a house alongside one rented by Nathalie De Goloubeff.

More and more D'Annunzio was forced to absent himself from the Capponcina, in his attempts to raise money and avoid creditors. He was working at Marina di Pisa because by all accounts the house in Settignano was uninhabitable thanks to the queue of tradesmen and others constantly beating a path to his door. By an extraordinary chance, at the beginning of September 1907 D'Annunzio won a prize in the national lottery. The amount was large, 42,500 lire, though not sufficient to pay his debts, and the last thing D'Annunzio wanted was for the sum to be eaten away by his creditors. Benigno Palmerio was sent to pick up the winnings, preferring to lie to the official paying out the money that the prize belonged to a consortium of D'Annunzio's servants, including himself. The result, according to Benigno, was that he could no longer himself step outside the Capponcina because of importunate requests for charity. Meanwhile D'Annunzio had found easy ways of dispersing the windfall, including a remittance of 3,000 lire to his mother, 1,000 each to his three legitimate children, wages for the servants, and 1,000 to be divided as a sop to his most pressing creditors.[53] Some of D'Annunzio's ploys to obtain money were more desperate than his attempts to avoid creditors: in March 1909 he signed film contracts with Saffi-Comerio (later Milano Films), obtained an advance and reneged on the agreement. The civil court at Milan found against him, and in July 1910 ordered him to repay the sum advanced, with interest and costs.[54] Another gambit was a contract signed in February 1910 with Pilade Frattini, a wealthy Brescian theatrical impresario, who gave him an advance of almost 40,000 lire for a lecture tour in Italy on 'Il dominio dei cieli' (The Mastery of the Heavens), the kind of nationalistic theme which D'Annunzio loved. The lectures were always identical except that D'Annunzio inserted into each a eulogy of the city where he

---

[53] Palmerio, *Con D'Annunzio alla Capponcina*, 230–8, describes these bizarre events; the sum won by D'Annunzio would amount to about £106,250 by 1997 standards.

[54] How D'Annunzio extricated himself from this particular predicament has never been explained; there is some discussion in G. Fabre, 'D'Annunzio nelle prime riviste del cinema italiano', *Quaderni del Vittoriale*, 4 (Aug. 1977), 55–92, esp. 71 n. 25.

currently found himself; it was a technique which he had used during the election campaign of 1897 in the score of speeches he had given in individual towns and villages in Pescara. After successful venues at eight major centres, including Milan, Turin, Bergamo, Venice, and Bologna (where Nathalie came to meet him for a week), the next audience, at Genoa, seemed too small for D'Annunzio's dignity, and he seized the opportunity to leave Frattini and others high and dry and abandon the enterprise. The ensuing lawsuit was declared void through *force majeure*.[55]

The pressure of debt had forced D'Annunzio to write more furiously than ever before, going to bed at five in the morning and rising a few hours later to press on. The struggle was in vain; any further advances which he might receive from Treves would not suffice to pay his enormous debts. Nevertheless he worked on, moving house even in Marina di Pisa in order to avoid his creditors, who put a distraint order on his horses there, and who finally forced him to take the charity of the Countess Flora Fenzi-Duclas, when he could no longer pay the rent on the by now modest house he was leasing. There are in the new novel few reflections of his current position or state of mind, lending further credence to the thought that by now D'Annunzio was detached not only from the grief and sufferings of others, but also from an awareness of his own dire situation, even though, privately, he did express some of his difficulties in a letter to his daughter Cicciuzza on 24 October 1909: 'Dear, dear little one, Forgive me. I am suffering a lot and working desperately. Tonight again I went to bed after five o'clock, and I rose at ten to begin again.'[56] But having said that, and although his next letter to Cicciuzza complains about his poor health and hard work (he had written, he said, 914 pages), the impression which remains is that he considered himself above such human problems as debt, sorrow, and indeed justice.

In this sense the hero of his new novel, Paolo Tarsis, is autobiographical, because he emerges at the end of the book triumphant over a potentially hideous fate in a failing aircraft, having flown across the Tyrrhenian to land safe on a Sardinian beach, leaving behind him madness, incest, and death. The complex story concerns two sisters, Isabella and Vana, in love with Tarsis, intrepid aviator

---

[55] Details of the civil court's judgement are reported in Antona-Traversi, *GD'A: Curriculum vitae*, i. 189–90.

[56] *Lettere di D'Annunzio a Maria Gravina ed alla figlia Cicciuzza*, 29.

and motor-racer. For the protagonists of the novel, evidence of the danger inherent in these pursuits is provided by the death in an accident of Paolo's dearest friend, Giulio Cambiaso, who had been in love with Vana. She seizes this opportunity to grieve over one whom she could thereafter consider her betrothed. Jealously Vana reveals to Paolo that Isabella and Aldo, her brother, are having an incestuous relationship. Isabella refuses to deny this to Paolo, who beats her unmercifully before one last tempestuous bout of love-making. In the morning they discover that Vana has jumped to her death over the famous *balze*, the cliffs on the way up to the family home in Volterra. Isabella, half-demented, wanders through the town, finally going insane and having to be confined in what is effectively an asylum. Paolo decides to take flight, literally, and leaves for the unknown, half expecting to plummet into the sea and die, until he realizes that land is visible and that by flying to Sardinia he has achieved what no other solo flier has done. In the final chapter he lands on a deserted shore, and meditates in the penultimate paragraph on the silence and sighing of the sea: 'And the word of the secret nurse who knows life and death, who knows that which must be born and that which must die, and the season for all things. "My son there is no god if you are not he".' Tarsis has burnt his foot on the aircraft exhaust during the final descent; the pain of the wound reminds him of the weakness of the flesh, 'restricting in a narrow point his victorious will'; he allows the sea to bathe his foot. But as he turns his head towards his aircraft, the thought occurs to him that he has achieved a first solo flight, 'And so in his soul it seemed that the spirits of the sea were healing the wound immersed therein.'

The novel has always had a mixed critical reception. On the one hand there have been followers of such opinions as those of Giuseppe Sozzi, that D'Annunzio produces the usual pairings of love and crime, voluptuousness and cruelty, 'which here present psychological variations more complicated and absurd than ever'.[57] On the other hand, it is possible to discern here something new and different in D'Annunzio's output, a changed tone in which the rhetorical flourishes of the traditional 'failed' superman give way to the ultimate triumph of the action-man hero, Tarsis–D'Annunzio.

---

[57] Sozzi, *GD'A* 240; Gatti, *GD'A* 254, emphasizes the strange lack of attention paid by leading critics to *Forse che sí forse che no*.

Charles Klopp, in his sensible account of D'Annunzio's *œuvre*, declares with unusual enthusiasm that the plot 'races forward with the dispatch and precision of a finely tuned internal combustion engine'. Klopp also speaks of the 'lexicological delight in precise technological vocabulary', which in his view, seen in combination with the 'effective natural imagery in the style of *Alcyone*, make the novel one of D'Annunzio's richer prose performances'.[58] In turn, however, it must be said that the technical vocabulary caused difficulty for readers who considered it pedantically over-precise, a problem which has not grown easier over the years. In an interview for *Tribuna* on 12 February 1910, D'Annunzio boasted that through *Forse che sí forse che no* he had introduced 2,000 neologisms into the language. Many remain preserved in the aspic of Giuseppe Passerini's dictionaries of Dannunzian usage;[59] only *velivolo* (aircraft) became a true part of the current language.

The novel is, however, another case of the Dannunzian superman, but a superman who this time points the way ahead to 1915 and the entry into war. Paolo Tarsis is the first Dannunzian hero who has nothing to do with intellectual pursuits, certainly nothing to do with the old pursuit of beauty as a means to aid the promotion of nationalism. He also overcomes the temptations of voluptuousness, in the case of Isabella Inghirami, the beautiful widow, who is certainly one of D'Annunzio's most interesting (some would say perverted) heroines, by treating her with disdain and force. Paolo avoids the distractions of painful relationships (Isabella's madness and Vana's suicide) by ignoring their consequences. The actual characterization of Isabella Inghirami involved a blend of many qualities from D'Annunzio's previous mistresses, including the most recent Nathalie-Donatella-Goloubeff, though much of the latter part of the story-line was simply copied from *Solus ad solam*, incorporating particularly Giusini's final moments of madness and Paolo–D'Annunzio's experiences of the clinic and the doctors. Those psychic disturbances are surmounted and subdued by asserting the heroic ideal of a superman of action. D'Annunzio certainly seemed to be enjoying his new-found ability to drive swiftly along the rural by-ways of Siena and environs. Antona-Traversi's pages are

---

[58] C. Klopp, *GD'A* (Boston, 1988), 62.
[59] G. L. Passerini, *Dizionario della prosa dannunziana* (Florence, 1912); id., *Dizionario della poesia dannunziana* (Florence, 1912); these were amalgamated in his *Vocabolario dannunziano* (Florence, 1928).

thick with accounts of D'Annunzio's motoring offences in western Tuscany; his red Florentia speedster with its motto *Per non dormire* (No sleeping!) was a danger to the small towns where, like Tarsis in the opening scenes of his latest novel, he raised dust-clouds with the velocity of his passage.[60]

There is no doubt that the publication of *Forse che sí forse che no* released D'Annunzio's energies for other means of ridding himself of his debts, though its very success probably brought home to him again that he could never repay such huge sums simply by his writing. And even the relatively profitable process of working on the lecture tour with Pilade Frattini could not have given him much encouragement that this, too, would be a successful route out of his troubles. It is true that the small audience drummed up by Frattini at Genoa had given him the excuse to cut short the boredom of lecturing, but the occasion coincided with the more golden opportunity offered by an Argentinian businessman, which D'Annunzio was not slow to seize. Giorgio Fabre, writing about the broken film contract with Saffi-Comerio, could not say how D'Annunzio managed to avoid the consequences of that particular lawsuit in July 1909, but it may be that by then D'Annunzio had prevailed upon his new millionaire victim, Giovanni Del Guzzo, originally an *émigré* from the Abruzzi, to pay the relatively minor debt. Del Guzzo had proposed that one solution to D'Annunzio's problems might be for him to give a series of lectures in Argentina to help celebrate the country's liberation from Spain and, simultaneously, take advantage of the potentially huge audiences at the World Trade Fair in Buenos Aires; in return Del Guzzo would pay the poet's debts in Italy, amounting to half a million lire. The two men met in Bologna on 14 March 1909 in the Albergo Brun. Reporting the meeting, Antona-Traversi reproduces the dedication which D'Annunzio appended to the presentation copy of the new novel given to Del Guzzo:

> To the Messiah,
> Invoked and come.
> To Giovanni Del Guzzo
> With Hosannas[61]

---

[60] Antona-Traversi, *GD'A: Curriculum vitae*, i. 147–52.

[61] Ibid. 166; there the sum of 480,000 lire is quoted as Del Guzzo's contribution to pay off D'Annunzio's principal debts.

While the agreement was being drawn up, D'Annunzio left for
Pescara on 17 March 1910. He had not been back there for over five
years, and found his mother overwrought and in a poor state of
health. A rare letter from Pescara on 20 March 1910 to his scapegrace brother Antonio in New York tells him, 'My presence has
made her more peaceful; and I hope with persuasive tactics to succeed in freeing her from her dark thoughts.' The same letter also
contains an allusion to a possible trip to Argentina: 'Perhaps I may
go to South America to restore my compromised financial situation.'[62] He left the Abruzzi on 21 March to meet Del Guzzo in
Genoa before the latter sailed; two days later, on 23 March, the
Argentinian signed semi-formal agreements with D'Annunzio, gave
the poet an advance of 15,000 lire, and departed for Argentina,
taking on board with him D'Annunzio's car and seventeen of his
manuscripts as a kind of guarantee. Incidentally, D'Annunzio had,
according to Palmerio, managed to keep the whereabouts of his
car a secret from creditors who might otherwise have distrained it,
by getting the good Benigno to hide it behind a friend's clinic in
Florence.[63] According to the agreement, D'Annunzio was to rejoin
Del Guzzo in Argentina after a brief trip to the French capital,
where he said he had to go for dental treatment. He left for Paris
on 25 March 1910, consigning to temporary oblivion his debts and
the Argentinian entrepreneur, whom he had dubbed 'the tenacious
Latin colonist' (*il tenace colono latino*).[64] It would be another five
years before D'Annunzio returned to Italy.

---

[62] *Lettere inedite di GD'A alla famiglia di origine*, 7.
[63] Palmerio, *Con D'Annunzio alla Capponcina*, 250.
[64] Ibid. 252; the whole of Palmerio's penultimate chapter describes the bizarre
arrangement with Del Guzzo.

9

D'Annunzio in France

ON 23 FEBRUARY 1914 D'Annunzio gave an interview for the *Daily Mail* and told the reporter that he had once gone to France to spend the Easter week in Paris. That, he added, had been four years earlier and from that day on, until his current journey to England, he had never been outside the borders of France. The poet's original intention in crossing the Channel had been to go to Liverpool where he planned to attend the Waterloo Cup; the *Mail* interview took place the day before D'Annunzio left London to return to Paris. He had made the journey to Liverpool in the hope of being able to course his own greyhounds at Altcar, but in the event he was to be frustrated by Britain's quarantine laws. The five days he spent in England, however, found an unusual echo in the quality newspapers; his name occurred in the Court Circular of the *Times* as a distinguished visitor staying at the Savoy, and his figure was to recur sporadically on those normally austere pages for the next six years, as he enjoyed greater or lesser coverage accompanied by lionization or denigration, according to the caprices of the British government.

In Paris La Goloubeff had moved from the family home to the Hôtel Meurice, and it was here that D'Annunzio came to stay on 25 March 1910. His wife Donna Maria had been living in the French capital for some time, calling herself Madame D'Annunzio,[1] and she it was who organized several soirées which enabled her to introduce him to fashionable public eager to welcome some new interest into their jaded salon society. One of Donna Maria's particular friends was Robert de Montesquiou-Fézensac, a Parisian Oscar Wilde, who introduced D'Annunzio to most of the major figures in literature and the arts in Paris at the time, from Anatole France

---

[1] For French speculative gossip concerning the relationship between D'Annunzio and his wife see *Le Cri de Paris* (15 May 1910). For D'Annunzio's immediate Parisian experiences, see A. Pellegrino, 'GD'A e R. de Montesquiou-Fézensac', *Rassegna dannunziana*, 24 (Dec. 1993), 43–51.

to Igor Stravinsky, from Maurice Barrès to Claude Debussy; many of them have left opinions of their first meetings with the Italian, some of which are less than complimentary; all suggest that the poet had hidden depths and talents; almost without exception his French appraisers are amazed at his influence over women. Among more serious commentators must be counted André Gide, who noted in his *Journal* the figure of D'Annunzio amongst the guests at a lunch they attended on 15 April 1910:

D'Annunzio, more pinched, more shrunken, wrinkled, smaller than ever, but also more sprightly. No tenderness or goodness in his glance; his voice rather adulatory than really caressing; his mouth more cruel than sensual; his forehead rather handsome. But in him genius goes beyond his natural gifts. More calculation than will; little passion, or at most a cold passion. Generally he disappoints any who appreciate [*se sont pris*], that is misunderstand [*mépris*], his work.[2]

There seems to have been no doubt that for six months D'Annunzio was the toast of many sections of Parisian society, as he went from luncheon parties at the Rothschild house to the race-course at Auteuil, from horse-racing there to greyhound-racing at St Cloud, from intimate rendezvous to private rooms at the Café de Paris, from musical soirées to literary launches, from a fancy-dress ball at Brunelleschi's to a reception for new members of the Académie Française, from boudoir to first night at the Opéra. Tom Antongini, a clever analyst of the decadent society of the time, has tried to show how Paris, when it elected a new superstar (whether it were a great writer, swindler, or fencer) 'never stops to discuss its idol; for every season it erects a new one', and in consequence, 'for a certain period which may last a fortnight or a year (the latter period, however, is rare!) the idol can do exactly as he pleases'. But whereas some stars, such as Josephine Baker or Pablo Picasso, took advantage of their brief brilliance to establish a more lasting reputation, however shallow their initial base, to Antongini's disappointment 'D'Annunzio neither saw his way to turn the exceptional moment to account, nor did he wish to do so'.[3]

[2] André Gide, *Journal* (Paris, 1939), 296; the comparison which Gide is making is with his observation of fifteen years earlier, when he first saw D'Annunzio in Florence on 28 Dec. 1895: see ibid. 62.

[3] Antongini, *D'Annunzio*, 210; the whole of his ch. 10, entitled 'The Exile', is useful as background for D'Annunzio's period in Paris and Arcachon.

For six months D'Annunzio's name was never out of the head-lines, and between his arrival in March 1910 and the close of the year newspapers and journals sought and published his views on a great variety of topics, from aeronautics to musicology, and, thanks to his presence in Paris, French reviewers, sometimes by revisiting his old triumphs, made sure that his literary works became fashionable.[4] But if it is true that D'Annunzio did not, as Antongini suggested, take advantage of such a popular position (if only perhaps to collect material for a new novel) the reason may be that D'Annunzio did not wish to jump through the hoops upon which Parisian society insisted; such behaviour would have been a limit on his freedom of action. He had, after all, outgrown that phase of his existence, probably, as Scarfoglio had noted, after the frivolity of his youth in Rome. This refusal to conform now influenced D'Annunzio's next, rather extraordinary, move into seclusion at Arcachon, a decision which should be seen in conjunction with a combination of other factors. In the first place his reception by intellectual society in Paris was, during his early months in France, somewhat mixed; there is much evidence that he still fascinated the women in the society salons he visited, and that probably increased the jealousy and disdain of his French counterparts. Secondly, Donatella–Nathalie Goloubeff, who by now had been given complete freedom by the easy-going Count Viktor, was hoping to keep D'Annunzio to herself in Paris, particularly since her husband had taken over responsibility for their children; D'Annunzio, on the other hand, was more interested in her abilities as a dog-handler for his hounds and no longer so fascinated by her long legs. Indeed, his eyes were already wandering elsewhere, in particular towards Romaine Brooks, the 37-year-old American painter, whom D'Annunzio may have known in Tuscany in 1909. Now separated from her English husband, she was a strong-minded person with money of her own (she was the sole heiress of Isaac Waterman's industrial empire) and, apart from her wealth, seemed to hold a strange fascination for D'Annunzio. He described her to Tom Antongini in the following terms:

Physically, Romaine Brookes resembles Eleonora Duse. She is a strange woman who lives in a marvellous 'hôtel particulier' on the Avenue du

---

[4] Some idea of his popularity is visible in the many newspaper reports and personal reminiscences collected by Antona-Traversi, *GD'A: Curriculum vitae*, ii. 44–77.

Trocadéro. It is completely black and grey, for these are the only tones she permits in her art, in the decoration of her home and in her dress. Although she is an American, she is both intelligent and a true artist.[5]

She also had lesbian tendencies, another fetish of D'Annunzio's which later made him pleased to make Radclyffe Hall's acquaintance. He called Romaine his 'barbarian' and gave her the pet name Cinerina (Little Ashen One) from the greys and black and whites of her paintings.

A further element in his initial sojourn in Paris which needs to be taken into account is that D'Annunzio had hardly arrived in the French capital before he began to spend money like water. He insisted on staying on the fourth floor of the Meurice, overlooking the gardens of the Tuileries; below him on the third floor was Guglielmo Marconi and on the second floor was the residence of the Italian ambassador. He secured an advance from his French publisher Calmann-Lévy, which, added to other borrowings, produced what was in effect a debt of 100,000 francs. It would take him only a short while to find himself in the very predicament which had forced him to abandon Italy earlier that year. His departure from Paris for Arcachon, then, might also have seemed a temporary solution to financial troubles, just as, during the first decade of the century, his gypsy-like existence in Italy had appeared to resolve some of his earlier financial problems if only because it allowed him to keep one step ahead of his creditors. Finally, it is also probable that D'Annunzio found himself embarrassed by the presence in Paris of so much glittering talent. He must have felt in need of a boost to his own publishing record, and experience had taught him that, while there was no substitute for raw sex as an inspiration for a work of literature, the frivolous affairs which were occupying him between his advent in March and the early summer of 1910 simply sapped his vitality.

Tom Antongini regretted that D'Annunzio was not using his experiences of society in order to accumulate new data for future literary work, as, for instance, he had done in Rome prior to writing *Il piacere*. Indeed for the whole of 1910 there are very few entries in the *taccuini*: half-a-dozen addresses in Paris including that of Mrs Brooks, a few remarks about Jacopo Bellini and observations on Persian miniatures, a note of his expenses for rental and for soap and toiletries, and for other minor items. The most important hint

[5] Antongini, *D'Annunzio*, 414.

is 'Voir Ducasse pour S. Sébastien',[6] a possible forecast of the only major literary piece which was to be forthcoming from D'Annunzio's sojourn in France. After all his exertions during those early months, what seemed to remain for D'Annunzio were feelings of melancholy disgust and physical exhaustion: 'I believe that never once in his long adventurous existence did D'Annunzio pass through a more phantasmagoric or more kaleidoscopic period, or a more useless one, than that which he spent in Paris between January and July 1910.'[7] Antongini's comment chimed with Edoardo Scarfoglio's lament of almost thirty years earlier. Then Scarfoglio had written bitterly of D'Annunzio's first return to Rome in 1882, and the squandering of his artistic talents by self-indulgence with frivolous adventures in the life of Rome's high society, wasting his time in the company of foolish people who had never read a line of his poetry: 'For six months Gabriele went from society balls to aristocratic luncheons, from horse-back riding to dinner with some emblazoned and pomaded cretin.'[8] But in Paris, no longer the 19-year-old social climber, D'Annunzio doubtless thought that there was no further need to submit himself to such minor aggravation.

By July, possibly with the help of Romaine Brooks, D'Annunzio had found a secluded residence, the Chalet S. Dominique at Le Moulleau, Arcachon. The villa belonged to Adolphe Bermond, a local dignitary whose friendship D'Annunzio gradually came to appreciate; the dwelling may have been leased initially under Romaine's name, partly for reasons of anonymity, but partly, one suspects, because the American artist was paying the rent. Romaine Brooks was, anyway, awaiting his arrival there at the end of July. Within a few weeks Nathalie was also installed in a neighbouring villa, La Maison (or La Villa) Blanche, and, presumably as a consequence, Romaine simultaneously left for Paris where one French observer, Paul De Montera, says she indulged her own taste in a love affair with Ida Rubinstein.[9] During this period, according to

---

[6] *Taccuini*, 593; the reference to Ducasse is preceded by only two pages of other notes for the whole of 1910.

[7] Antongini, *D'Annunzio*, 207; Antongini goes on to reflect that during the first six months there D'Annunzio spent a sum 'not inferior to 300,000 francs', about £15,000 sterling at that time.

[8] See above, Ch. 2 n. 15.

[9] P. De Montera, 'GD'A', in *Colloquio italo-francese su D'Annunzio in Francia*, Accademia dei Lincei (Rome, 1975), 23–58; richer is the volume he did with Guy Tosi, *D'Annunzio, Montesquiou e Matilde Serao* (Rome, 1972).

Guglielmo Gatti,[10] D'Annunzio also took refuge in another villa, the Villa Charitas, presumably while arguments raged over his body. Whatever the case, by the end of the year D'Annunzio was in permanent residence at the Chalet S. Dominique, had installed his faithful Abruzzese servant Rocco Pesce, and his mistress Donatella–Nathalie, while his factotum–secretary, Antongini, took lodgings in a local hotel,[11] and had already begun to make of the house the same kind of haven for his grotesque collection of antiques, fake and genuine, that he had done at the Capponcina and elsewhere. He also acquired his usual entourage of dogs and horses, some of which had been salvaged from Italy, where he had taken the precaution of registering some of his animals in the name of his lawyer Eugenio Coselschi. It was a fortunate ploy, since during the following May and early June a vast auction was held at the Capponcina and the poet's possessions were sold (at a fraction of the price paid) in order to placate some of his creditors. From the sale his friends managed to save only his books and a portrait of his mother by Basilio Cascella. Benigno Palmerio, his more than faithful vet-cum-factotum at the Capponcina, recorded the event with great sadness, his sorrow reaching a new climax when he learned of the fate of D'Annunzio's favourite thoroughbred, Malatesta, sold to pay part of the poet's debts.[12]

Romaine Brooks had departed rapidly from Arcachon, but D'Annunzio's relationship with the artist was to continue sporadically for years; in Paris (and years later in Venice) she painted three portraits of the poet. Here for the first time was a woman that he could not obviously dominate. One of her letters, written after her return from Arcachon has about it a refreshing candour, its tone much sharper than the not dissimilar letter which Duse had written in reply to D'Annunzio's request that she play Phaedra in 1909:

You write in your last letter that you are sad. I cannot understand it, because you have all you have asked of life and I foresee to the day of your

---

[10] Gatti, *Le donne*, 238; the vicissitudes of this period of the poet's life including an apparent attempt to rid himself of Donatella–Nathalie are described by Gatti, 257–61. A rather more romantic view of their relationship at Arcachon is given by Guy De Pierrefeux, *Le Surhomme de la Côte d'Argent: GD'A* (Mont de Marsan, 1928); this last account does not seem very reliable (for example, the author consistently misspells Antongini's name).

[11] Antongini, *Un D'Annunzio ignorato*, 204.

[12] Palmerio, *Con D'Annunzio alla Capponcina*, 254; see above, Ch. 8 n. 16.

death a long perspective of legs still to explore—what boundless joy! Even in heaven, dear poet, there will be reserved for you an enormous octopus with a thousand women's legs (and no head) which will renew themselves to infinity.[13]

In May 1909 Sergei Diaghilev had brought the Russian ballet to Paris; his choreographer was Michel Fokine and sets and costumes were the responsibility of Léon Bakst. Amongst the dancers were Pavlova and Nijinsky and the mime artist Ida Rubinstein. D'Annunzio, according to his own account, went backstage after the production of *Cleopatra*, having observed and admired the performance of Ida Rubinstein, and knelt to kiss her feet and wonderful long legs, murmuring as he did so 'Saint Sébastien'.[14] It has already been noted that D'Annunzio seemed for many years to have had an obsession with the martyred saint. He now set to work in earnest, researching at the Bibliothèque Nationale into the history and background of the legend. Between the end of 1910 and March 1911 he wrote up the results of his research, finishing the 'mystery' on 3 March 1911. D'Annunzio insisted on writing the play directly in French; he also refused to accept most of the corrections suggested by Montesquiou and by Hérelle, with whom he was once again briefly in touch. Consequently the play is full of Italianisms and strange 'Dannunzianisms', as the poet attempted to give his French the same kind of idiosyncratic style that he consistently gave to his Italian. On 20 March 1911 he wrote to Hérelle asking him to read the play and comment on the language. Hérelle's immediate reaction was that the work was written in ancient French and that he was not competent to judge its quality. D'Annunzio protested in a letter of April 1911 ('Au nom du ciel, mon cher ami!') that only one passage at the beginning of the play was in sixteenth-century French, and that Hérelle was mistaken. In fact the Frenchman later admitted that he had opened the proofs in a hurry and judged the language by the first page.[15] D'Annunzio was meanwhile discussing

---

[13] Winwar, *Wingless Victory*, 246; Winwar quotes here and on earlier pages from unpublished letters noted by her in the archive of the Vittoriale.
[14] The episode is described in GD'A, *Di me a me stesso*, 220 (the preceding pages have a further note on D'Annunzio as the 'speckled archer', for which see also Andreoli, *D'Annunzio Archivista*, 190 ff.); for Ida Rubinstein's reaction to D'Annunzio, see her 'Come conobbi D'Annunzio', *Nuova antologia*, 62/1322 (16 Apr. 1927), 426–40; an intriguing biography of the dancer is that of J. Depaulis, *Ida Rubinstein: Une inconnue jadis célèbre* (Paris, 1995).
[15] This exchange is well documented in *Lettere a Georges Hérelle*, 306–12.

arrangements with Gabriel Astruc, the leading Parisian impresario of the time, in the hope of taking over, in May 1911, the Théâtre du Châtelet, the largest venue available. He was also negotiating with Bakst to design sets and costumes; Ida Rubinstein was to play Sebastian, and Debussy to compose the incidental music. Indeed, as early as 25 November 1910 D'Annunzio had written an unusually ingratiating letter to Debussy, which brought about a meeting between the two men to discuss music for the play.[16] It was first produced by Michel Fokine in Paris at Le Châtelet on 21 May 1911.

The *Le Martyre de St Sébastien* is a 'mystery' in five 'mansions' with a prologue. Its main intention is to illustrate the conflict between pagan and Christian belief during the first century AD, but in effect it is another celebration of D'Annunzio's delight in spectacle and voluptuousness, with elements of sado-masochism thrown in to spice the performance. Surrounded by the totalitarian might of pagan Rome, Marco and Marcellino, Christian twins, are about to be put to death for their faith, while their mother and her five daughters plead tearfully with them in an attempt to make them abjure their God and save themselves. Sebastian, captain of archers, revealing himself to be a Christian, strengthens the youths' resolve to keep their faith, not only by his words, but also, in a practical demonstration of the power of God, by walking barefoot on the live coals laid ready for the two brothers. In turn Sebastian is condemned to death, and though his men attempt to save him by allowing him a way of escape, Sebastian insists on his martyrdom, invoking their arrows almost voluptuously; the archers fire at him, with a mixture of love and despair. Sebastian dies, but as his body slumps away from the tree to which the arrows have pinioned him he is at once taken up into heaven and gathered with the saints in paradise.

Just under a fortnight before the performance, on 8 May 1911, the French newspapers reported the Vatican decree, signed by Cardinal Della Volpe, by which D'Annunzio's plays, short stories, and novels (*omnes fabulae amatoriae*) had been condemned in the Congregation of the Catholic Index of prohibited books.[17] Half-suspecting that the Church would be hostile to his *Sébastien*, the

---

[16] *Claude Debussy et Gabriele D'Annunzio: correspondance inédite*, ed. G. Tosi (Paris, 1948), 51–2.
[17] For some of the newspaper reactions in Paris, see Antona-Traversi, *GD'A: Curriculum vitae*, ii. 195.

author had taken the precaution of dedicating the piece to Maurice Barrès, the French littérateur and member of parliament, well known for his Catholic leanings. D'Annunzio's absurdly florid letter of dedication reflects on his own audacity at confronting such a grave risk as creating his new masterpiece in French—nothing less than heroic, he declared, and yet no less wonderful than heroism is, he continued, its Latin equivalent, *intrepidity*, dyed with D'Annunzio's blood and with that of his peers.[18] Barrès, flattered, accepted, though he took the precaution of being far from Paris for the première. The archbishop of Paris, Monsignor Amette, issued a decree prohibiting Catholics from attending the performance, not least because the part of the saint was to be played by a woman, and a Jew at that, well known for her stage stripteases; the various Catholic prohibitions guaranteed that the theatre was packed for the first night. The play's immediate condemnation by the Catholic Church was a fair indication that the intended triumph of Christianity over paganism was not made clear by D'Annunzio's plot, but D'Annunzio and Debussy wrote a joint letter of protest to the Parisian newspapers, affirming that the work was 'profoundly religious, and a lyrical glorification, not only of Christ's admirable athlete, but of Christian heroism in its entirety'.[19] In June D'Annunzio sent Barrès the printed volume, 'I am sending you my excommunicated book; I heard through our friend Montesquiou that you were away during the week of the play's performances, and I didn't dare call you'. Barrès later included D'Annunzio's letter in his *Cahiers*, adding a long and not uncomplimentary comment on the composition, but noting also that 'It is certain that such a piece did not arise from some afflatus of Catholic inspiration, or Catholic-religious thought on the part of the author'. Saintly or not, the play was for Barrès a pagan fruit of D'Annunzio's own countryside, the product of a savage terrain.[20]

The response of reviewers to the performance of *Le Martyre* was mixed. Camillo Antona-Traversi's excellent study of critical reaction

---

[18] The text of the dedicatory letter is reproduced in GD'A, *Le Martyre de Saint Sébastien*, in *Tragedie, sogni e misteri*, ed. E. Bianchetti (Milan, 1946), ii. 382–6.

[19] Antona-Traversi's account of the controversial performance, *GD'A: Curriculum vitae*, ii. 106–7, conveniently reproduces the letter of D'Annunzio and Debussy, along with the archbishop's condemnation.

[20] M. Barrès, *Mes cahiers* (Paris, 1934–5), ix. 100–1, entry for 1911–12; Barrès had earlier commented favourably on D'Annunzio in a thumbnail sketch of his character: ibid. viii. 192–3.

in Parisian newspapers and his observations on non-French commentators elsewhere offer a rounded picture of the performance's reception at the time, from the sarcasm of *Rivarol* in *Action française*, 'D'Annunzio shouldn't leave all these loose ends when he accommodates his macaroni à la française', to an exaggerated eulogy in *Monde illustré* on 3 June 1911 by Denys Amiel. One particular disappointment for Rubinstein's partisans was the restricted nature of her performance; the ballet-going public associated her with brilliant mime and supple dance movements. In *Le Martyre* she was forced to verbalize and, unfortunately, her speaking voice itself was considered mediocre, and her French accent left much to be desired, while her inspirational legs, bound together during some of the performance, were of necessity under-used. Jean Cocteau's review beautifully described her as 'a stained-glass figure animated as it were by a miracle, but still lacking the free use of its new-found voice and gestures'.[21] Like D'Annunzio's other epic performances, *La nave* being another good example, the spectacle lasted five hours, ending at three in the morning, and though the 'mystery' played for a further nine evenings that month at the Châtelet, it had to wait for its Italian debut at the Scala, and an orchestra under the baton of Toscanini in 1926 (by which time D'Annunzio was a national hero in Italy), before it obtained its maximum success. The most recent production of the *Le Martyre* done for the BBC by Peter Weigl gives a good impression of its baffling longueurs, though Weigl tries to give his film a modern relevance by his attempt to fuse with the martyrdom of the Christian saint the martyrdom of contemporary anti-authoritarian demonstrators, beaten up by riot squads.

As a footnote to the partial success of *Sébastien*, it should be added that one result of the performance was to persuade D'Annunzio of the possibility that he might acquire a theatre of his own (not unlike the project he had once had for the shores of Albano), not least because in Paris funding seemed more readily available, thanks to the munificence of Maurice Rothschild. While his original intention was to inaugurate the theatre with a piece by himself, it was intended to be a universal theatrical venue, open to all playwrights and performances. The idea was to have a prefabricated and movable structure, a Théâtre de Fête, to be erected on the

---

[21] In *Comoedia* (1 June 1911).

esplanade of the Invalides. The Municipalité refused permission for its construction.

At the end of June 1911 D'Annunzio returned to Le Moulleau, taking with him a 24-year-old Parisienne, Amélie Mazoyer, a chambermaid whom he rebaptized Aélis, and who was to share the remainder of his life, dying long after him, at the age of 78, in 1965. D'Annunzio's immediate impression of Amélie, after she had been interviewed by Tom Antongini, was not very favourable: 'an ugly duckling', he said; after a few days at Arcachon, Antongini reported that she had assumed the elegance of 'an English governess of excellent family'. Aélis became an important if mysterious figure, kept mostly in the background, helpful in many of his love affairs as a go-between, albeit a jealous one at times, and also useful in making sure that his household was kept in good order, particularly at the Vittoriale. Antongini's final verdict on her was approving, 'Silent, faithful, incorruptible, she was for the poet indispensable for many long years'. Although Antongini suggests that Aélis left D'Annunzio after Fiume, and remained in Venice, this was only a temporary separation. By October 1922 she was permanently installed at the Vittoriale, where she was to assist D'Annunzio in his sex- and drug-induced pleasures.[22]

D'Annunzio, ever in need of cash, now began two new projects: the first was a return to cinematographic possibilities. Arturo Ambrosio, an impresario of the new medium, asked D'Annunzio to write the screenplays of six of his works, including five stage plays, in return for 4,000 lire per script. However, once having banked Ambrosio's advance of 10,000 lire, D'Annunzio abandoned all thought of continuing with the project and Ambrosio was forced to use the talents of Ricciotto Canudo as his screenwriter, in collaboration with Arrigo Frusta. Eventually the *Figlia di Iorio*, *Fiaccola sotto il moggio*, *Sogno d'un tramonto d'autunno*, *Gioconda*, *Innocente*, and *La nave* were adapted for films which Ambrosio produced between 1911 and 1912.[23] The second project was fulfilment (in part)

[22] Antongini, *D'Annunzio*, 262–4, describes the recruitment of La Mazoyer and her development into D'Annunzio's housekeeper–confidante; her diaries of the poet's later orgiastic existence at the Vittoriale were published in part by P. Chiara and F. Roncoroni, in *Tamara de Lampicka* (Milan, 1977); more recently A. Mazza has made use of these in his *L'harem di D'Annunzio* (Milan, 1995); Andreoli, *D'Annunzio Archivista*, notes *passim* the importance of Aelis's diaries and implies their under-use.

[23] F. Soro, *Splendori e miserie del cinema* (Milan, 1935), discusses the relationship between D'Annunzio and Ambrosio; further information is available in C. Quarantotto,

of his contract for the *Corriere della sera*: he began to publish a group of imaginative essays, *Le faville del maglio*, in several series which were to take three years, between July 1911 and September 1914, before the enterprise was completed. Interruptions in the series were brought about when D'Annunzio's attention was diverted by the Italian invasion of Libya in 1911, which provoked (or inspired) D'Annunzio's patriotic *Canzoni della gesta d'oltremare* (Songs of the Enterprise Beyond the Sea). Later the *Faville* were republished in volume form as *Il venturiero senza ventura*, *Il compagno dagli occhi senza cigli*, and *Il secondo amante di Lucrezia Buti*.[24]

The many essays are nothing more than romanticized versions of D'Annunzio's reminiscences, half factual, half fictional, mostly heroic. The prologue or *avvertimento* to the published volumes includes the following appraisal of his aim and achievement:

All these arduous prose works of mine were written in an unceasing attempt to illumine myself, with a constant will to sharpen my attention on my profound life, and with an assiduous effort to find that 'pure form' of me, to which my fervour, my courage, my suffering have been called and are destined. More than once, in writing to illumine myself, I have also written in praise of myself, without any hesitation; and it seems to me that I have added to my *Laus vitae* [Praise of Life] a *Laus mei* [Praise of Myself] no less marvellous in its rhythmic riches and imaginative power.[25]

Several of the essays derive from entries made in *taccuini* written in his adolescence, including memories, for example, of his period at the Cicognini. They reinforce the autobiographical quality of most of his earlier fiction, and explain incidents such as the 'Hour of the Chimera', which have already been considered above. As such the *Faville* had an intrinsic value, but they also revealed a new kind

---

'Cinema di D'Annunzio e cinema dannunziano (1908–1928)', in F. Perfetti (ed.), *D'Annunzio e il suo tempo* (Genoa, 1992), ii. 169–97. Most recently a sumptuous issue of the monthly journal *Oggi e Domani* comprising 220 pages was dedicated to Abruzzese film-makers, including a section on D'Annunzio's role in Italian cinema, bringing up to date and revisiting earlier studies, and covering issues such as the adaptation of his work for the screen, and contractual arrangements, for instance those with Ambrosio. See *Oggi e Domani*, 253/6 (June 1995), esp. 17–40; further essays are available in the entire issue dedicated to D'Annunzio and the cinema by *Quaderni dannunziani*, 4 (Aug. 1977).

[24] Now available in *Prose di ricerca*, ii. 147–411; for the alternative and problematic title of the first *Favilla*, *Violante dalla bella voce* (Violante of the Beautiful Voice), see De Michelis's definitive essay of that title in his *Roma senza lupa*, 111–96.

[25] *Prose di ricerca*, i, 5.

of prose style, which would be at its most revolutionary in the *Notturno* begun in 1916. D'Annunzio spent four years, between 1924 and 1928, re-elaborating the autobiographical writings and consolidating the myths which could serve as an obituary. Hence, strangely, the *Faville del maglio* published in the *Corriere della sera* may also be a presage of his resignation from the world of letters, not least because his vein of inspiration was rapidly running out. One final myth, strangely not exploited by D'Annunzio at the time, was the sensational theft from the Louvre of the *Monna Lisa* (23 August 1911). Although it finds no mention in the *taccuini*, he personalized the 'mystery' nine years later in Fiume, entitling it 'The Man who stole the *Gioconda*' and implying his own involvement in the handling if not the actual theft of the painting. The unlikely story is inevitably exaggerated by myth-makers.[26]

Italy had already manifested its ambition to found an African empire, and had had mixed fortunes in trying to annex and hold Somalia. In 1911 the Italian government was partly afraid that, if it did not also take over Libya, some other European power might make a pre-emptive move there; at the same time it declared itself disturbed by the chaotic political situation in Libya, which had arisen thanks to the misgovernment of the Turks. Whatever the motive, Prime Minister Giovanni Giolitti was persuaded to declare war on Turkey and to send troops to Libya, nominally, at least, to protect the Italian minority of Tripolitania, in danger because of administrative chaos on the ground in the region. On 5 October 1911 Italian troops disembarked at Tripoli, and D'Annunzio summoned up his old fervour, as heir to Carducci in the role of national bard, writing the *Canzoni della gesta d'oltremare,* those ten poems which were later collected and published in 1912 under the title *Merope*, intended as the fourth book of *Laudi*, despite the occasional nature of the poems and the lack of thematic connection with the earlier books. D'Annunzio attempted to make tenuous literary links with his previous collections by including a patriotic cry in his 'Canto augurale per la nazione eletta', taken from *Elettra* of ten years earlier, and by opening the series with a resignatory allusion to his poetic laurels, not unlike the reference to the cessation of his heroic struggles in *Alcyone*'s 'La tregua'. Piero Chiara, noting with journalistic cynicism that D'Annunzio was paid 1,000 lire per ode,

---

[26] *Tragedie sogni, e misteri*, ii, 1170–99; cf. Chiara, *GD.'A*, 221.

implies that the poet prolonged the series for a further nine poems for financial reasons.[27] It was not so difficult for D'Annunzio to write these neo-classical *canzoni*, the problem was rather for his reading public to understand all the erudite allusions, which he elaborated in his inimitable way by frequent recourse to classical thesauri and other dictionaries of the recherché Tommaseo–Bellini genre.

The most interesting and important of these poems was 'La canzone dei Dardanelli' (The Song of the Dardanelles), the title of which did not at first glance betray its preoccupation with the war in Libya. However, the situation in Tripolitania had reached a point where, after several months of effort, the Italian forces had established a bridgehead in Tripoli itself, but seemed further than ever from overcoming the Turkish troops in the interior of the country. One right-wing faction in Rome had proposed an attack at the heart of Turkey itself, considering that they had nothing to lose since they were already officially at war with Turkey, and believing that such an attack might draw back Turkish forces from their far-flung colonies. It was that plan of campaign which appealed to D'Annunzio and motivated his Dardanelles ode. In itself the daring plan was of interest, but what made D'Annunzio's poem even more significant was its peculiarly nationalistic content: while urging the attack on the Turkish mainland, the poet devoted much of his effort to vilifying other European nations for their indifference to the presence in civilized waters of the Turkish barbarians. Britain, 'the sober Thalassocrates, armed with teeth', is there accused of washing her hands of the affair. D'Annunzio was an effective satirist when reviling with vitriolic irony the inaction of the European powers, caricaturing them in generalizations which usually take their origin from some well-known act of barbarity. 'Armed with teeth' (*dentato*), is here a reference to Britain's naval power; he was later to use it as an insult against the full-dentured Americans. Another reference to 'the five-meals-a-day Briton' is taken from Rudyard Kipling's 'our five-meal meatfed men' in 'The Native-Born', published in 1896. Indeed most of the historical references in the poem are verifiable from well-known sources, and here Germans are represented as the slaughterers of women and old men, trampling the defeated mercilessly in the mud, the Austrian double eagle is compared to 'the

---

[27] 'D'Annunzio's odes, propagated by the 500,000 circulation of the *Corriere*, threatened to last at least as long as the war, so great was his need of hard cash': Chiara, *GD'A* 221.

head of a vulture which vomits the undigested flesh of its victims', and the emperor Franz Joseph is an angel of death, 'the angelicized hangman', whose allies include the Croat who cut off the hand of an Italian woman to obtain the rings on her fingers: 'These are the most Christian brothers [. . .] who have redeclared pious the virginity of the Dardanelles.'

The ode, sent like the others to Luigi Albertini at the *Corriere della sera*, was embargoed by Giolitti's cabinet, on the grounds that it would give offence to many important nations, Italy's potential enemies or allies. D'Annunzio insisted that the offending ode should be included in the volume *Merope* which Treves was to put together from the ten *canzoni*; Treves wisely printed only 100 copies, which were immediately seized by the police. A second edition came out soon afterwards with the censured parts marked by a line of dots and a note at the end signed by D'Annunzio: 'This Canzone of our disappointed Motherland was mutilated by the hand of the police, on the orders of Cavalier Giovanni Giolitti, Head of the Italian Government, on 24 January 1912.' Emilio Treves had gone personally to Arcachon in order to persuade D'Annunzio to eliminate the poem entirely. He was anxious to make a popular publication out of the new collection, not least because by February 1912 the sum that the Treves house had advanced without collateral to D'Annunzio amounted to 80,000 lire. Despite the censorship of Giolitti and company, a sin for which D'Annunzio never forgave the wily politician, there was plenty of publicity given to D'Annunzio's new polemical hymn. His son Gabriellino succeeded in getting the poem published in *La ragione*, the mouthpiece of the Republican Party, a political grouping which, while nominally the political heir of Mazzini, became then and thereafter the equivalent of the right wing of the British Conservative Party. After the composition and publication of the poems of *Merope*, D'Annunzio returned in 1912 to his *Faville del maglio*. By 1915, with the atmosphere changed in favour of intervention in World War One, and considering that Austria was then Italy's major enemy, the Dardanelles poem was published, along with the other *canzoni*, in an unexpurgated version.

In the meantime D'Annunzio, still in search of cash, had by 26 March 1912 written a pot-boiler, *La Parisina*, which exploited material not used for *Francesca da Rimini* in an alleged attempt to create the second play in the projected Malatesta trilogy. In fact, as Aldo

Rossi has demonstrated well, the need for a hasty publication meant that D'Annunzio copied shamelessly from the texts of two highly academic and (generally unreadable) collections of fourteenth- and fifteenth-century poetry, edited in the 1880s by Carducci and Severino Ferrari.[28] The play itself, which has a *Phaedra*-like plot in which Parisina, wife of Niccolò d'Este, falls in love with her stepson Ugo, was destined to be set to music by Pietro Mascagni, the very man that D'Annunzio in his vicious review of twenty years before had called a band-master. At its one performance at La Scala on 15 December 1913, the audience jeered the play and roared instead for Mascagni's *Cavalleria rusticana*. In 1921 it had an understandably more successful run at the Argentina theatre in Rome, notably since D'Annunzio by then could rely on his wartime reputation to sell tickets for virtually anything he had written.

The following month, April 1912, saw the deaths of two men with whom D'Annunzio had experienced a relationship which was unlike that he felt for any other person at the time. Giovanni Pascoli, the gentle poetic counterpart to D'Annunzio's pyrotechnic genius, died on the 6th. Pascoli had succeeded to Carducci's Chair at the University of Bologna, but had never lived up to the reputation of his great predecessor; his character was weak, and his health was probably undermined by his feelings of inferiority and uncertainty. With D'Annunzio his relationship had never been frank and friendly. Indeed, the differences in their personalities were too great for there to be any real friendship; there were often clashes and insults, particularly on the part of Pascoli, who felt jealous of D'Annunzio's fame and probably envious of his strength and his apparently heroic ability to shrug off all adversities.[29] The second death was that of Adolphe Bermond, the octogenarian from whom D'Annunzio had rented his house at Le Moulleau; a religious man, he had tried to divert D'Annunzio from what he considered the path of sin and debauchery, and by all accounts had established a good rapport with the poet, comforting him, for example, when, in order to pay his Italian debts, D'Annunzio's goods and chattels had been auctioned at the Capponcina (ironically Bermond's heirs later tried to sell the contents of the Chalet S. Dominique to secure rent arrears which

---

[28] See above, Ch. 4 n. 25.
[29] The relationship between the two poets is well summed up in A. Traina, 'I fratelli nemici: Allusioni antidannunziane nel Pascoli', *Quaderni del Vittoriale*, 23 (Sept.–Oct. 1980), 229–40.

D'Annunzio never paid). The obituaries for Pascoli and Bermond were good opportunities for D'Annunzio to write four occasional pieces for the *Corriere*, originally entitled *Per la morte di due amici* (For the Death of Two Friends), and republished almost immediately by Treves as *Contemplazione della morte* (Contemplation of Death). D'Annunzio's tribute to Pascoli is elegant, considered, and flattering to one whom he now called his friend. In fact he had never been so hostile to Pascoli as Pascoli had been to him, and his generous obituary shows a profound knowledge and understanding of Pascoli's poetry. D'Annunzio was asked by several public bodies, and urged by the students at Bologna, to take over the Chair which he had already refused on Carducci's death in 1907; now, politely, he refused it again, after the death of Carducci's successor. D'Annunzio's second eulogy, that of Adolphe Bermond, seized upon the religious devotion of the old gentleman and was interwoven with a mystical piety which puzzled critics, who thought, reading it, that D'Annunzio had repented and turned to Catholicism. It was a view similar to one reflected more ironically in British newspapers in the 1920s, on the occasion when D'Annunzio declared that he was considering entering a monastery. 'We may be sure', wrote the *Times*, 'that, if now Signor D'Annunzio is passing into the stage of sanctity, he will make it as exciting for himself and for everyone else as all his earlier stages.'[30] In these cases the cynics came closer to the truth.

On 12 March 1913 D'Annunzio completed (or reworked) a lyric play, *La Pisanelle ou La Mort parfumée*, another sado-masochistic story of family intrigue and murder, which had a finale that became famous: the courtesan protagonist Sainte Alétis suffocated by being submerged beneath an avalanche of rose petals. Ildebrando Pizzetti set the drama to music with Ida Rubinstein as its asphyxiated protagonist in a production at Le Châtelet which opened on 12 June. The play was to have less success than D'Annunzio's *Sébastien*, and the original text was not published until 1935 in Italy and 1941 in France, a fair indication that D'Annunzio thought little of its quality. The same view is implied in a letter from Ugo Ojetti on 18 June 1913: 'You should show more admiration for your *Pisanelle*. We who have heard it three times assure you that it really is a thing of beauty, beauty, beauty.'[31] The Italian text, which it was

---

[30] *Times* (4 Oct. 1922).
[31] *Carteggio D'Annunzio–Ojetti*, ed. C. Ceccuti, Florence (1979), 119.

hoped might make money through the *Corriere*, was issued in that newspaper in episodes, later reprinted in *La letteratura*, and finally came out in a volume published by Treves in 1914 with the Italian title *La Pisanella*. Such desperate efforts to publish as much as possible, to exploit even the mediocrity of *La Pisanelle,* is a further indication of D'Annunzio's dire need to raise cash. He still wished to keep up the rent of the Capponcina and of his former Pisan residence at Bocca D'Arno, in the hope of returning there in the near future, though by 1913 these were empty shells. The sale of his effects at the Capponcina had generated 130,000 lire, payable directly to his creditors; there still remained other financial obligations in Italy, as well as a growing weight of debt in France. Within a short time those financial problems would be solved permanently.

Some income was forthcoming from D'Annunzio's journalism, though the poor quality of some of his next offerings is a testimony to his desperation. During the summer of 1913 he sent to the *Corriere della sera* six episodes of a work entitled *Aspetti dell'ignoto* (Aspects of the Unknown), later to appear in 1916 as a separate volume published by Treves with a new title, *La Leda senza cigno* (Leda without the Swan), incongruously accompanied by an appendix, the autobiographical essay 'La licenza' (The Licence), which despite its title follows on the small volume and is twice the length of the main story.[32] The plot of this rambling and most unconvincing tale is almost that of a detective story, and, seen in the light of its original appearance as a newspaper serial, its attraction as an episodic thriller becomes more evident. A powerful, beautiful woman, La Sconosciuta (The Unknown One), is vainly in love with a musician dying of tuberculosis, who communicates the story to the narrator, his friend Desiderio Moriar ('Death Wish', in his turn attracted by the woman's mysterious fascination). The strange title of the story seems to be inspired by one episode in which the woman is moved to tenderness by the presence of one of Desiderio's greyhounds. The woman is herself dominated by a criminal type who finds for her a rich fiancé; she persuades the fiancé to insure his life in her favour and then arranges for him to have a fatal accident. Her criminal 'minder' threatens to betray her, torn between his desire for the insurance money and his fear that she may kill herself; this she

---

[32] The contents of the *Licenza* largely concern sporadic accounts of his life in France, part-romanticized and fictionalized; for its final publication see below p. 301.

soon does. The bizarre and incoherent tale is said by some critics to have the usual autobiographical content, though the mystery woman, also referred to by the narrator as 'The Unknown', is difficult to identify; for what it is worth, Philippe Jullian, D'Annunzio's French biographer, managed to unearth two or three obscure characters who might have provided the material for the account and whom D'Annunzio met in the Arcachon locality.[33] Frances Winwar had an even clearer understanding of the identity of the beautiful Sconosciuta, whose story D'Annunzio is said to have learned from his young composer friend, Gabriel Dupont.[34] Eurialo De Michelis, who usually favours D'Annunzio's creative efforts, dedicated a long essay to the work, but judged harshly the cohesion of the plot, which he said was 'Born from nothing, leading to nothing and culminating in nothing.'[35] What is interesting about the novel is the introspective character of the protagonist Desiderio Moriar, whose self-examination is given much greater importance than is required for the development of the plot; it would be that kind of introspection which would surface again in *Il notturno*. Meanwhile the advance which D'Annunzio received from Luigi Albertini for the serial rights of *La Leda* enabled him to stay in luxury at the Hôtel Meurice for the Paris production of *La Pisanelle*. He was also able to renew old acquaintanceships and pick up the traces of his *vie mondaine*, which he had not indulged in for five months.

In June 1913 D'Annunzio began to collaborate with Giovanni Pastrone, the proprietor of another Turinese film company, Itala Film. He set to work revising a silent film already shot in large part and taken from the original novel by Emilio Salgari, *Cartagine in fiamme* (Carthage in Flames); D'Annunzio altered the title to *Cabiria*, changed the names of some of the characters, and rewrote the captions, using much more grandiloquent expressions than those initially employed by Pastrone. In effect D'Annunzio assumed responsibility for the screenwriting, and pocketed a cool 50,000 lire for his pains.[36] The importance and originality of the film lay in the grandeur of its proportions and cast of thousands; it became a pioneering example of epic screen production (it lasted an unpre-

---

[33] Jullian, *D'Annunzio*, 215.   [34] Winwar, *Wingless Victory*, 263–4.
[35] De Michelis, 'La *Leda senza cigno*', in *Tutto D'Annunzio*, 436–52, here specifically 438.
[36] For the circumstances surrounding *Cabiria* see G. P. Brunetta, 'D'Annunzio nella storia del cinema', *Oggi e Domani*, 253/6, (June 1995), 30–6.

cedented three hours) and created a sensation in Turin, Milan, and Rome the following spring, before beginning a world tour. The technical improvements invented by Pastrone, added to the vastness of the enterprise, foreshadowed the later epic films of Eisenstein, D. W. Griffith, and others.

While he was working on *Cabiria*, D'Annunzio was also occupied with another tragedy, *Le Chèvrefeuille* (The Honeysuckle), translated into Italian as *Il ferro* (The Steel/Weapon), from which he was again hoping to make some quick money. The play was produced in Paris in December 1913, and during January 1914 by three different companies contemporaneously, in Rome, Turin, and Milan. The complex plot reverts to earlier superhuman ideals: Pierre Dagon, who considers himself above human laws, helps kill his incurably ill friend De la Coldre, with whose wife, Lawrence, he is in love. Lawrence's daughter, Aude, secretly in love with Dagon, nevertheless plans to avenge her father's death, her resolve strengthened because Dagon and her sister-in-law Helissent are also having an affair. Aude tells Lawrence of her new husband's infidelity and she stabs Dagon with a dagger subsequently picked up by Aude, who takes responsibility for the murder. The theme is a tired reworking of earlier blood-and-thunder family triangles and was withdrawn after seventeen performances; it was immediately translated into unreadable English and published in 1915 by Heinemann,[37] but it had to wait until 1935 before D'Annunzio endorsed its publication in book form in Italy.

Despite these evidently frantic attempts to make money with his pen, during the whole of 1913 D'Annunzio's financial affairs in France continued to deteriorate. More positively, the publicity produced by the regular publication of the *Faville* and other articles in Albertini's *Corriere della sera* was creating a kind of commercial goodwill for him in Italy; the cash thus generated was swiftly disbursed on old debts, but the money also provided for new luxuries, because, following the failure of his last two theatrical ventures, D'Annunzio more or less gave up hope of paying off what he owed, and for six months or so forgot his troubles by indulging in the escapism of Parisian high life.

[37] Its unreadability may be due to the fact that its translators, Cécile Sartoris and Gabrielle Enthoven were not themselves English; their somewhat importunate letters to D'Annunzio (still unpublished and in the archive at the Vittoriale) persuaded him to let them translate the play, which Enthoven later put on stage in New York.

Ironically, too, it now became convenient for him to leave Arcachon temporarily, since his creditors in the neighbourhood were becoming as vociferous as those he had left behind four years earlier in Tuscany. Not that Paris was much more serene for D'Annunzio; three valuable cabochon emeralds which Eleonora Duse had given him were pawned for at least the second time by Antongini.[38] Even Del Guzzo, 'the tenacious colonial', had returned from Argentina to attempt to persuade him to adhere to his original lecturing contract. At least from Del Guzzo the poet somehow retrieved the manuscripts of his earlier work, and these he planned to sell through a Milanese lawyer friend, Leopoldo Barduzzi. Out of the blue came an offer from the citizens of Pescara: for his fiftieth birthday anniversary the commune would build him a house with extensive grounds between the pine forest and the sea. D'Annunzio sent a telegram to the mayor, thanking him for his good intentions but emphasizing that he was self-sufficient and preferred to have the freedom to live where he chose. The idea, suggested Piero Chiara, of going back to the village he had left in order to conquer the world would have filled D'Annunzio with horror.[39] Nevertheless his need for money was as strong as ever and, perhaps remembering his lucky win at the Capponcina, he asked Albertini to put 30 lire on the national lottery in his name.

Among the diversions of the French capital was hare-coursing, the cruel blood sport of which, for years, D'Annunzio had been fond. He periodically transmitted to Albertini the news of some of the kills which his greyhounds made; in turn Albertini reported some of them in the *Corriere* in order to mollify his capricious correspondent. In fact, however, on the present occasion Albertini's hoped-for reward, a résumé of the new play *Il ferro*, did not materialize; for some unknown reason it was published instead in the *Secolo*. On 16 February 1914 D'Annunzio left on his famous journey to see the Waterloo Cup at Altcar, and found for the first time in the British press some of the fame which was to follow during the next years of war. With him went Nathalie De Goloubeff,

---

[38] Antongini, *D'Annunzio*, 221, describes the jewels and his two journeys across the Channel to what he described as an unpretentious but fabulously rich pawnbroker's in Victoria Street, which offered him a better price than its 'Parisian sister', 'the emeralds which, for many years, had had numerous opportunities of entering into cordial relations with all the pawnbrokers of Europe'.

[39] Chiara, *GD'A* 237.

who shared his passion for hare-coursing and probably helped pay the expenses of the journey; the pair were also accompanied by Aélis and by Suzanne Boulanger, whom he nicknamed Chiaroviso (Brighteyes), wife of the writer Marcel Boulanger, and by Odette Hubin, whom he nicknamed Nontivoglio (I don't want you). D'Annunzio and his four women stayed at the Savoy, from where at least two of the company, D'Annunzio and La Goloubeff, left next morning to make the misty train journey to Liverpool for three days of hare-coursing. The *taccuini* for the few days in Britain are crammed with interesting and interested entries: the landing at Dover, the impressions of the bustling capital, the damp English countryside, the preliminary meeting and lunch at Altcar, where the duke of Leeds presided over the draw for the different runs, the peculiar facial expressions of James Rothschild, the bookmakers, the odds on some of D'Annunzio's favoured runners. Back in London he visited art galleries, paying particular attention to certain world-famous exhibits, such as the Parthenon frieze, as well as many specifically Italian masterpieces of painting; his notes describe the attitudes and poses depicted and carved. It was during this visit that he caught the attention of the *Times*, and gave the interview to the *Daily Mail* with which the present chapter began.[40]

By 24 February D'Annunzio was back in Paris, in an apartment which he had rented in rue Kléber. The *Times* has snippets on his whereabouts and his activities during this period, including a report on 14 March 1914 that he had sprained his knee playing hockey in the grounds of the Italian embassy. Piero Chiara, highlighting the poet's rather indiscriminate use of women at the time, reveals that the sprained knee was a double ploy.[41] In the first place D'Annunzio had told Antongini that he was tormented by the continuously ringing telephone and by the host of invitations snowing him under; he would therefore put about the story of the sprained knee so that he could have peace and quiet (Antongini was an acknowledged master at this kind of deception). The story was well received in the press, embroidered by the *Corriere* (where the accident became a tennis injury), and provoked telegrams and good wishes, and even

[40] *Taccuini*, 626–50; a further interesting *taccuino* relevant to the trip to London was later found in the Vittoriale and published in *Altri taccuini*, 203–4.
[41] Chiara, *GD'A* 250–2; the Court Circular of the *Times* (14 Mar. 1914) gives the notice of the 'hockey accident'.

an unsolicited advance of 5,000 lire from Albertini.[42] At the same time, despite his injury, D'Annunzio was well enough to attend the boxing match between Carpentier and Janette on 21 March 1914 (and the *taccuino* for the evening is filled with well-captured moments of the fight, for possible use in some future opus).[43] However, a second mystery was concealed by the press release: D'Annunzio had contracted some form of venereal disease. In a letter to Treves shortly after the Carpentier fight D'Annunzio alludes to his sickness being a *male giovanilissimo* ('a most youthful trouble') and in another letter, to Luigi Albertini, dated 24 April, when he is still ill in bed, he confesses that his contagion came from a 'poisoner belonging to the class above suspicion'.[44] Gradually the poet convalesced, and began gently to indulge himself with theatre visits, the opera, walks around the zoo, and encounters with literary colleagues, though as late as 28 April he can still telegraph Ojetti saying that he is 'much better that day and hoped to get up the following Saturday'.[45] On 27 June 1914 he went to the theatre to watch Isadora Duncan dance. In the meantime Nathalie–Donatella resigned herself to the poet's indifference, isolating herself on a farm, the Dame-Rose, which she had leased near Meudon where the couple kept greyhounds, and where she had ambitions to breed champion coursers.

Antongini's account of D'Annunzio in Paris at the time omits any medical reference, but does suggest that boredom with the French capital would sooner or later have driven him either back to Arcachon or to Italy. To return to Italy was still too uncomfortable a prospect; Albertini constantly warned that his creditors would savage him. He would have returned to Arcachon, because, according to Antongini it was his intention to do some hard work. The dilemma was resolved for him in Sarajevo on 28 June 1914 when the student Prinzip assassinated Archduke Ferdinand and his wife Sophia. On 28 July Austria declared war on Serbia, and international alliances immediately clicked into place, forcing similar declarations: Germany against France and Russia, Britain against

---

[42] Antongini, *D'Annunzio*, ii, reports a letter concerning the 'excuse' of the twisted knee. (The Italian text calls the game 'Hokey'; the Heinemann translation reads 'playing Hooker'.)

[43] *Taccuini*, 653–4.

[44] Alatri, *GD'A*, 335, describes his plight at the time; for the many exchanges between D'Annunzio and Luigi Albertini, see the massive edition of L. Albertini, *Epistolario (1911–1926)*, ed. Ottavio Barié, 4 vols. (Milan, 1968), particularly vol. iii.

[45] *Carteggio D'Annunzio–Ojetti*, 126.

Austria and Germany. Italy and Austria were nominally allies, and D'Annunzio (in legal terms now an anti-French belligerent) was preoccupied with his own position in France, but on 3 August Italy declared its neutrality, and he was able to resume many of his earlier activities, including visits to the Dame-Rose farm, though here he needed safe-conduct passes to get him through the military patrols. From this point his annotations in the *taccuini* become more detailed, in possible preparation for dispatches to Albertini; typically, for instance, on the way to the farm on 9 August 1914 he noted the cavalry horses in the shade of the trees in the Bois de Boulogne waiting to be shipped to war; he meditated on the abolition of the individual as territorial reservists with berets and rifles stopped his carriage.[46] However, his main theme at this point in the *taccuini*, running through and beyond his comments on French military preparations, is the description of the farm, the feeding of the dogs, the horses, the rattle of the combine harvester, the croaking of frogs, the sunset, the moonrise, the dew on the meadows. He had had news that his favourite sister Anna (Nannina) was dangerously ill in Pescara; he noted in a *taccuino* the howling of one of the whelps ('baying at death' wrote D'Annunzio) and, in parenthesis, 'After the news of Nannina in danger'; Anna had, unknown to him, died the day before, on 8 August. This seems to have been his only reference to his sister's illness and death.[47] Thus, although D'Annunzio approved of the war for its own sake, and would soon throw himself into it with enthusiasm, there is plenty of evidence at this point that he was indulging in his usual diversions, particularly in the social sphere, without expressing much in the way of interventionist progaganda. But this would soon change.

Albertini wanted D'Annunzio to write articles from France supporting Italy's neutralist position, which it was the editorial policy of the *Corriere* to promote. This was far from D'Annunzio's thoughts. Instead, on 13 August 1914, he published an ode in *Le Figaro*, his 'Ode pour la résurrection latine', another jingoistic poem, in which he foretold the entry into the war of France's 'Latin sister', Italy; on the following day a translation of the poem was published without comment in the *Corriere*. D'Annunzio's view of the supremacy of the Latin race was, in its own way, as strongly

---

[46] *Taccuini*, 661–4.

[47] Ibid. 657; there are no other references to Anna in either of the two massive volumes of *Taccuini*.

held as the Nazi view of the supremacy of the Teuton, and he had consistently expressed such opinions over the preceding twenty years. Tom Antongini's reminiscences are full of illustrations of that tendency in D'Annunzio; he quotes, for instance, a letter, later published in *Le Temps*, in which D'Annunzio had commiserated with a French friend on the occasion of the assassination of Sadi Carnot in 1894. 'What is most consoling in this terrible misfortune is that, assuredly, the heart of Italy has never palpitated so strongly for her big sister, has never felt so strongly the communion of the Latin blood.'[48] And, as early as 1895, Georges Hérelle had noted in his journal that D'Annunzio had in mind to write 'a volume of poetic prose pieces which would be an appeal to the Latin races'. Fifteen years thence, D'Annunzio had prophetically feared, the Universal Exhibition planned for Paris in 1900 would be the final flourish of the Latin genius before the onrush of barbarity. The poet had elaborated his scheme to the Frenchman during their stay together at Francavilla:

Beyond the Latin races, there is only barbarity. My volume of *Poetic Prose Pieces* will probably be composed of two parts, of which the first will be the lyrical eulogy of the role played by the Latin races in the world throughout the centuries, and the second will persecute with lyrical imprecations the funereal influence exercised by the other races.[49]

After the defeat at Charleroi, the threatened advance of the German forces beyond the Marne, and the retreat of the French army, those 'Latin' sentiments come to the fore again in D'Annunzio; Antongini noted at the time that the anguish of the waiting was indescribable: 'D'Annunzio wrote in after-years: "The hour of the most cruel sacrifices has struck: the barbarian invasion seemed irresistible".'[50]

The articles which D'Annunzio sent back to the *Corriere* during August and early September 1914 give startling impressions of a Paris in emotional suspense at the fears of a German invasion, and then in panic as it was deserted by its citizens after the Battle of the Marne during the opening days of September; on 2 September the French government left for Bordeaux. D'Annunzio refused to leave Paris, even when enticed, as Antongini reported, 'by a pretty woman whom he had been courting for several months', who offered him 'a villa on the Côte d'Azur, tranquillity and—all the

[48] Antongini, *D'Annunzio*, 344.   [49] Hérelle, *Notolette dannunziane*, 36.
[50] Antongini, *D'Annunzio*, 348.

rest!'[51] The news became more alarming: Luigi Barzini, the best-known Italian war correspondent of the time, who had been an eye-witness of the French defeat, reported in person to D'Annunzio that there was no hope left for Paris; the Germans would probably be there within the week.[52] D'Annunzio instructed Antongini to lay in a good supply of tinned goods, 'To avoid the risk of rats figuring on our menu as they had on the Paris menus of 1870'. Antongini spent 4,000 francs, buying, as he said, sufficient supplies to feed all the inhabitants of the apartment in rue Kléber, 'the poet, myself, two women servants and twenty-two canaries—for fully a year'.[53]

At the Dame Rose farm, which D'Annunzio continued to visit sporadically, food shortages forced him to put down some of the dogs. He took his favourite bitch, Fly, to Paris, and the relevant entries in the *taccuini* describe him moodily walking the deserted streets. On 8 September 1914, a chance encounter with a friend and collaborator from his days in Italy, Ricciotto Canudo, evidently touched a chord with D'Annunzio, and had important repercussions shortly afterwards. Canudo had obtained a commission in an Italian force of so-called Garibaldian volunteers, and was about to leave for Lyons and the Front at Belfort, but, being penniless, he could not afford to pay for the appropriate uniform, which he had ordered and which he knew was waiting for him at the tailor's. D'Annunzio regretted that he could not give him any money because he hadn't any, 'but I can place at your disposal a man who, thanks to his consummate cleverness, can obtain your uniform without spending a penny'; so saying he entrusted Canudo to the skills of his usual quartermaster, Tom Antongini.[54] The latter has an amusing story of his meeting with 'A tailor with foresight':

After a long and fruitless argument with the obstinate businessman, I had recourse to the only plea which could possibly move him—patriotism. I said with pathos: 'You must not forget that tomorrow Monsieur Canudo may die for your country!' The tailor replied with a smile: 'I know it, and I admire your friend's gesture, but that is precisely the reason why I hesitate to give him credit for his uniform.'

[51] Ibid. 349.

[52] *Taccuini*, 677–8; the notebooks for this period capture particularly well the atmosphere of panic in the French capital.

[53] Antongini, *D'Annunzio*, 349.

[54] Canudo's penury is discussed in the *Taccuini*, 677–8; D'Annunzio's solution and Antongini's reflections on his visit to the Parisian tailor's are contained in Antongini, *D'Annunzio*, 355–6.

D'Annunzio scraped the money together by having Antongini sell the maid's sewing-machine. The most significant aspect of the encounter with Canudo is visible in a note which D'Annunzio left in the *taccuino* for that day.

Canudo is full of melancholy. They've told him to carry two revolvers: one for the enemy and a second for the volunteers, a motley crowd [*accozzaglia*] of different types, perhaps pusillanimous [*vile*]. How will this ideologue, extenuated by his aesthetic exertions, ever be able to face action? He will always feel his true life floating *above* the action, extraneous and far away.

The final two sentences are quotations or adaptations of lines from *Più che l'amore*, produced nine years previously. Canudo had some of D'Annunzio's own qualities of character. There is no doubt that the superman–aesthete who adventured his talents in politics or war was very present in D'Annunzio's thoughts on that melancholy evening at the Café de la Paix.[55]

A week after the encounter with Canudo, who was to win medals fighting three years later in action at Monastir, D'Annunzio went to obtain a safe-conduct pass to enable him to visit the Front; at the Invalides he met Joseph Simon Galieni, a first-generation French-man with his original roots in Lombardy, and now the military governor of Paris. General Galieni complimented D'Annunzio on his writings. 'At this moment I would give all my books for one of your actions', replied D'Annunzio.[56] The French, unwilling to be held responsible for the accidental death of a famous littérateur, were understandably chary about allowing D'Annunzio free scope to roam along the dangerous front line, and two journeys, under-taken on the 17 and 19–20 September, were mainly limited to areas well away from the current fighting, though he did reach Soissons which was then under bombardment, and there, despite the hesita-tion of the owner of the hired car ('Now that we've seen every-thing we may as well turn back'), D'Annunzio insisted on going into the heart of the city, pretending not to hear the suggestion. In the main square, Antongini reported, a shell had landed a few moments before, killing the driver of a wagon and his horse:

A great pool of blood, still warm, soaked the paving-stones of the deserted square. The car stopped before a tangled mass of wheels, harness straps and strips of flesh. An officer ran from a house towards us. He asked

<hr />

[55] *Taccuini*, 678.   [56] Ibid. 682–3.

D'Annunzio rather brusquely: 'Who are you and what are you doing here?' 'We are watching the bombardment', the poet replied with his usual gentle smile, and again he showed his safe-conduct pass. By a happy chance the officer was a passionate reader of D'Annunzio's works. The illustrious name on the pass mollified him completely. He permitted the poet to distribute fifty packs of cigarettes to the men, and to collect from them a dozen cards and letters to be mailed in Paris. The soldiers thanked and applauded him. These were the first steps towards the alliance![57]

Piero Chiara casts some doubt on the reliability of Antongini's matter-of-fact reporting, but the situation is confirmed by similar notes in D'Annunzio's *taccuini* of the time, and indeed in mood was not unlike those prosaic scenes which Hérelle had described in such matter-of-fact terms during the journey to Greece, and which D'Annunzio had then worked up into epic images. At the Front, he was, of course, all the time jotting down notes for his newspaper articles, and there is a notable artistic and imaginative divergence between his notes and the items for the *Corriere della sera* and later more creative descriptions in *La Leda senza cigno*, not unlike the contrast between the notes worked up from the *taccuini* written in Greece and the poetry of *Maia*. Thus, in the subsequent *Leda senza cigno* he breathes life into one of the broken spires of Soissons cathedral by imagining a crowd in the main square witnessing its decapitation by a German shell:

A sudden flash dazzled my gaze. The whole space trembled. The city caught its breath. A silence, human, more than human, spread from the centre, fell on everything, as when the crowd gathered in the square falls silent to hear the head of an innocent victim roll into the executioner's basket. One of the spires was seen to be sliced off; the city lifted skywards just an arm and a stump.[58]

Even better known and more spectacular was his description of the burning of Rheims cathedral, where the flame becomes the 'supreme architect', liberating the masterpiece in stone from its terrestrial weight, freeing it from the influence of its earthly builders and their mundane tools, lifting the whole edifice high into the night sky, joining cathedral with firmament. 'The cathedral was aflame

---

[57] Antongini, *Vita segreta*, 464: the fuller description of the scene is here translated by me from the Italian original; cf. *D'Annunzio*, 352.

[58] Clelia Martignoni comments on D'Annunzio's creative reporting here in the introduction to her edition of the *La Leda senza cigno* (Milan, 1976); in the same edition his descriptions of the bombardments occur at pp. 125–6.

in resurrection, and the soul of France was on its feet again in a Messianic reawakening.' In *La Leda*, the description of Rheims cathedral follows immediately on that of Soissons, and so convincing and startling was D'Annunzio's eyewitness account that stories were invented of his watching the flames from his automobile while taking notes. It is interesting to see the continuing creation of this and other myths surrounding the poet's figure at the time.[59] Charles Ricketts reports in his diary the account brought to him by Antonio Cippico:

Cippico to dinner. In Paris he met D'Annunzio, who is quite happy in an exquisite Louis XIV house near the Hôtel de Ville, making perfumes and experimenting in glass-blowing and moulding. D'Annunzio witnessed the burning of Rheims cathedral from his motor, and speaks of the terrible effect of the flames devouring the roof against a star-lit sky. He says the actual destruction is overstated and has affected mainly the restorations; this may or may not be the case.[60]

In fact the cathedral at Rheims was burnt at about the time D'Annunzio was in Soissons, on 18 and 19 September, and D'Annunzio did not see the ruins until he went there the following year with Ugo Ojetti, on 16 March 1915.[61]

D'Annunzio's absence from the scenes of destruction need not have impeded his creative brilliance. All the newspapers of Europe were full of the barbaric act at Rheims, and D'Annunzio would be able to incorporate such material into his reports and later into *La Leda senza cigno*. However, he went further: Guy Tosi has shown convincingly that the description of bombing and fire in La *Leda* relied heavily on passages from Louis Demaison's *La Cathédrale de Rheims* published in 1911 and from Auguste Rodin's *Les Cathédrales de France*, just then published in 1914. Tosi notes that D'Annunzio

[59] Guy Tosi has documented more factually the poet's visits in his *La Vie et le rôle de D'Annunzio en France au début de la grande guerre (1914–15)* (Florence, 1961), appendix V: 'D'Annunzio à Rheims' (157–74), and appendix VI: 'Sources livresques de l'évocation de Soissons' (175–6). Tosi's volume contains interesting plates of the cathedral in flames and of the streets round about during the time that Ojetti and D'Annunzio visited the ruins a year after the fire.

[60] C. Ricketts, *Self-Portrait*, ed. T. Sturge Moore and C. Lewis (London, 1939), 228.

[61] Two letters from D'Annunzio to Ojetti of mid-March 1915 prepare his friend for the expedition to Rheims: *Carteggio D'Annunzio–Ojetti*, 134–5; Ojetti's own description of the startling experience is reported in his *Cose viste*, i. 432–8; D'Annunzio's draft notes are in *Taccuini*, 719–21.

possessed both volumes and that in the Vittoriale library Demaison's volume contained the poet's characteristic marginal notes. An interesting series of passages from the works concerned, set out in parallel columns, adds the finishing touch to Tosi's thesis.[62] D'Annunzio, in those poetic allusions to a spiritual resurrection connected with the burning of Rheims cathedral, was celebrating the French revival on the Marne, the 'unexpected miracle' he called it,[63] which by 12 September seemed to have turned the tide, if only temporarily, against the Germans. Meantime he waited vainly for Italy to abandon her treaty with Austria and declare war. And, in the apparent absence of initiatives from Rome, he began to launch a campaign of his own.

On 30 September 1914, in the Parisian daily *Journal*, D'Annunzio published *Fluctibus et Fatis*, an appeal to the Italians to enter the war on the side of the Allies. The appeal was published next day in the *Corriere della sera*. The item contained what were going to be his standard criticisms of the senile government in Rome, and of its inept 'station-master prime minister' Giovanni Giolitti; it laid continuing emphasis on the innate superiority of the Latin races:

This war is not a simple conflict of interests, which might be transient, sporadic or illusory. It is far deeper than that and, I shall say it, something more divine, abolishing temporal evolution and the development of man with its bestial and primordial character. It is a struggle of races, a confrontation of irreconcilable powers, a trial of blood, which the enemies of the Latin name conduct according to the most ancient iron law.

With a more specific reference to the old tyranny of Austria, D'Annunzio underlined again his contention that Italy had only one lung; the lung on Italy's left side, the side of the heart, was still crushed beneath the heel of the Austro-Hungarian enemy. The words were prophetic of many of D'Annunzio's speeches and actions during the next five years, and were to culminate in his taking Fiume with a motley private army in 1919.

Meanwhile the atmosphere described in *La Leda* and in the *taccuini* continued for D'Annunzio to be one of feverish anticipation, mingled with disproportionately anxious preoccupations for his

---

[62] Tosi, *D'Annunzio en France*, appendix VI.
[63] He claimed the expression for himself in the *Aveux de l'ingrat*, *Prose di ricerca*, i. 824.

dogs at Dame-Rose as Europe crumbled. Thus his descriptions of the zone behind the front line illustrate a morbid curiosity in the destructive power of the war, not unlike some of the grotesque interest shown in the descriptions of the Lourdes-like pilgrimage to Casalbordino which Giorgio Aurispa and Ippolita Sanzio followed in *Il trionfo della morte*. In the *taccuini* he noted the odour of the putrefying, swollen carcasses of dead horses, the blackened, splintered landscape, the broken refugees with their improvised sackcloth head coverings. At the same time he was on tenterhooks lest the Germans should break through and take Paris.[64] But, for the record, his main concern in the *taccuini* during the whole of the period of his visit to the Front, beginning on 17 September 1914, was with the welfare of his greyhounds, and in particular with the death of Fly, his favourite. The expenses for his kennels alone ran into nearly 8,000 francs, and those figures, coincidentally, are noted in the *taccuini* immediately following his visits to the Front and immediately before reflections on the Italian volunteer force with which Ricciotto Canudo had gone to fight in the Argonne, under the leadership of Garibaldi's grandson, Peppino. His anxiety for the welfare of his greyhounds continues later that autumn when the Dame-Rose farm was requisitioned by the French to stable and graze the cattle which were systematically slaughtered to supply the troops. The picture which D'Annunzio drew of the situation was of beasts dying for lack of fodder (judged unnecessary if they were so soon to be slaughtered), up to their bellies in mud and manure, polluting the green runs where his hounds used to chase hares. The adjective he consistently uses to describe his situation, the atmosphere of Paris, the unceasing rain, and his mood is 'melancholic'.[65] Nathalie De Goloubeff was still at the farm; he had long grown tired of her company, but she was an enthusiastic dog-handler and skilled at rearing his greyhounds.

D'Annunzio's jingoistic articles in the *Corriere della sera* were gaining him a regular public; Luigi Albertini had become a senator, and, buoyed up by his new-found political power, no longer seemed so chary about publishing items which might embarrass appeasers in the government. The items for the *Corriere* and for

[64] The events of that frantic time are described in note form in the *Taccuini*, 687–729.

[65] The final gloomy page of the notes taken at the farm during his French exile is dated 4 Apr. 1915, *Taccuini*, 733.

other newpapers, including some articles syndicated for the Hearst chain in America, brought in for D'Annunzio considerable sums during 1914, but, as ever, he was continually in financial trouble. Only the intervention of the French home secretary, recognizing D'Annunzio's value in terms of anti-German propaganda, prevented the distraint of his goods at Arcachon when his creditors clamoured there in much the same way that they had done at the Capponcina. Indeed there is evidence that D'Annunzio had begun to cast around for a possible escape from such irritations by finding himself a 'safe house'. In October 1914 he approached a Madame Huard, lessee of the Hôtel de Chalon-Luxembourg, explaining that he needed somewhere 'far from the world' (*loin du monde*), in order to write a book on peace. He subsequently entertained the Huards to dinner, giving Madame Huard, as they left, a pair of pedigree greyhounds, elegantly accoutred in blue livery with red borders, which she later noticed had been tailored by Hermès. Since she and her husband were living in the Aisne, at Villiers, she agreed to sublet the beautiful old house to D'Annunzio. D'Annunzio's delight at finding such a splendid *pied-à-terre* is expressed in a letter of 2 January 1915 to Luigi Albertini (the editor was later to pay the rent for the new house). The same letter expresses his fear that Italy would not enter the war, 'I have within me a presentiment (which rarely lies to me) that Italy will not fight. What then?'[66]

Fortunately for Madame Huard the poet's presentiment played him false and Italy declared war on Austria before D'Annunzio could completely ruin the interior of the house. When she once visited the poet he invited her to come in and see the improvements (*améliorations*) he had made: the antique furniture which she and her artist husband had accumulated over their lifetime was no longer visible, replaced by sofas and *chaises longues*, ranged along the walls and piled high with cushions of all descriptions; in a 'black redoubt' illuminated by several candelabra, D'Annunzio had constructed a new water-closet (the Huards had carefully incorporated their bathroom into an ancient corridor); large mirrors and Romaine Brooks's dominant portrait of their tenant also caused Madame Huard some consternation. But by 3 May 1915 D'Annunzio had left the hotel, and on 15 May the Huards received a telegram advising them that the rent was awaiting them at the Banque Henri Martin. There they

---

[66] Albertini, *Epistolario (1911–1926)*, i. 309.

found no reference to D'Annunzio, but, the bank assured them, the payment had been made through a young lady, Corriere della Sera.[67]

For three months D'Annunzio seems to have led a boring existence, unable to write much beyond his newspaper reports; in May 1915 he once again had to pawn the emeralds which Eleonora Duse had given him (he was to retrieve them only two years later in 1917).[68] One bright spot on the horizon was that he seemed to be recovering from his dose of venereal disease. The time was ripe for some miraculous salvation from boredom, debt, and wet weather.

[67] I am grateful to Dr J. S. T. Garfitt for drawing my attention to the *Bulletin d'information* issued by the Parisian Association pour la Sauvegarde et la Mise en Valeur de Paris Historique, which gives interesting details of D'Annunzio's stay at the house. Frances Wilson Huard's biography of her husband, *Charles Huard 1874–1965* (Paris, 1969), 246, describes her first encounter with D'Annunzio; the payment of the rent is described ibid. 247.

[68] Antongini, *D'Annunzio*, 221.

10

Return from Exile:
Intervention and War

THE Italian brigade in the Argonne, under the leadership of Peppino Garibaldi, four years junior to D'Annunzio and grandson of the great hero, had fought bravely but in vain against the superior forces of their German opponents. Five hundred of the original 2,000 red-shirts had been killed, wounded, or lost in the fighting; the depleted force was disbanded on 5 March 1915.[1] D'Annunzio's *taccuino* for the next day is filled with 'the Garibaldian enterprise',[2] a proposal approved at the highest level to organize a propaganda campaign which might persuade the Italian people and government to intervene in favour of the Allies. The French, anxious to bring the Italians into the war on their side, had re-equipped the shattered Garibaldi volunteers (and had included among their supplies a useful propaganda issue of 2,000 red shirts, donated by Madame Paquin, a well-known couturière of the time);[3] the French wanted to send the company to Italy in order to stimulate that interventionist feeling. If the original plan failed there was hope that the brigade of pro-French enthusiasts might provoke a revolution. D'Annunzio, according to his own *taccuini*, acted as go-between, receiving the French conspirators, Jean Finot, vice-president of the Chambre, Etienne Clémentel, editor of the *Revue* and the *Cri de Paris*, and a Dr Guelpa, before conferring with Peppino Garibaldi the following day, 7 March 1915.[4]

When D'Annunzio awoke that morning, several factors, some inconsequential, some more substantial, coincided to increase his

[1] For an interesting account of this volunteer force, see C. Marabini, *La rossa avanguardia dell'Argonne* (Milan, 1915); also available as *Les Garibaldiens de l'Argonne* (Paris, 1917).

[2] *Taccuini*, 711.

[3] Tosi, *D'Annunzio en France*, 107; this is a useful translation of and part commentary on D'Annunzio's *Taccuini* for the period concerned.

[4] *Taccuini*, 716.

determination. He had long been enthusiastic for Italy's intervention on the side of the Allies, he was continually being pressed
to pay his creditors, he was keenly aware of the heroic actions of
the military in the immediate vicinity and in particular of the presence of courageous Italian volunteers at the Front itself, he still held
strongly to the memory of Ricciotto Canudo's gallant gesture, and
he was bored by the sameness of life spent between the deserted
French capital and the muddy fields of Dame-Rose farm, bored,
too, by the continuing presence of Nathalie De Goloubeff. On 7
March, just before his meeting with Peppino Garibaldi, D'Annunzio
opened, almost as an afterthought, a letter from someone who
proved to be a young poet and nationalistic newspaper reporter,
Ettore Cozzani, editor of *L'Eroica*, a modest newspaper in La
Spezia. The letter accompanied a photograph of a bronze statue by
Eugenio Baroni to be erected at Quarto, near Genoa, in honour of
Garibaldi's famous expeditionary force, 'the Thousand', which had
sailed from there in May 1860 to take Sicily, and thus begin the
final stage of Italy's liberation from foreign rule. D'Annunzio had
been studying the photograph of the statue in detail the day before.
When he read the covering letter it proved, to his surprise, to be
an informal invitation to speak at the unveiling of the statue. The
Dannunzian title of Cozzani's newspaper betrayed his nationalist
views; he was, in fact, a right-wing admirer of D'Annunzio, went
on to publish D'Annunzio's articles in his journal, and eight years
later he would write proudly of what he believed to be his role
in this important interventionist episode, and of D'Annunzio's
subsequent career as soldier–hero.[5] More immediately and more
importantly, Cozzani was a friend of Baroni, who had in fact just
completed the statue, commissioned by the city of Genoa. It was,
D'Annunzio wrote at the time, certainly a divinely poetic stroke of
providence (*provvidenza apollinea*).[6]

To explain his expression of joy it is necessary to consider his
position as a returning exile. It was true that, after four years in
France, D'Annunzio wanted to go back to Italy; Paolo Alatri also
notes that coincidentally, by the summer of 1914, Luigi Albertini had
confirmed that the poet's financial affairs in the Peninsula had been
regularized.[7] There seemed no impediment left to his departure.

[5] E. Cozzani, *GD'A* (Piacenza, 1923), a floridly produced eulogy with biographical elements.
[6] *Taccuini*, 713.   [7] Alatri, *GD'A*, 343.

However, his arrival in Italy as a simple rail-passenger from just across the border would have been nothing more than banal. How his circumstances had now changed. The relevant *taccuino* describes his feelings of exhilaration, after opening Cozzani's letter and realizing the significance of the invitation.[8] Now he could review the plan conceived with his French hosts; he could return alongside the re-equipped Garibaldians, celebrate the anniversary of their predecessors, and blend memories of the original heroic expedition of Garibaldi's Thousand, which had united Italy, with a new, irresistible, national political movement driven by himself, which might redeem the eastern coasts of Italy, Venice's former possessions. It would be a fitting recompense for his over-long exile: 'To arrive at Quarto, not as an ordinary speaker, but as the leader of Youth, mediator between two generations! To cross the Tyrrhenian in a ship laden with young blood waiting to be poured out! To offer up for sacrifice my own heart and the strength of those who believe in me!' As D'Annunzio meditated on the letter that morning, and waited for the arrival of Peppino Garibaldi, he imagined the impact upon the vacillating nation of the unveiling of the memorial to the glorious dead.

It is impossible that Italy, however blind and deaf, could not see the Sign or hear the Appeal, both of them kindled by the famed foreshore of Quarto, while two thousand young troops, armed and led by the grandson of the Hero, surround the solemn monument before leaving thence to conquer and die.

Although the words are jotted in staccato, note-like form in the *taccuino*, the rhetoric is ever present, and the style is appropriate to D'Annunzio's tense anticipation.

D'Annunzio and Peppino Garibaldi spent the evening of 7 March discussing the former's new ideas of a personal disembarcation at Genoa. Thoughts of the old conspiracy planned in Paris find no more place in his notes; the new enterprise becomes the stuff of poetic dream 'and tomorrow may become a reality', he tells Garibaldi. On 16 March, after the car journey to see the ruins of the cathedral at Rheims, the official invitation arrived from the mayor of Genoa asking D'Annunzio to inaugurate the monument at Quarto. He left Paris at once for the peace and quiet of Arcachon, the better to

---

[8] The incidents described in the following paragraphs and the relevant quotations are taken from *Taccuini*, 714–15.

compose his fateful speech, the 'Orazione per la sagra dei Mille' (Oration for the Festival of the Thousand).

Before his return to Italy D'Annunzio published two significant articles, the opening piece, 'La Très Amère Adriatique', on 25 April 1915 in *Le Figaro* (and simultaneously in the local Bordeaux daily *La Petite Gironde*), and the second, five days later on 30 April, again in *La Petite Gironde*, entitled 'Le ciment romain'.[9] The first, 'La Très Amère Adriatique', began with an exaltation of the genius of Rome, condemned petty-minded commercial interests content to acquire (*acquérir*) rather than conquer (*conquérir*), and foresaw in the coming war the opportunity to restore Italy to the grandeur of her classical past, through 'greatness of action and greatness of suffering'. Simultaneously the article regretted that the struggles for Italian independence had not reinstated the inheritance of Venice and returned the Adriatic to its rightful Italian heirs. It was another allusion to that left lung of Italy, crushed and infected by the barbaric Austrians. Virgil and Dante are called as his witnesses to the ancient Dalmatian boundaries of Italy, including the Carso and the mystic River Timavo. Those names were to crop up countless times in D'Annunzio's speeches and writings during the following five years, surfacing with particular bitterness after the armistice of 1918, and spurring D'Annunzio in his assault on Fiume in 1919. The second article was concerned with an appeal to the Latin nations to pull together in order to oppose what D'Annunzio saw as pan-Germanism and pan-Slavism, again preoccupations which were to dominate his thoughts for the next few years. The articles were also published simultaneously in the *Corriere della sera*. These were the ideas running through D'Annunzio's mind as he prepared the speech to be delivered in Genoa on 5 May 1915. He also wrote four sonnets, the so-called *Sonnets d'amour pour la France*,[10] which he sent to *Le Figaro*, their publication to coincide with his oration at Quarto. On 29 April 1915 D'Annunzio left Arcachon for Paris and thence for Italy on 3 May. He had sent a copy of his speech to Cozzani so that the journalist could show it to the prime minister, Antonio Salandra; he also sent one copy each to the two newspapers he had always favoured, *Le Temps* and the *Corriere della sera*, to be published on the morning of 5 May.

---

[9] Tosi, *D'Annunzio en France*, 129–30, analyses these articles.
[10] For some fruitful comments by Tosi on these sonnets, see ibid. 133.

One minor benefit for him of a flight from France was the possibility of finally and permanently abandoning his Donatella, Nathalie De Goloubeff. She returned to the Dame-Rose farm, where her once luxurious life-style was gradually reduced to squalor, not only as an oblique result of the Russian Revolution, which cut off her husband's source of income, but also because of a riding accident in the Bois de Boulogne which left her permanently lame. Her appeals to D'Annunzio for help did not fall entirely on deaf ears, according to Guglielmo Gatti, but D'Annunzio had seen the last of her and was no doubt relieved; he would never return to France except in one last flight over the battlefields.[11] The last phrase in that entry in the final 'French' *taccuino*, drawing a line beneath his definitive departure from Dame-Rose, wonders, 'Am I of the same species as those men chattering as they carry the trunks?'.[12] And fixed in his mind is the body of Fly rotting in a corner of the meadow. Nathalie's eventual fate was worse than that of many of D'Annunzio's other women: her husband Viktor abandoned Europe for the cheaper areas of Asia, leaving her a tiny allowance on which she lived until 5 November 1941. Then, according to Pierre Pascal, who knew her in her final six years of her life, she died a pathetic alcoholic, in the Hôtel de la Gare at Meudon-Valfleury during the German occupation. Nathalie's children were reputedly reduced to selling newspapers on the streets of New York.[13]

When D'Annunzio gave Cozzani the copy of his speech to show to Salandra, he emphasized that he was not willing to have it censored in any way. However, certain parts of his harangue strongly attacked the tyranny of Austria, at a time when, nominally at least, Italy was still Austria's neutral ally. Salandra could not therefore approve the presence of King Vittorio Emanuele at the unveiling ceremony, though the event was of national importance, and a royal presence might normally have been expected. The king sent the mayor of Genoa a telegram excusing himself from attending because of the pressure of 'cares of state'. Not to be put off, D'Annunzio began his speech, as he had originally intended, by addressing the

[11] Gatti, *GD'A* 295, retracted his earlier view of D'Annunzio's heartlessness *vis-à-vis* Nathalie, having found manuscript evidence at the Vittoriale which showed that D'Annunzio had sent help to his former mistress; see below, n. 13.

[12] *Taccuini*, 733.

[13] Details of Nathalie's ultimate degradation are given in Pascal, *Le Livre Secret*, notably in the preface, pp. xi–xxxvii; Gatti, *Le donne*, 279, gives a hearsay account which he later withdrew.

king, 'Your Majesty, King of Italy, absent, but present'.[14] The speech itself reads somewhat incoherently, and by general agreement its hearers found its content too erudite to be comprehended. There are references to the Dioscuri ('the Spartan twins'), to a little-known sonnet by the obscure Achillini, an epigram by Michelangelo in an esoteric reply by the artist to Giovanni Strozzi, an obscure reference to the battle of Marathon ('the promontory of Micale'), echoes of thirteenth-century *chansons de geste*, and a host of other literary and historical phenomena which in any circumstances would have required technical footnotes. Yet the speech is also punctuated by frequent exhortations to revive Italy's greatness, and allusions to self-sacrifice, faith in the fatherland, the spring of the reawakening country. The sound of the words was inspiring, and his audience, like the peasants of the Abruzzi in 1897, went away for the most part satisfied with his rhetoric. Some were not so pleased; in particular his peroration, possibly designed to appeal to Christian sentiments, had the opposite effect on some of his audience. Romain Rolland, who had known D'Annunzio from earlier days, as Eleonora Duse's friend, and had developed a growing contempt for D'Annunzio, not least because of what he saw as the poet's disgraceful treatment of the actress, adversely criticized the speech and launched a strong attack on the personality of D'Annunzio himself: 'This man, who is the incarnation of literary falsehood, dares to pose as Jesus! He *play-acts* Jesus, he recreates the Sermon on the Mount to incite Italy to violate her treaties and make war on her allies of yesterday.'[15] The reason for such critical consternation, as Rolland implies here and as he reiterated in 1919,[16] was the personal version of the Sermon on the Mount with which D'Annunzio concluded his speech. In nine beatitudes of his own, D'Annunzio hoped to stimulate his hearers to give their all to an Italy afire with nationalistic feeling. He began that peroration, 'Blessed are they that have

---

[14] The speech is reproduced in *Prose di ricerca*, i. 11–21, surrounded by minor addresses given in Genoa at the time (ibid. 7–10 and 22–37). The opening of the printed version of the *orazione* addresses 'Majesty, King of Italy' without reference to his absence.

[15] R. Rolland, *Journal des années de guerre* (Paris, 1952), 352; Rolland writes as a witness of these events.

[16] In January 1919, looking back over the war, Rolland did admit that D'Annunzio (unlike Daudet or Barrès, content to let others fight for their patriotism) had suffered for his country; nevertheless 'his rhetoric is no less odious. It is a slap in the face of Christ and Truth': Rolland, *Journal*, 1846.

most, because they can give most, dare most', and ended, 'Blessed are the pure in heart, blessed are they who return with victories, for they shall see the new face of Rome, the re-crowned brows of Dante, the triumphant beauty of Italy.'[17] To some, however, the close of the speech had great appeal, notably Ferdinando Martini, not usually ready, at least in private, to heap praise on D'Annunzio. In his diary for 2 May 1915 Martini noted the splendid effect of the speech and explained why there could have been no government representative present: 'The close is magnificent. For the rest it is not a speech that may be listened to by king and ministers. Whether we like it or not we are still allies of Austria: we shall not be so in a few days from now [. . .] but no official "consecration" would be possible.'[18]

Antongini advanced the unlikely theory that D'Annunzio was quite prepared to come to Genoa, give his speech, and return to Paris, and reports D'Annunzio as saying that his speech would simply be regarded as a piece of beautiful prose; there would be a few banquets and toasts: 'Then all will be the same as before and we shall set sail again for France.'[19] Even if that had been the case, the rapturous reception which the poet received from Italians at each of the stations on the line from Paris to Genoa would have convinced him that his destiny was thenceforth to be played out in Italy. The oration at Quarto was said to have had a mixed reception, but D'Annunzio's presence was sufficient to whip up enthusiasm, and he was to give a further seven speeches in and around Genoa in the next four days, including significant harangues to the student body and to a group of Dalmatian exiles.[20] But all his instigations to war were by then, if he had but known it, superfluous as far as the decision of the Italian government was concerned. D'Annunzio's demands had effectively been pre-empted: on 26 April 1915 Italy had signed a secret treaty with the Allies, the so-called Treaty of London, pledging herself to enter the war on the side of the *entente*.[21] The poet's rabble-rousing speeches then and later might

---

[17] *Prose di ricerca*, i. 21 (which also has the full text of the speech). Biblical paraphrase became a particular feature in D'Annunzio's political harangues.

[18] F. Martini, *Diario 1914–18*, ed. G. De Rosa (Milan 1966), 402.

[19] Antongini, *D'Annunzio*, 487.

[20] For these speeches see *Prose di ricerca*, i. 7–37.

[21] Enrico Caviglia in his controversial *Il conflitto di Fiume* (Milan, 1948), 84–9, gives the text of the Patto di Londra signed by Britain, France, Italy, and Russia, along with other useful documents relevant to the Treaty; Caviglia's sceptical book, written

have kept pressure on a weak Cabinet, which might have reneged on its earlier promises, but there is no certainty that D'Annunzio's actions and speeches had the effect upon Italian policy which many of his contemporary supporters believed.

After a brief interval womanizing in Genoa, much to the disgust of Ugo Ojetti, whose strictures, in a letter to Albertini, echoed what Scarfoglio had said of the poet's wasted youth, D'Annunzio prepared to move on to Rome. Ojetti was anxious that his friend should not squander the golden opportunity now offered by fortune to re-establish his influence and reputation in Italy.[22] The newspapers were already full of D'Annunzio's adventures with two women in the hotel in Genoa, and of the hotel bills left to be paid by Genoa's town council. With the hint of new scandals surrounding him, D'Annunzio left for Rome on 12 May, now surrounded by more or less hysterical crowds. That same evening, after his arrival in the capital, he improvised a harangue from his hotel balcony, recalling the glories of Garibaldi's campaign to recover Rome for Italy, calling for a reawakening of the country's genius, and rejecting the view that Italy was 'a museum, a hotel, a place for vacationing, a horizon painted Prussian blue for international honeymoons'.[23] On the following evening he again addressed the mob: his tone was abusively anti-governmental and anti-Giolitti. With one of his characteristic epithets he nicknamed the former prime minister *il vecchio boia labbrone* ('the old hangman with the flapping lip'), and urged the mob to gang together in order to hunt down their timorous, and implicitly traitorous, leaders. 'Form squads, civic patrols: do the rounds and lie in wait to take them, to capture them', D'Annunzio repeated.[24] His words chimed with the popular mood; only two days earlier, on 11 May, Benito Mussolini in his *Popolo d'Italia* had called upon the people to shoot in the back a dozen or so members of parliament and send at least a couple of ministers to gaol. Hugh Dalton, later to become a minister in Britain's

in 1921 was censured in page-proof in 1925 and published only in 1948, after the author's death; (Caviglia was one of the generals commanding the blockading force outside the enclave, and probably considered *persona non grata* by the fascist hierarchs, notably Luigi Federzoni, the 'home secretary' who censured his book).

[22] Cosimo Ceccuti quotes Ojetti's letter in the introduction to his edition of *Carteggio D'Annunzio–Ojetti*, 24.

[23] *Prose di ricerca*, i. 40–1.

[24] Ibid. 43 and 45; in Italian *boia* has diabolical undertones (often linked with God in a blasphemous curse) not present in the English 'hangman'.

coalition cabinet during World War Two, and afterwards Clement Attlee's short-lived chancellor, was in Rome at the time. Dalton noted the importance of Italy's entry into the war, and indeed of her neutrality the year before, and remarked upon the state of mind of the crowds in Rome, which he concluded was deliberate rather than hysterical. 'Hundreds of thousands of good people of all classes were walking slowly through the streets of Rome and other Italian cities, intoning with a slow and interminable repetition, "Death to Giolitti, Death to Giolitti".'[25]

D'Annunzio's attacks on the as yet unnamed Giolitti (*il vecchio boia labbrone*) were made in the same speech which exhorted his fellow citizens to more general violence, in terms which were to be recalled by Mussolini in his later harangues, and which, in view of future developments, it is worth recalling briefly here:

Comrades, it is no longer time for speaking but for doing; no longer time for orations, but for actions, Roman actions.

If it is considered a crime to incite the citizenry to violence, I glory in that crime. I take it upon myself alone.

If, instead of calls to alarm I could throw arms to the resolute, I would not hesitate; nor would I consider it necessary to feel any remorse for it.

Every excess of force is allowable, if it avails to prevent the loss of our Fatherland. You have to prevent a handful of pimps and swindlers from sullying and losing Italy.

The Law of Rome absolves all necessary actions.[26]

The situation was becoming politically untenable for the government, and intolerable for the reasonable citizen; the mob had attacked the parliament building, Palazzo Montecitorio, and, whipped up by D'Annunzio's rhetoric, now clamoured for Giolitti's blood. Some, who had gone off in a fire-engine hoping to attack the old appeaser in his home, were only repelled at the last minute by a military escort. On 13 May 1915 the government finally tendered its resignation, and next morning Ferdinando Martini, a member of the Cabinet, and an old acquaintance, if not friend, of D'Annunzio's, met with the poet along with Luigi Lodi. Martini revealed that the government had agreed as long ago as 26 April, when signing the secret Treaty of London, that they would pledge allegiance to

---

[25] H. Dalton, reported in the *New Statesman* (15 Mar. 1919), here 525–6.

[26] *Prose di ricerca*, I, 45; he later called this small speech his 'Arringa al popolo di Roma in tumulto' (Harangue to the Roman People in Tumult).

the *entente*, committing themselves to enter the war within a month; Martini further disclosed that a week after the Treaty, on 4 May 1915, they had agreed to dissolve the old Triple Alliance with Austria and Hungary. According to Piero Chiara the news was an open secret, at least at higher levels,[27] but it is difficult to believe that D'Annunzio would not have made use of such information earlier in his campaign if he had suspected the truth.

It is possible to imagine some of the thoughts that must have gone through his mind after the meeting with Martini, since, as things stood, all his rhetorical interventions would risk becoming nothing more than profound bathos when the news finally broke officially. D'Annunzio therefore devised a clever stratagem. He would make a speech which implied that he had known of the secret negotiations since before leaving Paris; he would suggest that the government had dissolved the Triple Alliance on 4 May, and imply that the Treaty of London was then meant to come into force. To this he would add that since 4 May Giolitti and others had worked with Berlin in order to frustrate Italy's pledges to the Allies. On the evening of 14 May 1915, using a convenient interval between the acts, D'Annunzio walked out on to the stage of the Costanzi theatre in Rome and delivered his brief but stirring message, revealing, as though he were in a privileged diplomatic position, that 'The government of Italy, which yesterday put its resignation into the king's hands, had abolished on 4 May, the eve of the Quarto celebrations, the treatise of the Triple Alliance'. He went on to say that he had known all about the national policy since leaving Paris. Without mentioning Giolitti by name ('The leader of the miscreants') he accused him of treason:

He therefore betrays his king, he betrays his country; against his king and against his country he serves the foreigner. He is guilty of treason, not because of any injurious word he might have uttered, not because of an excess of polemical phrases, but in reality, in truth, and according to the known character of that crime.[28]

On May 16 Vittorio Emanuele refused to accept Prime Minister Salandra's resignation; the rejection was more or less a declaration

---

[27] See Chiara, *GD'A* 276: 'Notizia che d'altra parte era ormai, almeno a alto livello, il segreto di Pulcinella.'
[28] *Prose di ricerca*, i. 47.

of the sovereign's support for intervention; nothing seemed to stand in the way of an open declaration of war. D'Annunzio's oratory might now have seemed superfluous, but he gave two final speeches in Rome. In the first, on the Campidoglio on 17 May 1915, he evoked the glories of the Roman past, the Capitol having been the traditional starting-point for heroic Roman military leaders to march out and subdue the foe, and he cited there the Emperor Germanicus as a good case in point because of his subjugation of the German tribes. D'Annunzio gave credit to the people for having stirred the country from its lethargy, and urged them to make lists of the names of politicians such as Giolitti, so that revenge might be taken in due course for their cowardice and treachery. Theatrically he drew from beneath the table where he was speaking the sword of Nino Bixio, one of Garibaldi's heroes, and kissed it in the name of future victories. The speech was received with the usual hysterical enthusiasm.[29] On 19 May Vittorio Emanuele gave D'Annunzio an audience in the royal palace, the Villa Savoia, and the pair walked and talked together for almost an hour. In France D'Annunzio had referred disparagingly to the king as 'that stationmaster with a mass of gold braid on his hat'; but it was recalled that, after the assassination of King Umberto I in July 1900, D'Annunzio had also written his hectoring ode on the young king's accession, with the implicit promise that he the poet–bard would come to his aid if and when the need arose. The meeting in the Villa Savoia must have seemed a fulfilment of that hope and prophecy, and soon afterwards D'Annunzio sent the king a copy of his *Forse che sí forse che no*, which Vittorio Emanuele had told him that he had read, adding the dedication:

> To His Majesty, King of Italy, who among the oaks
> of Villa Savoia deigned to remember this book,
> in an hour unforgettable for me.

D'Annunzio was always a Monarchist, but the experience in Rome removed what had been his personal disdain for Vittorio Emanuele and deepened his allegiance to the House of Savoy.

---

[29] Ibid. 53–8 (for the text of the speech). Rolland, noting the effect the poet had on the crowd, described the rabble-rousing performance as typical of a Marat, purveyor of the guillotine: 'He unleashes the frenzy of the populace against the only man who tries to oppose the public madness, Giolitti [. . .] a mélange of Robespierre and Tallien': Rolland, *Journal*, 365.

D'Annunzio's speech on the Campidoglio implied that Giolitti had consistently attempted to keep Italy out of the war and had constantly favoured continuing at least a neutralist alliance with the Austrian government; the words might have had further repercussions for the non-interventionists in the Italian government. Wisely, Giolitti left the capital for his home in Piedmont on 24 May 1915, the day that Prime Minister Salandra declared mobilization of the forces against Austria. At dawn on 25 May D'Annunzio addressed a dinner-party, with expressions of joy in anticipation of the sacrificial blood of his fellow Italians which was to be spilt, 'a sublime mystery unequalled in all the universe'. It is interesting to speculate on the reaction of his fellow diners to such rhetoric, once the die had been cast.

The tenth Muse, Energy [. . .] does not love measured words, she loves an abundance of blood. Her calculations, her measurements are different. She counts the forces, the nerves, the sacrifices, the battles, the wounds, the torments, the corpses; she notes the cries, the gestures, the slogans of heroic agonies. She computes the flesh laid low, the sum of nourishment offered to the earth so that, digested, it may be converted into ideal matter, rendered into perennial spirituality. She takes the horizontal body of a man as the only measure for measuring the vaster destiny.[30]

Those phrases and others like them might have seemed the outpourings of a drunken lunatic, but it is a well-known fact that at that time D'Annunzio drank very little alcohol. The words and others like them could not fail to strike a chill into the mind of any intelligent participant as dawn broke that morning, and perhaps when D'Annunzio remarked that the shiver the company might feel was not due to the cold air but to something more profound, he might have unwittingly come close to the truth.[31]

Italy's declaration of war on Austria on 24 May 1915 was the signal for D'Annunzio to revive his commission as a lieutenant in the Novara Lancers, a privilege which the War Ministry granted him as an extraordinary concession; at 52 years of age he must have been the oldest lieutenant in their forces. He was assigned to the headquarters of the duke of Aosta, commander of Italy's Third Army, but his commission was a roving one, allowing him access along

---

[30] *Prose di ricerca*, i. 65–70; for the quotation see p. 69.
[31] Ibid. 69; he continued: 'The blood begins to pour from our country's body. Do you not feel it? The killings begin, the destruction begins.'

the entire Front with permission to go to Venice and follow naval operations if he wished. However, from 24 May 1915 until he departed for the Front, D'Annunzio, to quote Antongini, 'lived in a sort of social parenthesis'.[32] He reverted to his old habits as 'a man of the world who goes from a reception to a dinner and from an intimate tea to an even more intimate night', sinking into the 'most abject state of frivolity' and, Antongini concludes, 'spent his strength daily on amorous adventures, made continually more simple for him by the glorious halo which he had worn since his return to Italy'. As the cynosure of fashionable life, D'Annunzio took advantage of every possible excuse to increase his status, causing some of his acquaintances to regard his antics with some disdain. Ferdinando Martini saw his performances as counter-productive among a public which was seriously concerned with reality, noting on 18 July:

He leaves a proud dedication [*orgoglioso epigrafe*] for the proprietor of the Hotel Regina; he goes down to Pescara seeking popular applause; he proceeds to Ferrara in order to present the Municipality with the manuscript of his *Parisina*; he leaves the city and writes that he carries the beauty of Ferrara within his *intrepid* heart. Foolishnesses [*Sciocchezze*] [. . .].

In fact on 30 June he had gone down to Pescara, nominally to visit his mother, whom he had not seen for five years. He stayed for just twenty-four hours before returning for a further fortnight's enjoyment of the fleshpots of the capital. On arrival his description of his mother chimes with his description of the fictional character of the senile Aunt Gioconda in *Il trionfo della morte*, unable to walk, unable to speak, sending out an incomprehensible miaowing, her hands moving convulsively.[33] Finally, Michetti seems to have persuaded him to leave the distressing spectacle the day after his arrival. Mario D'Annunzio, who went with his father on this occasion, described the melancholic meeting that D'Annunzio had with his mother surrounded, according to Abruzzese tradition, by all the family. Mario did stay longer with his grandmother and declared that his father was forced to return to Rome because of an engagement.[34] Despite D'Annunzio's long absence and his protestations of tenderness towards his mother, he preferred to avoid such distressing

---

[32] Antongini, *D'Annunzio*, 489–90.
[33] See Gatti, *GD'A* 301; for the character of Zia Gioconda in *Il trionfo della morte*, see the opening of Book II, ch. 1, which echoes Gatti's description and comments.
[34] D'Annunzio, *Con mio padre sulla nave del ricordo*, 123–4.

personal encounters, or at least to ensure that his freedom to enjoy life was not hampered by such inconveniences. He would never see his mother alive again.

On the other hand, he seems genuinely to have been excited by the mere accoutrements of a soldier, regarding himself almost as a member of a religious order.[35] On 14 July, having obtained funds from Treves to buy a couple of horses, and dressed in his smart new uniform, he left for the Front and took up residence at Venice's Royal Danieli. He later moved to the less accessible Zattere region of the city, in order to avoid his suffocating acolytes; there he found a fully furnished apartment, including the services of a cook and maid—all for 500 lire a month. From the outset it was obvious that D'Annunzio would engage only in individual and often extraordinary acts of warfare. Tom Antongini makes the point in his final comments before describing how D'Annunzio launched his new military career:

The General-in-Chief immediately perceived that the formidable moral force which D'Annunzio represented for the country and for the army would be, if not lost at least diminished, were he to be utilized in the body of the hierarchy and of the military organizations. Thanks to this intelligent conception on the part of the supreme commander, D'Annunzio, who had started the war as a lieutenant of cavalry, was permitted to be an aviator, an infantryman, a sailor and an organizer of expeditions, to which he invariably gave a distinctly personal complexion.[36]

And in fact one of D'Annunzio's first acts was to go on board the torpedo-boat *Impavido*, in a vain search for enemy shipping off the Dalmatian coast during the night of 20 and 21 July 1915; the enterprise is described in thrilling detail in *Il notturno*, the first of many such descriptions in those vivid reminiscences.[37] The next day he gave a funeral oration for the sailors lost on the cruiser *Amalfi*, torpedoed by the enemy on 7 July. Just over a week later, on 29 July 1915, he wrote a long letter to Prime Minister Salandra proposing an act of derring-do in the air.[38] His plan was to drop leaflets on Trieste, still in Austrian hands, indicating to philo-Italians in the

---

[35] See Albertini, *Epistolario (1911–1926)*, ii. 414.

[36] Antongini, *D'Annunzio*, 493.

[37] In *Prose di ricerca*, i. 309–15; the memoirs continue with other enterprises at sea.

[38] The letter, entitled 'Ho il dovere di combattere' (I have the duty to fight) was published in the *Corriere della sera* on 23 Aug. 1918 and, in a commemorative way, in *Nuova antologia*, 73/1585 (1 Apr. 1938), 241–4.

city the extent of their fellow nationals' efforts to free them from the shackles of the barbarian. When he first put this proposal to Salandra, the politician's reaction was negative: the enterprise would be risky, the chance of losing an expensive piece of flying equipment was not small, and there were no indications that the Triestines were particularly friendly towards Italy, whose intervention had already put Italian Triestines in bad odour with their imperial Austrian rulers; on the other hand, the presence of D'Annunzio himself, safe on Italian soil, was a useful propaganda boost to the Italian war effort; his death, *par contre*, would put greater heart into the Austrians.[39]

D'Annunzio, however, was insistent that he was no paper soldier, and on 7 August 1915, after trial flights the day before, with the approval of Antonio Salandra and Ferdinando Martini, he flew over Trieste as an observer in a plane piloted by Giuseppe Miraglia. Once over the city, he dropped miniature Italian tricolour flags attached to small waterproof containers which carried patriotic messages urging Italy's Triestine brethren to have courage, their salvation was at hand, the Italian forces were making progress, 20,000 Austrian prisoners had already been taken. The *taccuino* describing the flight trembles with the excitement of the new enterprise: the serenity of the terrain far below, the flak from Austrian anti-aircraft guns, canals and rivers snaking northwards, Miraglia like a bronze figure in the cockpit ahead, the low approach to Trieste, the beating of the poet's heart (for an instant louder than the throb of the engine), and so the return to Venice, with one last shot from the enemy.[40]

Five days later, on 12 August, D'Annunzio joined the crew of the submarine *Salpa*, about to make its hundredth mission, and his notes are full of character-sketches of the crew, technical details of the machinery surrounding him, the hiss of the water from the conning tower, the submerged journey, the freshness of the air as the boat surfaced again, all details logged ready for dispatch to the *Corriere della sera* or for a potential novel that was never written.[41]

[39] For a discussion of the government's dilemma, including other documentary evidence on the subject, see Alatri, *GD'A*, 366–7, and see F. Martini's comments above at n. 18.

[40] *Taccuini*, 738–45; the flight included an emergency when a bomb jammed in its launching position, adding the risk of an explosion when the plane landed.

[41] Ibid. 749–52.

And his individual enterprises continued during the coming months of 1915; in particular, the tactic of dropping leaflets, initially viewed askance by the hierarchy in Rome, had an enormous propaganda success in the Italian and foreign press, and was repeated over Trento in September. The *Corriere della sera* reported that the Austrian government had set a price of 20,000 crowns for D'Annunzio's capture. After his flights began, the *taccuini* become more detailed; they also contain complete notes for commemorative and other orations to be given to the combatants during the last months of 1915. Those orations sometimes included the reading of one of the poet's patriotic odes which were simultaneously sent on to Albertini for publication in the *Corriere*. The notebooks are further animated by the inclusion of the 'written dialogue' between D'Annunzio and his pilot, Giuseppe Miraglia, on block notes, that is, which were passed between their two cockpits, containing telegraphic queries and responses about the flight.[42]

D'Annunzio's successes in the military field increased the glamorous aura which surrounded him, and affairs with some of the most eligible women from the Venetian aristocracy were not difficult to come by. Partly to enjoy new sexual possibilities and partly to protect his privacy, in October 1915 D'Annunzio rented the Casetta Rossa on the Grand Canal. He also had a *pied-à-terre* at Cervignano, a monastic cell with a camp bed, which allowed him to be closer to the airfield, in case of emergency take-offs. At about the same time his daughter, Renata–Cicciuzza, arrived in Venice and was installed at the Danieli. Romaine Brooks had also come to Venice, and was busy painting D'Annunzio's portrait when, on 21 December 1915, Cicciuzza came to the artist's studio to bring her father news of the death in a test flight of his pilot Giuseppe Miraglia.[43] D'Annunzio wept by the pilot's corpse—perhaps a uniquely sorrowful experience for him.

By 15 January 1916 he was flying again with a new partner, Luigi Bologna. On the next day, after a vain attempt to fly again over Trieste, the couple were attacked in their flying-boat by Austrian

---

[42] Typical is the exchange in *Taccuini*, 758–9: 'Can you tighten the elastic of my goggles; they're slipping?'—'The spring won't hold'—'Are you sure we put water in?'—'Wounded coming back from the front line'; for another good example see below, p. 302.

[43] The incident, along with what follows, is described in *Il notturno, Prose di ricerca*, i. 197–9.

fighter aircraft and were forced to make an emergency landing on the sea at Grado. D'Annunzio dashed his head against the forward machine-gun, sustaining a blow to his right temple and eye. Ugo Ojetti described the immediate aftermath:

For a few hours he was almost sightless. He helped himself, gropingly, as best he could, dried the drops of blood from the bruise, but said nothing to anyone of what ailed him; he was almost ashamed, at his age, to tell his extremely youthful companions that he was tired or suffering. As soon as he had once more, towards noon, got back a minimum of sight, he insisted on leaving, on returning to Trieste, because those were the orders.[44]

The relevant *taccuino* for 16 January makes no mention of the accident, and next day, on D'Annunzio's insistence, the mission was accomplished, D'Annunzio launched his usual leaflets, and he and his pilot Bologna returned successfully. For the next week D'Annunzio continued to act as though nothing were amiss; he harangued military gatherings, delivered patriotic speeches, one at Milan's La Scala on 19 January in the interval after the first act of Verdi's *Battaglia di Legnano*, commemorated the unveiling of a monument to Miraglia on the 21st, and planned his participation in an aerial attack on Laibach for later that same day. He arrived at the airport from his various venues too late to take part in that particular raid, which ended disastrously for the squadron. The expedition was to be a glorious medicine for his wounded eye, stimulating his body's defences, he thought, to repel the blindness which was evidently afflicting him. The naïve idea had in it some of the mysterious faith which D'Annunzio as a young child had shown in binding his wounded hand with cobwebs. When he reported sick, he was told frankly by the army medical officer that he had lost the sight of his right eye and that he was in danger of losing the other; he was advised not to risk any sudden movement which might provoke a further deterioration in the sight of his left eye. However, faced with the prospect, Ojetti suggests, of 'remaining immobile, secluded for months at Cervignano',[45] D'Annunzio decided to leave for Venice the next morning, 'although he knew that every jolt of the car on its course might have blinded him completely

---

[44] U. Ojetti, *As They Seemed to Me*, trans. H. Furst (London, 1928), 6; this unusual volume contains three very informative essays on D'Annunzio.
[45] Ibid. 7.

and for good'. The arrival in Venice of Cicciuzza, now renamed Sirenetta by her father, had been providential. She was now able to move into the Casetta Rossa to look after D'Annunzio, who by then had been severely warned by Italy's leading eye specialist, Giuseppe Alberotti, that he must remain motionless with both eyes bandaged if he were to have any hope of saving the sight of his remaining good eye.

Impatient of staying motionless for so long, D'Annunzio, though he had to spend much of the time in bed, devised a method of writing his last truly creative work, *Il notturno*. He asked his daughter to cut up strips of paper, just narrow enough for him to run finger and thumb of his left hand along top and bottom in order to write a sentence or two on each strip. Between 23 February and 23 April 1916 he filled 10,000 of these strips, which Sirenetta then began to decipher and put together during May and June of that year:

My eyes are bandaged.

I lie supine on the bed, my upper body immobile, my head back, a little lower than my feet.

I lift my knees slightly to tip back the pad which is resting on them.

I write on a narrow strip of paper which holds one line. I have between my fingers a smooth-running pencil. Thumb and middle finger of my right hand, resting on the edges of the strip, make it flow along as the word is written.[46]

Although the opening of the book reproduces rather prosaically the mechanics of the operation, that staccato rhythm of composition had a novelty of its own, and gave rise to a new fashion of writing. *Notturno*-style prose became fashionable with a public still fed with a diet of classical Manzonian–Boccaccesque sentences built up from their Ciceronian models. It could well have given encouragement to young, less inhibited writers such as Alberto Moravia (whose first novel, the symbolically unpunctuated *Indifferenti*, dates from 1929), and helped to break once and for all the straitjacket of the élitist, academic style which had for centuries dominated Italian prose-writers. Beyond the superficial limitations of such banalities as the process of lying in bed writing on a clip-board, the staccato method also allowed him to fill his strips of paper with all sorts of delicate reminiscences, psychological insights into himself and

---

[46] *Prose di ricerca*, i. 171. D'Annunzio was always incapable of dictating his work.

others, dreamlike descriptions of a grey, mist-enshrouded Venice with water lapping at the walls of the ancient palaces. Gossamer memories of past idylls swam to the forefront of his mind and found expression in the book, alternating with the present bloody and fiery torment he perceived and felt at the back of his eyes. Critics have tried to link the style of the *Notturno* with D'Annunzio's slightly earlier prose work, dating back to *Forse che sí forse che no*, but there is no doubt that a difference exists. By the summer D'Annunzio was able once more to read with his good eye; he perused the manuscript of the *Notturno*, but made no alterations and intended no publication before sending it to Treves in July 1916. It could, even in its unrevised state, and even if not immediately publishable, serve as a pledge to Treves, in case D'Annunzio needed another advance or loan. The poet did no more work on the *Notturno* for a further four years, when, during his first months of residence at the Vittoriale in 1921, he revised the text, adding autobiographical reminiscences from the *taccuini* written long before his injury. The volume was finally published in November 1921.

Among the many female admirers and visitors whom D'Annunzio received at the Casetta Rossa during his convalescence were two of the French ladies with whom he had dallied in Paris, Suzanne Boulanger and Odette Hubin, who had last hit the headlines when they accompanied the poet to London during his trip to see the Waterloo Cup. The upshot of their visit was a renewed interest by D'Annunzio in the piece inspired by pleasant memories of his stay at Arcachon, *La Leda senza cigno*, to which he now added the *Licenza* (Licence), nearly two and a half times as long as the original *Leda*, and crammed with autobiographical reminiscences of the period in France; both *Leda* and *Licenza* were published by Treves in May 1916. The dedication to Chiaroviso (Brighteyes) was an allusion to Suzanne Boulanger.

In July the silver medal for gallantry was conferred upon him at a ceremony in St Mark's Square, and D'Annunzio gradually regained his old resilience. An unusual willingness to submit to military discipline is visible in his letters, often written in the form of reports, published by their recipient, General Luigi Bongiovanni, to commemorate D'Annunzio's death in 1938. Bongiovanni's tribute to D'Annunzio's bravery and devotion to duty seems sincere enough, and the letters bear out the poet's willingness to accept his superior's orders even during the period of his greatest renown, between April 1918 and March 1919.[47] Already, despite the warnings of his doctor and the unwillingness of his superior officers to allow him to fly again, D'Annunzio was eager to get back to the Front, and on 13 September 1916 he took to the air again with Luigi Bologna and eighteen other aircraft in a bombing raid on Parenzo. It was, he wrote later in the *Notturno*, the day of his rebirth, and the notes in his *taccuino* of the day record the drama of a flight which the doctors warned might destroy the sight of his left eye. Bologna turned constantly in his cockpit to check that the height was not harming his observer–bombardier and D'Annunzio's note-pad recorded laconically.

> Gigi Bologna
> Parenzo: 13 September 1916.
> 2200? I can see.
> 2600? I can see, I can see.
> 3000? I can still see—climb, climb.
> 3400? I can see. Climb.
> The lead group deviates towards Rovigno.
> Reduce the quota: to 1600.
> Right over the little square.
> Four hand bombs. All gone.
> Away—back to Sant'Andrea.[48]

A month later D'Annunzio was witnessing the ground fighting on the Isonzo, periodically in the company of the future hero, Giovanni Randaccio, in the desperate actions which enabled the Italians to take the Veliki and Faiti mountains. During the fight-ing on the Veliki D'Annunzio was to have a fateful meeting with another hero, Sante Ceccherini, at that time a colonel in the *bersaglieri*, whose physical presence and bravery impressed them-selves on the poet; Ceccherini, along with his colleague Colonel Coralli, seemed, he wrote, to have stepped out of the pages of an epic poem, and D'Annunzio noted in his *taccuino* for the 11 October 1916: 'Ceccherini, famous fencer; Herculean build; great square shoulders; large head; reddish; fine mouth beneath grey moustache. Bald. Seems dressed in leather like knights used to be when they

---

[47] Luigi Bongiovanni was commander of the Comando Superiore d'Aeronautica, in effect C.-in-C. of the air force. His 'Gabriele D'Annunzio aviatore di guerra' is published in *Nuova antologia*, 73/1584 (16 Mar. 1938), 151–69, and includes eighteen letters from D'Annunzio.

[48] *Taccuini*, 863.

took off their armour.'[49] As D'Annunzio climbed further up the mountain his notebook captured the grim atmosphere: 'In the mud empty tins, rags, broken bottles, planks, cartridges, dented helmets, torn sacks, a sodden boot or two'; the trenches and redoubts hacked out of solid rock; the sweat cold on his back, his feet freezing; wounded, dead, and dying soldiers around him; a constant search for planks, to make a resting-place above the surface of the mud; the continual passage down the mountainside of hideously wounded men. As D'Annunzio and his guides climbed higher, the Austrian bombardment became fiercer: great gongs clanging in the air: 'Ten beats of the gong, for the dance, one after another—the Austrian 105s—'; rocks splinter under the barrage; one skims past D'Annunzio's knee; incredibly a trumpeter passes, carrying a battered bugle, still used to call the troops to meals.[50] For his presence in the thick of these actions D'Annunzio was awarded his second silver medal for gallantry; he was also promoted captain.

In the period of the eighth battle of the Isonzo and during the months which followed, D'Annunzio had himself attached as a liaison officer to the 45th Infantry Division. The position allowed him to travel between commands, observing the war at close hand, while at the same time having the opportunity to harangue the troops with his patriotic speeches. He also took notes for potential literary work and wrote essays for publication in the *Corriere della sera* and other newspapers. At the beginning of December he returned briefly to Venice, where he was enjoying a burgeoning romance with a renowned patroness of culture, the Triestine Olga Levi Brunner, a singer and musician, who was living in the city with her husband at the Palazzo Giustiniani. For a month he shuttled between the frontline and the Casetta Rossa, and there spent Christmas with Renata–Cicciuzza–Sirenetta and his son Gabriellino. In August 1916 Renata had married Silvio Montanerella, a naval lieutenant and a former colleague of D'Annunzio's in the air squadron. Six years and nine children later, when Renata's marriage broke up, she attempted to approach her father in his retreat at Gardone, where she had rented a house for the summer holidays of 1922. D'Annunzio

---

[49] *Taccuini*, 887; Coralli was mentioned in the heroic *Merope* collection (in 'La canzone della diana' (Song of Reveille); a commemorative letter to Ceccherini from Fiume was published in *L'urna inesausta* (The Inexhaustible Urn), *Prose di ricerca*, i. 1048; for these and other details see below, p. 336.

[50] *Taccuini*, 895–6.

used his influence with the local authorities and police to make sure that she and her tribe were kept far away from him, to the extent that they were taken under a police escort to Verona and a prohibition put on their return to Garda. But all this was light years away.

In the meantime D'Annunzio, who had been bombarding Antongini in Paris with requests to have his name put forward for the award of the Croix de Guerre, finally obtained his desire on 12 January during a return to the Front. The medal pulled in its train other awards from Belgium and Serbia, and there were to be further, more prestigious, recognitions of his efforts on behalf of the Allies from other nations. D'Annunzio at once gave himself four months' leave and left for Genoa where, Piero Chiara notes, Romaine Brooks was awaiting his arrival.[51] On his return to Milan on 27 January 1917 the news of his mother's death was brought to him; he was too ill to leave for the funeral until 29 January, by which time his mother had been lying in her uncovered coffin for three days.[52] The occasion helped to demonstrate the respect and admiration which D'Annunzio enjoyed in large areas of the country, for, superficially or not, the death of the mother of the celebrated poet–bard became a cause for national mourning; it received widespread publicity in all the newspapers, and D'Annunzio was inundated with telegrams of condolence sent by hundreds of well-wishers, particularly by high-ranking individuals, from the commander-in-chief Luigi Cadorna to the home secretary Orlando writing on behalf of a grateful government. D'Annunzio was the best propaganda instrument that Italy had and it was obviously in the government's best interests to keep and increase his goodwill. For nearly two months D'Annunzio made few public appearances, and, in a not untypically malicious aside, Piero Chiara observes that 'The beautiful Olga Levi made provision to console his loneliness; he met her daily.'[53]

D'Annunzio stirred himself twice, to give a commemorative address on 3 April 1917 in memory of four aviators who had died in the fighting, and to send a message to the United States when they entered the war on 7 April 1917. The missive, published in all the important American newspapers, contained neo-classical allusions

---

[51] Chiara, *GD'A* 292.
[52] D'Annunzio, *Con mio padre sulla nave del ricordo*, 141–4, describes the situation and publishes D'Annunzio's telegrams during the three days.
[53] Chiara, *GD'A* 293.

to American history in language which, to be understood fully, needed many glosses. It also carried an ill-disguised reflection of D'Annunzio's opinion of that nation: what was once an enormous, obtuse mass of riches and power was now being transfigured into ardent and active spirituality.[54] Two years later in Fiume, he was to reiterate less diplomatically the more materialistic aspect of the message, adding to it other insults directed at Woodrow Wilson and his government. More immediately he had himself assigned to a bombing squadron and returned to the aerodrome at Cervignano. There, in co-operation with his son Veniero, by now qualified with a Swiss engineering degree, and working with Giovanni Caproni, the head of the Caproni aviation corporation, he prepared a report for General Cadorna on the strategic possibilities of the use of air-power. Several critics have seen in the report a remarkable prophecy of future air warfare, in which concentrations of bombers would attack not only hostile port installations and supply routes, but also strategic industrial targets in the enemy heartland. Whether or not his enthusiastic proposals were heeded by the High Command is uncertain, but his own enthusiasm for this new fighting arm knew no bounds and found expression in his speeches to aviators.

By 25 May 1917 D'Annunzio was at the battlefront on the River Timavo. Here there was greater danger than before. The *taccuini* become more detailed: the night of 25 May spent in a dugout, listening to the rats squeaking and rustling around his cot, stung by mosquitoes; the advance ordered for the afternoon of 26 May under the command of Giovanni Randaccio; the horrors of the wounded; no water to drink; his poison capsule in case of capture. The battle itself, as described in the *taccuini*, was a chaotic mixture of heroism, improvisation, and, to some eyes at least, cowardice. The attempt to cross the Timavo on a bridge made of single planks placed on oil-drums was in part successful, but the success simply provided the Austrian machine-gunners with easier targets. Those not slaughtered were forced to swim back as best they could. D'Annunzio writes that he tried to help some of the survivors out of the water; Giovanni Randaccio was mortally wounded alongside him. Some of the Italian troops waved white flags and attempted to surrender, despite the efforts of their commanding officers, reduced by now

[54] Laredo De Mendoza, *GD'A fante del Veliki e del Faiti*, 323–9, publishes the full message to the Americans.

to threats of firing on their own soldiers. D'Annunzio reports the cries of the men, 'We don't want to be taken back to the slaughter-house. Even those taken prisoner on 10 October have written to say that life is OK in Austria.' After the battle itself D'Annunzio wrote, 'I notice that battle leaves in the sensual man a melancholy similar to that which follows great voluptuousness—28 May 1917.'[55]

Giovanni Randaccio, helped from the battlefield by his adjutant, also wounded, died later in the hospital at Monfalcone; D'Annunzio was with him until the end, and on 7 June 1917 wrote a long, nationalistic article for the *Corriere* describing the action and the commander's heroism. Another entry in a *taccuino* dated a month later described Randaccio's memorial service at Aquileia, published in the *Corriere* on 3 July 1917. The notes in his *taccuini* were also subsumed into D'Annunzio's laudatory speech at the graveside and later published as a pamphlet distributed to the troops, to spur them on to greater deeds.[56] The common soldiery at least, if not their superior officers,[57] must by now have become tired of such exhortations, and when on 15 July 1917 two regiments of the Catanzaro brigade were ordered back to what they called the abbattoir of the Carso, they mutinied, killed three officers and four *carabinieri*, and laid siege to the house where they believed D'Annunzio to be staying, with cries of 'Death to D'Annunzio'. The mutiny was put down and thirty-eight soldiers were chosen by lot to be executed. In 'La fucilazione' (Execution by Firing-Squad), a series of notes which in the *taccuini* follow a few pages after the description of Randaccio's memorial service, D'Annunzio described the aftermath of the punitive executions. He clinically observed and described their wounds, the flies crawling on their brains, the studs on their boots, the bodies lined up for burial, the burial detail itself and the sound of picks and spades in the hard ground, digging out the deep grave.[58]

But in 1923, looking back over the incidents of that July, D'Annunzio wrote what was probably his most moving piece of prose. It described his observation of the whole incident, beginning

[55] *Taccuini*, 949; the preceding pages, included under the title of 'Andiamo sul Timavo', describe the events (pp. 923–48).

[56] Giovanni Randaccio is the subject of further Dannunzian prose in *Il libro segreto, Prose di ricerca*, i. 749–52.

[57] Though authors writing after the experience, such as Emilio Lussu in his fine novel *Un anno sull'altipiano* (Milan, 1967), give a portrait of officers disillusioned with the situation.

[58] *Taccuini*, 945–53.

with the description of the exhausted troops being ordered to return once more to the front line and his feeling of shame that such things had to happen. The pitiful sight of those Campanian, Pugliese, Calabrian, Sicilian peasants, squat, rugged, burnt by the sun, their dusty and ragged grey uniforms toning in with the limestone of the cemetery, the firing-squad, ashamed to raise its eyes above the great awkward boots of its victims, a hymn from the condemned men cut short by the fusillade from the firing-squad, the crumpled greyness blending with the grey mortar of the wall and the sterility of the cemetery, its only vegetation a patch of nettles, the mud and clay on the now exposed soles of their army boots. There is certainly something here of the 'art prose' for which certain Italian writers of the 1920s were famous, but the passage is shot through with unusual emotions for the normally indifferent D'Annunzio.[59]

In August 1917 D'Annunzio led three bombing raids on the Austrian bases at Pola; in September he planned a heavy raid on Cattaro, and, despite logistical difficulties and delays, the expedition was launched at the beginning of October. In between these activities he gave further speeches to the troops; he also withdrew occasionally to the luxury of the Casetta Rossa in Venice where there was no lack of fashionable women to console him. The raids on Pola were famous because of a Graeco-Roman 'battle-cry', 'Eia, eia, eia, alalà', which D'Annunzio insisted that Italian airmen should use to replace what he considered the barbaric 'Ip, ip, urrah!' with which they traditionally ended their bombing missions. So successful was his rhetoric that on this and on subsequent occasions during the next twenty-four years, it was the war-cry used by Italian fighting men in place of the more traditional if Teutonic version, familiar to Anglo-Saxons.[60] He also invented a slogan for his bombing squadron, *Iterum rugit leo* (The lion roars again), and a particularly vicious-looking lion (traditionally the symbol of St Mark and hence of Venice) was painted on the fuselage of his aircraft, reversing the original motto of Venice, which implied peace: *Pax tibi, Marce, evangelista meus* (Peace be unto thee, Mark, my evangelist).

[59] The account is published in *Il libro ascetico della giovane Italia* (The Ascetic Book of Young Italy), *Prose di ricerca*, i. 775–80, though his thoughts continue beyond the actual description.

[60] Masci, *La vita e le opere*, 284–5, has an interesting documentation of the new war-cry, publishing extracts from the *Giornale d'Italia* of 19 Sept. 1917, and the *Vedetta d'Italia* of 25 Apr. 1920, this last published in Fiume and particularly apposite.

Another famous slogan coined at this time was *Memento audere semper* (Remember always to dare), the reinterpretation of the initials MAS, the naval abbreviation for the swift and manœuvrable *motoscafi antisommergibili* (antisubmarine boats). The imaginative creativeness of D'Annunzio's slogans was by now nationally famous.[61]

D'Annunzio had proposed to the High Command a propaganda flight over Vienna, and in September 1917 had demonstrated that it was possible to remain in the air for the requisite period of time during an endurance trial of 1,000 kilometres over the Alpine territory of northern Italy. But the epic flight over Vienna had to wait for a further year, and D'Annunzio occupied himself with more banal bombardment of the enemy forces, including the planned attack on Cattaro to bomb the Austrian submarine fleet on 4 October 1917. The elaborate preparations for that particular raid take up an inordinate amount of space in the *taccuini*,[62] but the majority of commentators note that it had mixed fortunes, most of the fourteen aircraft losing their way, and only two reaching their objective.[63] For understandable propaganda reasons the flight was given out as a success and D'Annunzio was awarded a bronze medal for valour to go with the three silver medals he had won earlier.

In February of the next year D'Annunzio took part in one of the most famous of his enterprises, the Beffa di Buccari (the Buccari Joke). The plan was to take three of the small motor-torpedo boats into the heartland of Austrian Dalmatia, launch torpedoes against their shipping, and, in D'Annunzio's particular case, release three waterproof containers topped by the Italian tricolour, with the boast that Austria's fiercest enemy had come to mock the price on his head and that Italian sailors laughed at enemy nets and barricades and were always ready to 'dare the undareable' (*osare l'inosabile*). The raid was certainly a dangerous project: with only a limited fuel capacity, the three small boats had to be towed to within raiding distance of the Dalmatian coast before entering the narrows of the straits of Buccari and penetrating several miles inland, potentially at least under constant risk of being fired upon by enemy guns, at

---

[61] A few months after his summer bombing raids, the Bocconi stores in Milan's Piazza del Duomo burned down (in December 1917); D'Annunzio was asked for a suitable replacement name and his brainwave, La Rinascente, remains and flourishes to this day throughout the major cities of Italy.

[62] *Taccuini*, 973–1045.

[63] Chiara, *GD'A* 296–7, puts forward a view typical of commentators' verdicts.

sea and on land. The boats launched their torpedoes, D'Annunzio left his little bottles bobbing on the tide, and the three boats roared off into the night, though not without added piquancy when one boat's engines failed and two of the MAS had to wait for repairs to be made. As propaganda, the enterprise had great value, not least because D'Annunzio published his exciting account of the Beffa di Buccari in the *Corriere della sera* on 19 and 20 October 1918. It was issued shortly afterwards in a slim volume along with 'La canzone del Quarnaro' (an ode celebrating the adventure in very inferior verse).

There is no doubt that the Beffa di Buccari required courage and determination, though even D'Annunzio's published account suggested that the Austrian anti-torpedo nets successfully prevented any harm being done by the missiles they launched. He knew anyway, and noted as much in his *taccuini*, that there were no warships anchored there. The enterprise had a tremendous propagandistic impact, and, since no more than three silver medals were permitted to any one combatant, D'Annunzio was given another bronze medal for valour. But recently Elena Ledda, having examined Austrian war archives, and putting into relief a later radio interview with a surviving sailor, has made it clear that the torpedoes launched never exploded, though one ploughed a furrow on the beach next to a cement factory, which was the only installation, military or otherwise, in the vicinity; the so-called warships which the raiders observed looming up in the darkness were not military vessels—the largest was a passenger ferry, mothballed for the season, if not for the duration of the war, and D'Annunzio's account ends in bathos: 'Supposed warship is ferry of the Hungarian–Croatian line Venice to Fiume.'[64] Ivanos Ciani remarked drily at the anniversary conference in 1994, *i beffati eravamo noi* (the joke was on us).

Permission was finally obtained from government and High Command for the famous flight over Vienna, and on 9 August 1918 eleven planes took off from San Pelagio airfield at 5.50 in the

[64] *Taccuini*, 1081; the preceding twenty-six pages are taken up with the planning and with a description of the tenseness of the night's action (pp. 1055–81). Elena Ledda's article, 'Buccari: Per "osare l'inosabile". Storia di una beffa', is available in F. Perfetti (ed.), *D'Annunzio e la guerra* (Milan, 1996), 179–90; for completeness should be added A. Santoni's brief if inconclusive 'GD'A e la Beffa di Buccari', in F. Perfetti (ed.), *D'Annunzio e il suo tempo* (Genoa, 1992), i. 315–24; similarly inconclusive is the appended report (dated 13 Feb. 1918) by Captain Ciano, commander of the flotilla, ibid. 325–7; A. Bonadeo, *D'A and the Great War* (Madison, 1995), uncritically repeats this and other self-created myths.

morning. D'Annunzio was a passenger in the plane flown by Natale Palli; he carried a canister containing half a million leaflets, which bore two messages, one incomprehensibly literary, the import of the second being that the Italian aeroplanes could be dropping bombs on the citizens, but were instead sending a tricolour greeting.[65] The leaflets questioned Austria's allegiance to the Prussian militarists and suggested that further prolongation of the war could only result in suicide for Austria. The words did not reflect the actual situation at the front, where the Austrians, after their brilliant victory at Caporetto in October 1917, had thrown the Italian High Command into a panic, plans having been made at one point to abandon Venice if necessary to the advancing Austrian troops. However, the long flight over Vienna, from which all but one plane returned safely, electrified the world, making headlines in every newspaper. Not untypical is the report of the *Times* on 12 August 1918:

A New Ruggiero

Major Gabriele D'Annunzio, the intrepid Italian airman-poet, eclipsed his brilliant record last Friday by leading a flight of eight Italian aeroplanes over the Austrian lines [three of the original eleven had to turn back] [. . .] We have come to regard airmanship as the privilege of youth. Yet Major D'Annunzio is well past fifty [. . .] Dropping leaflets, the Germans may think, is not war; but even they cannot deny that it is magnanimous and magnificent. The Allies of Italy wish Major D'Annunzio long life and strength in future years to record in his inimitable verse achievements that outshine in their poetic quality the legendary flights of Ruggiero and Astolfo on the Ippogrifo. What Ariosto sang D'Annunzio has accomplished.

Based in Venice at this time there was a British correspondents' mission, and D'Annunzio was not slow to cultivate their friendship with gifts of inscribed editions of his works. Further glowing newspaper reports followed from the press organization, and continued indeed until D'Annunzio marched on Fiume just over a year later. An invitation from the British High Command to a celebratory lunch at the Savoy was telegrammed to the poet on 22 September 1918. The lunch had been arranged for 25 September and it becomes clear from the surrounding documentation in the archive at the

[65] The two messages launched by D'Annunzio are reproduced in Gatti, *GD'A* 325–6; G. Po, *Scritti messagi discorsi e rapporti militari* (Rome, 1939), 196, has further notes on the flight, derived from D'Annunzio's *Taccuini* (see ibid. 1139), which are deficient here because D'Annunzio gave the three notebooks concerned to Natale Palli immediately after the flight; see *Libro segreto*, *Prose di ricerca*, ii. 816–18.

Vittoriale that the invitation had followed earlier negotiations which ensured that D'Annunzio was to act as unofficial ambassador, carrying a message from the Italian premier, Vittorio Emanuele Orlando, to the victorious Allies.[66] D'Annunzio, piloted by Natale Palli, followed the route proposed by the British airforce authorities, but when he arrived in the skies over Paris on 24 September, he flew briefly over the Italian troop positions on the Aisne, and then returned to the aerodrome of San Pelagio. There is no explanation why he failed to make the appointment in London; he had earlier telegrammed Antongini to say that he would be in Epernay on the evening of 24 September, or perhaps the morning of the 25 September, proceeding to London.[67]

D'Annunzio had always made a point of delivering emotionally charged speeches over the bodies of his dead companions. With the war coming to an end his orations, or prayers as he called them, became more formalized and more concerned with Italy's claims for the just rewards of victory. One phrase which served as an irredentist rallying-cry for the invasion of Fiume in the following year, 1919, was the famous *Vittoria nostra non sarai mutilata* (Victory of ours, thou shalt not be mutilated). The words are taken from the 'Preghiera di Sernaglia' (Prayer of Sernaglia), the style of which exaggerated that trend for biblical paraphrase which had always been a feature of D'Annunzio's political rhetoric, and which had so shocked some of his audience at Quarto. So here the Sernaglia harangue concluded: 'What in God was said, is now restated: "The skies are less vast than thy wings, O Victory".'[68] His next oration went further: on 1 November 1918 'La preghiera di Aquileia' (The Prayer of Aquileia) recalled again the sacrifice of the Italian forces and the heroism in particular of Giovanni Randaccio. The tone recalls episodes from the Passion of Christ and the 'prayer' includes a startling paraphrase of the Lord's Prayer:

---

[66] The message, still preserved in its grey envelope, is kept in the archive of the Vittoriale, along with other documents concerned with this abortive expedition to London, none of them so far published in full: Archivio Generale, XIV and XVIII.

[67] Further details of these events are discussed in my 'D'Annunzio e la guerra: attraverso occhi inglesi', in F. Perfetti (ed.), *D'Annunzio e la guerra* (Milan, 1996), 179–90.

[68] For the Quarto oration see above, p. 288 and n. 14; the Sernaglia oration was published in the *Corriere della sera* (24 Oct. 1918); it is now available along with other speeches under the overall title of *Il libro ascetico della giovine Italia*, *Prose di ricerca*, i. 443–746, here 647–8.

O dead who are in earth, as in heaven,
Hallowed be your names,
Your spiritual kingdom come,
Your will be done on earth.
Give our faith its daily bread;
Keep alive in us sacred hatred, as we shall never deny your love.
Deliver us from every ignoble temptation;
Free us from every cowardly doubt,
And if necessary
We shall fight, not until the last drop of our blood,
But with you, until the last particle of our dust.
If necessary
We shall fight until Just God
Comes to judge the living and the dead.
Amen.[69]

Victory was in sight and D'Annunzio was preparing for the aftermath. He returned to the Front to take part in several actions before the armistice was signed; in particular he witnessed the final assault made by General Diaz against the Austrians on the Piave in order that Italy might assimilate as much territory as possible before any peace talks took place. The Italian push was successful and has been known ever since as the Battle of Vittorio Veneto, commemorated in many an Italian piazza and street name. On 3 November the armistice was signed. D'Annunzio's war was over, much to his apparent regret, though he had consolations, promotion to lieutenant-colonel and a gold medal for valour for the enterprises in which he had taken part during the previous three years. The citation read as follows:

A war-wounded volunteer for three years of bitter struggle, with inspiring faith, untiring activity, participating in the most audacious enterprises by land, sea and air, he wholeheartedly dedicated his noble intellect and his tenacious will, his thought and action in perfect harmony, to the sacred ideals of his native land, in the pure dignity of duty and sacrifice—War Zone May 1915–November 1918.

The medal was conferred by Emanuele Filiberto, duke of Aosta, on 10 April 1919, and D'Annunzio's speech of thanks is noted in his *taccuini*.[70]

---

[69] *Il libro ascetico della giovine Italia, Prose di ricerca*, i. 648–9.
[70] *Taccuini*, 1159–60; the citation itself is discussed by Alatri, *GD'A*, 400; an 'anthology' of D'Annunzio's citations for valour is given by E. Bianchetti in the *Prose di ricerca*, i. 986–1005.

Apart from official recognition and medals for valour from D'Annunzio's own and allied governments, the archive at the Vittoriale contains dozens of admiring letters from private correspondents containing expressions of admiration for his exploits and courage. From 'The Australians at Weymouth' Westham Camp, Weymouth, came a letter dated 18 August 1918:

I have been instructed by a very large number of Australians who are in this camp [. . .] to write to you and express to you their deep admiration of your spendid services to the Allied cause. And not only to the Allied cause, but to the cause of liberty and freedom of the whole human race.

From a whole range of individuals came similar letters. In view of the bad press to which D'Annunzio was to be subjected in Britain after 1919, it may be worth giving some publicity to a selection from some of these private and spontaneous expressions of admiration: the first such, dated 19 May 1915, was sent by Horace Ledger of Whitham, Essex, who wrote to say how proud he had been to make D'Annunzio's acquaintance, and recalled with great pathos that his son, 'who used to slip the greyhounds for us at St Cloud', had been killed in action near Ypres'; John J. Parker of Watting, Parker and Co., Chartered Accountants of Bristol, congratulated him particularly on the flight over Vienna, 'in the endeavour to bring light and reason to the misguided people of enemy countries, still groping, as they seem to be, in medieval darkness'; on 18 August a note from the Royal College of Physicians in Edinburgh complimented him and informed him that he had been elected Honorary Fellow of the college. And the letters continued over the years, recalling anniversaries of his actions or speeches during the war. W. B. Yeats wrote on 2 July 1924 reiterating an invitation for the Irish 'Aonach Tailteann', inviting him to come to Dublin 'as the guest of our nation'. H. L. Norton-Traill, a relative of Sir Henry Seagrave, was a regular correspondent in the files; on 7 May 1932 Norton-Traill wrote:

In this season we recall the memorable oration of 'the Comandante', delivered on 5 May 1915 from the 'Scoglio di Quarto'. The stirring words which fired the imagination of the Italian Nation resounded throughout the civilized world, and, as a contribution to victory have carried the eternal gratitude of England and of all the Allies.

It may have been Norton-Traill who brought Seagrave's twisted steering-wheel to the Vittoriale after the latter's death on Windermere in 1930; an allusion to something of the kind is made in a letter of 8 March 1932, and the wheel found a place of honour on the 'altar' of the reliquary room in the villa. There are many other testimonies of what seem genuine admiration from Anglophone correspondents, none so far published.

D'Annunzio, to judge by his actions and letters immediately after the war ended, felt purposeless. One aim and object seemed to be left unfulfilled: the redemption, as he and others saw it, of Italy's territories in Dalmatia. His celebratory ode on the victory over Austria, the 'Cantico per l'ottava della vittoria' (Song for the Octave of Victory) was in effect a promotion of that viewpoint; it claimed for Italy all the Dalmatian cities, a demand which went beyond the agreements of the secret Treaty of London. The ode was the last of his writings to appear in the *Corriere* (on 12 November 1918), whose editor, Luigi Albertini, was opposed to what he saw as Italian expansionism into territory which the Yugoslavs claimed with the same ardour as D'Annunzio; he understood that they were motivated by the same desire for liberty which had spurred on patriotic Italians fighting for Trento and for lands more obviously within the natural boundaries of Italy. The next year D'Annunzio turned his journalistic allegiance to Mussolini's recently founded newspaper, *Il popolo d'Italia*, and on 15 January 1919 published there his 'Lettera ai Dalmati' (Letter to the Dalmatian People).[71] It was the immediate prelude to the invasion of Fiume.

[71] The letter is available in the collection *Sudore di sangue* (Sweating Blood), *Prose di ricerca*, i. 801–19; see below, p. 321.

II

The Invasion of Fiume

D'ANNUNZIO'S career was about to scale new heights of controversy. His long-standing ambition to establish Italian sovereignty over territories outside the Peninsula which were by language, religion, culture, and historical precedent essentially Italian was understandable, justifiable, even laudable. He convinced himself and his acolytes that their actions were heroic, and pivotal for the development of Italian politics. There was certainly an epic quality to the ideas behind his seizure of the Yugoslav port of Fiume, and his actions in 1919–20 helped later to ensure that the city remained Italian for the next twenty-five years. Yet there was always an air of falseness about his takeover, an impression of play-acting, where the heroic was sometimes attended by the tragic and too often by the comic. More seriously, his capture of the port itself would divide the Italian people, help bring down at least three Italian governments (weakening for ever traditional party structures and alliances), set regiment against regiment, defer the signing of the European peace treaty, and create long-lasting distrust between Italy and her wartime allies. More significantly, and more immediately, the poet's long-held scorn for democratically elected authority was to condition the political attitude of two generations of Italians. His encouragement of irresponsible anarchy in the young (and not so young), and his personal aspirations to the totalitarian powers of dictator were only apparently paradoxical: as a dictator he would have no restraints upon his freedom of action or indeed upon his personal morality, and his behaviour reflected, at a more influential level, the anarchic irresponsibility of youth. When all the glamour and the excitement began to fade, and his more moderate followers began to abandon him, it was that totalitarian power which was his only consolation: 'the only joy in all this tedium'.[1] The poet's

---

[1] Letter to Sante Ceccherini of 11 Nov. 1920: 'E' necessaria che io mantenga questa prerogativa. E' la sola gioia in tanta noia' (Archivio Eredi Ceccherini). He had handed over command to Ceccherini the day before; see his statements to Ceccherini when the latter resigned definitively, below, p. 344, n. 65.

gradual eclipse in this, his most complex adventure, requires a certain amount of preliminary explanation.

By the end of the war Italian forces were left in command of most of the territories promised them in the Treaty of London of April 1915, including the Trentino, the south Tyrol, Venezia Giulia, the Istrian peninsula, Dalmatia, and almost the whole of Albania. But new problems now arose because of the intervention of the United States in the closing stages of the war. At the peace negotiations in Versailles President Wilson refused to accept the well-known Allied promises of territorial concessions to Italy, which France, Britain, and Italy had secretly negotiated over four years earlier in the absence of isolationist America. Woodrow Wilson's general position was to uphold the right of self-determination for recognizable nationalities, and more particularly to try to ensure that the whole of the Dalmatian coast formed part of the new nation of Yugoslavia. To add to the Italian government's diplomatic difficulties, Wilson shared with many of his fellow Americans a prejudice towards and distrust of Italy and Italians, motivated partly by what conservative America saw as egalitarian political views expressed by recent immigrants, partly by the corruption and violence later associated with criminal organizations such as the Mafia. Such distrust was exemplified between 1920 and 1927 in the unjust trial and execution of Nicola Sacco and Bartolomeo Vanzetti, nominally condemned for robbery and murder, but in fact executed by the American Establishment for their radicalism and anarchism.

For years before D'Annunzio's capture of Fiume, the files of the British Foreign Office bulged with information concerning the west coast of the Adriatic, which the British viewed as a potential trouble-spot. Notes and dispatches in the files culminate during the earlier part of 1919 with reports of ethnic conflicts in the city of Fiume itself. Until September the possibility of a takeover by D'Annunzio finds no mention in that avalanche of paper. The political explosion in Fiume had a long gestation period, and, as Renzo De Felice has pointed out on several occasions, it would be wrong to speak of the Fiume enterprise as a sudden piece of improvisatory initiative.[2]

---

[2] De Felice's splendid introduction to his edition of GD'A, *La penultima ventura: Scritti e discorsi fiumani* (Milan, 1974), makes this particular case as he sets D'Annunzio's actions in context; see also his *D'Annunzio politico: 1918–1938* (Bari, 1978), which despite its all-embracing title is mainly concerned with the Fiume adventure, and one of the best introductions to the affair.

And since we now know that, as far as many Fiumans were concerned, D'Annunzio was one of several possible leaders, it would be equally absurd to see his arrival on the scene as a fated advent. But it is also certain that D'Annunzio was not a man to let slip an opportunity, and the decisive quality of his actions was certainly crucial at a time of Italian government uncertainty.

On the other hand, it is true to say that D'Annunzio himself felt deep resentment at the Allies' failure, as he saw it, to ratify their pledges, and the 'bad faith' of the Allies incensed him more than any other aspect of the situation; he used the early months of 1919 to whip up feeling in support of his determination to hold on to the territories then occupied by Italian troops, in particular the Dalmatian territories. Fiume eventually turned out to be the greatest prize in the irredentist game, though, strangely, D'Annunzio's interest in the port, at least until late August 1919, had never been openly stated by him; indeed in his Dalmatian harangues he had not harped upon the name of Fiume as he had in the case of other 'lost' cities. The force of his oratory and the passion which he aroused in the Italian crowds in support of national claims for the 'lost' territories further alarmed the Allies, and, although his figure was often represented by journalists as clownish, D'Annunzio's escapade at Fiume during the period 1919–20 simply confirmed the distrust felt by the Americans, and convinced the British, if they needed convincing, of Italian bad faith, persuading both nations of the weakness and unreliability of the Italian government, and leaving a legacy of mistrust which conditioned their approach to Italy for the following fifty years, notably during the crises of the 1930s.

President Wilson seemed adamant in his insistence that the Allies should heed the request of the Yugoslavs to exclude the port of Fiume from any Italian sphere of influence. At the height of the Paris negotiations, on 23 April 1919, the American leader, going over the head of Prime Minister Orlando and Foreign Minister Sidney Sonnino, published an appeal to the Italians through the columns of the Parisian *Le Temps*, describing Italian aspirations as nothing less than imperialistic, and implying that the Italian negotiators were acting against Italian public opinion. Orlando and Sonnino indignantly withdrew from the talks, and the stage was set for a further dose of Dannunzian rabble-rousing, beginning with the brief exhortation 'La parola della patria' (The Word of the Fatherland) of 24 April 1919. In it D'Annunzio reflected on the integrity of

Italy's position in the face of the ignobility of the Allies with their xenophobia, and what he described as their lies and swindles; he also declared his pride at being an Italian: 'There is in the world nothing greater than this Italy of ours, unafraid to stand alone against everyone and everything, with its strength multiplied by its sacrifices.' The Italians should not yield as much as a fingernail (*non piegare d'un'ugna*).[3] In another speech, delivered in St Mark's Square on 25 April, he urged the Venetians to take up arms again and redeem what was theirs. The poet had chosen his time well; 25 April is the day of St Mark, patron saint of the city whose lost empire D'Annunzio was incidentally concerned with restoring. Walter Starkie, at that time one of the leading Anglophone experts on Italian life and letters (his study of Pirandello is still one of the best essays on the playwright), offered his readers a splendid eyewitness account of the occasion. Starkie's description begins with a statement of personal disillusionment at his first glimpse of D'Annunzio, 'a dwarf of a man, goggle-eyed and thick-lipped—truly sinister in his grotesqueness, like a tragic gargoyle. Is this the man that Duse loved?'[4] But Starkie was gradually forced to admit the magic of D'Annunzio's oratory as his voice played upon the emotions of the crowd 'as a supreme violinist does upon a Stradivarius':

Little by little, however, I began to sink under the fascination of the voice which penetrated into my consciousness, syllable by syllable, like water from a clear fountain. It was a slow precise voice accompanying the words right to the last vowel, as if he wished to savour to the utmost their echoing music. The tones rose and fell in an unending stream, like the song of a minstrel, and they spread over the vast audience like olive oil on the surface of the sea.

Starkie waxes unusually lyrical; here in a different context is a similar reaction to that of Arthur Symons, who listened spellbound to a reading of the Bible with commentary by the poet in Count Primoli's palace in Rome,[5] or to the sheer pleasure felt by Harold Nicolson in the plush intimacy of Countess D'Orsay's Florentine salon.[6]

---

[3] 'La parola della patria', *Prose di ricerca*, i. 855–8.

[4] W. Starkie, *The Waveless Plain: An Italian Autobiography* (London, 1938), here 124–5; D'Annunzio's speech, along with crowd reaction, described almost in terms of stage directions, is published in *Prose di ricerca*, i. 856–8 (Starkie's monograph, *Luigi Pirandello* (1st edn. 1928), was republished at Berkeley and Los Angeles, 1965).

[5] A. Symons, 'A Reading at Count Primoli's', in his *Eleonora Duse*, 113.

[6] See above, Ch. 1 n. 17.

The jingoistic speech in St Mark's Square was followed by open letters to an influential member of parliament, Luigi Luzzati, and to D'Annunzio's senator friend, Tommaso Tittoni, urging them both to hold firm in their resolve to keep Dalmatia. But probably his most fiery oratory was reserved for Rome in two speeches delivered at the Augusteo (on 4 May 1919), and at the Campidoglio (on 6 May 1919).[7] These harangues evoked the grandeur of the Roman past, and the recent sacrifices of Italy during the war. D'Annunzio added poignancy by recalling the heroism of Giovanni Randaccio and, unfurling the flag which had covered the hero's coffin, kissing its folds as he called out the names of the disputed territories.[8] At the same time he vilified the treachery of the Allies, and ridiculed the American intervention, caricaturing the American president: this was no man, but one of those ugly figurines you could buy for a farthing, this was no face but a mask, no mouth but a jaw stuffed with teeth, this was no countenance, it was a pair of lenses.[9] When D'Annunzio began to pour his scorn upon Woodrow Wilson, his invective did nothing to help the timorous efforts of the Italian delegacy at Versailles, while the poet's portrayal of Wilson 'with his long equine face' and his 'mouthful of thirty-two false teeth' was given wide coverage in newspapers in the United States.

In the case of the large port of Fiume, the Italians had to contend not only with Yugoslav claims, but also with other non-Italian national interests, which it would be impossible to consider fully here.[10] But as an example of those interests it is worth quoting from

---

[7] These last two speeches, 'Gli ultimi saranno i primi' (The Last Shall Be First) and 'Dalla ringhiera del Campidoglio' (From the Balustrade of the Capitol), are available in *Prose di ricerca*, respectively i. 861–77 and 878–84; the open letter to Luzzati is published ibid. 859–60.

[8] De Felice, in his introduction to *La penultima ventura*, puts the Venetian and Roman orations in their proper context.

[9] *Prose di ricerca*, i. 879.

[10] To the works by De Felice listed in n. 2 above should be added the most detailed and scientific account of the invasion of Fiume, that of P. Alatri, *Nitti, D'Annunzio e la questione adriatica (1919–1920)* (Milan, 1959). Most accounts of the Fiuman enterprise derive much of their information and indication of sources from this and from Ferdinando Gerra's classic *L'impresa di Fiume*, 2 vols. (Milan, 1974), Roberto Vivarelli's account, included in his splendid *Storia delle origini del fascismo*, 2 vols. (2nd edn., Bologna, 1991), 'L'impresa di Fiume', is the best modern summary of the Fiume escapade, and discusses both the political developments prior to the invasion and the consequences of D'Annunzio's actions, i. 491–587; Paolo Alatri brought up to date the history of the Fiuman question in his 'La storiografia sull'impresa dannunziana a Fiume', in F. Perfetti (ed.), *D'Annunzio e il suo tempo* (Genoa, 1992), 19–65; more recent papers include the collection E. Ledda and

Michael Ledeen's excellent account of the Fiume invasion a paragraph taken from the British *Shipbuilding and Shipping Record* of 1 May 1919, which pointed out to its readers the promising openings into lucrative and expanding markets that seemed available for the British merchant fleet through the exploitation of Fiume. Simultaneously the same shipping reporter sagely remarked that following Italy's new post-war naval expansion and ambition, Rome would not welcome foreign competition in that region.[11] Approaching the problem from another angle, it is also significant that, after the invasion itself, the *Times*, which, for six weeks or more, had been condemning unconditionally the piratical venture, admitted, in a leading article on 24 December 1919, the great strategic potential of holding on to the important harbour: 'With Trieste already in her hands, it would give Italy economic control over the only maritime outlets of a great portion of central Europe as well as of Yugo-Slavia.'

Ironically the enclave of Fiume, which was to be excluded from the negotiations, conformed to Wilson's directive about national sovereignty, since a majority of its people were Italian-speaking and felt themselves closer to Italy than to their Serbo-Croatian neighbours.[12] Already in October 1918 the citizenry of Fiume had elected a National Council (Consiglio Nazionale) and proclaimed their desire to become part of Italy. In the confused situation following Woodrow Wilson's insistence that boundaries be defined according to those clearly discernible national lines, the Italian government had sent a task force to Fiume as a counter to Serb troops which had infiltrated the town. The Allies responded by sending their own contingents, which included French and British detachments; Francesco Saverio Grazioli, the general commanding the Italian group, was placed in overall charge.

G. Salotti (eds.), *Un capitolo di storia: Fiume e D'Annunzio* (Rome, 1991); awaited are the papers from the 1996 conference: F. Perfetti (ed.), *Dannunzio e l'impresa fiumana* (Milan); a model essay is M. A. Ledeen's *D'Annunzio a Fiume* (Bari, 1975), trans. as *The First Duce: D'Annunzio at Fiume* (Baltimore and London, 1977), which, in particular, gives an American view of the affair. To counter the mock-heroics of many accounts J. N. Macdonald, OSB, *A Political Escapade: The Story of Fiume and D'Annunzio*, (London [1921]), makes salutary reading.

[11] Ledeen, *The First Duce*, 31.

[12] Macdonald, *A Political Escapade*, ch. 1, describes well the social make-up of Fiume, and adduces statistics, quoting the authoritative Depoli *Guida di Fiume*; Macdonald says that of a population of 49,806 the Italians made up 24,212 while the second largest group were the Croatians with 12,926.

D'Annunzio's views on the rights of Italy over the former Venetian possessions had been clear for a quarter of a century; his irredentist harangues at Genoa and at Quarto in May 1915 had reiterated his position, and his actions during the war years had positively demonstrated his enthusiasm for recovering what he continued to call the left lung of Italy. D'Annunzio always stressed that he had fought the war for Dalmatia—for the whole of Dalmatia. Events were now drawing inexorably to a crisis point, both for the poet and for the weak government in Rome, where Mussolini and his fascists were creating further political unrest. In April 1919, Giovanni Host-Venturi, a captain of the *arditi* and a fanatical Dalmatian patriot, organized the Legione Fiumana (Fiume Legion) presided over by Major Giovanni Giuriati, the influential chairman of the National Committee for War Claims. The intention of this new group was to organize volunteers and annex the port by force if necessary; patriotic ex-combatants were encouraged to make their own way to the city. The National Council of Fiume had been gathering strength and support from like-minded patriots, and in mid-June 1919 they collaborated in establishing what was known as 'an army for the defence of Fiume' with, briefly in charge of its administration, the playwright Sem Benelli, another singularly eccentric author, though not in the same league as D'Annunzio.[13]

The year 1919 had in fact begun with an interesting manœuvre on D'Annunzio's part, in which may be glimpsed the germs of future action. At the beginning of 1919, he worked on the composition of his 'Lettera ai Dalmati' (Letter to the Dalmatian People), which eventually, beginning on 14 January 1919, was published by several influential newspapers (including Mussolini's *Popolo d'Italia* on 15 January). The essay summed up in D'Annunzio's usual jingoistic tones the actions which the Italians had carried out during the war against Austro-Hungarian forces along the Dalmatian coast, with particular reference to the poet's own heroic raids on Pola, Premuda, and the Carnaro (through the Beffa di Buccari). Rejecting the 'enfeebling transatlantic purgatives offered by Dr Wilson', and the 'transalpine surgery of Dr Clemenceau',[14] D'Annunzio reiterated

---

[13] Benelli accepted the role as organizer of the Fiuman army on 12 June 1919, but by 26 June had withdrawn; see S. Gigante, *Storia del Comune di Fiume* (Florence, 1928), 201.

[14] The letter is available in *Prose di ricerca*, i. 803–20; the references to Drs Wilson and Clemenceau are at p. 816.

that he had dedicated himself entirely to the Dalmatian cause. The incoming prime minister, Francesco Saverio Nitti, who took over from Orlando following the latter's resignation on 21 June 1919, was as inclined to appeasement as Giolitti had been, and regarded D'Annunzio's view of a greater Italy as an irrelevance in a country which badly needed a period of peace and recuperation. American aid, or at least American approbation, was necessary for such recuperation, and not only did the Americans seem willing to support Italy's lira, but a starving Italy would also benefit from cheap American grain. American generosity was, understandably, driven by self-interest, but the last thing that Nitti wanted was to antagonize the United States, potentially Italy's greatest benefactor, In a letter to D'Annunzio dated 26 May 1919, defending his policies during 1918, Nitti pointed out that he had obtained from the United States of America goods worth not less than 6,000 million lire, thanks to huge credits granted by America (at the time Italy exported goods to America valued at only 127 million lire).[15] To that huge sum could be added a further $2,000 million in the form of Italy's debts to her next major creditor, Britain, to whom Nitti's government, by August 1919, owed in excess of £470 million.[16]

It was probably Nitti's diplomatic intervention which foiled D'Annunzio's first plan of attack: in June 1919 the poet came to know that General Ottavio Zoppi was about to leave the port of Venice with a transport ship taking his commando division to Libya. The poet tried to persuade Zoppi to 'wheel to the left', as he put it, and occupy the areas from which the Versailles negotiations seemed to be excluding Italy. Zoppi was amenable, but said he needed General Badoglio's approval. D'Annunzio had already spoken with Pietro Badoglio, who mollified him by declaring, with more rhetoric than realism, that he was ready to march on Lubljana

---

[15] Alatri, *Nitti, D'Annunzio e la questione adriatica*, 512–14; in view of D'Annunzio's later paranoid anti-Nitti hostility, it is worth considering a letter dated 10 June 1918, from the poet to Nitti, then at the Treasury, which is full of affability and friendship (ibid. 188); Nitti's letter of 26 May 1919 ends with 'a cordial handshake' (ibid. 513).

[16] A note dated 10 Dec. 1919 in the British Foreign Office papers details the parlous financial situation of the Italians and warns Lord Curzon personally not to allow Italy further credit, and this at a time when it was felt that further British loans might prove a good incentive for Italy to deal firmly with their renegade poet (FO.317.3512/162079). For this and other secret Foreign Office documents of the time, see J. R. Woodhouse, 'D'Annunzio e l'impresa fiumana: visto attraverso i documenti inediti del Foreign Office', in F. Perfetti (ed.), *D'Annunzio e l'impresa fiumana* (Milan, forthcoming).

himself with five divisions if the peace talks did not grant Italy what she was owed. Nitti's temporizing worked: Zoppi departed for Libya and D'Annunzio's inspired piece of improvisation came to naught.[17]

France had her own interests in keeping Italy out of Dalmatia, where Clemenceau was hoping to extend his country's personal sphere of influence in those areas recently abandoned by the former Austro-Hungarian empire. D'Annunzio had accused France of not supporting Italian territorial claims, and had been attacked in the French press as an ingrate, particularly, it was alleged, in view of the welcome he had enjoyed during his exile in France. He now launched four shafts at his 'second fatherland', entitled *Aveux de l'ingrat* (Avowals of the Ingrate), four articles in which he pointed out that he had saved France personally both by provoking Italy's intervention in 1915 and by drawing German military attention down to the southern front during the rest of the war. By reneging on the secret Treaty of London, France was being disloyal not so much to her ally Italy as to her son D'Annunzio.[18]

But both France and Britain were united in expressing disdain for the weakness of the Italian negotiators and for their inept government back in Rome. Clemenceau's words are reported with approval in the British Foreign Office minutes: 'The present Italian Government was unable to make itself obeyed by the army or the navy, and therefore could not properly be called a Government at all [. . .] Italy's allies were now being asked to sit still and contemplate D'Annunzio as the King of Fiume and to postpone all attempts to settle the problem'.[19] The withdrawal from the Versailles negotiations of Orlando and Sonnino had little effect on France and the other Allies, who simply used their absence to arrange matters the better to suit themselves, as the two Italian leaders found to their cost on their return to Paris. Back home in Italy their diplomatic failure had two immediate effects in the country as a whole: a strengthening of nationalistic tendencies, particularly among the disaffected and disillusioned ex-combatants, and an increased disdain for a parliamentary system which seemed to have

[17] There is useful documentation and discussion of the plan and its consequences in Gerra's *L'impresa di Fiume*, i. 34–5; the situation is touched upon briefly in Ledeen, *The First Duce*, 48–9.

[18] The articles are collected in *Prose di ricerca*, i. 821–54.

[19] FO.371.4264/150963, 11 Nov. 1919. (Foreign Office documents in the Public Records Office).

thrown up yet another weak government. Direct action of the kind which D'Annunzio had suggested to Ottavio Zoppi seemed to offer a more practical solution than the delays and inefficiencies of the parliamentary system. It was no coincidence that Mussolini's first *fasci di combattimento* (combat bands) were officially inaugurated by the fascist leader on 23 March 1919, and were soon to develop into an entirely new and unconstitutional militia. Zoppi's commando division had been made up of shock troops, the *arditi*, who during the recent conflict had impressed the world by their bravery and daring, qualities which D'Annunzio's subsequent invasion of Fiume would need in good measure. It was to the *arditi* that D'Annunzio later looked for his toughest and most unconventional irregular troops.

The start of 1919 saw another conjunction of events and ideas which Paolo Alatri rightly highlights as important to the coming enterprise: the creation by the Futurist pioneer, Mario Carli, of the idea of *arditismo*, an offshoot of Futurism, in which could be expressed a disdain for the kind of everyday mediocrity which entailed no risks and no gains; by contrast the movement exalted, rather, a passion for emotion, danger, and struggle found in the predatory soul, in the spirit of adventure, and in physical toughness. At Fiume in September 1919 Carli harangued the crowd as a warm-up to D'Annunzio's speeches. One such discourse, 'To all *arditi*, on land, sea, and in the air', while egotistic and full of self-praise, contains some of the theoretic inspiration to the new 'movement': 'The true Italy, the young Italy, the Italy which marches in the vanguard and cuts through diplomatic labyrinths with a good dagger-blow, is today at Fiume, either in person or in spirit.'[20] Carli tried to extract from what in peacetime were mere hooligan elements the characteristics of daring and courage which in war may well create heroes. For him *arditismo* was a frame of mind, a philosophy of life:

A quality revealed on a large scale by war—no monopoly of our Corps but a characteristic of all Italian youth. *Arditismo* has for our epoch the function which Romanticism had a century ago [. . .]. It is also and above all a spiritual tendency, a character spring, a constant attitude of the human personality, revealed in a hundred ways, in a hundred different forms.[21]

[20] M. Carli, *Con D'Annunzio a Fiume* (Milan, 1920); his speech is at pp. 44–6, here particularly p. 45. The situation and atmosphere are well discussed in Alatri, *GD'A*, 404.

[21] Carli, *Con D'Annunzio a Fiume*, 92; further Futurist theorizing by Carli is presented in 'L'aristocrazia degli Arditi', *Roma Futurista* (5 Jan. 1919); Carli later expanded on these ideas in his *Arditismo* (Milan, 1919).

Many of Carli's sentiments might have come from D'Annunzio's own pen; indeed for years the Futurists had been repeating themes which D'Annunzio had harped upon since his earliest youth. Even before the first Futurist Manifesto of 1909, the father of the movement, Filippo Tommaso Marinetti, had expressed equivocal appreciation of D'Annunzio.[22] And, in view of the Futurists' participation in the march on Fiume, it is important to see that after 1909 they supported independently actions of which D'Annunzio approved, including the Libyan campaign and Italian intervention in World War One. On 15 October 1913 their Futurist Political Programme had not only repeated the basic tenets of their new and outlandish poetic theories, but also took a political stand which coincided perfectly with the political ambitions of the Nationalist Party. Pacifism was denigrated, support was declared for strengthening Italy's military potential, on land and sea, a patriotic education for the proletariat was called for, a cynical, astute, and aggressive foreign policy was demanded; colonialism, anticlericalism, and antisocialism were three other watchwords. Following the publication in 1915 of the Futurist compilation *Guerra solo igiene del mondo* (War, the Only Health for the World), Marinetti (along with Mussolini) was among those arrested during the riots in Rome sparked off by D'Annunzio's oratory in April that year, and just a month later Marinetti himself was sent to the front as a volunteer. After the war, the Futurist *arditi* of Mario Carli were among the most violent opponents of the Socialist Party and formed the vanguard of the mob which attacked and destroyed the newspaper offices of the Socialist *Avanti* on 15 April 1919. They were to be appropriate companions in D'Annunzio's Fiuman Legion a few months later.

The recently constituted National Council of Fiume was well aware of D'Annunzio's long-standing predilection for their Dalmatian homeland, and on 7 April 1919 they sent Arturo Marpicati to Venice as an envoy to the poet, in a preliminary move to secure an inviolable link with their motherland, Italy. It was at this time that D'Annunzio launched into the speeches to mass audiences in St Mark's Square Venice and later in Rome, inveighing against Woodrow Wilson's interference and exhorting Italians to seize arms and make sure that the cry of Dalmatia was universally heard. Further

---

[22] F. T. Marinetti, *Les Dieux s'en vont, D'Annunzio reste* (Paris, 1908), 11–33; it must be added that, after D'Annunzio expelled Marinetti from Fiume on 30 Sept. 1919, the relationship between the two men cooled considerably.

anti-American statements, containing particularly aggressive attacks on President Wilson, were syndicated throughout the United States in the Hearst newspapers, causing consternation in diplomatic circles in Rome; Tommaso Tittoni, by now the new Italian foreign secretary, wrote in alarm on 24 July 1919 to his colleague Nitti, who responded on 27 July with what must have been in Dannunzian criticism the understatement of the century: 'I understand the harm which Gabriele D'Annunzio's most recent impulsive act can do us in America. I shall try to do my best to make him understand that his silence is necessary, but, as you well know, it is not an easy thing to do.'[23] D'Annunzio's popularity was much greater than that of the cautious Nitti: in February 1919 the Arts Faculty of Rome University had voted D'Annunzio an honorary doctorate, another sign, even though the decision had not been unanimous, of the way his ideas were chiming with the world around. The final conferment of the academic distinction coincided with Marpicati's visit.

D'Annunzio had by now been promoted lieutenant-colonel and had given his last two speeches splendidly apparelled in his officer's uniform; it was the pretext of military discipline which the ever-fearful government of Orlando next used as an excuse to order him to withdraw from Rome to Venice. Once there, however, D'Annunzio simply requested his own demobilization, and continued to give polemical irredentist speeches. Fiume itself had been occupied on 17 November 1918 by an ultra-nationalistic brigade of Sardinian Grenadiers, the most venerable regiment in the Italian army, welcomed enthusiastically into the enclave by the local population. For several months the Grenadiers remained in sole command, before, that is, the Allies landed contingents of their own. The situation assumed a new urgency when, according to one witness, Giuseppe Sovera, trouble arose after ill-disciplined Indo-Chinese and African troops forming the French detachment pressed their drunken attentions on local women. Whatever the truth of that circumstance (the women might well have been suborned as *agents provocateurs*), clashes occurred between French and Italian troops.[24] Against the account given by Sovera and others motivated by genuine feelings of patriotic fervour and youthful passion must be considered the

---

[23] This and other messages between the two men are reproduced in Alatri, *Nitti, D'Annunzio e la questione adriatica*, 188–9.

[24] See G. Sovera Latuada, 'Giuseppe Sovera's Role in the Inception of D'Annunzio's Raid on Fiume', *Modern Language Review*, 87/2 (1992), 338.

stark narrative of the Benedictine priest J. N. Macdonald, who emphasized by contrast the brutality of the attacks by local Italians upon non-Italian elements in Fiume during the period immediately preceding the invasion of 12 September. In particular he notes the racist violence against the French Annamite troops, the use of children as *provocateurs* (paid a commission of 10–16 kronen for their services), the treacherous murder of unarmed and disarmed French soldiers by elements of the Fiuman volunteer force, and the complete failure by the Italian commander-in-chief, General Grazioli, to impose any kind of authority or discipline on the men under his command. Macdonald's account, cut short three months before the end of the affair, is supported by an avalanche of telegrams sent to the British Foreign Office by British agents and officials in and around the enclave.[25] One consequence of the Italian attack on soldiers from the Allied contingents on 9 July 1919 was that Clemenceau ordered a French battleship to proceed to Fiume,[26] and a rumour spread that the Allies would expel the Italian contingent and impose their own conditions. This was bad news for the irredentists: the prospect of ousting a determined Allied force of American and English peacekeepers was more daunting than simply infiltrating an Italian company already in nominal charge of the city. A steady and relentless pressure was building on the Italian interventionists to act quickly, and D'Annunzio, along with other promoters of a greater Italy, had frequent meetings during the next two months, in Venice and Rome.

British preoccupation with the growing tension in the area is reflected in the ever-increasing thickness of the Foreign Office files marked ITALY, ADRIATIC, AUSTRIA, FIUME. One telegram from Admiral Sinclair, new commander of the Third Flotilla, Light Cruisers anchored off Fiume, described the cruelty and ineptitude of the local Italian police force, who had recently shot and killed nine of the locals and injured between fifteen and twenty more, 'children returning from a picnic' who had refused to cry *Viva* for the Italians. Such unthinking chauvinism over such a trivial affair convinced the admiral that the Fiume question could not be settled

[25] Macdonald's main indictment may be seen at pp. 68–94 of his *A Political Escapade*.

[26] Movements of this and other naval forces were monitored in secret telegrams sent from the British Third Flotilla, Light Cruisers stationed off Fiume, commanded at the time by Admiral Hope; see FO.371.3509/99847.

without bloodshed.[27] A week later Lieutenant-Colonel Peck, commander of the British ground forces at Fiume, telegraphed to say that young Fiuman volonteers had begun to wear Italian uniform and that he suspected that they were being supported by General Grazioli.[28] On 5 September Arthur Balfour wrote to Lord Curzon, his successor at the Foreign Office, urging him to keep a British destroyer off Fiume, notwithstanding what the Italians might say about its being unnecessary, and, a week afterwards, F. G. F. Adam, later to become principal secretary at the Foreign Office, declared in a marginal note that he was not prepared to accept the word of an Italian naval officer.[29] The same day Members Hogge and Raper asked questions in the Commons concerning the government's policy in the Adriatic. Bonar Law made a non-committal reply, but the brief report in the *Times* was cut out and pasted up in the Foreign Office file, the forerunner of many such clippings used as fundamental information to stimulate discussion among the secretaries.[30] Two days before the invasion proper, a conversation with Admiral Sinclair prompted a report by another of the secretaries, S. R. Harris, directed to Lord Curzon's office; it must have arrived simultaneously with the telegram from Sinclair's successor off Fiume, which first mentions rumours that D'Annunzio was awaited in the port.[31]

The poet's attention was again temporarily distracted by three divergent but not untypical preoccupations. The first was a pressing need to vacate the house at Arcachon: his goods and chattels were in danger of being seized by creditors there; D'Annunzio somehow found 20,000 francs (1920 value about £1,000) to delay the crisis, and decided to clear the house of his possessions. The second distracting element was a new female temptation in Venice, where the return of the Hohenlohe family, the original proprietors of the Casetta Rossa had forced D'Annunzio to leave his fashionable

[27] FO.371.3509/120247; Admiral Sinclair had taken over command that summer from Admiral Hope.
[28] Peck's reports are models of sage objectivity (see for instance the thick summaries in FO.371.3510/130227) and must have been invaluable as a guide for Foreign Office decisions; eulogies of Peck by the diplomats in London are periodically to be found in the marginal jottings of his reports.
[29] FO.371.3509/127903; Adam was later to become an important player in the negotiations.
[30] FO.371.3509/127903, in effect the opening file on D'Annunzio's escapade.
[31] FO.371.3509/127511; Sinclair retired at this point to his estates in Scotland.

little house. This time the new star on his horizon was Luisa Baccara, a pretty and talented musician, who now took the place of Olga Levi, and whom D'Annunzio began to bombard with gifts as a prelude to fresh conquest. Luisa Baccara was to be one of his most faithful companions to the end of his days. The third distraction was less domestic: a cunning bribery attempt by Prime Minister Nitti, who tried to suborn D'Annunzio by offering him a commissariat in charge of the Italian air force, or some similar ministerial office of his choice. D'Annunzio, encouraged by Mussolini, ignored the offer and was later to revile Nitti in the most lurid language of which his famous oratory was capable; in particular Nitti's failure to support the idea of an Italian Fiume incensed D'Annunzio. He coined the nickname Cagoia[32] for the prime minister, which was to remain with the statesman thereafter, and is still associated with Nitti's name, particularly in right-wing circles. Writing of this in a letter of 5 October 1919, D'Annunzio urged Mussolini to publicize the nickname as widely as possible—his own men were making up songs about the unfortunate politician—and D'Annunzio coined another adjective to suggest opposition to Nitti's weak regime, *anticagoiesco*.[33]

In the meantime the rumour concerning the withdrawal of Italian forces from Fiume was in part borne out when the force of Grenadiers which had formed the Italian presence in the city was ordered out of the enclave by the Allied Commission. To avoid demonstrations by the locals, the Grenadiers were instructed to leave at night, specifically on 24 August 1919, but the ruse was exposed, the city's bells were rung by local supporters, flags were draped on the ground in front of the retreating troops, and women and children attempted to prevent the departure by lying in their path. The atmosphere seemed more than favourable for an Italian take-over. However, more immediately, the Grenadiers left for army quarters at Ronchi before their planned transfer to barracks in Rome, their place in Fiume being taken by an Italian infantry company. On 28 August 1919 Giuseppe Sovera, then one of the company commanders of the Grenadiers, left for Venice with four letters from Host-Venturi, to be delivered to D'Annunzio, Mussolini, Luigi

[32] The word is untranslatable but perhaps 'shititis' renders the meaning.
[33] *Carteggio D'Annunzio–Mussolini*, ed. R. De Felice and E. Mariano (Milan, 1971), 13 and 15. For *Cagoia* implying political vacillation, see Chiara, *G.D'A.*, 317.

Federzoni, leader of the Nationalist Party, and Giovanni Giuriati. Sovera's purpose was to sound out what support each might give to a possible insurrection.[34] He was able to relay D'Annunzio's positive reaction when he returned to camp at Ronchi, where a group of seven officers (*i giurati di Ronchi*) took an oath to free Fiume from foreign occupation, and on 5 September sent one of their number, Claudio Grandjacquet, bearing an appeal to D'Annunzio to lead their expedition. The fact that the poet was seen as only one of four potential leaders of an insurrection may indicate a circumstance which has been completely lost to view until recently, namely that until late August 1919 D'Annunzio never showed any particular enthusiasm for capturing Fiume. As has been noted, his earlier irredentist speeches had never specifically mentioned Fiume, though he had named nearly every other major town in Dalmatia; indeed, Carlo Ghisalberti has shown that D'Annunzio's silence was probably a deliberate snub to a city which had, he thought, consistently refused to recognize his talents. Only during the month before the actual invasion did he begin to mention Fiume as his particular target.[35] But by 7 September he had agreed to leave Venice and join the Grenadiers in their quarters at Ronchi; for the moment, however, dinner engagements with Ida Rubinstein and Luisa Baccara detained him, a further indication perhaps of his lukewarm attitude at that time to the specific capture of Fiume.

On 10 September a group of officers went to see the poet in Venice in order to add pressure, and next day D'Annunzio left for Ronchi. Before his departure for the camp on 11 September he wrote to Mussolini, indicating that he had a high fever but that he intended to launch the great adventure the morning afterwards and take Fiume by force of arms.[36] Two days later, at 5 a.m. on the morning of 12 September he was taken from the camp there in a Fiat Tipo 4 which headed a force of 196 Grenadiers in twenty-six army trucks purloined from a local barracks by one who was later to become his dauntless and enterprising quartermaster, Guido Keller; on the way they were joined by three armoured cars, and

[34] Sovera Latuada, 'Giuseppe Sovera's Role', 339.

[35] For the strange omission of Fiume from D'Annunzio's previous speeches see C. Ghisalberti, 'La lunga via per Fiume', in F. Perfetti (ed.), *D'Annunzio e l'impresa fiumana* (Milan, forthcoming).

[36] His tone to Mussolini is that of commander to subaltern: *Carteggio D'Annunzio–Mussolini*, 9.

by a miscellany of armed supporters who had been steadily making their way on foot towards the objective of Fiume.[37] Pausing only at the Trieste–Fiume crossroads for D'Annunzio to harangue the troops, the convoy moved closer to the famous Bar of Cantrida which marked D'Annunzio's personal Rubicon. They were met by a former group of General Zoppi's *arditi*, who had been sent to halt their progress, but who were soon won over to the cause and provided D'Annunzio with further welcome reinforcements. A mile from the barrier General Pittaluga demanded D'Annunzio's withdrawal, at which point D'Annunzio made the famous Napoleonic gesture of inviting Pittaluga to shoot him, offering him his medal-draped chest. The mock heroics of this and other actions are put into proper perspective by J. N. Macdonald, whose caustic remarks sum up the reality of the situation:

On the stage of any country, such a scene might not appear so utterly ludicrous, but in the world of fact it would have been impossible in any rather than a Latin nation—a General entrusted with the command of an important area, threatened by a rebel Lieutenant-Colonel at the head of a thousand men, after a few moments of feigned resistance, eventually taking the arch-rebel's hand and encouraging him in his project.[38]

The rebellious column moved on to the barrier itself, where it was the turn of another high-ranking officer, General Ferrero, to try his powers of persuasion. One of the armoured cars decided the issue by crashing through the bar, followed closely by the 'Legion', by now swollen in strength and growing all the time as stragglers and volunteers joined it *en route*. At 11.45 a.m. on 12 September 1919 Fiume fell, without a blow being struck, and bells, sirens, and cheering crowds made it clear that the 'invasion' was welcome to the more boisterous Italian section of the populace.

[37] Guido Keller is a fascinating minor player in the drama: see his biography by A. Ferrari, *L'asso di cuori: Guido Keller* (Rome, 1933). Estimates of the size and make-up of the force vary according to the political stance taken by commentators. Giannantoni's *Vita di GD'A*, 500, mentions fifty troop transports and seven armoured vehicles; Alatri, *GD'A*, omits the number of transports and adds that there were four armoured vehicles; Ledeen, *The First Duce*, 66, plumps for twenty-six troop transports; more naïve testimonies are recorded as an appendix to E. Ledda's interesting compilation, *Fiume e D'Annunzio* (Chieti, 1988). Sovera Latuada's account renders well the panic and the tension of the situation before the vehicles were procured: 'Giuseppe Sovera's Role', 340.

[38] Macdonald, *A Political Escapade*, 96; the incident was reported by most Italian newspapers: see *Il popolo d'Italia* of 13 Sept. 1919.

By the time D'Annunzio entered Fiume his motley crew amounted to some 2,500 men, adventurers, disillusioned veterans, notably the tough *arditi*, Futurists, and schoolboys, but now they also included that frontline detachment of Sardinian Grenadiers under Carlo Reina, who had previously garrisoned Fiume and who were passionately enthusiastic about returning there to recover the territory for Italy. By the afternoon of 12 September, while the Italian government was hesitating about its official position, D'Annunzio had already lowered the Allied colours, raised the Italian flag, and, from the balcony of the governor's palace, harangued the local populace and his enthusiastic volunteers; all these events were observed and reported on by the British military observers.[39] Pictures of the event also show how D'Annunzio had theatrically draped over the balcony the flag in which had been wrapped the coffin of Giovanni Randaccio, well known to everyone present as the local hero who had died fighting bravely alongside the poet in the struggle to free Dalmatia in 1917. D'Annunzio asked the approval of the towns-people below in the square for his plan to annex the city to Italy, and the crowd gave him total and enthusiastic support.

Next day, 13 September 1919, General Pittaluga handed over military control to D'Annunzio. The Allies in Paris considered the matter to be a problem to be resolved in the first instance by the Italian government, and following the reasoned (and aristocratic) pleas and reassurances of General Di Robilant, all the Allied troops, except the French and the Yugoslavs, were persuaded to leave the city by 14 September, in order to allow the Italians to settle their own rebellion in their own way; even the French and Serbs were gradually convinced that it would be better to withdraw. A telegraphed report from Sir Rennell Rodd, British ambassador in Rome, no doubt added the confidence of complacency to the Foreign Office's decision to sanction troop withdrawals; in it he summed up the recent naval telegrams, made a synthesis of newspaper reports (which he considered indicated Italian popular disapproval of D'Annunzio and his activities), and added a reassuring note concerning the legendary severity of General Badoglio, sent to Fiume to demand the rebels' surrender. The one note of doubt in Rodd's on the whole ingenuous communication was whether Badoglio, or anyone else, could

---

[39] Telegrams from Admiral Sinclair and Lieutenant-Colonel Peck were sent assiduously to Lord Curzon's office during these first two days.

persuade Italians to fire upon their own compatriots. Indeed, if Rodd could have known of a secret dispatch sent by Badoglio to Nitti on 27 October 1919 he might have been even less sanguine: 'Your Excellency considers that D'Annunzio can be convinced with words and can withdraw from his objectives. That is completely unrealistic. D'Annunzio and company will withdraw from Fiume only when their object is accomplished. All reasoning, all discussion is perfectly futile.'[40] In an unconsciously amusing digression, Ambassador Rodd mentioned the Italian-government-backed project to sponsor a flight by D'Annunzio to Japan, which was now, he feared, a feint with which D'Annunzio had played along in order to put officialdom off the true scent, the attack on Fiume.[41]

The aristocratic mien of Di Robilant, the renowned severity of Badoglio, and the false peace of mind generated by Rodd's telegram strengthened the Foreign Office in its decision to allow things to drift further. Opposition to the British (and Allied) action, or lack of action, seems to have been limited to the *New Statesman*, which published an intelligent article on 4 October 1919, warning of the dangers of political indifference in such a potentially explosive situation. D'Annunzio's actions were more robust and energetic: Giovanni Giuriati was at once nominated head of his improvised Cabinet, Carlo Reina, head of military staff, and Orazio Pedrazzi was placed in charge of the press office. In addition D'Annunzio chose Eugenio Coselschi as his personal secretary and Guido Keller as freelance quartermaster and morale-booster. Four Italian vessels in the harbour, including the cruiser *Dante Alighieri*, were persuaded to remain and for a while formed part of D'Annunzio's navy, despite the efforts of Vice-Admiral Mario Casanuova who was sent post-haste to Fiume with the destroyer *Stocco* to attempt to withdraw the ships. When the vice-admiral arrived, he was forced to admit his inability to take action or to control his sailors and telegraphed Rome to that effect.[42] And when General Badoglio warned the soldiers in D'Annunzio's ranks that they were guilty of

---

[40] Alatri, *Nitti, D'Annunzio e la questione adriatica*, 285.

[41] This important document, FO.371.3509/129005, was sent at 13.17 on 13 Sept., received in London at 08.45 on 14 Sept., read and judged by the secretaries in the Foreign Office on 15 Sept., and finally initialled by Curzon on 16 Sept.

[42] For the text of his telegram and for the vice-admiral's dilemma, see GD'A, *La penultima ventura: Scritti e discorsi fiumani*, ed. R. De Felice (Milan, 1974), introduction, p. xx.

desertion, the poet reacted with another fierce denunciation of the Italian government's stance.

D'Annunzio's disillusionment with the as yet powerless Mussolini was equally great. De Felice and Mariano's edition of their correspondence publishes in full a fascinating letter sent to Mussolini by D'Annunzio on 16 September, reproaching him for his inaction. Mussolini cunningly reproduced what he called a facsimile of the letter in his *Popolo d'Italia*; in fact, with a clever use of scissors and paste, the Duce had first excised the adverse comments which D'Annunzio had directed at him personally, and at the unsupportive Nitti government. It is interesting to see the phrases which Mussolini expunged (here placed in square brackets) before publishing the remaining pro-fascist fragments:

My dear Mussolini,

[I am astonished at you and at the Italian people.]

I have risked all, I have accomplished all, I have gained all. I am master of Fiume, of the territory, one part of the armistice line, ships, and of soldiers who are willing to obey only me. Nothing can be done against me. No one can remove me from here. I have Fiume; I hold Fiume for as long as I live, unconquerably.

[You tremble with fear! You have there the most abject con-man ever brought to light in the history of the scum of the universe and you let him set his porcine foot on your neck. Any other country—even Lapland— would have overthrown that man, those men. And there you are prattling away while] we struggle on from moment to moment, with an energy which has created from this enterprise the most beautiful exploit since the departure of Garibaldi's Thousand. [Where are the combatants, the shock troops, the volunteers, the futurists?]

Other uncomplimentary phrases followed, all of which Mussolini excised from his published version:

[Is there nothing to hope for? What about your promises? At least prick that belly which weighs you down, let some of the air out. Otherwise I shall make my way there when I have consolidated my power here. But I shall not deign to look you in the face.][43]

Mussolini's immediate response was the forged facsimile published on 20 September; thereafter that 'supportive' letter of D'Annunzio's was republished many times in the fascist press and literary collections until 1941. Only in 1954 was the original text published, and

---

[43] *Carteggio D'Annunzio–Mussolini*, 9–10.

by then D'Annunzio's critical support in the country was so weak that no one was willing to exhume the facts which might vindicate that early contempt for Mussolini and his fascists.[44] For the moment Mussolini needed the support which he imagined might be forthcoming from associating himself with the popular hero, and, anyway, he had no alternative at the time. He immediately began to raise money for D'Annunzio's enterprise, and on 25 September wrote to him suggesting a six-point plan to annex Fiume, including a march on Trieste, the overthrow of the monarchy, and the establishment of a Directoire of which D'Annunzio would be president.[45] D'Annunzio did not immediately respond to Mussolini's proposal, and much of the money raised for Fiume went, as Mussolini had anyway intended, into the Fascist Party coffers.

For D'Annunzio one effect of the capture of Fiume was surely meant to be the overthrow of the weak Nitti government; he was not alone in his surprise that the government had not already collapsed. On the contrary, however, Nitti dissolved parliament in an orderly fashion on 28 September 1919 and proclaimed new elections for 16 November. As if to counter Mussolini's plan for a Republican insurrection, on 30 September 1919 the Monarchist D'Annunzio expelled from Fiume two strong supporters of the anti-monarchical policy, the two most prominent Futurists of the time, Filippo Tommaso Marinetti and his lieutenant, Omero Vecchi. Soon afterwards Mussolini chose to come to Fiume to consult with D'Annunzio on 7 October. The poet by then must have been feeling full of self-confidence; many aeroplanes, flown by aces of World War One, had joined his forces and, the day before Mussolini's arrival, General Sante Ceccherini, one of the most revered of the recent war heroes, had come to Fiume and declared himself in favour of the annexation of the enclave. D'Annunzio was wholly delighted with the support of the general who had so impressed him personally with his courage and physical presence in the heat of battle. On 12 October 1919 D'Annunzio celebrated the 'sacred thirty days' since the taking of the city with a speech to the citizens which both exalted the capture of the city, and, more lengthily, praised the courage and sagacity, strength and inspiration of General

---

[44] The original was finally published by D. Susmel, *Carteggio Arnaldo–Benito Mussolini* (Florence, 1954), 223.
[45] *Carteggio D'Annunzio–Mussolini*, 21.

Ceccherini.[46] In the Ceccherini papers there is a signed memorial presented to the general to commemorate both his arrival in Fiume and his last previous meeting with D'Annunzio in the battle for the Veliki mountain:

> To Sante Ceccherini.
> . . . And as I gave you a small makeshift flag, you opened your tunic; and your chest shone as though your tricolour soul were shining through.
> Osservatorio delle Bombarde: October 1916
> Fiume d'Italia: October 1919[47]

The poet made Ceccherini his second-in-command, and, by 11 November 1920, when the regime began to crumble, created him, willy-nilly, inspector general of the troops and commander of the armed forces. The general settled in Fiume with his wife and daughter and for some ten months gave his firm and sincere support to 'the Cause'; then his growing scepticism and gradual disillusionment with affairs in the city culminated in his leaving Fiume in November 1920 after the Treaty of Rapallo, which effectively conceded all of the Fiumans' demands, but which D'Annunzio refused to accept.

The Italian elections of 16 November 1919 proved a shock to all on the right; instead of veering towards Mussolini's fascists, that part of the electorate which reacted against the old Liberal Party had chosen instead to support the Popular Party and the Socialists. Mussolini's own constituency gave him a derisory vote and no fascist deputies were elected. One symptom of Mussolini's political weakness between 1919 and 1920 is the number of ingratiating letters which he wrote to D'Annunzio at this time, ranging from pleas for any articles which the poet cared to write for his newspaper, *Il popolo d'Italia*, to specious statements which declared him ready to fight on D'Annunzio's behalf: 'I am your soldier' (where soldier implies that he had 'taken D'Annunzio's shilling' or *soldo*). But even though for Nitti and company the change of government seemed to be going smoothly and without right-wing upsets, there was still

---

[46] The speech, 'Nel trigesimo', is published in *Prose di ricerca*, i. 1068–71; the manuscript used by D'Annunzio was given by the poet to General Ceccherini (in an attempt to keep his goodwill) with the persuasive inscription 'To General Sante Ceccherini on the anniversary of his arrival. Fiume 6 October 1919–6 October 1920', but by then the game seemed to Ceccherini to be hardly worth the candle; the document is still in the archive of the Eredi Ceccherini.

[47] Archivio Eredi Ceccherini; D'Annunzio's actual words were 'una piccola bandiera di fortuna'.

an opportunity to provoke a revolt by extending the occupation of Fiume. Two days before the elections, at the head of 600 legionaries, D'Annunzio, making use of the warships that had been left at Fiume, led an expedition down the coast to Zara, where he had a meeting with the governor of Dalmatia, Admiral Enrico Millo, who swore that he would maintain the terms of the secret Treaty of London and hold fast to territory that was rightly Italy's. Millo's defiance of specific orders from the Rome government emphasized Nitti's weakness, and perhaps in consequence General Badoglio was finally authorized to offer D'Annunzio most of the concessions he had demanded concerning the annexation of Fiume. The poet insisted on remaining as head of the National Council of Fiume and stipulated that the amnesty to be conceded to all combatants in the Fiume enterprise should also be extended to Admiral Millo. The Fiuman National Council voted to accept the Rome government's generous terms on 15 December 1919, despite D'Annunzio's delaying tactics. At the same time it should be added that Giovanni Comisso, in the authoritative account of his service as a subaltern in Fiume, alleged that the populace was deceived by the Rome authorities into thinking that a positive vote for accepting Nitti's terms would also ensure that D'Annunzio would remain in power.[48] But the 'Comandante' saw the great adventure ending in an anticlimax of diplomatic acquiescence and this was probably why, although he had obtained nearly all his demands from Rome, he insisted upon putting the matter to a popular referendum, heavily prejudiced in favour of his remaining in Fiume as Regent. The wording ran as follows:

Do you agree to welcome the proposal of the Italian government, declared acceptable by the National Council at its session of 15 December 1919, which releases Gabriele D'Annunzio and his Legionaries from their oath to hold Fiume until annexation has been decreed and put into effect?[49]

In spite of emotional appeals by D'Annunzio the voting still seemed to be going in favour of accepting Nitti's terms. The plebiscite was then deliberately interfered with; some voting slips were stolen; attempts were made by strong-arm groups to prevent the declaration of the result; D'Annunzio ordered the suspension of the count and declared that the accord with Badoglio had been broken off.

[48] G. Comisso, *Le mie stagioni* (Milan, 1951), 33–4.
[49] For the text of the plebiscite see Alatri, *GD'A*, 438–9.

Giuriati condemned the poet's decision and resigned as head of D'Annunzio's 'Cabinet' on 23 December 1919, joining forces with Reina, who had already left at the beginning of the negotiations with Badoglio, having concluded that the government's terms were reasonable. These moderates were soon replaced by less scrupulous revolutionaries, including Alceste De Ambris, a well-known anarchist-cum-trade unionist, who took Giuriati's place and whose help D'Annunzio invoked in his later attempt to write a new constitution for the Fiume, the Carnaro Charter, which in theory at least would give some sort of legal justification to a continuing occupation.

The most probable explanation for D'Annunzio's dismissal of the popular vote was that he was fundamentally unwilling to let go of the absolute power which he now experienced for the first time in his life. Apart from the trappings of political and military power, he had a constant supply of women to gratify his sexual appetites and he was able to engage in other self-indulgent practices for which no one was in a position to reprove him (he seems also to have been experimenting with drug-taking at this time). He was as near as he ever came to being a Renaissance despot: Fiume was for the poet the high point of his life. The adventure, rather like an improbable schoolboy escapade, revived his youth at a time when he was declaring that he would give the whole of the *Alcyone* to be 24 years old again. Psychologically, despite his great intelligence and his creative genius, which had certainly put him into the first rank of Italian writers, D'Annunzio never seemed to develop beyond adolescence. It has been noted that there is no evidence that D'Annunzio ever showed regret or compassion or even consideration for others once they had gratified a temporary whim; selfish egotism governed his every action And one of the most significant legacies he left to fascism was the vulgar, indeed obscenely dismissive, motto *Me ne frego*, which had adorned his letter-head for several years already, and which he would send even in friendly letters to innocuous acquaintances, such as Ojetti.[50] It had been the watchword of the *arditi*

---

[50] See *Carteggio D'Annunzio–Ojetti*, 122, on notepaper headed *Me ne frego*, he writes, 'My dear Ugo, welcome. Welcome Madam Nanda! [. . .] Would you like to come to Villacoublay tomorrow, Sunday?' A stronger variant on *Me ne frego*, the more vulgar *Me ne strafotto* was also inscribed on banners, one of which greets tourists as they enter the museum at the Vittoriale. *Fregarsi*, the plebeian expression for 'to masturbate', has now become so much a part of everyday Italian that the most strait-laced matrons will use it to express their indifference, without a thought for its original meaning.

during World War One, and D'Annunzio had the motto inscribed on flags in Fiume in order to show his contempt for the Allied ultimata and for the government of Italy in particular. *Me ne frego* certainly typified his egocentric genius. His advocates might ask, 'Who is to judge such a man by parochial standards?', but perhaps in accordance with what has just been referred to as his arrested adolescence, the adventure of Fiume always gives the impression of a gigantic boy-scout jamboree, or of youth playing at war, but, tragically, using real ammunition. Osbert Sitwell captured some of the less serious atmosphere in his visit to Fiume as a correspondent for the *Nation* during the final days of D'Annunzio's regency:

D'Annunzio had invited an eminent Italian conductor to bring his orchestra over from Trieste and give a series of concerts, and had provided for him a fight for the orchestra to witness. Four thousand troops, among whom were the Garibaldian veterans whom we had seen—one aged seventy-eight and the other eighty-four—had taken part in the contest and one hundred men had been seriously injured by bombs. The members of the orchestra, which had been playing during the quieter intervals, fired by a sudden access of enthusiasm, dropped their instruments, and charged and captured the trenches. Five of them were badly hurt in the struggle.[51]

The eminent conductor was Arturo Toscanini. Sitwell probably exaggerated for the benefit of his newspaper audience but Comisso also mentions Toscanini's performance and the 'battle' and says that some instruments were shattered by shrapnel fragments; another part of this seemingly unlikely story is casually confirmed by a letter of D'Annunzio sent to Guido Treves on 3 July 1922. With the letter he enclosed a speech, 'unknown in Italy', ready for printing, which was, he wrote, delivered after an exercise of the *arditi* with hand-grenades, machine-guns, and flame-throwers, 'I had forty wounded, and one of the musicians, an orchestral professor was also injured, on the lip'. The stirring speech included phrases directed at the orchestra, of the kind: 'You are more than a perfect orchestra. For the *arditi* of Fiume you are a resonant battalion of assault troops [*un sonante battaglione di assaltatori*].'[52]

---

[51] Sitwell, *Noble Essences*, 123–4.
[52] Comisso, *Le mie stagioni*, 46; cf. 'Dal *Notturno* al *Venturiero senza ventura*: 32 lettere inedite a Guido Treves', an anonymous article containing unpublished letters of D'Annunzio, in *Nuova antologia*, 73/1584 (16 Mar. 1938), 128. The speech 'La legione orfica' (The Orphic Legion), dated 20 Nov. 1920, is available in GD'A, *La penultima ventura*, 383–6, here 386; not untypically D'Annunzio referred to Toscanini as Re Arturo (King Arthur): see Andreoli, *D'Annunzio archivista*, 189.

For the legionaries, campsite rhetoric and camaraderie alternated with dressing up in military uniform, often personalized, as Sitwell colourfully noted, to suit the character of the individual concerned:

We gazed and listened in amazement. Every man here seemed to wear a uniform designed by himself: some had beards, and had shaved their heads completely, so as to resemble the Commander himself, who was now bald; others had cultivated huge tufts of hair, half a foot long, waving out from their foreheads, and wore, balanced on the very back of the skull, a black fez. Cloaks, feathers and flowing black ties were universal, and every man— and few women were to be seen—carried the 'Roman dagger'.[53]

D'Annunzio gave almost daily harangues, which were regarded as entertainment in themselves. But there were other diversions available:

The officers, and especially the 'Commander' are having a very good time. The consumption of alcohol and wine is considerable. It is a known fact that Gabriele D'Annunzio spends most of his evenings at the Restaurant Ornitorinco, with his mistress, where he drinks numerous bottles of champagne, and from where he seldom returns before late in the morning.

That particular confidential account of D'Annunzio's excesses was received with some amusement by the Foreign Office secretaries who filed the secret report from a 'perfectly reliable' source, noting in the margin 'D'Annunzio seems to be having the time of his life at Fiume. This is an interesting picture of life there.'[54] The rank and file were not slow to follow their leader's decadent life-style and the city soon became a byword for immorality. Drugs, particularly cocaine, were in common use. Indeed, in a letter to Ceccherini dated 18 October 1919, D'Annunzio complained about slanderous rumours, and wondered whether it was worth the trouble to work and worry so much 'to keep alive such a crowd of rabble stuffed with phrases and crammed full of drugs' (*tanta canaglia imbottita di frasi e infarcita di droghe*). Comisso's account goes on to describe the atmosphere of free love, and the liberal sexual conventions (to which he, along with Guido Keller and D'Annunzio's American

[53] Sitwell, *Noble Essences*, 118–19. Sitwell's account is more than confirmed by L. Kochnitzky, *La quinta stagione, o i Centauri di Fiume* (Bologna, 1922), in particular his description of the orgiastic dancing ('unchecked Bacchanalia'), which filled the piazzas and characterized the Festa of San Vito, 15 June 1920 (p. 52).

[54] The anonymous report, from 'an ex-British Vice-Consul', is preserved in the Public Record Office, FO.371.3512/178857.

liaison officer, Henry Furst, subscribed heartily) which, without question, he states, allowed homosexual *arditi* to wander off hand in hand to the twilit hillsides. Venereal disease was rife and Comisso interrupts his normally idyllic account in order to describe a visit to a hospital devoted entirely to that scourge.[55] Father Macdonald attributed D'Annunzio's capricious and outrageous speeches to the possibility of venereal disease: 'The Poet's constant orgies, and the disease from which he was commonly reported to be suffering, so affected his brain as to render him irresponsible alike for his words and for his actions.'[56]

On a slightly higher cultural level, there were also concerts, such as the one described by Sitwell, and recitals by Luisa Baccara, to which D'Annunzio would issue particular invitations to select officers and dignitaries. One such, dated 26 June 1920, was solicited by Sante Ceccherini, and the poet, in a typically friendly letter, responded:

My very dear friend,

Luisa Baccara tells me that she is happy to be able to help you out by offering a concert in honour of your Florentine friends.

This being so, fix up a day and a time so that we can make the announcement.

26 June 1920   Your
                                     Gabriele[57]

There were also social visits by such distinguished personages as Guglielmo Marconi, for whom D'Annunzio was anxious to put on a good show of military pomp.[58] And when it became difficult, because of the expected blockades, to provision the town, D'Annunzio arranged for one of his officers, Captain Mario Magri, to organize raiding-parties, in order to find the necessary food and

---

[55] Comisso, *Le mie stagioni*, 41–2 and 45.

[56] *A Political Escapade*, 128; Macdonald later refers to D'Annunzio's *excesses* in a favourite restaurant, the *Cervo d'oro* (Golden Stag), after which he decreed that 'the restaurant should be known as *Ornitorinco d'oro* (Golden Platypus). The suggestion was applauded, but very few of the guests perceived the nauseous allusion' [to the platypus's disgusting if mythical digestive system]. Comisso, (p. 35) wrote that Keller stole a stuffed platypus and placed it on the poet's table to mock his baldness. Mario D'Annunzio, *Mio padre, Comandante di Fiume* (Genoa, 1956), 92, says that the badly painted inn sign resembled a platypus.

[57] Archivio Eredi Ceccherini.

[58] A note to Ceccherini, dated 22 Sept. 1920, tells the general of Marconi's arrival that day at 14.00 hours: 'He must be treated with honour; we shall go to await his arrival; please give orders for a military presence when he lands' (Archivio Eredi Ceccherini).

material. To the men who made up those raiding-parties D'Annunzio gave the name of *uscocchi* (corsairs), originally a term reserved for Serbian pirates; these buccaneers ranged far and wide, re-routing vessels with fat cargoes to the docks of Fiume. They often enrolled as seamen on board ships so that they could force the legitimate crew to sail round to Fiume. Their first sally netted the merchant ship *Trapani* just before the end of 1919; their most profitable coup was on 5 September 1920 when they boarded the steamer *Cogne* in Catania harbour; the ship was bound for Argentina, laden with a cargo of silk, cars, watches, clocks, and other luxury goods. The worth of the cargo is disputed, but the whole had a total value of something like 200 million lire—a vast sum in those days. When the *Cogne* sailed into the port of Fiume, D'Annunzio offered to sell its cargo to the Italian government, which, understandably, declined to purchase, and declared any sale illegal. D'Annunzio immediately threatened to put the whole cargo up for auction on the quay-side, as he had done with other booty, including all the equipment which the Allied detachments had unwisely left behind in the city. Eventually, after negotiations with the government and the ship-owners mediated by a consortium of wealthy businessmen, D'Annunzio and his gang received a ransom of 12 million lire for the ship and its cargo.[59] Piratical coups became so frequent that some doubt has been cast upon the traditional view that these were all daring raids by D'Annunzio's buccaneers. Alatri suggests that the *Cogne* affair, for instance was simply an excuse for the supportive Senator Borletti, to organize donations from groups of business-men in Milan, thus affording them the opportunity to subsidize a movement whose repercussions might encourage right-wing politics on the mainland. Further doubt is cast upon the authenticity of the piracy by Father Macdonald, whose suspicions reinforce some of Alatri's ideas:[60] noting how appropriate certain captured cargoes were to specific needs of Fiume at given periods, he suggests that these were proof that the 'capture' of certain ships was an unofficial way of provisioning D'Annunzio's beleaguered garrison. Piracy

[59] Gatti, *GD'A* 374, gives a useful selection of local newspaper accounts of the capture of the *Cogne*.

[60] See Alatri, *GD'A*, 451, and Macdonald, *A Political Escapade*, 156: 'At first the pretence was kept up [. . .]. Later the fiction that the ships had been comman-deered by the rebels was no longer kept up.' Macdonald also noted the apparently inexhaustible supply of Red Cross parcels sent from the mainland and offloaded at Fiume.

interested the British newspaper-reading public, and these actions found a ready market in the *Times* and other journals. At one point the acts of piracy became convincing enough and seemed serious enough for the British Foreign Office to allow visas on 23 October 1919 to Italian secret agents enabling them to pass through Gibraltar in order to prevent D'Annunzio's fifth columnists from corrupting the crew of the Austrian ship *Mrav*.[61]

Spirits among the largely unpaid troops were not always high, and there was always a risk of a withdrawal of support. Partly to provide a diversion, partly to shock opponents outside the enclave, D'Annunzio captured Arturo Nigra, one of the blockading generals who was particularly opposed to the rebels. Seized by the *arditi* on 26 January 1920, the general was held captive for a fortnight. The poet wrote proudly to Sante Ceccherini:

My dear Sante,
    Last night I captured General Nigra, the detested adversary [*l'esoso avversario*]; I hold him prisoner and hostage, keeping all my options open.
    The capture was executed with supreme elegance. The order, given at 19.00 hours was carried out at 2.00 in the morning.
                    Good Morning to you![62]

The presence of General Nigra in the city also had a practical purpose: it prevented a recurrence of threats and incursions against the vulnerable airport, which lay outside the perimeter of the town; an explanatory if anonymous proclamation concerning the kidnapping appeared in the *Vedetta d'Italia* on 10 February 1920.

There were other similar incidents. One of a minor kind took place on 18 April 1920, when the *uscocchi* captured forty-six first-class horses from the Italian troops based at nearby Abbazia, where, incidentally, the British mission was by now also resettled. The Italian detachment threatened to increase pressure on the blockade if the horses were not returned. The *uscocchi* then rounded up forty-six of their own starving nags which D'Annunzio's men could no longer feed, and these living skeletons were handed over in exchange, except fourteen, which the troops took the opportunity of eating.[63] The forces of the establishment were, naturally, livid,

[61] FO.371.4264/144589.   [62] Archivio Eredi Ceccherini.
[63] The events are reported in the *Vedetta d'Italia* for 24 and 28 Apr. 1920; D'Annunzio's main riposte was a clever speech, 'The Horse of the Apocalypse' of 27 Apr. 1920, now available in GD'A *La penultima ventura*, 241–8.

and the newspapers chortled merrily. So far the adventure had been going along like something from *Swallows and Amazons*. But a few days after the horse-rustling incident, a company of *carabinieri* attempted to leave Fiume to join their regiment. D'Annunzio issued an order:

All the Carabinieri and the Battalion Firenze, which had already begun its march to go past the Bar, must be allowed past the Bar without delay. This evening Fiume must be purged of all traitors.

Fiume d'Italia   6 May 1920   19.00 hours[64]

But the 'traitors' encountered a hostile group of *arditi*, and at the frontier post two soldiers were killed.

In other respects the regime had, only a couple of months into the occupation, produced hardship and privation in the town, and was in danger of becoming oppressive to many of the locals, in spite of the fact that well over half of Fiume's population was Italian; hence the willingness of the Fiuman National Council to agree to hold the plebiscite to decide whether to accept the Italian government's terms for a *modus vivendi*. It should be added that those terms included the proclamation of a free Fiume, defended by Italian troops, who would also guarantee its sovereign rights and independence, with no possibility of later negotiations changing its status. Nevertheless that prosaic prospect of losing supreme command and reverting to the banality of an administrative governorship must have appalled D'Annunzio.[65] Life was too exciting in so many new ways; to become even semi-respectable as a governor would put inhibiting limits on his dissolute, indeed debauched, life as the Duce of what was in effect a free state. Some indication of the way that D'Annunzio hesitated over Badoglio's terms, and his reluctance to lose his absolute power, is visible in some of the notes in the *taccuini* for the evening of 18 December 1919:

The day of the vote. Sense of tragedy in the city. 'We shall leave with our dead at the head of the column.' The atrocious song. The excitement. The

---

[64] Archivio Eredi Ceccherini.

[65] Some confirmation of that was later revealed in D'Annunzio's final letter to Sante Ceccherini, when, requested to lay down his power after the Treaty of Rapallo of 11 Nov. 1920, the poet protested at the cruelty of the imposition: 'I am the Commandant, and I remain the Commandant' (Archivio Eredi Ceccherini, letter dated 24 Nov. 1920); cf. above p. 315 and n. 1.

walk in the old city. Weeping women. The Roman arch. The stone. The vote. Arrival of the messenger from Rome. Visit to the National Council. The plebiscite annulled.[66]

But the situation in the city deteriorated until its anarchy and immorality were denounced by all who witnessed the events there. D'Annunzio's *taccuini* become a catalogue of exotic flesh, as he hints at the diverse women he enjoyed. The population of Fiume suffered privations and began to murmur against the occupation. Hundreds of children had to be evacuated to Milan and environs in mid-February 1920. Thereafter D'Annunzio had to work hard at his speeches and his emotional appeals to keep the crowd on his side. He gained some encouragement from the fall of Nitti's government on 11 May, and of a third, re-formed, Nitti administration on 9 June 1920, though the subsequent re-election of Giovanni Giolitti proved D'Annunzio's ultimate downfall.

On 27 August 1920 D'Annunzio published the Carta del Carnaro, the Carnaro Charter, a remarkable document which gave universal suffrage to the people, insisted on schools free of political and religious propaganda and influence, guaranteed freedom of the press, free trade-union association, and listed many other liberal measures. Its statements are the exact antithesis of anything that was to be promulgated by Mussolini's government in the coming decades, and it is one of the documents which most strongly argues for D'Annunzio's indifference, if not hostility, to what he considered the vulgar regime which has so often been seen as a consequence of his actions. The Charter itself was not without its little idiosyncrasies. Its sixty-five clauses contain many references to the Muses. 'The kingdom of the human spirit has not yet begun', one clause announced. To create such a realm there was to be a cult of music as a social and religious institution (*una istituzione religiosa e sociale*, statute no. 64). This rather impractical-sounding project was in keeping with D'Annunzio's character and outlook: music and the arts were useful to society because they stimulated thoughts of a higher, more noble, kind. Osbert Sitwell, in many of his remarks, is a good witness to D'Annunzio's attitude; for example, when Sitwell was first admitted to the presence in 1920 D'Annunzio's first question to him was: 'Well, what new poets are there in England?'

[66] *Taccuini*, 1175–8.

Sitwell comments, 'Not, you will notice, "What new generals are there?" or "Who plays centre-forward for Arsenal nowadays?".' Sitwell, unlike most of his contemporaries, was sympathetic to the genuine love of literary culture which D'Annunzio invariably showed, and Sitwell's contemporary comments on the barbarity of Eton and of his fellow Brits were well known.[67] If any confirmation of Sitwell's attitude were needed, it may be seen in the contrast between his opinions and the viewpoint expressed in the *Times* on 13 September 1919, the day before that newspaper began its attacks on the poet. The report is one of the usual eulogies of D'Annunzio's war career; I limit myself to one sentence: 'Signor D'Annunzio has proved himself as good a man of action as any healthy normal Englishman, who would no more read a line of poetry than he would write one.' A version of Sitwell's essay published in 1925 included an appendix which contained just clauses 64 and 65 of the Carnaro Charter.[68]

The reactions of the British Foreign Office to these antics of D'Annunzio's were predictable.[69] Cabinet papers show that it regarded the initial invasion as a temporary hitch in the peace negotiations. The regular reports from its military command in Abbazia increased the distrust felt by F. G. F. Adam, a product of Eton and King's College Cambridge; initially he had considered that the government of Nitti was acting in collusion with D'Annunzio in an attempt to make Dalmatia permanently Italian. (In fact D'Annunzio's public contempt for Nitti was well known in Italy.) The *Daily News* of 16 December 1919, swallowing hook line and sinker Orazio Pedrazzi's propaganda, had headlines which Adam found disturbing: 'D'Annunzio Wins'; 'Italy to have Complete Sovereignty at Fiume'; 'Rebels to Return to Army as Heroes'. The cutting, pasted up in the Foreign Office papers, had a marginal note, 'encouraging the newspapers to deny D'Annunzio's success'.[70] By 24 December 1919 the *Times* had launched a series of articles ridiculing D'Annunzio as a madman:

[67] Sitwell, *Noble Essences*, 123.

[68] O. Sitwell, *Discursions on Travel, Art and Life* (London, 1925); 'Fiume and D'Annunzio' is at pp. 217–41. Walter Starkie included the same clauses in his *Waveless Plain*, 373–5.

[69] Further details on what follows are available in J. R. Woodhouse, 'D'Annunzio a Fiume: Testimonianze inglesi inedite o rare', in *L'Italia contemporanea: Studi in onore di Paolo Alatri*, 2 vols. (Naples, 1991), ii, 151–66.

[70] FO.371.3512/164931.

Like an adventurer of the Renaissance he made himself master of Fiume and acts accordingly. He thinks himself above all laws, proclaims that he is led by divine inspiration, says he is a seer, dreams of living for ever the life of a rebel, and talks wildly of bringing his sword to aid rebels all over the world—in Ireland, Egypt, India and Arabia.

His feelings, his words, and his actions are strangely unintelligible to any sane man. He really incarnates the characters of his decadent literature. It is a melancholy spectacle. Even those who had always condemned D'Annunzio as a mountebank begin now to fear that his case is more to be pitied than reproved. His psychology is all in this reflection, which he made the other day to a friend—'It is sad that this marvellous Middle Age should end thus'.

Adam noted in the margin on 27 December: 'D'Annunzio is near the end of his political career.'[71]

As usual, descriptions from the *Times* of hysterical scenes in Fiume were carefully cut out and pasted up in Cabinet papers, with comments from Adam to the effect that he was amused and satisfied with the way things were developing. One of the proposals which underlay the references to Ireland, Egypt, India, and Arabia in that article of 24 December and one which most annoyed the British was the so-called Lega di Fiume (League of Fiume) which had been dreamt up initially by the Belgian poet Léon Kochnitzky, whom D'Annunzio had welcomed to Fiume as a poetic ally. The League was intended to unite all oppressed peoples, and Kotch, as D'Annunzio called him, initially included in the association not only the Irish, the Egyptians, the Maltese, the Flemings, the Montenegrans, the Catalans, and other minorities, but even the exploited colonies of Chinese labourers in California. D'Annunzio treated Kotch's wild dreams as such and the Belgian soon abandoned Fiume a disillusioned man. But it did not require D'Annunzio's genius to realize that an alliance of Balkan peoples to prevent Serb domination of the area would help to keep Fiume independent. He also saw Ireland as a good irritant for the British, and the League harped upon the indomitable Sinn Fein. Four days after Adam's view that D'Annunzio's career was at an end, Lord Curzon added another marginal note, dated 31 December 1919: 'It is difficult to know how to act, and in these cases I follow the advice of the late lamented Lord Salisbury, who always used to say in the Foreign Office, "When

---

[71] The cutting, and the remark of Adam, are in FO.371.3512/165318.

you are really uncertain about anything, do nothing".' Thereafter in reports from Fiume 'No action' was often written in the margins, interspersed with those occasional amused reactions to reports in the *Times* of D'Annunzio's debauched visits to night-clubs. But despite Adam's unusually hasty judgement, it took another year before the *Times* could report on 30 December 1920: 'D'Annunzio Surrenders'. A mistaken report in that newspaper on the following day suggested that D'Annunzio had left Fiume by aircraft; the item provided a self-created excuse to write a leading article on D'Annunzio's abdication. The author, presumably the long-serving editor Geoffrey Dawson, there talks about the 'pitiful collapse of D'Annunzio's mock heroics' and goes on to underline another aspect of the situation which would figure in subsequent reports on D'Annunzio's activities: 'Italians have a keen sense of the ridiculous, and D'Annunzio's final proclamation, with its announcement that he is "still alive and inexorable", but no longer disposed to make the sacrifice of his life he had intended, is intended to appeal to it.'

But before the final débâcle, the Carta del Carnaro had been published, and on 8 September 1920 D'Annunzio was elected Regent by the governing council. He issued postage stamps, some adorned with a massive portrait bust of himself, while others sported inspiring views of the countryside around the enclave. The anniversary of the capture of Fiume was celebrated on 12 September with military pomp and circumstance, but by now the festive atmosphere was an obvious attempt to shore up the crumbling edifice. D'Annunzio's more respected and respectable followers had almost all deserted him. At the beginning of November 1920 Sante Ceccherini was to to intimate his disillusionment at D'Annunzio's promotion of incompetent favourites, and D'Annunzio wrote him daily letters to win back his goodwill. The poet's despair is visible in a letter written, not to the general, but to his wife, on 8 November:

My dear friend,

Help me, if you can, to avoid the great grief which is threatening me. You know how much I love and admire Sante. You know that I could never console myself for having lost him.

I have written to him,

I trust in your goodness.

I am dead from fatigue, but I shall not be able to sleep.

If you can, telephone me just one good word so that I can give some respite to my poor burning brain.

Telephone 'Sleep tranquilly'.
Yes?
I kiss your hands.
Good night to you and Ena.
>Your
>Gabriele d'Annunzio

Fiume
8 November 1920[72]

Thereafter several personal letters to Ceccherini attempted to mollify him and ensure that he stayed. Negotiations were in the meantime also continuing among the Allies, until on 11 November 1920 the Treaty of Rapallo, signed between Yugoslavia and Italy, established an independent state of Fiume. The last obstacle to D'Annunzio's withdrawal had been removed, and he was issued with an ultimatum to evacuate the town, with a deadline of 6 p.m. on 23 December 1920. The Vittoriale archive contains an almost tearful letter dated 21 November 1920, addressed by Ceccherini to his 'Commandant and dearest great friend', pleading with D'Annunzio to change his mind. And in the Ceccherini archive an equivocal but ultimately blustering reply from D'Annunzio states 'I have to consider you both [Ceccherini and his second-in-command colonel Sani] as deserters to the Cause in the face of the enemy'. On 24 November he reiterates, 'I am the Commandant and remain the Commandant. Thank you for what you have done for me and for the Cause. I thank you even for this grief. And I send you every good wish.' One final letter from Ceccherini dated 26 November suggests that he and Sani should make a last appearance with D'Annunzio, surrounded by the rest of his officers, in order that their sudden withdrawal should not arouse suspicions of a weakening of D'Annunzio's authority. Whatever the outcome of that suggestion, the drama moved to an inexorable close: the deadline had been given and, on Christmas Eve, Italian government troops began their advance. The timing had been well thought out by the experienced Giolitti: there were no newspapers on Christmas Day, and the Rome government was determined that by then the city would be retaken. There was stiff resistance, 150 casualties and fifty-six fatalities, evenly divided on both sides. Then a naval shell from the *Andrea Doria*, skilfully lobbed through the window of D'Annunzio's headquarters, narrowly missed his head: he surrendered.

---

[72] Archivio Eredi Ceccherini.

He left Fiume on 18 January 1921, said to be the last of the Fiuman legionaries to leave. The adventure was over. Walter Starkie allows a young Venetian acquaintance to sum up for him the final humiliation:

Poor decrepit old bard! I pity him. The youth of Italy has turned away from him. The Futurists have shouted him down and blown their motor-horns at him. Whom has he got on his side except a handful of 'Arditi' who remembered the *Beffa di Buccari* and remain yawning at their posts in the 'Vittoriale' for old times' sake? He stands pathetically on the shore beckoning to the rising sun, but the boat has put out to sea without him and his voice is lost in the wind.[73]

But what D'Annunzio had fought for remained. Fiume was in essence to stay Italian, along with the former Venetian possessions on the Dalmatian coast, until the Allies took them away from Mussolini's defeated Italy after World War Two.

The consequences of D'Annunzio's cavalier attitude to authority, his defiant march on Fiume, and his readiness to use armed force to sustain a nationalistic purpose were all-important examples for Mussolini and became precedents for what was to happen in Rome during the next two years. D'Annunzio lent no direct support to the fascist cause, but it was his attitude, inculcated by example into the youth of Italy at a crucial time, which provided all that Mussolini later needed. Roberto Vivarelli sums up well the effect of D'Annunzio's 'disobedience' upon the general political climate: 'In this way the sceptical distrust of the citizenry towards their free institutions increased more and more, and more and more any feeling of devotion to the public good, the necessary presupposition of every free and well-ordered civil society, withered and died.'[74]

And, rather as the Futurists had made a cult of 'arditism', so the *arditi* themselves created the notion of 'Fiumanism', a tendency that has its echoes even nowadays in Italy (and perhaps elsewhere in Europe) and one which reinforced the anti-authoritarian attitudes which Vivarelli examines. Indeed as we approach the new millennium, as the atrocities of the recent civil war in Yugoslavia become daily more evident during United Nations investigations, so the Fiuman Society is, fifty years on, investigating earlier atrocities

---

[73] Starkie, *The Waveless Plain*, 376; it is a view which chimes with Sitwell's more elegiac conclusion in his *Noble Essences*, 125.

[74] Vivarelli, *Storia delle origini del fascismo*, i. 587.

carried out against Italians by non-Italian elements in the town, following the collapse of the fascist regime at the end of World War Two. Passions still run high, and some of the zealots find inspiration in 'Fiumanism'. J. N. Macdonald threw this new abstraction into relief in his account of the first nine months of the invasion eighty years ago. As part of his source material Macdonald made good use of the weekly news-sheet of the *arditi* themselves, the *Testa di Ferro*, which defined Fiumanism in these terms:

Fiumanism is no longer a name; it is a precise and palpitating fact. At last we have a great and clear mission in the world. We are the advance guard of all nations on the march to the future. We are the island of wonder, which in its journey across the ocean will carry its own incandescent light to the continents stifled in the darkness of brutal commerce. We are a handful of illuminated beings and mystic creators, who will sow through the world the seed of our force—a force which is purely Italian and will germinate into the highest daring and violent irradiations.[75]

Macdonald makes it clear that in his view such abstractions were a mere smoke-screen to conceal the violent and often drunken racist hooliganism witnessed by him and others.[76]

Lord Curzon's Foreign Office secretaries were quick to move on to other matters as soon as D'Annunzio had been expelled from Fiume, and his name swiftly disappeared from British newspapers, but the consequences of Fiume were incalculable for the future development of European politics. More parochially, Britain's distrust of Italy and a general lack of confidence in Italian governments, apparently incapable of governing, became a natural part of policy thinking *vis-à-vis* Italy, conditioning the views and attitudes of Salisbury, Eden, and Chamberlain. For Mussolini, a further more subtle bonus was that D'Annunzio's abrupt and simultaneous withdrawal both from Fiume and from serious commitment to national politics left the field free for him. By taking over D'Annunzio's mantle, Mussolini also took over part of the intellectual respectability attached to the poet and the undoubted man of learning, and thus was also able to insinuate his message into the mind of the literate Italian middle and upper classes. On the wider stage

[75] Macdonald, *A Political Escapade*, 171.
[76] Giovanni Comisso describes the destruction of all Slav businesses as a reprisal by D'Annunzio following the killing of two Italian naval officers by the Yugoslavs at Spalato: *Le mie stagioni*, 54.

disrespect for democratically elected authority was to lead, through Mussolini's reckless inheritance of power, to a contemptuous disregard for the League of Nations. And, despite D'Annunzio's attempts to prevent an Italo-German axis, Mussolini's example could only foster the kind of nationalistic feelings which Hitler was later to exploit.

The Vittoriale:
Theatre of Memory

THE expulsion from Fiume was a considerable blow to the poet's pride, its bitterness increased by the thought that it had been accomplished at the instigation of Prime Minister Giolitti, D'Annunzio's political *bête noire*, and in his eyes a particularly contemptible figure. Having reached that particular peak of personal power, it was difficult to see what he could do next. His immediate reaction was a desire to withdraw from the company of all but his most intimate acquaintances—notably Luisa Baccara and Aélis, who joined him in Venice after he left Fiume on 18 January 1921. Just three days earlier Guido Treves, heir to the publishing house, had sent him a telegram suggesting the possibility of his renting a villa, sequestered from its former German owner, and located at Fasano on Lake Garda.[1] In Venice he still had the vast apartment in Palazzo Barbarigo, which he had rented after Fritz Hohenlohe had returned to the Casetta Rossa. There, awaiting him by courtesy of the French government, were the wagonloads of furniture and personal effects rescued from his creditors at the Chalet S. Dominique in Arcachon. To these he was to add various truckloads of belongings accumulated during his fifteen months in Fiume. Antongini describes the chaotic collection and the apartment, which 'appeared to him in the light of a vast depository rather than of an actual residence'.[2] D'Annunzio himself roamed aimlessly through the rooms eyeing the incredible disorder with a mixture of exasperation, melancholy, and high nervous tension. It should be said that most of those goods were not intrinsically valuable; astonishingly, as far as his acolytes

---

[1] This prophetic indication of D'Annunzio's future domicile was, according to Vito Salierno, an attempt to revive the business relationship between the house of Treves and D'Annunzio, Emilio Treves having died in 1916; for the telegram and a discussion of the incident, see Salierno, *D'Annunzio e i suoi editori*, 177.

[2] Antongini, *D'Annunzio*, 548.

were concerned, he had not used his position of power to seize valuables from the territories over which he had held temporary sway. All the effects, however, had some talismanic memory for him.

During the next weeks of seclusion in Venice D'Annunzio received various offers of villas and houses, rather similar to the offer made to him by Pescara over a decade earlier. Instead of accepting immediately, he asked six faithful friends to look for isolated houses, preferably far from railway lines and easily defensible from potential hordes of faithful if sentimental members of his old legions. To each property-scout he gave identical instructions, concluding, according to Antongini in a voice between tragic and jocose, 'If within eight days, none of you have found a suitable house for me, I shall throw myself into the canal, since I have no intention of camping any longer in this Venetian mausoleum'.[3] From his list of desirable locations he had mentally eliminated Sicily and the whole of southern Italy, and had drawn up a catalogue of specific requirements for his perfect residence: a garage for two cars—stables for at least three horses—a good concert grand piano—a bathroom—a laundry and pantry—heating—suitable arrangements for procuring, 'at a moment's notice', wood and coals—an enclosed garden—at least four servants' rooms. To the most trusted of all his 'marshals', Tom Antongini, he delegated responsibility for the locations around around Lake Garda. It was well known that in 1909 he had sided with the Nationalists, and particularly with their leader Luigi Federzoni, in Italian protests against the Germanization of the lake. He now informed Antongini why he had chosen him for that locality:

I have given you Lago di Garda because I feel that my Fate impels me to live there. You alone know my tastes, my vices and my virtues; the others see in me only the Comandante of Fiume, but luckily the tastes of the Comandante of Fiume are not those of Gabriele D'Annunzio.[4]

Within a week the explorers had returned to report to D'Annunzio at Palazzo Barbarigo. All proposals were dismissed except that of Antongini.

The house Antongini had chosen was the Villa Cargnacco, to all appearances a sizeable farmhouse with seventeen rooms of varying

---

[3] Antongini, *D'Annunzio*, the description of the scouting expeditions which followed is taken from Antongini.
[4] Ibid. 549.

sizes, secluded, in large grounds, soon to be extended by further purchases, and surrounded by beautiful shrubs and trees, some 300 yards from the village of Gardone Riviera, on a height dominating the lake and looking eastwards towards the Adriatic. Its plain and modest appearance was soon to be altered, but at first sight it hardly seemed grand enough for the Comandante; certainly the other five 'property marshals', whose explorations had revealed elaborate, castellated dwellings on the other lakes, did not take Antongini's discovery very seriously. Old pictures of the dwelling show the mortar of its façade crumbling somewhat, an old-fashioned iron balcony over the front door. In front of the house was a cobbled courtyard with olive trees; cypresses dotted the hillside. Below the main building, on a level with its terraced gardens, was a smaller house with eight rooms; there were several rougher outbuildings. Behind the main buildings, a small stream ran through the property at the bottom of a narrow ravine. Most of these features are still visible today, even in their reconstructed form. The villa had been built in the eighteenth century and had been sold in 1877 to the Austrian engineer Luigi Wimner, once mayor of Gardone, whose heirs had sold it to Heinrich Thode in 1910. Thode was a well-known professor of art history with an extensive library, which Antongini noted with pleasure had been left at the house when Thode and his second wife, as 'belligerents', were forced to leave Italy at the beginning of World War One. Thode's first wife, Daniela Senta von Bülow, was the step-daughter of Richard Wagner, while Daniela's mother, Wagner's second wife, was Cosima Liszt, daughter of the famous composer. Antongini commented with jubilation that when he was being shown around the house its custodian had, 'in tones of religious awe', pointed out a concert grand piano in the music room, which he said had belonged to Franz Liszt. There were also various musical souvenirs recalling the German composers, including volumes containing Wagner's autograph dedications, later to be bones of contention between D'Annunzio and the more legitimate heirs of Thode.[5]

With these accoutrements and associations, there was little wonder that it should appeal to D'Annunzio:

[5] More details are available in M. Bernardi, 'Storia del Vittoriale: Come D'Annunzio comprò la Villa di Cagnacco', *Quaderni del Vittoriale*, 20 (Mar.–Apr. 1980); see also Plates 13 and 14.

No sooner had D'Annunzio set foot in the villa of Cargnacco, walked through two or three of its rooms and opened a window into the garden than his decision was made. [. . .] From the first moment when D'Annunzio visited a house his mind was busy, almost subconsciously, planning alterations: in his imagination he was pulling down doors, widening windows, heightening walls, building on new rooms, and already visualizing the probable aspect of his new home.[6]

By 30 January D'Annunzio had leased the property for a year at a monthly rent of 600 lire; the villa at Fasano, which Guido Treves had proposed on 13 January 1921, would have cost three times as much. The poet made his plans for modernizing and, to use his expression, de-Germanizing, the house. At the beginning of February he was in Gardone, staying at the Grand Hotel with Luisa Baccara, and occasionally going up to the site to see how the alterations were proceeding. He had two pressing problems to overcome: the first was to get rid of the Bazzani–Cobelli family, who had looked after the property for many years and who were well installed in at least half a dozen of the rooms which D'Annunzio regarded as desirable for himself, including what was later to become his 'Dalmatian Oratory', which the family had discovered was a good place to hang their salami and hams for seasoning. They were persuaded to transfer their goods and four daughters to the adjacent cottage; it later became the guardaroba for the Vittoriale complex. The second problem was the perennial difficulty of funding the various repairs and modifications, which even at the outset included the installation of new central heating, electricity plant, and telephone. D'Annunzio began to play off, one against the other, the publishing houses of Mondadori and Treves, in the hope of getting higher advances. Arnoldo Mondadori, head of the publishing house, came to a meeting in Gardone on 25 March 1921; on 16 April D'Annunzio gave him the following ultimatum:

My dear friend, as I told you, I need to put my domestic affairs in order in Pescara. My mother has no tomb, my mother's house is in ruins; besides which I need to straighten out other family interests. Hence I must request, as a first instalment, 500,000 lire. I am very sorry to have to say that if this most justifiable request of mine is not satisfied, I have to ask you to leave me in peace.[7]

[6] Antongini, *D'Annunzio*, 554.
[7] For this negotiation and the letter to Mondadori, see P. Chiara's article, 'D'Annunzio e Mondadori', *Nuova antologia*, 116/2138 (Apr.–June 1981), 204. Punning on the publisher's name, D'Annunzio rechristened Mondadori 'Montedoro'

But on 6 July 1921 D'Annunzio signed an exclusive contract with the Treves company and received an advance, through their director, Giovanni Beltrami, of 200,000 lire.[8] The poet was playing a very clever, if unscrupulous, game. In 1921 the house of Treves supplied too few copies of the *Notturno* to satisfy public demand, and the poet would later use that failure to justify his preference for the new dynamism of Mondadori's presses. On 31 December 1931 he wrote to Guido Treves: 'Every day I receive complaints. The booksellers are without copies; someone asking for fifty volumes receives only six; others wait in vain; the impetus is halted. [. . .] And old habits must be broken once and for all; the ancient windows must be opened to let in the wind of fortune'.[9]

In December 1921 he mentioned *en passant* to Guido that the possibilities offered by Arnoldo Mondadori had nothing to do with his irritation at the old-fashioned policies of the Treves company.[10] Soon after signing the contract Beltrami discovered that D'Annunzio was negotiating for a 450-page volume to be published by Emanuele Castelbarco in his *Botteghe della poesia* series. The publisher's remonstrations were in vain; in a letter of 22 October 1922, D'Annunzio telegrammed Beltrami that Treves risked losing him as their author if the Castelbarco publication were impeded: 'With sorrow I declare to you that any hostile act against the book at this time will be considered by me as a definitive break between me and the Treves house—STOP—I shall undertake the consequences with my usual energy—STOP.'[11] Despite brilliant advocacy by Beltrami in a reply dated 23 October 1922, D'Annunzio's mind was obviously made up, and the campaign continued. In September 1923 he wrote a

(Mountain of Gold) for the advances he obtained from him; Mondadori, in turn, used a similar term to refer to D'Annunzio: see M. Giammarino, *Incontro con D'Annunzio* (Rome, 1988), 9. Further details of the relationship with the houses of Mondadori and Treves are available in Salierno, *D'Annunzio e i suoi editori*; the intrigues between D'Annunzio, Guido Treves, and Arnoldo Mondadori in the period 1921–6 have recently been re-examined by M. G. Sanjust, '"Chi 'l tenerà legato?": D'Annunzio e Treves', *Critica letteraria*, 91–2 (1996), 141–62.

[8] For details of the contract and of the correspondence between Beltrami and D'Annunzio see the stimulating article by V. Salierno, 'G. Beltrami e D'Annunzio: dalla Beffa di Buccari al *Venturiero senza ventura*', *Rassegna dannunziana*, 14/29 (May 1996), 21–34.

[9] 'Dal *Notturno* al *Venturiero senza ventura*', 124.

[10] Ibid. 125; D'Annunzio's letter is dated 7 Dec. 1921: 'Poor Mondadori is not to blame; I saw him for just a few moments; he was profuse in his praise of your edition.'

[11] From the correspondence in the Vittoriale archive, Guido Treves, inv. 25512.

particularly long letter complaining of the printer's inefficiency and delays, but their association continued for a further year, until Treves published *Il venturiero senza ventura e altri studi del vivere inimitabile* in 1924[12] and negotiated for the second volume of *Faville del maglio*, which was finally published in 1928. Some of the old cordiality seems to have returned to the letters exchanged with Guido Treves and Giovanni Beltrami, and D'Annunzio was never backward in telling his publishers how hard he was working for them:

On 21 [September] I shall begin to work 21 hours a day—three hours for food and sleep.

I shall come to Milan in a few days.

I am most unsettled, turbulent; some nights I have attacks of lycanthropy.[13]

The true relationship with the Treves house, despite the excellent work by Vito Salierno, will not be revealed until the full correspondence with Guido Treves is uncovered and published. It seems that D'Annunzio was able to separate in his mind his attacks on the publishing house, its antiquated machinery and lack of any spirit of adventure, and the personality of Guido Treves. Thus, as late as 23 April 1930, he invited the seriously ill Guido and his wife to holiday and recuperate on the estate in the Villa Mirabella, and his letter is full of affection. Five days afterwards he intimated that he could break previous contracts with Mondadori (returning the monies received so far) and take up again his rapport with the house of Treves.[14]

Meanwhile, after a government decree of 10 April 1921, the Villa Cargnacco officially passed into the possession of the local authority and it became possible for D'Annunzio to buy the house and grounds outright, though not, initially, the furnishings, for which he negotiated with Thode's widows for a considerable time.[15] To buy the property he obtained a loan of 360,000 lire from the Bank of Rome, though this sum never seems to have been paid back by him personally; after his death it was left to Arrigo Solmi, at that time president of the new Foundation of the Vittoriale, who is said

---

[12] It is worth noting, if the atmosphere was indeed so hostile, that on 23 July 1924 D'Annunzio congratulated Guido Treves on the volume, signing off 'I embrace you with all my heart, in gratitude and in my vows [*in gratitudine e in voto*]', see 'Dal *Notturno* al *Venturiero senza ventura*', 130.

[13] Salierno, 'G. Beltrami e D'Annunzio', 23.

[14] 'Dalla "Capponcina" al "Vittoriale"', anonymous article in *Nuova antologia*, 73/1585 (1 Apr. 1938), 361–83, here 370 and 371.

[15] See above, p. 355.

to have paid off the debt with monies which had accrued from the poet's royalties. Some of the expense would be mitigated after 1923 when D'Annunzio was allowed by Mussolini's new government to donate to the Italian people the already partially reconstructed villa, now renamed, with one of his inimitable coinings, the Vittoriale.[16] By that date it was in Mussolini's interest to keep the former popular hero away from the political limelight. How better to do this than to pander to his whims and keep him happy constructing his own physical obituary on the distant western shores of Lake Garda? It must have been gratifying to Mussolini, despite his professed support for the poet, to see D'Annunzio expelled from Fiume. Their joint plan for a march on Trieste and possibly on Rome had been quietly dropped by the fascist leader. When D'Annunzio emerged exhausted from the adventure in Fiume, coming as it had done on top of his years of service during World War One, his only declared ambition was to lose himself once more in creative writing.

But events around D'Annunzio were moving at a swift and inexorable pace. On 15 May 1921 Prime Minister Giolitti included in his list of potential political allies the names of thirty-five fascist candidates, and the party of Mussolini, which at the previous election had collected few votes and no seats, now found itself recognized at last and, because of Italy's system of parliamentary elections which was based on proportional representation, supported by Giolitti and his allies with sufficient votes to secure seats in the House. There is little evidence that the election results had any effect at all upon D'Annunzio. For the rest of that year he occupied himself with domestic matters, choosing paint and fabrics, making the occasional journey to Milan and Venice, continuing the game with Mondadori and Treves (and finally obtaining an advance of a million lire in royalties from the latter for an edition of his *Opera omnia*). He also worked to complete the *Notturno*, the account of his physical and psychological experiences and memories written during the period of 'blindness' at the Casetta Rossa; the volume had been informally promised to the Treves house since its composition in 1916. Published in December 1921 the book sold in record numbers, exhausting Treves's print-runs and subsequently generating a new trend for his earlier, less apparently fashionable, works: by February the

---

[16] The implications of the name (which implied in Late Latin 'pertaining to victory') are twofold: the 'result of victory' and the 'reward of victory', but there also is an obvious triumphalist ring to the word.

Notturno, in the translation by André Doderet, had begun to appear in the *Revue des deux mondes*. D'Annunzio also wrote six articles under the general title *International Naval Disarmament* for Randolph Hearst's *New York American* between 28 November 1921 and 30 April 1922, for which, according to Antongini, he received between $1,000 and $1,200 each. Antongini reported that D'Annunzio, desperate to find material for the final article, brought out an old piece written for the *Corriere della sera*, modifying it slightly. The modifications, multiplied in translation and in the garbled transmission though the telegraph system, rendered the article unrecognizable to the sub-editors of the *Corriere*, which published its own translation of the American text 'unaware that it was an old tenant of its own columns'. Antongini suggested to D'Annunzio that they try sending back a translation of the 'new' *Corriere* article to see what version would finally appear in the Hearst newspaper.[17]

D'Annunzio's position *vis-à-vis* Mussolini and the fascists was unclear, indeed he seems to have been courted for several years by left-wing activists diametrically opposed to Mussolini. For two years, between March 1922 and May 1924, he was official leader of the Federazione Lavoratori del Mare (Federation of Seaworkers), and tried to defend them against the worst effects of industrial oppression on the part of owners, who in their turn supported the fascists. At the same time that he was welcoming workers to the Vittoriale he also hosted a visit from the Russian foreign minister Jorgi Tchitcherin, his guest there for two days.[18] An apocryphal story circulated that Lenin had described D'Annunzio as the only revolutionary in Italy.[19] D'Annunzio's political views were always very equivocal, and in particular his rapport with the fascist regime, which, as Vivarelli wrote, is 'difficult to comprehend and lends itself to serious misunderstandings'.[20] Mario Carli gives as good a

---

[17] Antongini, *D'Annunzio*, 483; it should be added that Antongini's amusing anecdotes do not always convince Italian critics of their authenticity or of his veracity, though most critics use many of his statistics for their own purposes.

[18] The *Times* of 3 July 1922, in one of its few post-Fiume items on D'Annunzio, contains a curious report on the meeting of these two apparently incompatible minds.

[19] For this and other details of D'Annunzio's anti-fascist pronouncements, as well as his apparent sympathy for the workers, see Alatri, 'La ripresa dell'attività politica', in his *GD'A*, 502–11. It must be added that if Lenin actually said anything of the sort he was probably venting his sarcasm against the lack of revolutionary fervour in the Italian Socialists.

[20] Vivarelli, *Storia delle origini del fascimso*, 36.

summary as any in his study of D'Annunzio in Fiume, where he plumps for D'Annunzio, his own man:

D'Annunzio today is called 'comrade' by the Fiuman proletariat, just as yesterday he was called 'corporal' by the *arditi*, and 'sergeant' by the *bersaglieri*. Do not be surprised at anything: tomorrow he could be celebrating a fakir's ritual, or dancing the light fantastic with the most civilized Arabs of Egypt. It is the privilege of genius, this transition into a thousand forms of creation, and it is his secret how he remains immutably and miraculously himself.[21]

Certainly the fascist hierarchy seemed uncertain which way D'Annunzio's political feelings were running. Paolo Alatri sees the poet in this period as a pacifier, attempting, if anything, to build a bridge between the left-wing agitators, ready to strike for their rights, and the fascist *squadristi*, ready to make their opponents drink the ritual castor oil or beat the strikers into insensibility. The spirit of reconciliation reached a point where Tom Antongini was given the task of arranging a meeting between D'Annunzio, Mussolini, and Nitti, scheduled for 15 August 1922. Two days before, at eleven o'clock on the evening of 13 August, D'Annunzio had a mysterious fall from the garden window of the music room of the Vittoriale, while he was listening to an informal recital by Luisa Baccara. The fall effectively prevented the scheduled conciliatory meeting, but there are and will remain doubts concerning the facts of that particular evening. Was it simply a question of dizziness? Was he pushed, deliberately or accidentally, by one of the people in the room, among them Luisa's sister Jolanda? Or could it have been the action of Aldo Finzi, also said to be present that evening? Finzi had been with D'Annunzio in the famous leaflet flight over Vienna, but he was now a high-ranking official in the fascist central office. Was it a political act to prevent D'Annunzio from weakening the forces which two months later were to drive the fascists to march on Rome? Antongini is mysterious on the subject, possibly unwilling, in 1938 when his book was published, to indict the regime for attempting to kill D'Annunzio.[22] How serious were his

[21] Carli, *Con D'Annunzio a Fiume*, 125.

[22] The account of D'Annunzio's 'archangelic flight', as he termed it, from the window is omitted from the English translation of Antongini's biography; see Antongini, *Vita segreta*, 558. His account concludes: 'This mystery is interesting enough to merit a separate study'; in his later *Un D'Annunzio ignorato*, 194, Antongini again comments on the enigma, and wonders why the fascist government made so little fuss of such a serious accident to Italy's leading poet and littérateur.

injuries? His new French translator, André Doderet, arrived to see him a month later and noticed nothing amiss. His doctors, whose diaries D'Annunzio seems to have confiscated, were worried about his recovery after three days of an apparent coma. D'Annunzio himself, in the 'Avvertimento' (Notice) prefacing his *Libro segreto* implies, through his mouthpiece Angelo Cocles, that he had attempted suicide.[23] That particular observation continues with a description of his medical condition, obviously gained from the notes made by his doctors. D'Annunzio's children, Renata and Mario, who visited their father shortly afterwards, blamed the Baccara sisters for having caused the 'accident', but D'Annunzio was so indignant at that suggestion that he banished his children from sight and temporarily forbade them to return to the Vittoriale. D'Annunzio's archangelic flight has only recently begun to be investigated and may indeed have to remain a mystery, though an explanation will be attempted below.[24]

Mussolini had planned a spectacular march on Rome in order to consolidate his power and precipitate a crisis in Giolitti's Liberal administration which might increase pressure for a fascist coup. According to Antongini, D'Annunzio was not opposed to what Mussolini had in mind, 'but in his heart of hearts he was convinced that nothing decisive was to happen, and that it was necessary to leave everything to time'.[25] Mussolini had anyway, by various ploys, succeeded in keeping D'Annunzio calm with regard to the march on Rome (which was brought forward to 28 October 1922), and at least he seems to have persuaded the poet not to oppose the venture. In a letter of 28 October he wrote:

I do not ask you to line up at our side, though this would avail us greatly; but we are sure that you will not set yourself against this marvellous youth which is fighting for your and for our Italy. Read the proclamation! At a later time you will certainly have a great word to offer us.[26]

Antongini suggests that there was no reaction on D'Annunzio's part either to the march or to the subsequent call by Vittorio Emanuele

[23] *Prose di ricerca*, ii. 643–4.

[24] The notes of the two doctors were found later in the Vittoriale; most recently Pietro Gibellini has published an edited version of their observations, along with other Dannunzian texts relative to the case, without necessarily coming to any definite conclusion, though he does refer to D'Annunzio's 'lucid delirium': GD'A, *Siamo spiriti azzurri e stelle: Diario inedito*, ed. P. Gibellini (Florence, 1995) p. xxiv.

[25] Antongini, *D'Annunzio*, 402.   [26] *Carteggio D'Annunzio–Mussolini*, 27.

for Mussolini to form a new government. D'Annunzio's letters at this time, both to Antongini and to Mussolini, betray what seems to be a world of complete unreality. At the high point of the crisis, for instance, he writes to Antongini what the latter described as a magnificent but obsolete letter:

One's country is the work of assiduous creation. This work must consist in creating an even greater country and acting as one's own legislator.

This is a simple truth that must be placed again on the deserted altars. *In me manet et ego in ea* (It remains in me and I in it).

The future is before us, not like a dubious labyrinth but like a firm Roman road. *Patet aditus* (The entrance is open).

For a young nation the Triumphal Arch may sometimes be compared to a rainbow.

Serenitatem adfert (It brings serenity).

And I wish all Italy to understand my Latin, which is that of the Consuls and that of the Humanists.

Be you also among the 'doers of the word'.

I embrace you, Ave![27]

In the circumstances the words seem a mad parody of D'Annunzio's earlier aphoristic harangues. But the meaningless rhetoric, at such a crucial point in the nation's political fortunes, along with D'Annunzio's mysterious fall, which he never wished to have investigated, may indicate another factor which has only recently begun to be investigated frankly by critics and historians: his dependency on drugs. Visitors on the tour of the Vittoriale are told of the poet's hypochondria and are usually shown the large walk-in cupboard full of phials and jars of proprietary medicines; in fact D'Annunzio had a mini-pharmacy in the Zambracca, that room where he regularly took his meals alone, and where he was found dying on 1 March 1938.

D'Annunzio had, in 1908, broken off his affair with Alessandra di Rudiní, his once beloved Nike, because he declared that he could not contend with her addiction to the demon drugs, notably morphine, on which she had become increasingly dependent following her operations; her habit was later aggravated because of her over-compensation for his subsequent infidelity and indifference to her. At Fiume drugs had been freely available; Luisa Baccara, by all accounts, had become an addict, and D'Annunzio's own

---

[27] Antongini, *D'Annunzio*, 402.

experimentation with drugs may have started at this time, though many front-line officers had experimented with them during the war. The most recent study of D'Annunzio's life at the Vittoriale, Attilio Mazza's lurid *L'harem di D'Annunzio*, makes use of the semi-literate diaries of Aélis to support the view that D'Annunzio was seriously addicted to cocaine and that on the evening of his famous fall he was in the window seat of the music room fondling Luisa's sister Jolanda.[28] Was he full of cocaine that evening? And did his fuddled brain concoct the strange letter to Antongini on 29 October 1922, in the period, that is, between the fascist march on Rome and Mussolini's appointment as prime minister? Vittorio Pirlo, the knowledgeable son of D'Annunzio's pharmacist (and a former mayor of Salò) has stated publicly his judgement that D'Annunzio was fondling 'Jole' when he fell, or was pushed, from the window. Dr Pirlo, asked whether D'Annunzio took cocaine, declared that it was a well-known fact. The poet was to use the drug to help him in what he called his orgies or vices (*orgie*; *vizi*), and though he seemed perfectly lucid, particularly in his business correspondence with his editors, there is no doubt that he occasionally created a drugged dream world of his own.[29]

Whether or not this was his state of mind at the time of Mussolini's assumption of power, high-flown but meaningless words were exchanged between Mussolini and D'Annunzio after the march on Rome and the former's appointment as head of government two days later on 30 October 1922. D'Annunzio warned Mussolini, for instance, 'Victory has the clear eyes of Pallas. Do not blindfold her'; Mussolini reassured him, 'The vigorous fascist youth which is restoring the nation's soul will not put a blindfold on victory'.[30] D'Annunzio could certainly command great loyalty in the country; in particular the Fiuman legionaries were willing to follow him anywhere, indeed he found it difficult at times to move around outside the Vittoriale without the enthusiastic presence of his veterans. Many of them had re-entered their old civilian trades and professions, and there was a possibility of D'Annunzio's popularity spreading through the trade unions, and of his becoming something of a

[28] Mazza, *L'harem di D'Annunzio*, 100; Mara Giammarino goes as far as to say that Luisa Baccara pushed him: *Incontro con D'Annunzio*, 10.

[29] See the pages on what he himself called his 'orgies' in Andreoli's ed. of *Di me a me stesso*, 70 ff.

[30] *Carteggio D'Annunzio–Mussolini*, 29.

political danger to the fascist hierarchy. Mussolini, anxious not to provoke D'Annunzio, had assured him that his favourite union, the Federation of Italian Seaworkers, would not be affected by a fascist project to amalgamate all unions within the fascist syndicates. It has become a cliché of the politics of the time that Mussolini over-estimated D'Annunzio's political influence while D'Annunzio under-estimated Mussolini's capability for political action. But D'Annunzio was at that time still full of self-confidence: on 9 January 1923 he was still enclosing the word 'fascismo' within inverted commas, as though this new movement had no real identity at the time, and he noted: 'In the so-called [*detto*] "fascist" movement has not the best been generated by my spirit? Today's national revanche was announced by me—a good forty years ago, alas—and was promoted by the Leader of Ronchi.'[31]

But Mussolini's authority at this stage was by no means dictat-orial; his supporters had collectively more power than he had as an individual; by December 1922 they were pressing for restrictions on bodies and corporations which fell outside their party control. General De Bono, a leading light in the Fascist Grand Council, and Mussolini's head of police, sent out a circular to the prefects of all the provinces urging them to crack down on the kind of anarchic organizations which used D'Annunzio's name to band together and create public disorder. De Bono noted in particular the National Federation of Fiuman Legionaries, and suggested secret and unan-nounced raids on their premises. Similar attacks, strongly supported by the powerful shipowners' lobby, were made during the course of 1923 on the headquarters of the Seaworkers' Union. Until 1925 D'Annunzio continued to write letters of protest to Mussolini con-cerning such treatment, but his influence during that period grew ever weaker. By March 1923 he had requested an official guard who might defend his solitude against the importunate enthusiasts who were inclined, even with the best of intentions, to disrupt his lit-erary work. Mussolini was delighted to comply and sent Giovanni Rizzo, who thereafter remained by the poet's side, transmitting his every action to the Duce. This was not always to D'Annunzio's disadvantage, indeed he seems to have deliberately leaked informa-tion to Rizzo in order to have it reported in higher circles. It meant that Mussolini knew exactly how to keep D'Annunzio pacified

31 Ibid. 38.

(mainly by giving him huge sums of money for his expensive projects), but it also meant that D'Annunzio might forget his financial
anxieties for ever, or at least for as long as Mussolini remained in
power. D'Annunzio became very fond of Rizzo, and, thanks to
the pressure he was able to exert on Mussolini in later years, managed to obtain the policeman's promotion through various grades
until he reached the high rank of prefect of police. In return for
D'Annunzio's favours Rizzo established a local police organization which effectively turned the area around the Vittoriale into
D'Annunzio's private feudal territory.

Antongini dates D'Annunzio's renunciation of public affairs to
shortly after the extraordinary letter of 29 October 1922:

With the advent of fascism, Gabriele D'Annunzio's political activity came
to an end.

The magnificent craftsman, the incomparable creator of masterpieces,
came back to ordinary life.

The proclaimer of the war, the hero of the heavens, of the sea, of the
slopes of the Carso and of the miraculous gesture of Fiume entered the
realm of Legend.[32]

Significantly, by November 1922 D'Annunzio had begun to write
to Mussolini using the familiar 'tu' form of address. Some hints of
the poet's withdrawal from public affairs were reported in British
newspapers, not without some irony. Simultaneously Italian newspapers published cartoons of D'Annunzio in Franciscan habit, one
cartoon by the famous cartoonist Manca showing him opening the
monastery door ingratiatingly to a Luisa Baccara lookalike holding
a pre-Raphaelite lily in her delicate hand.[33]

There is a tradition, false or true as may be, that Abruzzese men
withdraw from the world in late middle age, and enjoy an easier
life; the phenomenon is known as the *ritiro abruzzese* (Abruzzese
withdrawal). D'Annunzio's early letters from Garda are sent from
the Romitorio del Cargnacco (the Hermitage of Cargnacco). In
such a letter to Mussolini dated 1 December 1922 he makes the point
that he could go into exile as in 1912: 'I prefer exile to the daily

---

[32] Antongini, *D'Annunzio*, 402; the translation mistakenly has 'heir of the
Heavens' instead of 'hero'—the original is *eroe*; see *Vita segreta*, 560.

[33] D'Annunzio in caricature is a subject on its own; see E. Ledda, *D'Annunzio in
caricatura* (Gardone Riviera, 1988), a catalogue of the exhibition published during
the commemoration of the fiftieth anniversary of D'Annunzio's death, which reproduces the caricature described, no page numbers, but p. 18.

torment.'[34] However, D'Annunzio was still nominally fighting on behalf of the Seaworkers' Union, and no less than twenty appendices to the correspondence with Mussolini contain the many settlements attempted between the government, the employers' organizations (Confindustria), and the Seaworkers' Federation FILM (Federazione Italiana dei Lavoratori del Mare), and Mussolini had no reason to be complacent about the poet's political allegiances. D'Annunzio had certainly not taken the easy way out during his fifties, indeed he had boasted that at the age of the armchair and slippers he was risking life and limb in the cockpit of an airplane. He might yet prove an awkward antagonist. Nevertheless the words *ritiro* and *esilio* (exile) began to recur in letters written by D'Annunzio to friends and relatives, as well as to Mussolini and Rizzo. It soon became obvious to Rizzo that it would require little to persuade D'Annunzio to abandon his former allies in the Seaworkers' Union, as he had those in other federations. Piero Chiara reproduces part of a report which Rizzo made to Mussolini: 'The Comandante has two aspirations: firstly that his name goes down to posterity as a great man [. . .]; secondly that financially he has all he needs to live, as he always has lived, without preoccupations. As for the Seaworkers' Federation, he could not care less.'[35] Mussolini continued to ply him with presents and privileges: nomination to the Senate as part of the poet's sixtieth birthday celebrations, an honour which D'Annunzio rejected, preferring (and accepting) the gift of the prow of the warship *Puglia*, which had memories for him of the Adriatic campaign. The stunning souvenir was hauled up the hillside to Gardone Riviera and set into the west side of the gardens, looking over Garda, where it still amazes visitors by its impressive size and the frightening height of its sheer sides above the valley in which it stands. Other perquisites followed, including the MAS, or an identical boat, on which D'Annunzio had sailed into Buccari;[36] this now served him as a thrilling speedboat on the waters of the lake, where on the shore he refurbished with Gothic magnificence a castellated boat-house, the Torre San Marco. He was also presented with the aircraft in which he had flown over Vienna, as well as with smaller memoirs of his war experiences. One of his

---

[34] *Carteggio D'Annunzio–Mussolini*, 30–1.   [35] Chiara, *GD'A* 371–2.
[36] Alberto Santoni's most recent account follows the tradition that it was the actual boat on which the Buccari raid was carried out: see Santoni, 'GD'A e la beffa di Buccari'.

letters to Mussolini, dated 7 May 1923, suggested the levelling of a nearby hilltop in order to accommodate a small airfield,[37] but the request was one of the few that Mussolini preferred to ignore, and other placatory gestures were made to D'Annunzio instead. On 15 March 1924 Fiume was finally annexed officially to Italy and Mussolini convinced the king to confer upon D'Annunzio the title of Prince of Montenevoso. Whether this was a spontaneous gesture on Mussolini's part is arguable. No doubt any favour he could do for D'Annunzio weakened the latter's motivation to oppose what the fascists were doing, and it was easier to fall in with the poet's wishes. It is not difficult to follow the implications of certain letters of the period, in which D'Annunzio wrote that the government ought to recognize his services to the nation and nominate him Prince of the Adriatic or Prince of Montenevoso; one such is dated 25 February 1924:

The Government and the Nation have the most imperious duty to recognize me finally [. . .] Let the country recognize, *you* recognize, then, the vast and varied part which I played in the 'Holy War' [. . .] You can call me Prince of the Adriatic—yes; Prince of Montenevoso—yes. The coronets are still lacking.[38]

Four days later Mussolini's reply addressed D'Annunzio as 'My excellent Prince'.

On 22 April 1924 Eleonora Duse died in Pittsburgh during yet another tour in America. D'Annunzio was publicly moved. He had met Eleonora in Milan by chance for the first time in eighteen years in August 1922, after she had sent him a telegram from Paris asking for his permission to put on *La città morta*. There had been an earlier sporadic correspondence between the two, though Duse, who ignored a score of invitations to visit the Vittoriale, was obviously keen to maintain her independence and distance both from D'Annunzio and, incidentally, from Mussolini, who offered to subsidize her theatre.[39] She preferred to tour in Europe (her final appearance in London was as late as June 1923) and in the following year left on her final journey, to the United States. D'Annunzio did write and ask Mussolini to ensure that the body of the actress

[37] *Carteggio D'Annunzio–Mussolini*, 54.
[38] Ibid. 100; similar conclusions are drawn by Chiara, *GD'A* 371, and Alatri, *GD'A*, 522.
[39] Pontiero, *Eleonora Duse*, 330.

was brought back to Italy at once.[40] Mussolini would have done so, anyway; it was a question of national prestige, but it served him speciously as another favour to D'Annunzio, and every little helped in keeping the exile mollified. Duse's death coincided with the publication on Treves's presses of D'Annunzio's reworked *Faville*, and just a month later he was busily editing the memoirs which made up *Il secondo amante di Lucrezia Buti*. Commenting on his work rate at the time, D'Annunzio remarked to Treves, in a letter of 24 April 1924, that he was hoping thus to console himself from that 'too harsh a misfortune', the death of Eleonora.[41]

After all of Mussolini's efforts to placate the poet, it must have caused him no little chagrin to read a newspaper report in *Il mondo* on 30 July 1924. The article, an interview with D'Annunzio, referred among other details to the assassination (though at the time it was no more than the disappearance) of Giacomo Matteotti, the leading Socialist member of parliament, whose battered body was found some fifteen days later north of Rome; he had been beaten to death by a fascist gang. The reporter on *Il mondo* simply mentioned that D'Annunzio had said that the fetid ruin had saddened him. Mussolini sent a panic-stricken telegram to Giovanni Rizzo on 30 July 1924 enquiring what D'Annunzio meant by 'fetid ruin'.[42] What D'Annunzio was alluding to was unclear, but, with the death of Matteotti, Mussolini found himself at the centre of a political storm which threatened his situation more than any before or after, and the thought of having D'Annunzio as a potential opponent again stimulated him to other favours. The dictator paid 100,000 lire on behalf of the government for the manuscript of *La gloria*, proposing to set up a Dannunzian manuscript archive; and during the year he continued to make minor concessions to D'Annunzio, which culminated in the promise of a Christmas present for 1924: the government would decree the Vittoriale a national monument. On 25 November 1924 D'Annunzio wrote to Costanzo Ciano, himself heavily involved in the negotiations with the Seaworkers'

[40] *Carteggio D'Annunzio–Mussolini*, 363–4.
[41] 'Dal *Notturno* al *Venturiero senza ventura*', 130.
[42] Ibid. 115; according to some commentators, it was D'Annunzio's failure openly to denounce the Matteotti murder which finally condemned him in the eyes of anti-fascist intellectuals; see Oscar Pio Granchelli's intervention in *D'Annunzio e la sinistra*, proceedings of a Round Table discussion involving Renzo De Felice, Gabriele De Rosa, Filippo Mazzonis, and Mario Sansone, who chaired the event (Pescara, 1978), 5.

Federation, to say, 'After what I have done and written, without stain and without fear, I wash my hands of it', and, as if to underline his nonchalance at his renunciation of his 'union' affiliations, he added trivially that his Airedale bitch had given birth to three whelps, to one of which, a female, he had given the name Finimola.[43] By the start of 1925 Mussolini was sure that D'Annunzio did not wish to interfere in the political aftermath of the Matteotti murder, and in May he made a personal visit to the Vittoriale, in part to set the official stamp of approval on the acceptance of the Vittoriale itself by the state as a national monument. He stayed with the poet for two days, 25–7 May. After he and his entourage had said farewell to D'Annunzio on the forecourt of the house, the poet went up to the balcony and addressed a small crowd who had gathered below, stressing his agreement with the Duce's political attitudes, and reading out the telegram of solidarity which he and Mussolini had just then sent to the king. 'The meeting', writes Alatri, 'signalled the reconciliation between the two, but also the surrender of the Comandante to the Duce, if not actually to Fascism.' Alatri elsewhere makes the point that D'Annunzio suffered in public reputation because his many protests to Mussolini were always made in private correspondence.[44]

For the next thirteen years D'Annunzio made no serious political moves, though he may have attempted in vain in 1937 to interfere with the growing alliance between Mussolini and Hitler. He continued to be courted, or placated, periodically, by the fascist hierarchy, granted the title of general in the reserve air brigade in September 1925, when it was decided to create a Ministry of Air, an occasion which gave him the opportunity to order three splendid new uniforms. Mussolini paid dear for keeping D'Annunzio amenable. Every week brought new requests from the Vittoriale: a new high road between Bolzano and Brescia, which D'Annunzio had costed at 33 million lire, the adoption as parliamentary candidate of the poet's son Mario, a senatorship for his friend Alfredo Felici, blank shells for salvoes fired from the *Puglia* to celebrate various anniversaries, pensions for his Fiuman war widows, state funerals for dead veterans, a score of names of friends and cronies put forward for promotion in state enterprises, including the faithful

---

[43] *Carteggio D'Annunzio–Mussolini*, appendix XX, p. 493.
[44] Alatri, *GD'A*, 527; see also Alatri, 'D'Annunzio: Mito e realtà', *Clio*, 24/4 (Oct.–Dec. 1988), 539.

Tom Antongini given a sinecure in Paris. Mussolini is credited with the *bon mot* that D'Annunzio was like a broken tooth: he had to be eradicated or covered in gold. D'Annunzio's influence could also be malign: a local inn near the entrance to the Vittoriale was demolished to keep away what D'Annunzio considered the loose women housed there, but also potential tourists and sightseers; houses around the family home in Pescara were demolished to throw the building into greater relief and to obtain a river view from the rear windows; his daughter Renata kept far from the Vittoriale; his son Gabriellino's future wife arrested by Mussolini's police because D'Annunzio suspected her of poisoning his son (literally, or with venereal disease). All this and more is logged in the letters exchanged with Mussolini between 1922 and 1937.

His requests to Mussolini became at times no more than petty: a letter of 22 January 1928 complains that he is being persecuted by local traffic police imposing fines for speeding.[45] Periodically, too, D'Annunzio wrote indignant letters to the Duce, protesting that his contribution to the grandeur of the nation was passing unheralded, and he was particularly annoyed that on 27 May 1929 his name should be omitted from the ceremonies to commemorate Italy's entry into World War One.[46] Perhaps the most enduring favour conceded to D'Annunzio had been the founding on 21 June 1926 of a national institution for the editions of the *Opera omnia* of Gabriele D'Annunzio, supported by 5 million lire of state funding and under the patronage of King Vittorio Emanuele. *Alcyone*, the first of the forty-four volumes proposed, came out exactly a year later. This was the culmination of the contest between Treves and Mondadori. By 25 November D'Annunzio had secured Mondadori's support with a declaration that 'The house of Treves will not have my new work'.[47] On 25 December 1925 he asked Mussolini 'to free him from the labyrinthine intrigues',[48] and by 12 May 1926 Mussolini had sanctioned the setting up of the national edition of D'Annunzio's *Opera omnia*, confirming that Mondadori had the contract.[49] D'Annunzio also received huge advances from Mondadori for the rights to publish a more popular edition of his complete works.

---

[45] *Carteggio D'Annunzio–Mussolini*, 237.   [46] Ibid. 276.
[47] The drama is discussed in Salierno, *D'Annunzio e i suoi editori*, 206; the letter is discussed in Chiara, 'D'Annunzio e Mondadori'.
[48] *Carteggio D'Annunzio–Mussolini*, 173.   [49] Ibid. 189.

The official government recognition of his house as a national monument, a second great favour, enabled him to pursue his grandiose building projects, which in their way provided him with a new form of creativity akin to writing. D'Annunzio felt that such creativity extended to his Sperellian qualities as an interior designer: he considered that his decorative techniques, including his arrangement of the bric-à-brac with which the Vittoriale was crammed,[50] bore his particular stamp of genius. Indeed Tom Antongini witnessed D'Annunzio's pride at the effect which the music room had upon visitors, including Antongini's own daughter: 'The poet said to my daughter, who remained rapt in ecstasy on the threshold, so greatly was she struck by all this beauty and harmony: "You are the only person who has realized that I am a better decorator and upholsterer than I am a poet or novelist".'[51] The question of D'Annunzio's taste in decoration is debatable. But what was clear was that at the same time as immortalizing himself in elegant print he also desired to enlarge and improved the fabric and furnishings of the Vittoriale, so that it could be equally worthy of his immortal fame. Unable to write creatively any longer, mainly concerned with editing past work and reminiscences, and with a goodly income guaranteed for the first time in his career, he devoted himself to constructing within the Vittoriale's grounds what has been described already as his own physical obituary, a huge theatre of memory, in stone, steel, and mortar. He hired an architect, Gian Carlo Maroni, painters, Adolfo De Carolis and Guido Cadorin, a sculptor and goldsmith, Renato Brozzi, and an army of workmen and specialist artisans and craftsmen to do their bidding. Until 1938 D'Annunzio had to live surrounded by all the inconveniences of a building site; in a sense his tolerance of the noise and squalor was another heroic creative effort, in this case necessary to produce the Vittoriale.

Beginning with the original modest building, D'Annunzio renovated the outer shell, covering the façade with emblems, coats of arms, statues and bas-reliefs which recalled incidents from his earlier life, and presented the appearance, albeit somewhat grotesquely, of the residence of a medieval *podestà*, such as those at Volterra or Arezzo. Inside, the rooms, by now converted or developed as thirty-

---

[50] A. Mazza, *D'Annunzio e il Vittoriale: Guida alla casa del poeta* (Gardone, 1989), produces a modest but colourful and comprehensive guide to the house and its interiors.

[51] Antongini, *D'Annunzio*, 561.

six different spaces, including corridors and landings, were filled with a vast miscellany of objects, including many casts of famous statues such as Michelangelo's slaves for the tomb of Pope Julius or the heads of the horses from the pediment of the Parthenon, which he had seen one day in the British Museum as long ago as 1914. To the casts he added bric-à-brac which might have been bought at any of the antiquarian shops in local villages: Chinese pots, buddhas, coloured glass balls, cushions by the dozen, small bronzes, decorative plates, glass vases for votive tears, swords, a veritable Noah's ark of animals in all conceivable materials, bracelets, chains, machine-guns.

Many of these objects were arranged by the poet himself in an 'artistic' manner, in which he flattered himself he was uniquely expert:

Certainly sovereign art inspires me, taste for form and colour directs me in choice and composition, a most ingenious awareness illuminates me in the way to regulate gaps and heights between objects; to lift one figure higher than another I use a majolica box for my base, a strip of gold cloth is useful to me to disguise the effect of the cube, a quick way of estimating the mass of a bronze reassures me that some fragile glazed material beneath it will not give way beneath the weight.

To the accumulation of objects he might add, 'to the surprise of the simple people around me', an old nail, a shred of precious cloth, a remnant of gold ribbon, an old paint-box.[52]

With the exception of his main study, which he called his Officina (Workshop), and the art-deco dining room, glowing in gold and red, the other rooms were (and are) dimly lit, and any window heavily curtained or glazed with impenetrable stained or painted glass. Drapes of all kinds of material proliferate (the ceiling of the music room is hung with thick tapestry-like cloth reminiscent of a Saudi tent). The effect of this lack of light and air, added to the cluttered environment, was and continues to be as oppressive as it is impressive. The rooms were given typically Dannunzian names: the Corridor of the Via Crucis, Room of the Leper, Room of the Leda, The One-Handed's Writing Room, the Blue Bathroom, containing more than 2,000 objects, mostly plaques, majolica plates, vases, and small glazed ceramic animals, the Dalmatian Oratory (the austere antecamera for official guests, where Mussolini was made to wait), and the Room of the Relics (even more crammed with

[52] *Prose di ricerca*, ii. 709–10.

bric-à-brac than the others). Lucia Re, who did a survey of the Vittoriale for Rizzoli's *Journal of Decorative and Propaganda Arts*, has an atmospheric synthesis of this last room, which conveys the cluttered ambience:

The 'Room of Relics' is dominated by two compositions in the form of a pyramid and an altar [. . .]. The pyramid of Asian idols is composed of a series of statuettes of dragons, of Confucius and of Buddha, crowned by a fifteenth-century wooden sculpture of the Madonna and Child, flanked by a series of small polychrome statues of various saints. The altar, with a bas-relief of the Lion of St Mark above it, is covered with precious Baroque reliquaries and other religious paraphernalia; at its centre is a crushed steering wheel (a particularly incongruous detail). This belonged to the powerboat in which Sir Henry Seagrave died during a race which D'Annunzio had himself proposed.[53]

On the wall opposite the 'altar', among many other objects, is a tapestry, said to be of the sixteenth century, which shows a priest holding up five fingers to a group of men and women. The setting is Arcadian, children in the background seem to be holding up five fingers in imitation of the priest. Above the tapestry is carved the motto, 'Five are the fingers, five are the sins', recalling D'Annunzio's acceptance of lust and prodigality as natural propensities, rather than mortal sins.

Many, if not most, of the rooms were decorated with such mottoes, some of which D'Annunzio had used during his earlier life as headings or watermarks for his books or writing-paper and ex-libris, or which he had collected and noted down over the years in the *taccuini*: *Immotus nec iners* (Unmoved but not inert), *Memento audere semper* (Remember always to dare), and hundreds of others.[54] One particular room, the Cassaretto, has its ceiling covered with paintings of scrolls containing such mottoes. D'Annunzio's demagogic style often depended upon such succinct, ironic apophthegms (not always in Latin), his most imitated (and still current) being the dismissive sneer which had characterized his defiance at Fiume: *Me ne frego*. At a time when most of the populace was barely

[53] L. Re, 'Il teatro della memoria di GD'A: Il Vittoriale degli Italiani', *Journal of Decorative and Propaganda Arts*, 3 (Winter 1987), 38.

[54] P. Sorge, *Motti dannunziani*, (Milan, 1994), has put together an anthology of such slogans, adding a brief introduction and explanations of some of the more arcane mottoes.

literate, it was useful to be able to put over a viewpoint by using such slogans, which by definition embraced within themselves an inevitably mnemonic quality, and which sometimes contained the kind of wit or irony visible in medieval heraldic inscriptions. D'Annunzio used them as the rhetorical counterpart to the slogans of wall-posters which were often the most efficacious way memorably to convey information to the masses, unable to read newspapers and still without the radio.

The proverbial phrases served as exhortations to the poet himself in literary and heroic spheres, including military contexts: *Non nisi grandia canto* (I sing only great things), *Per non dormire* (Not to sleep) along with *Ognora desto* (Ever awake), implying his heroically insomniac efforts at creative writing, while *Dant vulnera formam* (Wounds grant form), which prefaces the first edition of the *Notturno*, bridges the gap between the wartime exploit which brought about the loss of his eye, and the literary 'form' to which the wound gave birth. Mottoes also served as inspirations to his companions in arms; such was the well-known *Memento audere semper*, concocted from the offical abbreviation of the *motoscafi antisommergibili* (MAS), or *Semper adamas* (Ever adamant), which he coined for the First Naval Squadron. The Fiume adventure was particularly fecund in mottoes; two such, which have a biblical ring, were *Chi non è con noi è contro di noi* (a paraphrase of Christ's 'He that is not with me is against me'), and *Si spiritus pro nobis quis contra nos?* (a paraphrase of Paul's 'If God be for us, who can be against us?'). Many of these sayings were worked up into bookplates or etched as works of art for their own sake by Adolfo De Carolis. Other, traditional, proverbs, which might seem banal out of a Dannunzian context, were given new life by De Carolis's powerful images. Thus *Cosa fatta capo ha* (Once it's done it's done) looks both menacing and inspiratory when painted across a black sky over four plunging daggers held by sinewy hands, with FIUME in capitals at the base of the etching. All of the mottoes have about them a medieval or Renaissance aura, those carved on stones in the garden and inlaid with red paint are similar to ancient Irish inscriptions, others, in scroll-like form like those in the Cassaretto are medievally heraldic. As far as D'Annunzio was concerned they all added memorable echoes to the buildings and monuments which were going up around his new hermitage; all helped to supply further striking autobiographical souvenirs to him and his public.

In the seclusion of the Vittoriale D'Annunzio gradually with-drew more and more from the public eye. He had his own court of admirers and servants: Luisa Baccara and Aélis Mazoyer supplied his wants and ruled the household. Those wants included a regular supply of women, to whom, despite the fact that they were often prostitutes from Salò, he would give his usual pet names, as though they were Renaissance princesses. He no longer had the time or the patience to spend years in a semi-marital state as he had done with the major female figures in his past life. Annamaria Andreoli's edition of D'Annunzio's intimate thoughts concerning his experiences after settling in to the Vittoriale is thick with references to what he calls his orgies with various women, assisted at times by cocaine (*il veleno*—poison) whenever, without that artificial aid, he felt him-self gradually losing his sexual urge, his will-power dying, forcing him to yield and feel shame. But the drug worked: 'The orgy is triumphant—beyond dawn.'[55] Perhaps the most startling of these accounts is his experience with a lesbian on 12 May 1929, when, after copulation, the woman continues her gyrations, and D'Annunzio, willing himself to be a woman, revels in the violence of his lover's, bruising embraces. He is, however, aware of the danger of having his testicles crushed by the increasing compression of the woman's thighs.[56] The final orgy detailed in the volume, said to last twenty-four hours (followed by eleven hours of unbroken sleep) is dated 5 October 1933. The poet was just over 70 years of age. In the great catalogue of women that D'Annunzio enjoyed, it is curiously amus-ing to see that the editor has left blank three lines in which the poet lists the names of young women from Gardone, still alive at the time of Andreoli's edition, who might otherwise have been shamed or libelled.[57]

There were, it is true, more respectable women who continued to visit him in the Vittoriale, in particular the actress Elena Sangro, whom he pet-named Ornella, who continued their association until 1935 (she was to make her final film, with Fellini, in 1962). Another 'respectable' visitor was the reporter Mara Dussia (Mara Giammarino), a beautiful blonde sent by Arnoldo Mondadori to interview the

[55] *Di me a me stesso*, 99; his sexual adventures, largely at the Vittoriale, are recorded between pp. 71 and 131.
[56] Ibid. 101–2: 'Cependant je suis attentif au danger de laisser mes couilles écrouées par le resserrement toujours plus violent de ses cuisses.'
[57] At p. 112.

poet. Renamed Maria for the evening by D'Annunzio, she described how he attempted to seduce her, by offering her a diaphanous shawl to model, by reciting poems, by what she took to be an attempt at hypnotism, and possibly by the sheer exhaustion of walking and talking with him until six in the morning.[58] Meanwhile D'Annunzio's wife Maria Hardouin had come to live at the property, in the large house which he called Villa Mirabella, and although she was not allowed into D'Annunzio's private apartments, the so-called Priory, their relationship became friendly, particularly after 1929.

Despite his sexual diversions, D'Annunzio's old age was, in his own view, humiliatingly corroded by ailments, which rendered him unable any longer to fascinate women, though from afar the curious continued to endanger their safety by venturing into his web. Radclyffe Hall was one such who had a narrow escape when she came with her partner, Una, Lady Troubridge, and spent some time with the poet in 1934. D'Annunzio was fascinated and always titillated by lesbian sex and encouraged her to visit him, plying her with gifts. But though she came to Garda on other occasions in 1935 and 1936, it was not possible for her or Una to see the Comandante, as she insisted on calling him in her ingratiating letters, because of his indisposition. One unpublished letter from D'Annunzio to Radclyffe praised her *Well of Loneliness* (which she presented to him in translation) and invited her to stay in the grounds of the Vittoriale and write his biography. The letter, which is, to say the least, disjointed, ends with a half-remembered quotation, perhaps from Robert Bell's *Early Ballads*, '"Love will find out the way". Sans doute vous aimez comme nous, vos early ballads. O open the door to me!'[59]

D'Annunzio's literary production during this period consisted of what might be called a series of 'assembly jobs'. Between 1934 and 1935 he crammed into the second half of his final large compilation, *Il libro segreto*, most of the unfinished fragments of prose and poetry which he had jotted down in notebooks over the previous twenty years and until then had failed to publish. The opening part

[58] Giammarino, *Incontro con D'Annunzio*, *passim*; it should be added that the slim volume, dictated by the reporter in her eighties, does not give the impression of being the most reliable of testimonies.

[59] The letter is in the *inedita* of the archive at the Vittoriale; for a brief account of Una Troubridge, Radclyffe Hall, and D'Annunzio, see R. Ormrod, 'D'Annunzio and Radclyffe Hall', *Modern Language Review*, 84/4. (Oct. 1989), 842–5.

of the *Libro segreto* is a narcissistic series of memoirs, headed 'Via crucis, Via necis, Via nubis' (Way of the Cross, Way of Death, Way of Cloud), containing defensive regrets at his past, and complaints about the negative effects of old age. The second part is entitled 'Regimen hinc animae' (Here is the Realm of the Soul) and contains the various fragments. The book was published three years before D'Annunzio's death under the pseudonym of Angelo Cocles. If there is a new message to be gleaned from its pages it is that, despite D'Annunzio's apparent determination to seize the day and make the most of what time he had left, there is a disillusioning sentiment that even his immortal, inimitable (in his view) literary efforts are vain.

D'Annunzio's health grew worse after 1935. He rarely went beyond the limits of the estate. And then, on 30 September 1937, he summoned up the strength to meet Mussolini who was just returning from Berlin having made an informal agreement with Hitler, which would turn out to be the 'Pact of Steel' between the two nations. During the whole of his correspondence with Mussolini D'Annunzio mentions Hitler only once, and then only to caricature him:

You are about to repudiate fiercely the *marrano* Adolf Hitler, whose ignoble face is obscured under the indelible splashes of whitening and paste from his overflowing decorator's brush, which on top of his cane or pole has become his ferocious clown's sceptre, not without a tuft extending at the root of his 'nazi' nose.[60]

As Mussolini's train returned via Verona on that last day in September, D'Annunzio went to meet him at the station. Of all the versions of their brief conversation the most likely appears to be that D'Annunzio protested against any alliance with the old barbarian enemy; Mussolini was content to allow D'Annunzio to give his view and, because of his obvious decrepitude, to ignore him as politely as possible. After the meeting at Verona, on 13 December 1937, Mussolini announced Italy's withdrawal from the League of Nations, and D'Annunzio applauded the action. At about the same time

---

[60] *Carteggio D'Annunzio–Mussolini*, 319; accusing Hitler of being an apostate Jew (*marrano*, or pork-eater) no doubt added to what D'Annunzio saw as his irony here; more elaborate satires of Hitler in the form of Pasquinades are discussed in P. Gibellini, *Logos e Mythos: Studi su GD'A* (Florence 1985), 251–9; Gibellini's findings and D'Annunzio's manuscripts are more fully aired and discussed in Andreoli, *D'Annunzio archivista*, 51 ff.

D'Annunzio accepted Mussolini's proposal to make him president of the Italian Academy, following the death of Marconi.

Among the last of the visitors to the Vittoriale in D'Annunzio's final months were Max Beerbohm and his wife; they appear not to have seen the Comandante, but were entertained by Luisa Baccara, who played for them and gave them commemorative medallions. Beerbohm's letter of thanks, dated 24 January 1938, is full of friendly admiration, addressing D'Annunzio as 'Maître, and fellow-countryman of Rossetti', and leaving an impression of the mansion:

If Aladdin could come back to life and were admitted to that house and domain, he would say to himself, rather ruefully, '*My* palace was comparatively insipid. *My* palace was rather pot-au-feu.' And he would add, 'Moreover, Signora Baccara was not there to act as hostess. And Signora Baccara did not play Bach there'.[61]

But the lightness of Beerbohm's letter conceals a gloomier picture of the recluse in his impenetrable hermitage. Accounts of the decay in D'Annunzio's physical health and appearance vary little; most are in agreement that there had been a sudden collapse during the final two years of his life. Antongini describes the poet's face as 'ravaged beyond description. His very features have been deformed by a diabolical hand', and Ojetti, who visited him at the end of August 1937, portrays him as a crumpled ruin of a man.[62]

The final moments are among the most mysterious of D'Annunzio's existence. Among his servants was a certain Emy Heufler, a blonde girl from the Italian Tyrol, who served D'Annunzio in many roles, dubious as well as legitimate. According to the reliably investigative journalist Alfredo Todisco, the poet and she would sometimes spend three days locked away from the other inhabitants of the Vittoriale, perhaps, he suggests, in a cocaine-induced coma. The poet's fierce dislike of Hitler and the Germans was well known, and his conversation with Mussolini at Verona had been simply the latest indication of his dislike of a *rapprochement* between Latins and Teutons. For the German secret service D'Annunzio might have seemed to present a stumbling-block to a future alliance. On the evening of 1 March 1938, while he was working in his study, he

[61] The letter is published by Emilio Mariano in *Quaderni dannunziani*, 4/5 (Apr. 1957), transcribed from the Archivio Generale of the Vittoriale, IX. 5.

[62] Antongini, *D'Annunzio*, 805–6; U. Ojetti, *Taccuini* (Florence, 1954), 476–84; for other hearsay witnesses see Alatri, *GD'A*, 563.

suffered a heart attack or cerebral haemorrhage and died. Emy Heufler left the Vittoriale immediately and went to Berlin, where she worked in the offices of Ribbentrop. Todisco suspected that she might have been an agent of the Nazis.[63] Mussolini, with the leading members of the Fascist Grand Council, arrived the next day. The funeral took place on 3 March and on 4 March the body, having lain in state in the *Puglia* for just a day, was buried in the grounds and later placed in the huge sarcophagus in the centre of the mausoleum which D'Annunzio's architect Maroni had built for him at the highest point of the Vittoriale estate. Around him were the tombs (or cenotaphs) of nine of his former comrades in arms; Maroni had reserved for himself the tenth sarcophagus.

D'Annunzio's death was received by a period of national mourning which spread beyond the boundaries of Italy, even to those areas where the poet was no longer *persona grata*. In Britain the press was magnanimous in its attitude, almost to a man; only the Labour *Daily Herald* treated him with scant regard, but even in that newspaper there was nothing particularly hostile. The *Times* headed its obituary 'The Spirit of the Cinquecento', and was most eulogistic there and in a long leading article on him:

Poet, novelist and politician, dramatist and demagogue, aesthete and soldier, Gabriele D'Annunzio, Prince of Monte Nevoso, is dead. No poet of our time has led a fuller life than this Byron of the modern world [. . .] showed himself a fighter of dauntless courage and a politician who swayed the fortunes of Europe [. . .] bore his wounds with stoic fortitude.

The *Times* linked his fortune closely with that of Mussolini, as did the *Telegraph* and the fascist *Action*. The most objective and probably the most just obituary was that of the *Guardian*, which summed up his literary merits, dwelt on the Fiume adventure, and calculated his importance in getting Italy to enter World War One, but surprisingly in view of its liberal associations made no strong correlation between him and the fascists. For the British public D'Annunzio's fame was to remain buried with him for the next fifty years.

[63] A. Todisco, 'C'è stata una donna nella morte di D'Annunzio', *Corriere della sera*, (15 June 1975).

Bibliography of works consulted

I have many debts to my predecessors, and what follows can only be a selective list of what I have read and heard on D'Annunzio during the past thirty years. That said, I have tried to include those works which I consider most useful.

D'ANNUNZIO'S WORKS

Collected Works

Le cronache de La Tribuna, preface by Ruggero Puletti (no editor's name given), 2 vols. (Bologna, 1992). Contains all the important articles published in the Roman journal 1884–88.

Opera omnia, 48 vols. + 1 vol. indices (Milan, 1927–36). The Edizione Nazionale of D'Annunzio's work.

Opere poetiche, ed. E. Palmieri, 8 vols. (Bologna, 1941–59). The best annotated edition containing most of D'Annunzio's poetry.

Pagine disperse, ed. A. Castelli (Rome, 1913). A useful anthology of miscellaneous writings only now becoming available in more scientific editions.

Poesie, teatro, prose, abbr. and ed. M. Praz and F. Gerra (Milan and Naples, 1966). A useful anthology of what Mario Praz judged the best in D'Annunzio's production.

Roma senza lupa: Cronache mondane (1884–88), ed. A. Baldini and P. P. Trompeo (Milan, 1948). For many years the only anthology of D'Annunzio's columns in *Tribuna*; cf. *Le cronache de La Tribuna* above.

Tutte le opere, ed. E. Bianchetti, 11 vols. (Milan, 1939–76). The edition used in the present biography and containing: *Altri taccuini* (1976); *Prose di ricerca, di lotta e di comando*, 3 vols. (vols. i and iii 1947; vol. ii 1950); *Prose di romanzi*, 2 vols. (1940); *Taccuini* (1965); *Teatro: Tragedie, sogni e misteri*, 2 vols. (1939–40); *Versi d'amore e di gloria*, 2 vols. (1950).

Individual Editions

The Child of Pleasure, trans. Georgina Harding (London, 1898).

Crestomazia delle lirica di Gabriele D'Annunzio: Interpretazione e commento, ed. E. Palmieri (Bologna, 1944).

Di me a me stesso, ed. Annamaria Andreoli (Milan, 1990).

Giovanni Episcopo, ed. Clelia Martignoni (Milan, 1971).
Il libro delle vergini, ed. Riccardo Scrivano (2nd edn., Milan, 1990).
Il trionfo della morte, ed. Giansiro Ferrata (5th edn., Milan, 1980).
La Leda senza cigno, ed. Clelia Martignoni (Milan, 1976).
La penultima ventura: Scritti e discorsi fiumani, ed. R. De Felice (Milan, 1974). An indispensable annotated edition with an excellent introduction to the Fiuman adventure.
Siamo spiriti azzurri e stelle, Diario inedito, ed. Pietro Gibellini (Florence, 1995).
Solus ad solam, ed. Federico Roncoroni (Milan, 1979).

Correspondence

The following are the main volumes containing important collections of D'Annunzio's letters; other individual letters or smaller collections are available in specific critical works or in scattered journals too numerous to include here, though, where utilized, such letters have been cited in the footnotes.

Albertini	Letters in L. Albertini, *Epistolario*, ed. O. Barié, 4 vols. (Milan, 1968).
Antongini	T. Antongini, *Quarant'anni con D'Annunzio* (Milan, 1957). See under Critical Studies for Antongini's other works.
Badoglio	*Carteggio D'Annunzio–Badoglio*, ed. E. Mariano, *Quaderni dannunziani*, 4–5 (1957).
Beltrami	V. Salierno, 'Giovanni Beltrami e D'Annunzio: Dalla Beffa di Buccari al *Venturiero senza ventura*', *Rassegna dannunziana*, 29 (May 1996), 21–34.
Bideri	A. Cappelletti, *Due carteggi dannunziani* (Naples, 1929).
Bongiovanni	Luigi Bongiovanni, 'Gabriele D'Annunzio aviatore di guerra', *Nuova antologia*, 73/1584 (16 Mar. 1938). Includes eighteen letters from D'Annunzio.
Capuana	*Lettere a Capuana*, ed. Anna Longoni (Milan, 1993).
Conti	'Lettere al "Dottor Mistico" (Angelo Conti)', ed. E. Campana, *Nuova antologia*, 74/1603 (1 Jan. 1939).
De Ambris	R. De Felice, *Sindacalismo rivoluzionario e fiumanesimo nel carteggio D'Annunzio–De Ambris* (Brescia, 1966). 'Nuove lettere di Alceste De Ambris a Gabriele D'Annunzio', *Clio*, 9 (1973).
Debussy	*Claude Debussy et Gabriele D'Annunzio*, ed. G. Tosi (Paris, 1948). *D'Annunzio–Debussy. Mon cher ami: Epistolario 1910–17*, ed. C. Mazzonis (Florence, 1993).
Di Rudinì	*Alessandra di Rudinì e Gabriele D'Annunzio da un carteggio inedito*, ed. G. Gatti (Rome, 1956).
Duse	*Carteggio D'Annunzio–Duse*, ed. P. Nardi (Florence, 1975).

Gentile   *Carteggio inedito D'Annunzio–(Giovanni) Gentile*, ed. E. Mariano (Milan and Rome, 1970).

Gravina   *Lettere di D'Annunzio a Maria Gravina ed alla figlia Cicciuzza*, ed. R. Tiboni (Pescara, 1978). For other correspondence with Maria Gravina and her daughter see below under Miscellaneous Correspondence.

Hérelle   *Gabriele D'Annunzio à Georges Hérelle*, ed. G. Tosi (Paris, 1946).
Lettere a Georges Hérelle, ed. M. G. Sanjust (Bari, 1994).

Leoni   *Lettere a Barbara Leoni*, ed. B. Borletti and P. P. Trompeo (Florence, 1954).

Mancini   F. Roncoroni publishes letters of La Mancini in his excellent introduction to D'Annunzio's *Solus ad solam* (Milan 1979); other letters are available in *Prose di ricerca*, vol. iii (Milan, 1975).

Mazoyer   'D'Annunzio à Amélie Mazoyer, lettere e messaggi inediti', ed. A. Pellegrino, *Rassegna dannunziana*, 19 (Mar. 1991).

Mussolini   *Carteggio D'Annunzio–Mussolini*, ed. R. De Felice and E. Mariano (Milan, 1971).

Ojetti   *Carteggio D'Annunzio–Ojetti*, ed. C. Ceccuti (Florence, 1979).

Rizzo   G. Rizzo, *D'Annunzio e Mussolini: La verità sui loro rapporti* (Bologna, 1960). Contains letters and messages exchanged with Rizzo, his in-house policeman–spy.

Treves, Emilio   *Lettere di Gabriele D'Annunzio all' editore Emilio Treves*, ed. M. Guabello (Biella, 1938).

Treves, Guido   'Dal *Notturno* al *Venturiero senza ventura*: 32 lettere inedite a Guido Treves', *Nuova antologia*, 73/1584 (16 Mar. 1938).
'Dalla "Capponcina" al "Vittoriale": 41 lettere a Emilio e Guido Treves e a Renato Brozzi', *Nuova antologia*, 73/1586 (16 Apr. 1938).
Lettere ai Treves, ed. G. Oliva (Milan, 1999).

Zucconi   *Lettere a Giselda Zucconi*, ed. I. Ciani (Pescara, 1985).

Miscellaneous Correspondence

Miscellaneous and important letters to his family and Abruzzese friends often quoted in the present volume have been published as follows:

'Ho una gran voglia di mettermi a lavorare', ed. A. Alberti, *Nuova antologia*, 77/1694 (16 Oct. 1942).

'I giorni della "chiusa adolescenza": Lettere al padre, alla madre e alle sorelle', ed. R. Tiboni, *Nuova antologia*, 74/1620 (16 Sept. 1939).

'L'avventura elettorale: 37 lettere inedite di Gabriele D'Annunzio', ed. U. Russo, *Oggi e Domani*, 6/3–4 (1978), 35–41. Largely concerned with the 1897 election compaign in Ortona.

'Lettere al padre e alla madre', ed. E. Bodrero, *Nuova antologia*, 73/1590 (16 June 1938).

Scritti dannunziani, ed. R. Tiboni (Pescara, 1992). Collects Tiboni's writings on GD'A and adds other *inedita*.

BIBLIOGRAPHICAL STUDIES

ANTONA-TRAVERSI, CAMILLO, *Gabriele D'Annunzio: Curriculum vitae*, 2 vols. (Rome, 1932–4).

BALDAZZI, ANNA, *Critica dannunziana nei periodici italiani dal 1880 al 1938* (Rome, 1977).

FORCELLA, ROBERTO, *Gabriele D'Annunzio: Guida bibliografica*, vols. i–ii (Rome, 1926–8); vols. iii–iv (Florence 1936–7).

FUCILLA, JOSEPH G., and CARRIÈRE, JOSEPH M., *D'Annunzio Abroad: A Bibliographical Essay* (New York, 1935).

MASCI, FILIPPO, *La vita e le opere di Gabriele D'Annunzio in un indice cronologico analitico* (Rome, 1950).

VECCHIONI, MARIO, *Bibliografia di Gabriele D'Annunzio* (Pescara, 1955).

CRITICAL STUDIES

ABRUGIATI, LUIGIA. See Tiboni, Edoardo, and Abrugiati, Luigia.

ALATRI, PAOLO, *Nitti, D'Annunzio e la questione adriatica (1919–20)* (Milan, 1959).

—— *Scritti politici di D'Annunzio* (Milan, 1980), introduction.

—— *Gabriele D'Annunzio* (Turin, 1983).

—— *D'Annunzio negli anni del tramonto* (Venice, 1984).

—— 'D'Annunzio: Mito e realtà', *Clio*, 24/4 (Oct.–Dec. 1988).

—— 'La storiografia sull impresa dannunziana a Fiume', in F. Perfetti (ed.), *D'Annunzio e il suo tempo* (Genoa, 1992).

ANDREOLI, ANNAMARIA, *D'Annunzio* (Florence, 1985).

—— *D'Annunzio* (in photo-history) (Florence, 1987).

—— *Album D'Annunzio* (Milan, 1990).

—— *D'Annunzio archivista: Le filologie di uno scrittore* (Florence, 1996).

ANGELI, DIEGO, *Cronache del Caffè Greco* (Milan, 1930).

ANTONGINI, TOM, *Vita segreta di D'Annunzio* (Milan, 1938); English trans. *D'Annunzio* (London, 1938).

—— *D'Annunzio aneddotico* (Milan, 1939).

—— *Un D'Annunzio ignorato* (Milan, 1963).

BADOGLIO, PIETRO, *Rivelazioni su Fiume* (Rome, 1946).

BARBERI SQUAROTTI, GIORGIO, *Il gesto impossibile: Tre saggi su Gabriele D'Annunzio* (Palermo, 1971).

BARILLI, RENATO, *D'Annunzio in prosa* (Milan, 1993).

BARRÈS, MAURICE, *Mes cahiers* (Paris, 1934–5).

BEMBO, PIETRO, *Prose della volgar lingua*, ed. C. Dionisotti (Turin, 1960).

BENSON, EUGENE, 'Gabriele D'Annunzio: The New Poet and his Work', *The Yellow Book*, 11 (Oct. 1896).

BERNARDI, M., 'Storia del Vittoriale: Come D'Annunzio comprò la Villa di Cagnacco', *Quaderni del Vittoriale*, 20 (Mar.–Apr. 1980).

BERTAZZOLI, RAFFAELLA, 'Le *Elegie romane* tra Goethe e D'Annunzio', in Pietro Gibellini (ed.), *D'Annunzio Europeo* (Rome, 1991).

BISICCHIA, ANDREA, *D'Annunzio e il teatro tra cronaca e letteratura drammatica* (Florence, 1991).

—— *Gabriele D'Annunzio: Poeta, soldato, drammaturgo* (Milan 1996).

BONADEO, ALFREDO, *D'Annunzio and the Great War* (Madison, 1995).

BRANCA, VITTORE, 'La scrittrice Eleonora Duse', *Corriera della sera* (19 Apr. 1969); elaborated in *Nuova antologia*, 126/2178 (Apr.–June 1991), retitled 'Vocazione letteraria di Eleonora Duse, con una serie di documenti inediti'.

BRIGANTI, ALESSANDRA, *Il parlamento nel romanzo italiano del secondo 800* (Florence, 1972).

BRUNETTA, GIAN PIERO, 'D'Annunzio nella storia del cinema italiano', *Oggi e Domani*, 253/6 (June 1995).

CALIARO, ILVANO, *D'Annunzio lettore–scrittore* (Florence, 1991).

CALTAGIRONE, GIOVANNA, *Dietroscena: L'Italia post-unitaria nei romanzi di ambiente parlamentare 1870–1900* (Rome, 1993).

CARDUCCI, GIOSUÈ (ed.), *Cacce in rima dei secoli XIV e XV* (Bologna, 1896).

CARLI, MARIO, 'L'aristocrazia degli Arditi', *Roma Futurista* (5 Jan. 1919).

—— *Arditismo* (Milan, 1919).

—— *Con D'Annunzio a Fiume* (Milan, 1920; repr. San Severo, 1993).

CASTRONOVO, VITTORIO, *La stampa italiana dall'unità al fascismo* (Bari, 1970).

CAVIGLIA, ENRICO, *Il conflitto di Fiume* (Milan, 1948).

CELATI, GIOVANNI, *Il vate e il capobanda: D'Annunzio e Mascagni* (Rome, 1992).

CERVONE, PAOLA, *L'anti-Badoglio* (Milan, 1993).

CHIARA, PIERO, *Vita di Gabriele D'Annunzio* (Milan, 1978; here the 1981 edn. is used).

—— 'D'Annunzio e Mondadori', *Nuova antologia*, 116/2138 (Apr.–June 1981).

—— with Roncoroni, Federico, *Tamara de Lampicka* (Milan, 1977).

CHIARINI, GIUSEPPE, 'Alla ricerca dell'inverecondia', *Domenica letteraria* (19 Aug. 1883).

CIANI, IVANOS, 'Alla scoperta della Sardegna', *Rassegna dannunziana*, 14 (Dec. 1988).

CIANI, IVANOS, 'La nascita dell'idea del *Canto novo*', in E. Tiboni and L. Abrugiati (eds.), *'Canto novo' nel centenario della pubblicazione* (Pescara, 1982).

CIMMINO, NICOLA FRANCESCO, 'Appunti inediti sul *San Sebastiano*', *Dialoghi* (July–Aug. 1953).

—— *Poesia e poetica in Gabriele D'Annunzio: Problemi di critica dannunziana* (Florence, 1960).

CIRCEO, ERMANNO, *L'Abruzzo in D'Annunzio* (Pescara, 1995).

COMISSO, GIOVANNI, *Le mie stagioni* (Milan, 1951).

COZZANI, ETTORE, *Gabriele D'Annunzio* (Piacenza, 1923).

DAMERINI, GINO, *D'Annunzio e Venezia* (Milan, 1943; repr. Venice, 1993).

D'ANNA, RICCARDO, *Roma preraffaellita* (Rome, 1996), proceedings of the Lincei, *Memorie*, ser. IX/7, fasc. 3.

D'ANNUNZIO, GABRIELLINO, 'Ricordi dannunziani', *La lettura*, 12/11 (Nov. 1912).

D'ANNUNZIO, MARIO, *Con mio padre sulla nave del ricordo* (Milan, 1950).

—— *Mio padre Comandante in Fiume* (Genoa, 1956).

—— *D'Annunzio politico: 1918–1938* (Bari, 1978).

DE FELICE, RENZO, *D'Annunzio politico (1918–28)* (Rome and Bari, 1978).

—— with Pampaloni, Geno, and Praz, Mario, *D'Annunzio* (Florence, 1978).

DE LA RAMÉE, MARIE LOUISE [Ouida], 'The Genius of D'Annunzio', *Fortnightly Review*, 67 (Mar. 1897).

DELLA GATTINA, FERDINANDO PETRUCELLI, *I moribondi di Palazzo Carignano* (Milan, 1862).

DE LEIDI, CRISTIANA, 'Gli illustratori di *Isaotta Guttadauro*', *Rassegna dannunziana*, 28 (Nov. 1995).

DE MICHELIS, EURIALO, *Tutto D'Annunzio* (Milan, 1960).

—— *D'Annunzio a contraggenio* (Rome, 1963).

—— *Roma senza lupa* (Rome, 1976).

—— *Ancora D'Annunzio* (Pescara, 1987).

DE MONTERA, PIERRE, 'Gabriele D'Annunzio', in *Colloquio italo-francese su D'Annunzio in Francia*, Accademia dei Lincei (Rome, 1975).

—— with Tosi, Guy, *D'Annunzio, Montesquiou e Matilde Serao* (Rome, 1972).

DEPAULIS, JACQUES, *Ida Rubinstein: Une inconnue jadis célèbre* (Paris, 1995).

DE PIERREFEUX, GUY, *Le Surhomme de la Côte d'Argent: Gabriele D'Annunzio* (Mont de Marsan, 1928).

DODERET, ALPHONSE, *Vingt ans d'amitié avec Gabriele D'Annunzio* (Paris, 1956).

DRAKE, RICHARD, *Byzantium for Rome* (Chapel Hill, 1980).

DUNCAN, ISADORA, *My Life* (London, 1968).

DUSE, ELEONORA, and BOITO, ARRIGO, *Lettere d'Amore*, ed. R. Radice (Milan, 1979).

ELLMANN, RICHARD, *James Joyce* (Oxford, 1982).

FABRE, GIORGIO, 'D'Annunzio nelle prime riviste del cinema italiano', *Quaderni del Vittoriale*, 4 (Aug. 1977).

FATINI, GIUSEPPE, *Il Cigno e la Cicogna: Gabriele D'Annunzio collegiale* (Pescara, 1919; repr. Florence, 1935).

—— *D'Annunzio, Pascoli e altri amici* (Pisa, 1963).

FERRARI, ATLANTICO, *L'asso di cuori: Guido Keller* (Rome, 1933).

FLORA, FRANCESCO, *Gabriele D'Annunzio* (Naples, 1926; repr. Messina, 1935).

FRACASSINI, TOMASO, *Gabriele D'Annunzio convittore* (Florence, 1916; repr. Rome, 1935).

—— 'Dannunziana', *Nuova antologia*, 74/1609 (1 Apr. 1939).

GATTI, GUGLIELMO, *Le donne nella vita e nell'arte di Gabriele D'Annunzio* (Modena, 1951).

—— *Alessandra di Rudinì e Gabriele D'Annunzio, da un carteggio inedito* (Rome, 1955).

—— *Vita di Gabriele D'Annunzio* (Florence, 1956).

—— 'Il *Convito* di Adolfo De Bosis', *Quaderni dannunziani*, 8–9 (1958).

—— 'Un contrasto nell'amicizia fra D'Annunzio e Michetti', in id., *Gabriele D'Annunzio, Studi-Saggi* (Bologna, 1959).

—— 'Lo scandalo della bella Giusini', *Stampa sera* (2 Aug. 1959).

—— 'Dopo una lite D'Annunzio non volle più vedere la figlia', *Il resto del Carlino* (31 Jan. 1966).

GERMAIN, ANDRÉ, *La vie amoureuse de D'Annunzio* (Paris, 1925).

GERRA, FERDINANDO, *L'impresa di Fiume*, 2 vols. (Milan, 1966); here quoted in Longanesi's edn. (Milan, 1974).

GHELLI, SILVIO, *Austria nemica* (Milan, 1916).

GHISALBERTI, CARLO, 'La lunga via per Fiume', in F. Perfetti (ed.), *D'Annunzio e l'impresa fiumana* (Milan, forthcoming).

GIAMMARINO, MARA, *Incontro con D'Annunzio* (Rome, 1988).

GIANNANTONI, MARIO, *La vita di Gabriele D'Annunzio* (Milan, 1933).

GIBELLINI, PIETRO, 'Fiori di carta: La fonte della flora di *Alcyone*', in E. Tiboni and L. Abrugiati (eds.), *Natura ed arte nel paesaggio dannunziano*, (Pescara, 1980).

—— *Logos e Mythos: Studi du Gabriele D'Annunzio* (Florence, 1985).

GIDE, ANDRÉ, *Journal* (Paris, 1939).

GIGANTE, SILVIO, *Storia del Comune di Fiume* (Florence, 1928).

GIGLIO, RAFFAELE, *Per la storia di un'amicizia: D'Annunzio, Hérelle, Scarfoglio, Serao* (Naples, 1977).

GRANATELLI, LAURA, *Arrestate l'autore! D'Annunzio in scena*, 2 vols. (Rome, 1993).

GRANCHELLI, OSCAR PIO *et al.*, *D'Annunzione e la sinistra*, proceedings of a round table discussion chaired by Mario Sansone (Pescara, 1978).

GREENE, GEORGE ARTHUR, *Italian Lyrists of Today* (London, 1893).

GRIFFIN, GERALD, *Gabriele D'Annunzio: The Warrior Bard* (London, 1935).

GROSSI, ALDO, *La poesia del fiume e del mare in Gabriele D'Annunzio* (Chieti, 1963).

GUABELLO, MARIO, *Barbara la bella Romana* (Biella, 1935).

GUICCIOLI, ALESSANDRO, 'Diario del 1897', *Nuova antologia*, 76/1657 (16 Apr. 1941).

—— 'Diario del 1904', *Nuova antologia*, 78/1699 (1 Jan. 1943).

HÉRELLE, GEORGES, *Notolette dannunziane*, ed. I. Ciani (Pescara, 1984).

HERFORD, CHARLES, 'Gabriele D'Annunzio', *Bulletin of the John Rylands Library* (1919) 5 (1918–20).

HERGESHEIMER, JOSEPH, introduction to Gabriele D'Annunzio, *Tales of My Native Town*, trans. G. Mantellini (London, 1920).

HUARD, FRANCES WILSON, *Charles Huard 1874–1965* (Paris, 1969).

HYNES, SAMUEL LYNN, *The Edwardian Turn of Mind* (Princeton, 1968).

INFUSINO, GIANNI, *D'Annunzio a Napoli* (Naples, 1995).

JANDOLO, AUGUSTO, *Le memorie di un antiquario* (Milan, 1938).

JOYCE, JAMES, *Letters*, ed. R. Ellmann (New York, 1966).

JOYCE, STANISLAUS, *My Brother's Keeper*, ed. R. Ellmann (New York, 1958).

JULLIAN, PHILLIPE, *D'Annunzio* (Paris, 1971); English trans. London, 1972.

KLOPP, CHARLES, *Gabriele D'Annunzio* (Boston, 1988).

KOCHNITZKY, LÉON, *La quinta stagione o i Centauri di Fiume* (Bologna, 1922).

LAREDO DE MENDOZA, Saverio, *Gabriele D'Annunzio aviatore di guerra* (Milan, 1931).

—— *Gabriele D'Annunzio fante del Veliki e del Faiti* (Milan, 1932).

LAWRENCE, DAVID HERBERT, *Twilight in Italy* (London, Penguin edn., 1960).

LEDDA, ELENA, *Fiume e D'Annunzio* (Chieti, 1988).

—— *D'Annunzio in caricatura* (Gardone Riviera, 1988).

—— 'Gabriele D'Annunzio nella prima guerra mondiale', pt. 1, *Rassegna dannunziana*, 23 (May 1993); pt. 2, ibid. 24 (Dec. 1993).

—— 'Buccari: per "osare l'inosabile". Storia di una beffa', in F. Perfetti (ed.), *D'Annunzio e la guerra* (Milan, 1996).

—— and Salotti, Guglielmo (eds.), *Un capitolo di storia: Fiume e D'Annunzio* (Rome, 1991).

LEDEEN, MICHAEL A., *D'Annunzio a Fiume* (Bari, 1975); English trans. *The First Duce: D'Annunzio at Fiume* (Baltimore, 1977).

LEGA, GIUSEPPE, *Cinquant'anni di giornalismo* (Rome, 1930).

LODI, LUIGI (ed.), *Alla ricerca della verecondia* (Rome, 1927). Essays by Ettore Panzacchi, Enrico Nencioni and Giuseppe Chiarini.

LORENZINI, NIVA, *D'Annunzio* (Palermo, 1993).

LUSSU, EMILIO, *Un anno sull'altipiano* (Milan, 1967).

LUTI, GIORGIO, *La cenere dei sogni* (Pisa, 1973).

MACDONALD, J. N., *A Political Escapade: The Story of Fiume and D'Annunzio* (London [1921]).

MARABINI, CAMILLO, *La rossa avanguardia dell'Argonne* (Milan, 1915); French trans. *Les Garibaldiens de l'Argonne* (Paris, 1917).

MARIANO, EMILIO, 'Il patto d'alleanza fra Eleonora Duse e Gabriele D'Annunzio', *Nuova antologia*, 86/1801 (Jan.–Feb. 1951).

— (ed.), *L'arte di Gabriele D'Annunzio* (Milan 1968).

— 'La *Francesca da Rimini* e i suoi significati', *Quaderni del Vittoriale*, 24 (Nov.–Dec. 1980).

MARINETTI, FILIPPO TOMMASO, *Les Dieux s'en vont, D'Annunzio reste* (Paris, 1908).

MARTINI, FERDINANDO, *Diario 1914–18*, ed. Gabriele De Rosa (Milan, 1966).

MASCAGNI, PIETRO, 'Come nacque *La Parisina*', *La lettura*, 14/1 (Jan. 1914).

— 'Mascagni, Parisina e D'Annunzio', ed. A. Lualdi, *Quaderni dannunziani*, 30 (1965).

MAZZA, ATTILIO, *D'Annunzio e il Vittoriale: Guida alla casa del poeta* (Gardone, 1989).

— *L'harem di D'Annunzio* (Milan, 1995).

MAZZALI, ETTORE, *D'Annunzio artefice solitario* (Milan, 1962).

MONCALVO, GIGI, *Alessandra di Rudiní dall'amore per D'Annunzio al Carmelo* (Milan, 1994).

MONICELLI, FRANCO, *Il tempo dei buoni amici* (Milan, 1975).

MORELLO, VINCENZO, *Gabriele D'Annunzio* (Rome, 1910).

MOSSO, MIMI, 'Le prime lettere di Gabriele D'Annunzio al suo editore', *Illustrazione italiana* (6 May 1923).

NARDELLI, FEDERICO VITTORE, *L'arcangelo: vita e miracoli di Gabriele D'Annunzio* (Rome, 1931); English trans., with sporadic notes by Arthur Livingstone, London, 1931.

NARDI, PIETRO, *Vita di Arrigo Boito* (Milan, 1942).

NENCIONI, ENRICO, 'Le poesie e le pitture di Dante Gabriele Rossetti', *Fanfulla della domenica* (15 Feb. 1884).

NICASTRO, GUIDO, *Il poeta e la scena* (Catania, 1988).

NICOLSON, HAROLD, *Some People* (London, 1927).

NITTI, FRANCESCO SAVERIO, *Rivelazioni: Scritti politici*, iv: *D'Annunzio, la guerra e Fiume* (Bari, 1963).

OJETTI, UGO, *Cose viste*, 7 vols. (Milan, 1937). Ojetti's monumental work has references *passim* to D'Annunzio.

— *As They Seemed to Me*, trans. Henry Furst (London, 1928). Three of Ojetti's essays on D'Annunzio are included in this volume.

— *D'Annunzio: Amico–maestro–soldato (1894–1934)* (Florence, 1954).

— *Taccuini* (Florence, 1954).

OLIVA, DOMENICO, *Note di uno spettatore* (Bologna, 1911).

OLIVA, GIANNI, *I nobili spiriti: Pascoli, D'Annunzio e le riviste dell'estetismo fiorentino* (Bergamo, 1979).

ORMROD, RICHARD, 'D'Annunzio and Radclyffe Hall', *Modern Language Review*, 84/4 (Oct. 1989).

OUIDA. See De la Ramée, Marie Louise.

PALMERIO, BENIGNO, *Con D'Annunzio alla Capponcina* (Florence, 1938).

PARATORE, ETTORE, *Studi dannunziani* (Naples, 1966).

PARODI, SEVERINA, *Catalogo degli Accademici della Crusca* (Florence, 1983).

PASCAL, PIERRE, *Le Livre secret de Gabriele D'Annunzio et de Donatella Cross* (Padua, 1947).

PASSERINI, GIUSEPPE, *Dizionario della prosa dannunziana* (Florence, 1912).

—— *Dizionario della poesia dannunziana* (Florence, 1912).

—— *Vocabolario dannunziano* (Florence, 1928).

Pellegrino, Alberto, 'Gabriele D'Annunzio e R. de Montesquiou-Fézensac', *Rassegna dannunziana*, 24 (Dec. 1993).

PERFETTI, FRANCESCO (ed.), *D'Annunzio e l'impresa fiumana* (Milan, forthcoming).

PESCETTI, LUIGI, 'D'Annunzio, Marradi e Chiarini', *L'Italia letteraria* (25 Mar. 1934).

PETRONIO, GIUSEPPE, *D'Annunzio* (Rome, 1977).

PIANTONI, GIANNA, *La Cronaca bizantina, Il Convito e la fortuna dei pre-Raffaelliti a Roma* (Rome, 1972).

PISTELLI, MAURIZIO, *Il 'divino testimonio': D'Annunzio e il mito dell'eroica Rinascenza* (Modena, 1995).

PLUTARCH, *Lives* (London, 1939).

PO, GUIDO, *Scritti, messaggi, discorsi e rapporti militari* (Rome, 1939).

PONTIERO, GIOVANNI, *Eleonora Duse: In Life and Art* (Frankfurt, 1986).

PRARIO, LUCY NAPOLI, *Tre abiti bianchi per Alessandra* (Milan, 1954).

PRAZ, MARIO, *La carne, la morte e il diavolo nella letteratura romantica* (Milan, 1930); English trans. *The Romantic Agony* (Oxford, 1933; here quoted in the 1962 Fontana edn.).

—— *Il patto col serpente* (Milan, 1972).

QUARANTOTTO, CLAUDIO, 'Cinema di D'Annunzio e cinema dannunziano (1908–1928)', in F. Perfetti (ed.), *D'Annunzio e il suo tempo* (Genoa, 1992).

RAIMONDI, EZIO, *Il silenzio della Gorgone* (Bologna, 1980).

RAPAGNETTA, AMEDEO, *La vera origine familiare e il vero cognome di Gabriele D'Annunzio* (Lanciano, 1938).

RE, LUCIA, 'Il teatro della memoria di Gabriele D'Annunzio: Il Vittoriale degli Italiani', *Journal of Decorative and Propaganda Arts*, 3 (Winter 1987).

RENZETTI, LINO, *La casa natale di Gabriele D'Annunzio: Ieri e oggi* (Chieti, 1989).

RHODES, ANTHONY, *The Poet as Superman: The Life of Gabriele D'Annunzio* (London 1959).

RHYS, ERNEST, *Everyman Remembers* (London, 1931).

RICKETTS, CHARLES, *Self-Portrait*, ed. T. Sturge Moore and C. Lewis (London, 1939).

RIDENTI, LUCIO, *La Belle Époque* (Rome, 1966).

RIZZO, GIOVANNI, *D'Annunzio e Mussolini: La verità sui loro rapporti* (Bologna, 1960).

ROLLAND, ROMAIN, *Gabriele D'Annunzio et la Duse* (Paris, 1947).

— *Journal des années de guerre* (Paris, 1952).

ROSSI, ALDO, 'D'Annunzio giovane, il verismo e le tradizioni popolari', in E. Tiboni and L. Abrugiati (eds.), *D'Annunzio giovane e il verismo* (Pescara, 1979).

RUBINSTEIN, IDA, 'Come conobbi D'Annunzio', *Nuova antologia*, 62/1322 (16 Apr. 1927).

RUSSO, LUIGI, *Gabriele D'Annunzio* (Florence, 1939).

RUSSO, UMBERTO, 'L'avventura elettorale: 37 lettere inedite di Gabriele D'Annunzio', *Oggi e Domani*, 6/3–4 (Mar.–Apr. 1978).

SALIERNO, VITO, *D'Annunzio e i suoi editori* (Milan, 1987).

SANJUST, MARIA GIOVANNA, '"Chi 'l tenerà legato?": D'Annunzio e Treves', *Critica letteraria*, 91–2 (1996).

SANTONI, ALBERTO, 'Gabriele D'Annunzio e la Beffa di Buccari', in F. Perfetti (ed.), *D'Annunzio e il suo tempo* (Genoa, 1992).

SAPEGNO, NATALINO, *Compendio di storia della letteratura italiana*, 3 vols. (Florence, 1946).

— 'D'Annunzio fu più retore che poeta', *La Stampa* (17 Apr. 1963).

SARTORIO, GIULIO ARISTIDE, 'Nota su D. G. Rossetti pittore', *Convito*, 2 (1895).

SAVOCA, GIUSEPPE, and D'AQUINO, ALIDA, *Concordanza del 'Poema paradisiaco'* (Florence, 1988).

— *Concordanza della 'Chimera'*, (Florence, 1988).

— *Concordanza dell' 'Isotteo' e delle 'Elegie romane'* (Florence, 1990).

— *Concordanza del 'Canto novo'* (Florence, 1995).

SCARANO, EMANUELA, *Dalla 'Cronaca bizantina' al 'Convito'* (Florence, 1970).

SCARFOGLIO, EDOARDO, *Il libro di don Chisciotte* (Rome, 1885); now ed. C. A. Madrignani and A. Resta (Naples, 1990).

SCHIAFFINI, ALFREDO, 'Arte e linguaggio di Gabriele D'Annunzio', in E. Mariano (ed.), *L'arte di Gabriele D'Annunzio* (Milan, 1968).

SERAO, MATILDE, 'La figlia di Iorio', in L. Vergani (ed.), *Eleonora Duse* (Milan, 1958).

SIGNORELLI, OLGA, *Eleonora Duse* (Rome, 1955).

SITWELL, OSBERT, *Discursions on Travel, Art and Life* (London, 1925).

— *Noble Essences* (London, 1950).

SODINI, ANGELO, *Ariel armato* (Milan, 1931).

SOLMI, ARRIGO, *Gabriele D'Annunzio e la genesi dell'impresa adriatica* (Milan, 1943).

SOMMARUGA, ANGELO, *Alla ricerca della verecondia* (Rome, 1884).

—— *Cronaca bizantina (1881–1885)* (Milan, 1941).

SORGE, PAOLA, *Motti dannunziani* (Milan, 1994).

SORMANI, ELSA, *Bizantini e decadenti nell'Italia umbertina* (Bari, 1975).

SORO, FRANCESCO, *Splendori e miserie del cinema* (Milan, 1935).

SOVERA LATUADA, GABRIELE, 'Giuseppe Sovera's Role in the Inception of D'Annunzio's Raid on Fiume', *Modern Language Review*, 87/2 (1992).

SOZZI, GIUSEPPE, *Gabriele D'Annunzio nella vita e nell'arte* (Florence, 1964).

SQUARCIAPINO, GIOVANNI, *Roma bizantina* (Turin, 1950).

STARKIE, WALTER, *The Waveless Plain: An Italian Autobiography* (London, 1938).

STEPHENS, FREDERICK, *Dante Gabriel Rossetti* (London, 1894).

SUSMEL, DUILIO, *Carteggio Arnaldo–Benito Mussolini* (Florence, 1954).

SUSMEL, EDOARDO, *La marcia di Ronchi* (Milan, 1941).

SYMONS, ARTHUR, introduction to Gabriele D'Annunzio, *The Child of Pleasure*, trans. Georgina Harding, (London, 1898).

—— *Studies in Prose and Verse* (London, 1904).

—— *Eleonora Duse* (London, 1926).

—— *Selected Letters*, ed. K. Beckson and J. M. Munro (London, 1989).

THOVEZ, ENRICO, *L'arco di Ulisse* (Naples, 1921).

TIBONI, EDOARDO (ed.), *D'Annunzio giornalista* (Pescara, 1983).

—— (ed.), *Verso l'Ellade* (Pescara, 1995).

—— and ABRUGIATI, LUIGIA (eds.), *Canto novo nel centenario della pubblicazione* (Pescara, 1982).

TODISCO, ALFREDO, 'C'è stata una donna nella morte di D'Annunzio', *Corriere della sera* (15 June 1975).

TOSI, GUY, *D'Annunzio en Grèce et la croisière de 1895* (Paris, 1947).

—— *La Vie e le rôle de D'Annunzio en France au début de la grande guerre (1914–15)* (Florence, 1961).

TRAINA, ALFONSO, 'I fratelli nemici: Allusioni antidannunziane nel Pascoli', *Quaderni del Vittoriale*, 23 (1980).

TROMPEO, LUIGI, *Ricordi romani di Gabriele D'Annunzio* (Rome, 1938).

ULIVI, FERRUCCIO, *D'Annunzio* (Milan, 1988).

VALERI, NINO, *D'Annunzio davanti al fascismo* (Florence, 1963).

VIVARELLI, ROBERTO, *Storia delle origini del fascismo*, 2 vols. (Bologna, 1991).

WEY, FRANCIS, *Rome* (London, 1872).

WILLIAMS, ORLO, 'The Novels of D'Annunzio', *Edinburgh Review*, 218/443 (1913).

WINWAR, FRANCES, *Wingless Victory* (New York, 1956).

WILLIAMS, ORLO, 'The Novels of D'Annunzio', *Edinburgh Review*, 218/443 (1913).

WINWAR, FRANCES, *Wingless Victory* (New York, 1956).

WOODHOUSE, J. R. [The disproportionately large number of articles listed indicates the English orientation of this reassessment rather than any intrinsic importance the items may have.]

—— 'La fortuna inglese del *Trionfo della morte*', in E. Tiboni and L. Abrugiati (eds.), *Il trionfo della morte* (Pescara, 1981).

—— 'Il *Canto novo* e i nuovi rimatori inglesi: Un'occasione perduta?', in E. Tiboni and L. Abrugiati (eds.), *Canto novo nel centenario della pubblicazione* (Pescara, 1983).

—— 'D'Annunzio's Election Victory of 1897: New Documents, New Perspectives', *Italian Studies*, 40 (1985).

—— 'Curiouser and Spuriouser: Two English Influences on D'Annunzio', *Italian Studies*, 42 (1987).

—— 'La fortuna inglese della *Fiaccola sotto il moggio*', in E. Tiboni, M. Rapagnetta, and U. Russo (eds.), *La fiaccola sotto il moggio* (Pescara, 1987).

—— 'Gabriele D'Annunzio e la cultura anglosassone: La testimonianza del silenzio', in E. Tiboni (ed.), *Gabriele D'Annunzio a cinquant'anni dalla morte*, vol. ii (Pescara, 1988).

—— 'D'Annunzio a Fiume: Testimonianze inglese inedite o rare', in *L'Italia contemporanea: Studi in onore di Paolo Alatri*, 2 vols. (Naples, 1991).

—— 'Creative Plagiarism: D'Annunzio's Varied Sources' in G. Bedani, R. Catani and M. Slowikowska (eds.), *The Italian Lyric Tradition* (Cardiff, 1993).

—— 'D'Annunzio e la guerra: Attraverso occhi inglesi', in F. Perfetti (ed.), *D'Annunzio e la guerra* (Milan, 1996).

—— 'D'Annunzio and Yeats', *Journal of Anglo-Italian Studies*, 5–6 (1998).

—— 'D'Annunzio e l'impresa fiumana: Visto attraverso i documenti inediti del Foreign Office', in *Rassegna dannunziana*, 38 (2000).

Index